Poets of Action

Poets of Action

incorporating essays from *The Burning Oracle*

G. WILSON KNIGHT

METHUEN & CO LTD
11 NEW FETTER LANE LONDON EC4

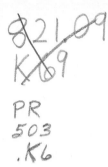
First published 1967 by Methuen & Co Ltd
© 1967 by G. Wilson Knight
Printed in Great Britain by
Butler & Tanner Ltd, Frome and London

Distributed in the U.S.A.
by Barnes and Noble, Inc.

Contents

Prefatory Notes

This reorganization of *The Burning Oracle*, for many years now out of print, follows a logical plan. In place of the old essays on Shakespeare and Pope, which have found new homes in *The Sovereign Flower* and *Laureate of Peace* (reissued as *The Poetry of Pope*), I have incorporated an abbreviated version of *Chariot of Wrath*, my war book on Milton as a national prophet; and also my Byron Foundation lecture on Byron's prose.

The result remains true to the original sub-title 'On the Poetry of Action'. The four major writers here handled were narrative artists deeply concerned with action; and so was Marlowe, briefly discussed on pp. 66–9 below,[1] whose *Tamburlaine* is nearer epic than drama. All these men had governmental and political interests and experience, and three of them risked their lives in the cause of political liberation. Milton, Swift and Byron stand alone in our history as men of compelling literary genius whose powers were geared to national or international action.

External action is an expression of man's dynamic being, and at its activating centre are his sexual instincts. On these our poets of action, except Swift whose involvement, at least in *Gulliver's Travels*, is rather different, have much to say.

Spenser, Marlowe and Milton offer bold insights into a deeply human but disconcerting inter-relation of the divine, or seemingly divine, and the forbidden, sometimes the lascivious (pp. 10–11, 24–7, 29–32, 37–8, 66–9). That this particular penetration into what might, because it may seem to involve pleasure the more exquisite for its daring, be called 'positive evil' (cp. Byron's 'god of evil', p. 242), should be the preserve of experts in the literature of narrative and action suggests that we are here at the roots of man's national and international confusions. The relation is the clearer when we note that in Milton's *Paradise Lost* an ugly humour both follows the Fall and

---

[1] In this preface 'p.' and 'pp.' refer to pages in my present volume.

characterizes Satan's exultation at the success of his artillery
(pp. 30, 39). In Marlowe the central unhappy complex may be
felt within the cruel humour which pervades his wider action:
the sadistic comedy of *Tamburlaine*, the horse-play of *Doctor
Faustus* and the macabre farce of *The Jew of Malta*. All this is at
once aesthetically unsatisfying and appallingly true to the
world of our experience. It is as though the authentic reporting
of the human state forces an ugly humour and a disrupted art.[1]

Shakespeare and Byron are not in this way involved; or at
first, anyway, appear not to be. Both poets generally write of
human confusions as though they were, during composition, to
quote the Sermon on the Mount, so 'pure in heart' that they
have seen 'God', and can accordingly preserve artistic control
of whatever paradoxes they handle. Their humour is kindly.

I would point here to my essay 'The Shakespearian Integrity',
originally in *The Burning Oracle* and now in *The Sovereign
Flower* (included in *Shakespeare Criticism 1935–60*; see p. 242
note), an essay which should be read in conjunction with my
present volume, especially p. 31. In it I used *Venus and Adonis* to
show how Shakespeare's harmonious artistry grew from a rare
love-identification, simultaneously inward and sensuous, spiritual and physical, which enabled him to order his universe
without confusions (*The Sovereign Flower*, 215–18). He is
certainly aware of sexual anomalies. The paradox of lust is
exactly handled in Sonnet 129, and throughout *The Rape of
Lucrece*. Tarquin endures a conflict of 'hot-burning will' and
'grace' (247, 712); he knows that his deed will bring a 'fleeting
joy' at the cost of enduring misery (212–13; 690); that the
immediate sweetness so renders him regardless that 'what is vile
shows like a virtuous deed' (252). The psychology points on to
Macbeth. But observe that firm distinctions are preserved: there
is *no deep-planted and essential inter-relation of enjoyment and evil*.
Tarquin would prefer an accepted love-union were that possible.
It just happens, in this instance, not to be possible, since
Lucrece is married (240–1).

'Fair' and 'foul' may be said to change places in *Macbeth*, but

---

[1] Some recently published appreciations of Marlowe's *Dido and Aeneas* lead me
to suppose that my comparative neglect of that drama, here and elsewhere, may
have done Marlowe a certain injustice.

the incompatibility is projected within an appropriate setting of 'fog and filthy air' (I. i. 11–12). In Shakespeare ethical judgement goes in double harness with imaginative association; when in *Antony and Cleopatra* the tonings are bright, our judgements are being accordingly, and exactly, modified and directed. One cannot say this of *Comus* or of Homer and Helen in *Doctor Faustus* (pp. 24–5; 68). At the heart of our discussion we may place Pope's remarkable line 'How glowing guilt exalts the keen delight!' (*Eloisa to Abelard*, 230; see p. 242, note). Is there, or is there not, some deeply human, perhaps necessary, truth there?

Byron writes with Marlowe, Spenser, Milton and Pope to build on. He does, it seems, go far to include the disparity, and labours, as his succession of sympathetically conceived dark heroes shows, to make from it through a series of transvaluations, a new good. He knows all about the yearning for some 'forbidden' 'celestial fruit' and man's 'uneradicable taint of sin' (*Childe Harold*, IV. 120, 126); in *Manfred*, Astarte is an ambivalently inclusive sexual figure of purity, illicit love, and condemnation (p. 198); in *Cain* he deliberately changes the Devil from Satan to Lucifer, with a corresponding shift in the reading of the Fall; and in *Heaven and Earth* he dramatizes sympathetically the forbidden union of humanity and seraphs. His survey is inclusive; he is fully conscious, deliberately working it all out, searching for his transvaluations. And he seems to attain a resolution. In *Don Juan* the Juan and Haidée cantos (pp. 239–42) celebrate a deliberate reversal of the Fall, showing desire innocent, as in *Venus and Adonis*. After that, Byron's light handling of exotic lust acts as a purification (p. 246); his analytic survey of the sexual is throughout keen (pp. 242–3, 250–1, 258, 262), and he can dissolve its problems in a rich humour (pp. 257–60). He might seem to have mastered the Miltonic confusion. His single phrase 'that indecent sun' (p. 259) goes far to prove it. See p. 242 below, note.

In both Shakespeare and Byron we find an exquisite fusion of the inward and the sensuous. The fusion is clear in Shakespeare's perception of Adonis' blood-life and physical personality, what I called in 'The Shakespearian Integrity' a body 'lighted from within'; and in Byron's lines 'the precious porcelain of

human clay', and 'like to a lighted alabaster vase' in *Don Juan*
(pp. 244, 248). From such instinctive physical-spiritual love-
identifications both poets could expand to that general transfiguration of the ugly and the evil defined perfectly in Shakespeare's Sonnets 113 and 114 (*The Mutual Flame*, 119-21;
Shakespeare and Religion, 239, 288-9). Whatever is repudiated is
repudiated within an inclusive imaginative coherence that is,
in its own way, a forgiveness and a purifying; though there is
less impersonal acceptance and transfiguration in Byron
because he is labouring, sometimes through direct satire, for a
number of moral transvaluations. He is, as it were, doing the
same job as Shakespeare in a more advanced, or intellectual, way.

Perhaps it is a question of direction, of where we start.
Shakespeare and Byron start with a tendency to acceptance,
and proceed to their various orderings. Marlowe and Milton,
and probably Spenser too, start from sexual unease and guilt,
and produce art-forms wherein instinctive delight jarringly
accompanies what is simultaneously known to be evil, the evil
being perhaps sometimes, as in Pope's revealing line, a necessary *part of the delight*; a delight, as it were, in daring, parasitic
on a rigid morality; and from there it is a single step to the
puritanical regarding of any delight as a symptom of evil. The
humour of Shakespeare and Byron is warm and generous, that
of Marlowe and Milton ugly and cruel, in Milton accompanying Adam's move to licentiousness and sense of sin directly
after the Fall (p. 30; and see pp. 39, 68). In Byron a 'golden'
(pp. 258-9) humour dissolves guilt. Both Shakespeare and
Byron, starting from acceptance and forgiveness, proceed un-
impeded to their greater harmonizations (for Shakespeare, p.
31 below); to those 'easy numbers' which shame the 'slow
endeavouring art' of Milton's Sonnet on Shakespeare; and the
words apply even more readily to *Don Juan*.

And yet, even so, man himself is not as yet healthy or harmonious, and Swift is before us as a towering figure to show it.
Are Marlowe, Spenser and Milton perhaps facing a dislocation
that *must be faced*? More, is there a further revelation within this
very 'mental twist' and 'shivering delight' (pp. 11, 31) of our
fallen humanity that is yet to be uncovered? – the forbidden
fruit in Eden which was able to make men as gods, as both

Milton in *Paradise Lost* and Byron in *Cain* remind us (pp. 30, 37-8, 201). Perhaps Shakespeare and Byron have uncovered it and Byron's transvaluations are part of the result. The art of both, even so, discreetly veils that electric moment of 'delight' accompanying 'guilt' noted in Pope's extraordinarily exact line; and perhaps, failing a perfected synthesis, such a veiling is wise.[1] There are many difficulties. It is moreover possible that homosexuality is also sometimes involved, though the surface poetry does not say so; we may note that the sensuous imagination in both *Venus and Adonis* and *Don Juan* is directed, as in *Eloisa to Abelard* and so often elsewhere in poetry, on a male figure.

Our discussion is fraught with uncertainties. There is a subtle relation between the sexual complex and the wider fields of action, of crime, war-daring and politics.

What does seem certain is this. Milton in both his prose and his poetry almost too fearlessly involves himself in all the worst paradoxes of both sexology and politics, those two great determinators of man's earthly existence which were left unplaced by the Christian revelation and are by Shakespeare and Byron so perfectly placed that they might well seem, to our distracted society, as irrelevant as is Christianity itself. The trouble is, we are just not ready for the greater harmonies. We know only too well the dislocations; in both his prose and his poetry Milton speaks direct to our present anxieties.

It is just because his attempt was so uncompromising that Milton's art incurs criticism. Both he and Spenser laboured to assimilate the heroic tradition to Christianity, and failure was inevitable; even Shakespeare, in his supreme and final statement *Henry VIII*, could not make his Cranmer as dramatically interesting as Wolsey (*Shakespeare and Religion*, 32-4). What is wanted is, without denial of any authentic, nature-planted, thrill, to bring instincts into harmony with righteousness; the sex-drive and the power-drive into harmony with love.

Such are some of the considerations that must be brought to

---

[1] We cannot attribute this veiling to the necessities of public performance. Marlowe pleased his public, and the exact quality of the complex we are discussing is expressed in Shelley's *Cenci* ('fearful pleasure', IV.i; *The Golden Labyrinth*, 215-17) with no loss of dramatic propriety.

bear on the critical strictures applied in the following pages to the artistry of Spenser and Milton. The *interpretative* approach of my second Milton chapter may appear to stand in strange juxtaposition to the *critical* approach of the first. And yet the one followed naturally, if not inevitably, from the other. The faults first observed were later found to be symptoms of a dislocation which was rendered clear, and in a sense justified, from a wider survey including Milton's prose and political activities, within which those very faults could be felt as contributory elements to a richer understanding (p. 129).

Between my first essay and my second my thoughts had been stimulated by certain remarks of my friend Francis Berry to the effect that Milton stood pre-eminent in sheer poetic *power* (p. 105); and that he was, in all probability, whatever we say of his artistry, the greatest *man* in English history. Such thoughts, together with the impact of World War II, led on to my *Chariot of Wrath*, which was written hurriedly in 1941, Milton's prose, mostly new to me, being read, and the book composed, in under a month. It must not however be supposed that I had not previously admired Milton, for *Paradise Lost* was among my earliest poetic delights, in the year 1915, or before; just as *Othello*, which I criticized for its Miltonic affinities in *The Wheel of Fire*, had been in boyhood, and for long after, my favourite Shakespearian play.

I recall also that Francis Berry, sometime in the nineteen-thirties, after reading certain aspersions of mine on Marlowe's shameless dramatization of sadistic *enjoyments* in *Tamburlaine*, remarked that it was just this that made him so great. Subsequent experience has made me aware of a justification in that remark which I did not at the time recognize. We have all watched, on a world scale, events which correspond to Marlowe's treatment. The enjoyment dramatized is part of the problem and to blunt it might be said to shirk the issue.[1] Both Marlowe and Milton suffer from their fearless realism. They attempt to render into art qualities almost impossible to harmonize. They are simultaneously realistic and embarrassing; they give us truth without *catharsis*.

---

[1] Here lies the importance of Browning's *The Heretic's Tragedy*, so admirably high-lighted in Thomas Blackburn's recent *Robert Browning*, 1967, 201–4.

Western man is becoming more and more keenly aware of his own more dangerous compulsions. Pope in his *Essay on Man* did much towards the acceptance and softening of instinct, without denial of its primacy. Drawing nearer, we have the supreme doctrine of sublimation in Nietzsche's *Thus Spake Zarathustra* and the all-important teaching of John Cowper Powys (pp. 30, 113, 242, notes) as to the handling of dangerous, sexually located thrills and fantasies.

Sexual psychology is related to politics, the link being the sadistic instinct, which may be regarded as an extreme of the itch to power. On the political front the problem is before us, more urgent than ever. It is, briefly, this: how to blend State and Church, War and the Sermon on the Mount. The required note has been poetically sounded by Shakespeare in Portia's 'Quality of Mercy' lines in *The Merchant of Venice* and by Isabella's on justice in *Measure for Measure* (*Shakespeare and Religion*, 229–30); and by Byron's *Fitzgerald* sonnet (*Lord Byron: Christian Virtues*, 287–9; *Byron and Shakespeare*, 336; pp. 149, 229 below, notes); but single speeches are not enough. War has, of course, been often satirized, but what we want is, not a condemnation, but a fusion; a fusion of the heroic and the Christian, power and love; and a fusion in terms of narrative and action, allowing, provisionally at least, rights to *both* sides, including all more questionable thrills and enjoyments; otherwise we have merely a one-way tract. In Byron's *Sardanapalus*, which comes near to what we want, the balance tilts a little too obviously in favour of the softer values; there is more transvaluation than fusion. In his life and work together, felt with all their sexual conflicts and dark heroisms as one great whole, Byron certainly established on all fronts as inclusive a harmony as is, for us, conceivable; but we have to take the whole sweep of his life and work into account together; and it may be easier to live the harmony than to express it within a close and exact poetic artistry. Living a solution is far more important, certainly, than writing it; but it is not always, and from every viewpoint, more difficult. Our main concern in this volume is with writing; with the poetry of action.

The lack of strong narrative in our contemporary poetic output symptomizes our Hamlet-like bafflement before the urgent problems that face us. Solution in poetry is a step towards solution in society; and we must accordingly look for, and treasure, any strong contemporary accomplishment within the poetry of action.

I turn again to Francis Berry. He has, as a poet, and a great one, come closer to what we need than any of his predecessors. In *Spain, 1939* (p. 145 below), *The Iron Christ* (*The Galloping Centaur*, 1952) and *Morant Bay* (1961) he has brought insight into atavistic and sexual impulsions and yearnings to an understanding of communal violence; with no taint of satire, with profundity and purpose, he has related the psychology of action to a Christian sensibility. In his two most powerful narratives he has achieved that for which three centuries of English poetry have been striving.

I am well aware that my following essays need to be supplemented by other contemporary studies. I would point students especially to the following: for Spenser, to C. S. Lewis's pages on *The Faery Queen* in *The Allegory of Love* (1936), which have done much to further my general understanding, and also to Alastair Fowler's *Spenser and the Numbers of Time* (1964), cited by my brother W. F. Jackson Knight in the revised and enlarged edition of *Roman Vergil* (Peregrine–Penguin, 1966), and to be read, I would suggest, in conjunction with both my brother's Vergilian commentaries and George E. Duckworth's *Structural Patterns and Proportions in Vergil's Aeneid* (1962); for Milton to John Cowper Powys's essay, unique in its judgements on the sonnets, in *The Pleasures of Literature* (1938; U.S.A., as *The Enjoyment of Literature*), William Empson's *Milton's God* (1961), Francis Berry's *Poetry and the Physical Voice* (1962), R. J. Zwi Werblowsky's *Lucifer and Prometheus* (1952) and Harold Fisch's *Jerusalem and Albion* (1964); for Swift, to Middleton Murry's *Jonathan Swift* (1936; pp. 176–8 below) and the authoritative account in Bonamy Dobrée's *English Literature in the early Eighteenth Century* (1959); and for Byron, to my own more elaborated studies *Lord Byron: Christian Virtues* (1952), *Lord Byron's Marriage* (1957) and *Byron and Shakespeare* (1966). I would here express my gratitude for the support and encouragement which these three studies have received from that fine Byronist, Sir Herbert Read.

I apologize for this haphazard and personal list. I know well enough that there are many others deserving attention.

In the following pages I use for purposes of numerical reference one-volume Oxford editions for Shakespeare, Marlowe, Milton's poetry, and Swift; for Milton's prose, the Columbia edition of the works under the general editorship of Frank Allen Patterson; for Byron's poetry, the seven-volume edition edited by E. Hartley Coleridge and for his prose the *Letters and Journals* edited by R. E. Prothero, Lord Ernle. For my quotations I have used, nearly but not quite always, a modernized spelling for which I am myself responsible. In passages set out as poetry I have, when the metre demanded it, abbreviated verb-formations ending in -ed to 'd. When quoting I have often allowed myself freedom in punctuation and in the use of italics to assist my argument. After forty years' of anxiety and indecision I have given up attempts at consistency in the capitalization of Sun and Moon or the possessive case of words ending in 's'. Instead, I go by context and sound. Comus's is perhaps reasonable, but *Moses's*, 'Moseses', is not; nor *Jesus's*. *Sardanapalus's* might be allowable were we not then simultaneously involved in an adjacent *Salamenes's*, 'Salameneses', which is unbearable. I would myself advise those starting their literary careers to settle for s' throughout, as we do with the possessive case of plurals.

I follow my usual practice in printing the letter 'p.' only for pages in this book; page numerals of other books appear without it. I have given my earlier texts a surface tidying in matters of clarification, syntax and punctuation; a supplementary reference has occasionally been added, but all new *thoughts* are dated.

My thanks are recorded to Mr Michael Phillips who undertook the arduous task of transferring my references to Milton's prose from the Bohn to the Columbia edition, besides checking my references to his, and Spenser's poetry. Dr Sylvia England has checked some of my references and Professor Paul J. Alpers has guided me in the adjustment of a couple of Spenserian dates. Once again Dr Patricia Ball has helped me, finding the line references for Byron's dramas and checking the numerals for his poetry elsewhere. I thank Mr John D. Christie for directing his faultless eye on my proofs and for allowing me to dedicate this volume to him in grateful return for the devotion, care, and brilliance which he has brought, and brings, to the editing of my brother's posthumous papers.

Exeter, April 1967   G. W. K.

To John D. Christie

I

The Spenserian Fluidity

First published in *The Burning Oracle*, 1939

Through Spenser Elizabethan England first becomes fully vocal. His frequent excess, though sometimes deplorable, is of the stuff nevertheless that fills the mould of *Twelfth Night* and *Othello*. He offers a fountain of Elizabethanism, neat. Ideals of Queen-worship and courtiership, especially clear in his admiration of Sidney, are strong in him; also an English pastoralism entwined with Greek mythology; and a sensuous love. He is both national and lyric. Part of his life a civil servant in Ireland, he aspired to be more, and his disappointment has left poetic records of satiric bitterness. But failure did not stifle his more vivid apprehensions, and it is that more positive and characteristic quality that I shall emphasize.

The Shepherd's Calendar (1579) shows a typical profusion, an up-gushing of poetic life. Each eclogue is a miniature lyric playlet, the sequence patterned on the procession of the twelve months. In his archaic language Spenser is here self-consciously English, acknowledging Chaucer and attempting to repudiate other, especially continental, sources. Hellenic mythology is, as in Lyly, a natural expression for a native voice. From out a medley-setting of Theocritus and an English spring, Queen Elizabeth is hymned with extravagant praise and shower-garlanded with a stanza of flowers. One of E. K.'s[1] notes to *April* is valuable:

> So that by Pan is here meant the most famous and victorious king, her highness' Father, late of worthy memory, King Henry the Eighth. And by that name, ofttimes (as hereafter appeareth) be noted kings and mighty potentates: and in some place Christ himself, who is the very Pan and god of shepherds.

[1] The poem appeared in 1579, edited and annotated by an authority signing himself 'E. K.' [1967]

Notice the close texture of Greek mythology, Christianity, and the throne of England. *The Shepherd's Calendar* is both delicately autobiographical and allegorically allusive: 'By the kid may be understood the simple sort of the faithful and true Christians' (E. K.'s note to *May*). The Roman Catholic Church, Gabriel Harvey, Spenser's own love-affair, appear in turn and in fancy dress. The close-entwining of royalistic and heraldic meanings within the flower-stanza of *April* has been skilfully analysed by Janet Spens (*Spenser's Fairie Queene: an Interpretation*, 1934; 74–5). Red and white roses bind civil warfare into an offering to Tudor supremacy, a miniature forecast of Shakespeare's historic succession culminating in *Henry VIII*. Complexity of symbolic or allegoric suggestion is enmeshed in the contemporary and actual fact or event, whether of the poet's own life or the nation's. Contemporary reference is native to the Elizabethan mind. Abstractions are not, as in medieval literature, allowed dictatorial rights over it; they are twisted into a close texture of a new sort. To the Elizabethan poet the ideal is incarnated and at hand; politically in the Queen, personally in his own love. Neither the medieval nor the modern distinction between the actual and the imaginative can properly be supposed to exist.

Inspection of Spenser's four *Hymns* (pub. 1596; the first two purportedly composed much earlier) reveals the Eros-cult which is his belief-core, and, indeed, almost central to Renaissance poetry. From them we can pass to *The Faery Queen*.

The *Hymn in Honour of Love* addresses its deity with all the fervour of a pagan worshipper, the love being of the sexual-romantic kind. Eros is a 'great godhead', 'thou mighty god of love', 'great god of might that reignest in the mind', a phrase neatly pointing a recognition of psychological sovereignty. The analogy is frequent: 'sovereign king', 'sovereign lord of all', 'lord of truth and loyalty', 'victor of gods, subduer of mankind'. There is stress on love's power, yet the god is at heart gentle, inspiring a 'gentle fury', taming lions and tigers. It is that first creative force playing on Chaos, the Holy Spirit of Genesis; Venus, beauty-goddess, the life-former, blends the four elements in harmony. Notice the replacing of Biblical by classical deities. Spenser distinguishes his ideal from lust; it appeals to man's 'immortal mind', is a matter of 'eternity' and 'beauty'. Such Platonic intuitions would perhaps silence too glibly a profound problem, but Spenser does not shirk the unrest of an unsatisfied aspiration which drives men to distraction through 'enravished' sight of a divine excellence, till 'all other bliss seems vain'. He realizes its tragic quality and attendant evils, plunging the lover in 'hell' and that worst monster jealousy that turns 'all love's delight to misery'; the thoughts forecast *Othello* as the greater part of the poem recalls Berowne's defence of Love in *Love's Labour's Lost* (IV. iii. 290–365) and kindred Shakespearian imaginations. The whole is strongly charged with light-imagery. There is perhaps too facile and adjectival a use of it. A line such as 'the flaming light of that celestial fire' illustrates an extreme of what is here an habitual overstress, almost a technical vice. There is not enough housing of his fire in continually new, concrete shapes, but the experience transmitted is clear. The poem ends in flowery delight and with a prayer that the lover may, after his pain, attain paradise:

> Then would I sing of thine immortal praise
> An heavenly hymn such as the angels sing,
> And thy triumphant name then would I raise
> Bove all the gods, thee only honouring,
> My guide, my God, my victor, and my king . . .

His adoration is theologically uncompromising.

The *Hymn in Honour of Beauty* is similar, and strongly Platonic. Christian thought is present, but the goddess is 'Cyprian Queen' of 'sovereign might'. This beauty of 'goodly pattern' ignites love, it is a 'light', a 'lively fire' shining in a face and darting 'amorous desire' into the beholder's soul. The inwardness and physical transcendence of it is argued from our not falling in love with pictures or natural scenery: the beauty which inspires love must involve vitality. The externals of human beauty seen as 'white and red', 'golden wire', 'sparkling stars' must fade, but not so the spirit-fire moulding the physical form in its likeness. Spenser does not altogether shirk the crucial problem of beauty of face joined to evil of soul; but neither does he solve it. He again waxes fierce against 'that hellish fire-brand disloyal lust'; as well he may, since it is the main reason why the cult of Eros has not ages ago been royally established. The trust is, however, finally in the true lover, who sees more profoundly than others, admires 'a more refined form', in a sense focusing 'the mirror of his own thought'; an act of knowledge channelling full subjective instincts. A reciprocity is set up between lovers' eyes:

> For lovers' eyes more sharply sighted be
> Than other men's, and in dear love's delight
> See more than any other eyes can see,
> Through mutual receipt of beames bright . . .

It is a revelation, a 'dawning day'. Something is created, or apprehended. This sense of the significance of lovers' eyes is paralleled in Lyly and Shakespeare. Spenser ends his *Hymn in Honour of Beauty* with more regal touches: 'thy great majesty', 'great sovereign', 'great goddess of my life'. It is a force that 'can restore a damned wight from death'. It could scarcely be more highly honoured.

The two Heavenly Hymns parallel and complement these. The four together neatly balance opposing principles in the Elizabethan mind. Janet Spens (51, 111) observes that the *Hymn of Heavenly Love* describes a downward giving rather than an upward reaching: *agapé* rather than *eros*. It is, as Father E. C. Le Bel has shown, a fairly direct transcription of Christian doctrine. Love starting from the Father begets the Son and from them is derived the Holy Spirit. Spenser phrases as best he can the illimitable bright splendours of angelic life, stress falling on the infinite and, as before, on light. He discusses the Fall, Incarnation, and Redemption. King-imagery, as before, is potent: 'high heaven's king', 'sovereign might'. Christ is 'eternal king of glorie' with 'sovereign bounty' and 'sovereign mercy'. The Hymn ends with exhortations to rise above lesser loves to Christ, couched in the usual blaze of fire-imagery and Platonic excitement. Although the reverse movement and explicit doctrine contradicts the earlier pagan aspirations, they remain only part of the poetry. In so far as we attend to the massed impressions, the substance appears not so very different. It is characteristically Platonic, characteristically scintillant. Spenser's explicit repudiation of his former 'lewd lays' while offering to sing of 'true love' for a change may be nearer an artistic device than confesssion of conversion. The Elizabethan poet was not normally convertible, since both terms of the opposition were with him comfortably together from the start, and to the end. This balance the four *Hymns* in turn express. The Elizabethan is only doing on purpose what many poets since have done by instinct, aiming to eat his cake and have it too. This is often a poetic necessity.

Poetry cannot be entirely theological and transcendental. God must be continually imagined in ever-new materialist terms: as some sort of 'sovereign', 'high eternal power', 'maker', or, in the Hymn to *Beauty*, 'this world's great work-master'. In the fourth Hymn Spenser has a neat problem: how to sing of that Beauty which transcends nature? What do we mean by eternal, divine, spiritual? The concrete quality of poetry cannot rest content with such abstractions. The same road is taken by poet after poet: his mind-structure being naturalistic and yet his final aim being transcendent, he focuses a reality best termed 'universalistic'. The holistic tendencies of poetry are well seen in such instances.

So we are asked to look on the frame 'of this wide universe', and thence to dream others 'infinite in largeness'. We are told of 'endless perfectness' and 'infinite delight'. Impressions of space are expanded:

> First th' Earth, on adamantine pillars founded,
> Amid the Sea engirt with brazen bands;
> Then th' Air still flitting, but yet firmly bounded
> On every side, with piles of flaming brands,
> Never consum'd nor quench'd with mortal hands;
> And last, that mighty shining crystal wall
> Wherewith He hath encompassed this All.

Contemplation of the universe rather than 'nature', of *Antony and Cleopatra* rather than *King Lear*, is the way to divine apprehension, spurning earth:

> Air more than water, fire much more than air,
> And heaven than fire appears more pure and fair.

Though all elements are finally transcended, the Heavenly Beauty is frequently imaged as a sun. We are to concentrate on the 'king' and 'queen' of the sky who 'the heavens' empire sway'. 'King' and 'sun', as so often, touch metaphorically: 'their Captain's flaming head' is a good phrase. There are regal suggestions, as in 'the glorious face of the divine eternal Majesty' and the 'sovereign Powers and Potentates' which are said to contain 'all mortal Princes and imperial states'. This Beauty is a 'majesty divine' compared with which Sun and Moon are dark, itself a 'bright sun of glory'. Therefore throw yourself humbly 'before the footstool of his Majesty', whose 'throne' is built on eternity and whose 'sceptre' is righteousness. Sapience is his queen, 'the sovereign darling of the Deity', she is 'clad like a queen in royal robes', on her head is set 'a crown of purest gold', and all is 'subjected to her power imperial'. 'Beauty sovereign', 'sovereign praises', 'sovereign light' – the poem is dense with royalistic impressions and imagery, perhaps over-insistent, of sun and fire.

What Spenser is doing should be clear. To read any absolute division into the two halves of the sequence is to read that sequence as something other than poetry. His impressionism remains constant, and though this is not the whole of his poetry it is a great part of it. The human is first seen as divine; the divine is later imaged in human, with in Sapience feminine, terms. At one extreme there are sexual, at the other Christian, apprehensions. They are different-coloured beads threaded on the one golden string of royalistic and fire-impressions inter-twisted with a Platonic idealism. This balance in opposition or synthesis of Christian and erotic feeling is vital throughout Renaissance and post-Renaissance poetry. Only less interesting is the close relation, almost equation, of kingship and personal aspiration. A king is, as it were, a super-self, and the term may be used to suggest a super-apprehension, or its object. It blends naturally into a sense of the divine, being soaked in centuries of sacramental feeling.

In *The Faery Queen* (1590–96) Spenser seems to have taken all poetic impressionism as his province. It is stocked with folklore, myth, and legend of all sorts and crammed with influences Italian, medieval and classical. The poem is peculiarly rich in pagan lore. Spenser's metaphysic of fertility and creation is often nearer to the pagan and the naturalistic than to the Christ-ian. *The Faery Queen* is more a storehouse for poets of the future than itself a poem. In this, if in no other sense, he is, as he has often been called, 'the poets' poet', and a study of *The Faery Queen* in detail should help anyone who finds Colin Still's interpretation of *The Tempest* in terms of ancient legendary and ritualistic correspondences a fantastic conception.[1] Behind all our poetry there is a communal store of semi-consciously possessed legendary material: Spenser seems to have possessed it consciously. As so often, the Elizabethan is fully aware, his mind flooded, where later poets rely on mysterious, not-to-be-accounted-for promptings, controlled or otherwise, from unconsciousness.

But *The Faery Queen* is not concerned mainly with ancient recollections: it is supremely Elizabethan as well. Its forked meanings are clear from Spenser's own statement in *A letter of the Author's expounding his whole intention in the course of this work:*

> In that Faery Queen I mean glory in my general intention, but in my particular I conceive the most excellent and glorious person of our sovereign the Queen, and her kingdom in Faery Land. And yet in some places else I do otherwise shadow her . . .
>
> (*Poetical Works*, ed. J. C. Smith and
> E. de Selincourt, 1924 ed.; 407)

A neat statement of the universal and particular in poetic blend, though so tight and exact a fusion as is suggested applies more generally to the work of Lyly than to that of Spenser, whose significances are often arbitrary and laxly related, as his final phrase suggests. But he is throughout more than a fancy-poet, and also more than a medieval allegorist, though both these he certainly is too. He builds a nationalist and royalist purpose into the scheme. It is 'the eulogy of a patriot addressing a united people', writes B. E. C. Davis (*Edmund Spenser*, 1933; 75), 'the nearest approach to a national epic in the cycle of English poetry'. He suggests that the constitution of Spenser's Faery Land presents a happy medium between monarchy and oligarchy that reflects 'in vague outline' the commonwealth of Tudor England. The poem is dedicated to the Queen, who as Gloriana is supposed to dominate. In the introduction to Book II there is praise of the Queen; reference to recent explorations and discoveries; and a final sense of mystery and magic in the immediate and actual projected into the equation of England

[1] I refer to Still's *Shakespeare's Mystery Play*, 1921; revised, as *The Timeless Theme*, 1936. See my study *The Crown of Life*, 226. [1967]

and Faery Land under the 'fairest Princess under sky'. The Queen's chastity, so often found to make a neat blend in the Elizabethan mind of its two dominating positives – royalistic splendour and sexual excellence of one divine sort or another – is to be related elsewhere to Belphoebe and also to Mercilla. Prince Arthur is, in part, Leicester. Arthur's 'magnificence' is the Renaissance ideal in full show:

> The general end therefore of all the book is to fashion a gentleman or noble person in virtuous and gentle discipline.
>
> (*Poetical Works*, as above; 407)

Not, be it noted, to make a saint. The search for eternal truth (Una), the supplanting of deceitful semblances (Archimago and Duessa) are aspects of the humanistic ideal. Again,

> So in the person of Prince Arthur I set forth magnificence in particular, which virtue for that (according to Aristotle and the rest) it is the perfection of all the rest, and containeth in it them all, therefore in the whole course I mention the deeds of Arthur applyable to that virtue, which I write of in that book.
>
> (*Poetical Works*, as above; 407)

That holiness would not have been one of Aristotle's 'virtues' need not trouble us. Renaissance poets try to *include* Christianity in a new, humanistic, comprehension. This is their poetic instinct, whatever their religious assertions. With them the present and actual incarnates the divine; from that sense is born their poetry. This is true equally of their royalistic and their erotic perceptions, which are not finally distinct. Both are blended with Christianity rather than subject to it.

Besides the specifically ancient or contemporary there are throughout *The Faery Queen* essences of the universal and the timeless. I mean the vivid naturalism and imagistic grace, the luscious stanzaic woodlands and glades of impressionism and event; the featuring of beasts and people, good or evil; of lovely life and hideous fears; the use of cosmic forces, sun or earth; of the seasons; of night and day; death and life in interdependence; and of divine purposes generally.

Nevertheless the poem is, as a whole, unsatisfying. It claims more than it fulfils. The various knights and their quests are surely too shadowy, too slightly distinguished and objectified.

And even if they were not, the dominating and binding presences of Gloriana and Arthur do not dominate and bind as they ought. It is difficult to feel the poem as a whole and would be even if it were finished. We get from it a vague quality rather than a structure. This is partly because the symbolic technique is faulty. Although Spenser attempts to inweave his general thinking with the national life of his day, yet, faced by his vast self-proposed scheme, he falls back on a medievalistic allegory which he never quite controls. When one of his monsters vomits pamphlets we are shocked; too much realism in the beast's creation renders his deeper significance ludicrous; the blend of allegory and realism has not been properly performed. He misses symbol of the more profound sort: that incarnation of significance in fictional person, or beast, so exactly true that every bend of the mould fits, in its degree, the desired shape of the contained fluid. Spenser's moulds are themselves undisciplined and variable. Dante had his rigid theological beliefs and the medieval allegorists normally started with some precise and ruling intellectual structure. Shakespeare has his realism, his unswerving sense of the way things happen, as well as his sources. Spenser has no such discipline: there is nothing to stop his poem going on for ever, and, worm-like, its organic perfection suffers little from its having been chopped off halfway. It is true that in Shakespeare various meanings can be drawn from one symbolic figure: Caliban, for example. But Caliban is first a unit. 'This is the law of symbolism', writes Charles Williams in discussion of Spenser, 'that the symbol must be utterly itself before it can properly be a symbol' (*Reason and Beauty in the Poetic Mind*, 1933; 55). Whatever Caliban may mean, he is first Caliban, a rounded artistic whole. Spenser's significances are flat, and however many flatnesses are superimposed you do not create a multifacial globe. One sees in his work a transition between old-style allegory and a more rounded symbolism. He is struggling for it. He talks well of 'general' and 'particular' intentions, but in the completed result these are not tied up in a tight knot, it is all loose. His seeming complexity is never a complex profundity.

Though the main plan is, it seems, a magnificent failure, this does not preclude excellences in the parts. Its national, religious, and social implications are probably weaker than those personal and psychological, but these are often exquisite.

The poem is concerned heavily with man's erotic and sensuous nature, the problem of good and bad love. 'Love', writes B. E. C. Davis (217, 220), is 'a cardinal motive' in all Spenser's poetry; it 'lies at the very foundation' of his 'cosmos'. In *The Allegory of Love* C. S. Lewis has well analysed Spenser's meticulous impresssionism in conveying states of decadent and healthy sex-instincts. In the Bower of Bliss there is stress on idleness, artificiality ('metal ivy'), eye-lust, and an excessively conscious sex-appeal, as in the bathing nymphs:

> Then suddenly both would themselves unhele,
> And th' amorous sweet spoiles to greedy eyes reveal.
>
> (II. xii. 64)

In contrast, the Garden of Adonis offers nature rather than art, frank sex-intercourse and a stress on creation (*The Allegory of Love*, 1936; 324–6; 330–3). The naked Graces at VI. x. are, comments Lewis (331), 'engaged in doing something worth doing'; that is, dancing in a ring 'in order excellent' (VI. x. 13). Lewis analyses another related and tricky opposition: of passionate yet adulterous love, persistent in medieval poetry, to married faithfulness. The end and aim of the sex-substances in *The Faery Queen* seems to be this marriage-ideal: a thought with manifold implications for the study of Elizabethan drama. Chastity to Spenser 'means Britomart, married love'. The 'romance of marriage' replaces the 'romance of adultery' (*The Allegory of Love*, 340).

We must therefore not complain too readily that Spenser's attractive evils, as in the Bower of Bliss, prove him a dangerous moralist. Rather he is at work on a very subtle problem. Certain stanzas may suggest a failure, such as we find in *Comus*, to be sure about his own judgements; but then he may not be sure; which, of course, may be an artistic limitation. C. S. Lewis writes: 'The Bower of Bliss is not a place even of healthy animalism, or indeed of activity of any kind. . . . It is a picture, one of the most powerful ever painted, of the whole sexual nature in disease' (332). The attraction – and the accompanying descriptions are often attractive – is part of the disease, and the problem as old as the Garden of Eden. It is similarly insistent in Marlowe and Milton, though there is no trace of it in Lyly or Shakespeare. The puritan, whether Spenser or Milton, opposes, as did D. H. Lawrence, not a physical instinct but an insidious mind-perversion from which few of us can claim complete freedom. It is the enjoyment of an idea rather than a reality, and ideas can have an attractive intensity no reality quite touches. Properly to act and live an experience the mind must be subdued, dissolved, itself unpossessing; creative things are often accomplished half-aware; while excessive awareness tends to the immoral. Nevertheless some intensity of perception may perhaps be known in the very mental twist of such evil, some sense of the life-fire not known otherwise, depending partly on the breaking of conventional codes, whatever they be; an enjoyment of daring, parasitic on traditional principles. In so far as we describe or imagine an ultimate paradise, where neither creativeness nor ethical codes are properly relevant, a degree of essential freedom may again be helpful, if only to suit the perversions of our minds. Both the Bower of Bliss and the Garden of Adonis have their rights, and maybe this is why Spenser allows so much exquisite description, involving bird-song, to accompany temptation. The problem is obscure. We shall meet it again in our study of Milton.

Spenser's puritanism is, in a sense, sex-flooded. In the Garden of Adonis we hear: 'Frankly each paramour his leman knows' (III. vi. 41); which is not true of the Bower of Bliss. The Temple of Venus is a place of 'joy and amorous desire' (IV. x. 38) where, writes B. E. C. Davis (219), 'every object serves to stimulate passion and the instinct to reproduce, unchecked by moral or religious scruple'. Again (228), 'No moral law or religious inhibition mars the "sweete love" and "goodly merriment" of the Garden of Adonis, the "spotlesse pleasures" and unbridled Hedonism of Venus' Isle.' This is Spenser's central hope: untainted creative joy outside and beyond the world of good and evil, from a Shakespearian height where the Bower of Bliss will perhaps appear an insubstantial rather than an evil dream. The continual search in Spenser's narrative for truth and reality, the supplanting of imposters and righting of erroneous choice, is an aspect of our problem. The deceits of lust correspond within

Spenser's story to deceptive occurrences: though these may
have ecclesiastical references, there are psychological references too. Spenser's humanism asserts that virtue is finally the
only realism: a fulfilment of nature, not a thwarting of it. This
he knows, and describes; yet does not, like Shakespeare, reveal.

His poem does not quite live the gospel it preaches. It lacks
architectonic strength. It is fluid. Of the two qualities needed,
that of a time-sequence and a strong, controlling, spatial design,
it valuably possesses only the first. Its spatialized scheme, though
vast, is insubstantial. Exquisite descriptions of human art and
various rich solids are frequent, but the poem as a whole has
neither architectural stability nor solid richness. There is an
addition of image to image, of verbal music to verbal music, a
diffusion rather than concentration, an essentially stanzaic
sequence, but no complex intertwisted multiplication of significances. There are modifying contrasts, but no dramatic intensity. Often Spenser seems more interested in his abstract
doctrines than in his created world; or, if his world grips him,
he seems to forget, for a stanza or two, his message, which is
temporarily smothered by the luxuriant impressionism. The
nature of his creation changes indecisively. Aristotle's idea that
the constructing of a weighty central plot is a greater art than
characterization or rhetoric comes to mind. Spenser's fluid,
shifting significances make a boneless, piecemeal work. There is
a lack of tough moral fibre in his constructional technique. Any
amount of things happen, but you get slight sense of vital action.
It is a dream-world, a 'faery' world, perilously near decadence.
It is sensuous, yet unreal. Janet Spens writes (69–70) that 'he
never deals so much with the sensuous fact as with the mental
translation of the fact – with the use which the soul's faculty
makes of the impact and stir of the physical sensation; and he is
more excited by the infinitely various web which man has woven
to adorn and clothe the physical than by the simple physical facts
themselves'. She notes elsewhere (122, 130) that the root evil
in Spenser's world is the medieval *accidie*: that is, sloth, melan-
cholia, inactivity. If this be true, there is an interesting relation
between the poem's technical weakness and those sensuous and
mental errors the poet so skilfully diagnoses. *The Faery Queen* is
an eye-feast, an ear-feast, a mind-feast: but it is not a shared

action, it is without dramatic suspense. People do things, but at a distance, like figures on a tapestry. It is hard to feel events in relation to the whole. There is really no organic heart. Though Gloriana and Arthur are meant as such, they do not so function, do not receive from the whole action and pump back living significances. Consequently the body-structure lacks organic warmth. It tends to split, dissolve: the whole into books, books into cantos, cantos into events, events into descriptive luxuriance. The proper organic process is reversed. To compare it with a contemporary: in Thomas Sackville's Induction to *A Mirror for Magistrates* (1563) we have at least fine separate imaginate blocks (death, hell, Buckingham) in whose service images are powerfully used, thronging all their joint force into each little whole. Even in Spenser's shorter movements each whole is liable to obscurity by its parts. It is less than the sum of its parts. Instead of building up and cohering, the poem is always decomposing. Its finest units, being so independently fine, are, even if in themselves organic, rich rather with a cancerous and upstart vitality, drawing attention from that whole they should serve. Hence the baggy, bulgy, loose effect, the fluidity. 'Flowing water', writes Miss Spens (78) 'always fascinated Spenser.' Naturally. This fascination corresponds to a relaxed sensuousness, and that to an immorality of technique which just misses conviction, is over-mentalized and all but decadent. Spenser may explicitly favour his Garden of Adonis, with its upsurge of creative life; but we must go elsewhere for that. *The Faery Queen* is itself one vast Bower of Bliss.

That is, it may be, an overstatement. I admit that I do not feel at home here. Possibly, were the poem complete and I had it in all detail and as a whole thoroughly comprehended, its design might appear satisfactory and its parts contributory. But it is very difficult to reach this, and difficult in a sense that the mental possession of Dante's poem is not. Spenser asks, and I think has undertaken, too much. It is a transition poem, aiming at an epic or medieval-heroic manner not deeply suitable to the age. Greek tragedy stands between us and Homer; the New Testament between us and Vergil; and Shakespeare between us and the *Morte D'Arthur*. The dramatic and complex continually supervene on the epic and the adventurous. A new dimension of significance interwoven with every action is, in the Renaissance world especially, urgent for expression. Spenser's poem has no *active* meaning, is not dramatically alive, because he has not found the action he believes in: action which, as in Shakespeare, is newly created, not a legendary reminiscence of a past chivalry. Greek tragedy and the New Testament are both powerfully realistic and metaphysical. Spenser's story is usually unworthy of his thought, of his metrical and stanzaic skill, of his impressionistic profusion. The action, as such, is weak.

True, Spenser with his subtle and comprehensive designing and his intention of a Gloriana and Arthur centrality attempts the typical patterning and dominant, fusing symbol that so often lend meaning and power to long works: he has the idea, though his vast scheme is too unwieldy for it. Many Shakespearian essences, moreover, are here. The heritage of the ages is combined with a contemporary royalism; human instinct, and especially Renaissance sensuousness, subtly analysed; pagan and Christian mythology entwined. Shakespeare's political thinking is forecast. I quote again from B. E. C. Davis (228): 'The national pests disfiguring the land of Faerie – Error, Deceit, Tyranny, Anarchy, Lust, Detraction – all spring from the cardinal evil principle, Disorder.' The various knights are at work quelling the various forces of disorder. Spenser is, like all poets, at home among cosmic forces of all sorts; but something is wanting.

That 'something' is to be related to (i) the New Testament and great tragedy generally; (ii) individual human personality as an indissoluble and realized unit. The two are clearly related. Often in *The Faery Queen* there is a subtle sensuous inconsistency, or if not that, an artistic indecision: he can insert a lovely birdsong stanza in his Bower of Bliss, or associate the most ghoulish horrors with an *intellectual* heresy. There is a certain want of imaginative common-sense, and perhaps artistry, as though ethical principles were not in the wider issues of this work perfectly integrated with aesthetic associations into his imaginative scheme. Though it witnesses a certain integrity, this indecision – when he is sure of evils he leaves you in no doubt, as in the masque of sins at the end of Book I – precludes the creation of strong human action and a convincing artistic structure. There is not that impact of terrific importance and native direction in the human adventure found in the New Testament drama and in Shakespeare. These generally force a dramatic, often tragic, expression. Conversely dramatic form helps to force creative profundity. Drama, with its close plot-texture and disciplinary limits, its centralized and realistic human concern, was the condition of full Elizabethan expression. The Elizabethan mind was too flooded with a diversity of ideas and images; Shakespeare knew no more than Spenser, but gained by being forced to say less. Steep banks make a stream deep, swift, and forceful – 'forceful' rather than 'fluid' – which without them is slothful, leisurely, and expansively shallow. Moreover the greatest dramatic expression depends also on a sense of human personality which I feel Spenser, to a final judgement, lacks. He is rarely inside his fictions, enduring their joys and terrors. Shakespeare writes from a hard core of trust in human personality, his own or others', which Spenser's fluid impressionism does not reach, so getting underneath his dramatic figure or action, creating from within and forcing others to share from within; and finally, the structure of his art-form has, with little explicit doctrine, the tough-corded sanity of an unswerving experienced realism.

The Hymns present Spenser's visionary thought, while his sensuousness is most perfect in *Epithalamion*, wherein his fluid tendency, which becomes an explicit river-symbolism in *Prothalamion* and the union of Thames and Medway in *The Faery Queen* (IV. xi), functions beautifully in torrential celebration of his own marriage; but in referring these twin impulses, intellectual and emotional, to epic action, he fails. *The Faery Queen* has nevertheless certain passages of deep tragic meditation; its recurrent metaphysic of fertility is important; and pieces of symbolic description presenting pictures, legends in static design, sculptured figures, and so on, hold profound psychological meanings.

The poem perhaps improves after the more famous, but perhaps less powerful, first two books, moving from religious polemic towards, at times, a blazing humanism, a pagan-ritualistic apprehension wherein the closely related glories of sun-fire and human love are finely advanced. The praise of Venus, sovereign of

B

creation, is especially valuable (IV. x. 37–47). Spenser's ranging
cosmic intuition draws level with Bacon's *Advancement of Learning*
and Pope's *Essay on Man*, as in the dialogue between Artegall
and the Giant concerning the divine ordering of the physical
universe (v. ii. 30–50). The poetry grows more plain, virile,
and athletic (as at III. xi. 25); with similes of sharp, realistic
observation and sense of elemental vigour (see IV. vi. 14; v. ii.
50), and a remarkable projection of animal life in fierce action
(see v. ii. 15; v. xi. 12). There is, once at least, a Shakespearian
inwardness of dramatic sympathy in description of Britomart's
varying anxiety and distress, compared finally to a child's wayward grief (v. vi. 1–14); and once strong action becomes itself
significant in Britomart's penetration of fire to rescue Amoret
from sensuous enchantment (III. xi. 21–xii. 45). Britomart is
Spenser's most satisfying person. She is a comprehensive conception, in her masculine dress and armour signifying an integra-
tion of sexual principles, as does Venus at IV. x. 41; a creature
of romantic action, challenging purity, and – we are told,
though perhaps scarcely made to feel – ardent love. Dedicated
to a dream-lover, she is meant to attain successful human consummation, though her attractiveness symbolizing the feminine
and finally matrimonial ideal is rather strained by her twice
conquering in fight her future lord before their union. Artegall
cuts a sorry figure: 'Ah, my dear Lord', says Britomart to him
during a characteristic rescue, 'What May-game hath mis-
fortune made of you?' (v. vii. 40). She herself, however, accur-
ately personifies what the fiction as a whole does not attain: the
marriage of strong action with emotional purity.

Spenser's expressly *gentle* humanism, which precludes any
convincing presentation of heroic conflict as such and leads to
excessive reliance on spiritual content as opposed to realistic
form – and this is what we mean by allegory – nevertheless itself
draws him finally nearer to the consistently trusting humanists,
Lyly, Shakespeare, and Pope, than to the somewhat aesthetically turbulent and variously forceful distrusters, Marlowe and
Milton. His attempt to convey in philosophic and epic form a
flooding sensuousness which penetrates so many creeks and
ramifications of human desire, good or bad, heralds a new line
of poetry to be concerned with (i) the erotic impulse as the

central drive to an expanding apprehension of man's at once earthy-natural and fiery-cosmic setting, and (ii) the problem of action, involving conceptions royalistic and communal; while both are to be related to man's tragic destiny and the spirit, though not necessarily the dogmas, of Christianity.

II
Milton: the Poetry

First published as 'The Frozen Labyrinth' in *The Burning Oracle*, 1939

I

This cannot be an easy essay: no great writer in English presents so many opportunities for critical confusion as does Milton. Fortunately his early poems serve as a clarifying introduction. The *Nativity* ode *On the Morning of Christ's Nativity* (1629) has many typically Miltonic images. Here are some: the sun's 'burning axletree', 'the well-balanc't world on hinges hung', the 'enamell'd arras of the rain-bow'. In these observe the concretizing of the natural, the mechanical approach to the cosmic. The star, we hear, 'hath fixt her polish'd car', and attends with 'handmaid lamp'. Often a smooth and polished surface is suggested, a rounded and perhaps shining completion. This particularizing yet romantic concreteness turning out references to 'urns and altars', 'chill marble', and a 'furnace blue' blends with an exquisite realization of pagan ritual.

L'Allegro and *Il Penseroso* (1632) are mosaics of impression. They resemble inlay-work or embroidery, choice pieces meticulously arranged according to a preconceived design. Other ingredients are a subtle use of folklore and country superstition; an equally subtle and yet truly Elizabethan sense of pastoral merriment; a varied play of light and darkness; a loving memory of literature, classical, Chaucerian, Elizabethan; and of Greek philosophy. Each image in the sequence is of gem-like worth, reflecting the unearthed riches of a studious and cloistered mind.

Aspects of nature are often solidified into persons, sometimes helped by reference to fabrics. The ethereal and evanescent are rendered weighty, as in the 'labouring clouds' of *L'Allegro*. We meet images from human civilization, clothes, sculpture, something of nature's Shakespearian and dynamic otherness being lost. In *Il Penseroso* we find the nightingale 'smoothing the rugged brow of night'; Melancholy comes in 'a robe of darkest grain' and a 'sable stole of cypress lawn', forgetting herself 'to marble' with a 'leaden downward cast'; the 'civil-suited morn' is 'kerchief'd in a comely cloud'. There is little feeling for organic, pulsing life as such: all is levelled under a weighty impressionism. Effects are usually pictorial and still, to be contrasted with the tingling apprehension of nature's vital movement in, say, Goethe. And yet results may be admirable, as in the royalistic grandeur of this, in *L'Allegro*:

> Where the great sun begins his state,
> Rob'd in flames and amber light,
> The clouds in thousand liveries dight.

Light is rendered solid, its glory both refracted and concretized, weightily embodied and momentously, darkly, colourful.

Such a love for the solid leads naturally to the architectural dignity of oaks, noted as 'aged' in the one poem and 'monumental' in the other. In *L'Allegro* 'twisted eglantine' gets the outer design, though less of the sap, of the flower; there is a chequer-board effect in 'russet lawns and fallows grey', a mosaic suggestion in 'meadows trim with daisies pied', a solidification of liquid in 'spicy nut-brown ale'; dawn is 'dappled', the lark sings from his 'watch-tower in the skies'. In *Il Penseroso* 'glimmering bowers' suggests human artistry as much as foliage; so do the 'arched walks of twilight groves'. Milton habitually feels foliage and vegetation as an over-arching canopy. Such impressions are summed in *Il Penseroso*:

> But let my due feet never fail
> To walk the studious cloister's pale,
> And love the high embowed roof,
> With antique pillars massy proof,
> And storied windows richly dight,
> Casting a dim religious light.

Milton's love of architectural weight, dim light, and legendary colour suffused by religious solemnity is perfectly condensed, and the whole illustrates the first point I wish to make: Milton's innate sympathy with the weighty, monumental, and architectural.

Milton's poetry contains strong feelings for music and other sounds. The *Nativity* ode asks for a 'solemn strain' to offer the Infant God. There is 'no battle's sound', the winds are 'with wonder whist' for the occasion. The shepherds are greeted by divine music elaborated through two stanzas, a harmony of 'blissful rapture' unifying Earth and Heaven; and three more stanzas are given to their harping 'in loud and solemn quire'. We are told that this repeats the first creation-music: it is associated with 'crystal spheres', 'the bass of Heaven's deep organ', and is called an 'angelic symphony' and 'holy song' which, if it 'enwrap' our 'fancy', will reintroduce the golden age, reverse time, kill sickness and make the 'dolorous mansions' of Hell pass away. Music is Milton's natural approach to cosmic resolutions. Later we have the 'trump of doom' thundering with 'horrid clang' such as once was heard on Mount Sinai. At Christ's birth oracles are 'dumb', no 'voice or hideous hum' runs 'through the arched roof', Apollo flies 'with hollow shriek', there are no more 'breathed spells', the 'resounding shore' hears weeping and laments, Lars and Lemures 'moan with midnight plaint', flamens are disturbed by a 'drear and dying sound'. Cymbals ring in vain for Moloch, and Osiris ceases to trample the grass 'with lowings loud'. There is often a suggestion of resonance and echo, as though sounds were enclosed in a building. Milton's apprehension of pagan sanctities, and indeed of nature generally, points towards Keats.[1]

L'Allegro is, perhaps strangely, less full of sound than *Il Penseroso*. We have the 'hounds and horn' to wake the morning, 'echoing shrill' through woods; the ploughman whistling, the cock who 'rings' his 'matins', the 'busy hum' of human cities. There are 'merry bells' and 'jocund rebecks', people are lulled to sleep by 'whispering winds', Shakespeare 'warbles his native woodnotes wild'. *Il Penseroso* is musically more rich. Melancholy, though a creature of 'peace and quiet', hears the muses singing round 'Jove's altar'. There is to be 'mute silence' except for the nightingale, 'musical' and 'melancholy' 'chantress' who shuns the 'noise of folly'; the 'far-off curfew' sounds across water sing-

ing 'with sullen roar'; far from 'resort of mirth' we hear only the
cricket or the 'bellman's drowsy charm'. We listen to Orpheus
warbling to his string and symbolic melodies in the 'sage and
solemn tunes' of old romance, where 'more is meant than meets
the ear'. There are winds 'piping loud' and 'rustling leaves', the
bee 'singing' at work, waters 'murmuring', the music of the
'unseen genius of the wood', pointing on to *Comus*. Both poems
have their appropriate sounds, and each has its crowning music
passage. The first from *L'Allegro* is this:

> And ever against eating cares,
> Lap me in soft Lydian airs
> Married to immortal verse,
> Such as the meeting soul may pierce
> In notes, with many a winding bout
> Of linkèd sweetness long drawn out,
> With wanton heed and giddy cunning,
> The melting voice through mazes running;
> Untwisting all the chains that tie
> The hidden soul of harmony.

Music dismisses 'cares'; the marriage of music to words is followed by a meeting of the soul and music; 'linkèd sweetness'
recalls 'leading him prisoner in a red-rose chain' in Shakespeare's *Venus and Adonis* (110), harsh metal turned to flowery
delight; direct opposites are blended, resolved, as in Coleridge's *Kubla Khan*, the 'winding bout' paradoxically 'long drawn
out'; 'heed' and 'wantonness' converge, also 'cunning' and
'giddiness', under the spell of music; 'mazes', an important
symbol to be found throughout Milton for distress and confusion, are the scene of a happy chase; while the heavy chains
that manacle the mind are 'untwisted' – words suiting the solidity and weight of Milton's imagery – to reveal and unleash a
carefree and universal harmony. In such lyric music Milton can
lose his weightier self. But most of his references are to 'solemn'
music, and *Il Penseroso* has also its star music passage, neatly
following and blending into the ecclesiastical and architectural
description already quoted to build a perfect condensation of
the specifically Miltonic:

> There let the pealing organ blow
> To the full-voic'd quire below,

In service high and anthems clear,
As may with sweetness through mine ear
Dissolve me into ecstasies,
And bring all heaven before mine eyes.

Here we are at the very heart of Milton. The short *Arcades* (c. 1633) has music lines of high interest. Music is there felt as intrinsic to all ultimate understanding, the bed-rock of creation, a matter of 'sweet compulsion', again a paradox and again recalling our *Venus and Adonis* line, or St Paul's happy bondage (Ephesians, iii. 1); a power that conquers destiny, lulling the 'daughters of necessity', that is, resolving antinomies of free-will and fate; keeping nature at her work and drawing it to the divine. However, to know this resolution whilst listening to music, or drinking (like Burns's hero in *Tam o' Shanter*, 'o'er a' the ills o' life victorious'), is one thing; to possess it on a wider front of literary action quite another, as we shall see when we come to *Paradise Lost*.

Architecture is spatial and static, music dynamic and temporal. Milton is strongly sensitive to both. We can say, by metaphor, that in the greatest literary art-forms these two qualities, the architectonic and narrative, are perfectly fused, as in Shakespeare. Outside the Sonnets Shakespeare has comparatively little to say of architecture, and though we ourselves may often use metaphors from building and design for our own analyses, they cannot do more than provisionally reflect the organic and natural energies of Shakespeare's work. As for sound, thunder-tempests and music are in Shakespeare our final terms of reference; but they are nothing in themselves apart from the human action. Music description or suggestion of it in metaphor is comparatively slight, nor is the dramatic use of music excessive. In the greater plays it occurs at the limit, so to speak, crowning, but never replacing, other positive effects, the other more human melodies of passion and action: it may be heavily stressed at a high moment, as in *King Lear*, *Antony and Cleopatra*, and *Pericles*; and in *The Tempest*, Miltonic in its fondness for sounds and especially solemn music, it helps to mark the culmination of a movement composed of many plays. These twin arts so persistent imagistically in Milton's early work may both be felt implicit in the more poetic fusion of Shakespeare, where how-

ever we cannot disentangle passion's music and action's thunder
from dramatic and architectural stability. Neither art exists *as
itself* in Shakespeare. The *Nativity* ode, though it offers a satisfying lyric integrity, remains fluid in its addition of stanza to
stanza: there is no complex inter-knitting of central action with
design, nor is that necessary. *L'Allegro* and *Il Penseroso* present a
dualism of mood important to our understanding of Milton, but
the texture of each is loose: no more is needed than a succession
and addition of 'objective correlatives' to the feeling in question.
The poems are static. The images are themselves pictorially
still, making a sequential arrangement of tiny solids with no
sense of any dynamic, evolving energy. The task of marrying
movement and action to design, the realizing of an organic cohe-
sion of motion and solidity, of the melodic and the architectural,
remains unattempted, though the arts corresponding to each
of these elements *in isolation* are insistently, almost excessively,
emphasized.

Paganism and sensuous feeling are strong in Milton from the
start. In the *Nativity* ode Christ is himself, as in Spenser, where
He once shares the title with Henry VIII, indirectly associated
with the 'great Pan'. Though *L'Allegro* and *Il Penseroso* in opposition hold the germ of Milton's main conflict, the richness of
both witnesses his sensuous vigour, just as their suffusing solemnity and scholarly cast of thought witness his ascetic control.
In *Comus* (1634) Milton attempts a complex work turning on a central opposition of sensuous temptation and religious abstinence.

It repeats former essences with a more spontaneous upgush-
ing of pure Elizabethanism, which does not blend any too
easily with the poem's ethical nature. *A Midsummer Night's
Dream* has been a helpful, and understood, influence. The setting continues Milton's love of architectural nature, and the
prevailing darkness his feeling for subdued light. The wood is
both an over-arching dimness and a maze:

                              their way
    Lies through the perplex'd paths of this drear wood,
    The nodding horror of whose shady brows
    Threats the forlorn and wandering passenger.   (36)

The heroine is lost 'in the blind mazes of this tangled wood'

(181), it is a 'leavy labyrinth' (278), with 'paths and turnings' (569). The Lady's song (230) addresses Echo – Milton loves *echoing* sounds – who lives unseen by the river 'Meander', the song itself suggesting a winding, labyrinthine movement that recalls the 'winding bout', 'sweetness long drawn out', 'giddy cunning' and 'mazes' of the dualism-resolving song in *L'Allegro*. The express purpose of both is to match labyrinthine distress with labyrinthine harmony. The wood of *Comus* suggests the mazes, especially the psychological mazes, of human life. Darkness has cruelly muffled the stars

> That nature hung in heaven, and fill'd their lamps
> With everlasting oil, to give due light
> To the misled and lonely traveller.   (198)

Observe the concrete mechanizing and civilizing of nature in 'everlasting oil'. *Comus* is a moral parable of spiritual error and divine guidance, recalling certain parts of *The Faery Queen*, and *The Tempest* as interpreted by Colin Still (see p. 7, note). Chastity here is the safeguard against both unruly fears and disordered imaginations, since light, we are told, may reign in the soul whatever the surrounding darkness (381–2). As the Lady meditates on Christian virtues a sable cloud is seen to 'turn forth her silver lining on the night' (224). Notice the textile quality of 'lining'.

The poem is psychological and moralistic. Comus and his rout suggest the evils of unrestrained, especially mental, lasciviousness. The opposition is ethically direct and the logic coherent in so far as we neglect the poetry; but once admit that, and a difficulty appears. Comus is far too attractive. His misbehaving rout and Bacchic exuberance generally may be readily placed, but he as often reminds us of the more guiltless joys in *L'Allegro*. He defends (93–144) his point of view in natural and cosmic terms fine as the Helen-poetry in Marlowe's *Doctor Faustus*: his argument enlists the 'starry choir', 'spheres', the procession of months, years, seasons; vast sounds, seas; the moon, 'wavering' morris-dancers, fairy dance on sands, books and fountains. He reminds us of Oberon and Titania, and of many mythological or romantic intimations before and since ranging from elfin loveliness to cosmic grandeur. There are other tonings, but the difficulty remains. 'A light fantastic round' (144) replaces the 'light fantastic toe' of *L'Allegro*. In his invitation later on (706–55) Comus's reasonings are far from unconvincing. He accuses the Lady of a too exclusive chastity in words recalling a New Testament parable; and had he accused her of a somewhat too self-conscious chastity our sympathies would hardly be in doubt. How closely Milton is dramatizing a conflict in his own mind, to be made even more explicit in *Lycidas*, appears when Comus blames her for following 'budge doctors of the stoic fur', fetching precepts from 'the cynic tub': the Miltonic condensation and solidification of image is on occasion very awkward, as also in 'Jonson's learned sock' in *L'Allegro*. Comus urges the fecundity of nature in poignant phrases, the one so praised by F. R. Leavis in *Revaluation* for what he considers an un-Miltonic sincerity significantly among them. Milton never elsewhere shows so convincing a cosmic apprehension. Comus concludes by asserting that if all nature followed the Lady's course the result would be creative disaster.

It must be admitted that the Lady's answer (756–99) is equally fine: it has a dignity that recalls Shakespeare's Hermione and Queen Katharine, and Webster's Vittoria Corrombona. The defence emphasizes the danger of enlisting nature on the side of vice instead of 'temperance': chastity is a 'sun-clad power'. The speech has fire and vigour enjoying a humanly dramatic and Elizabethan force unique in Milton.

The evil here is, as in Marlowe, mental, something 'that fancy can beget on youthful thoughts' (669). I am not suggesting that it is not evil; but what, precisely, is it? We are not directly told. In so far as we seek definition in atmospheric and poetic suggestion – our main, and in any case our final, guide – we have all cosmic and natural excellence such as Shakespeare incorporates into *Antony and Cleopatra* ranged with the evil force, whereas the brothers and the Lady are, throughout their early moralizing, dull. After a lengthy speech by one brother it needs more than the other's reply 'How charming is divine philosophy' (476; we might contrast the exquisitely humorous parallel spoken by the Nurse in *Romeo and Juliet*, III. iii. 158–9) to get our sympathy. The statement that nature itself demands continence and that virtue is the only true freedom, we need not deny; but 'virtue' is as undefined as the evil of Comus, except by the poetry, which upsets the ethical balance. We may say that the temptation – there is authority in the text – is the straight one of sexual intercourse, but this is really to lay too heavy a stress on the play's realism, since that could scarcely be a serious temptation under the circumstances. The drink offered by Comus suggests something more inward and more subtle.

Music and sounds play a heavy part; they are in this darkened wood our main terms of reference. There is a 'soft pipe' to still winds and 'hush the waving woods' (86–8); the Lady hears a noise of revelry and listens, describing the 'ill-managed merriment' of 'jocund flute' and 'gamesome pipe' (172–3). Her Echo song (230) itself carries music-references. Comus and his rout enter with a 'riotous and unruly noise' (92–3). He compliments the Lady on her singing (244–70), comparing music to a fog-dispelling power, a phrase whose psychological undertones are plain. The brothers talk of farmyard sounds (345–7), philosophy is 'musical as is Apollo's lute' (478). The Shepherd's music is said to delay a stream and sweeten musk-roses (494–6): music has material power. The Attendant Spirit's description of Comus tells how the sorcerer's cup is mixed 'with many murmurs' (526); he speaks of his own 'rural minstrelsy' (547) and the 'barbarous dissonance' (550) of Comus's followers. The lady's song is such as 'might create a soul under the ribs of death' (561–2): the unforced compression of the thought is Elizabethan. The temptation is staged in a 'stately palace', typical of Milton, to 'soft music' and tables spread with 'dainties' (658–9), pointing on to *Paradise Regained*. After the rescue the Attendant Spirit again speaks of pastoral music and Sabrina is invoked by song. The mask ends with song and happy, even rollicking, dance.

My friend Francis Berry has called my attention to an interesting stress on the importance of Comus's rod for the Lady's release from the 'enchanted chair' where she is fixed as a 'statue' (658, direction: 661; 818–19). This is my reading. Mental inhibition is shadowed by the frozen paralysis during resistance imposed by Comus. The reversal of Comus's rod (816) is needed to unbind the spell: which suggests a *redirection of the same instinct*. But the rod is lost, instinct sunk in repression. Therefore assistance is invoked from Sabrina, a virgin river-goddess who

controls the 'Severn stream' with 'moist curb' (825), symbolizing, it seems, some mastery of passions. Her 'chaste palms moist
and cold' contrast with the 'gums and glutinous heat' of lust
fixing the Lady to the 'marble' seat (916-18). She is associated
with liquid freshness from 'snowy hills' as against 'summer's
drouth' (928). A poetic emphasis on transparent waters and
their jewelled beds further indicates (i) cold, if natural, purity,
and (ii) high ethical transcendence. Words like 'virgin' and
'chaste', as well as 'holier' (943), 'Heav'n' (970), 'virtue' (1022),
and 'grace' (938) are significant. Though 'victorious dance'
succeeds 'sensual folly' (974-5) and the Attendant Spirit, left
alone, talks finally of Cupid and Psyche (1004-5), nevertheless
the resolution seems to come rather through a transcendence,
explicitly a second thought, than the more human process implied by the reversal of Comus's rod. The imaginative distinction is subtle, and must not be pressed too far.[1]

I have compared *Comus* to *The Tempest*, its conflict, though
narrower, being similarly universal (966-75); Richard Prentis
has recently noticed its stylistic resemblance to some lines in
Prospero's mask; and the Attendant Spirit vividly recalls Ariel
at the end. Milton starts his life-work with the grave manner
and solemn music of Shakespeare's close. Moreover, if we
allow *Samson Agonistes* to correspond very roughly to *Hamlet* in
point of (i) self-disgust, (ii) feminine disillusionment, (iii) a
supernaturally enjoined revenge, and (iv) final holocaust, we
find Milton ending where Shakespeare's greater work begins.
Milton has, to borrow a phrase from T. S. Eliot's poetic criticism
of our own age in *The Rock*, advanced 'progressively backwards',
his poetry maintaining a petrified resistance, like the Lady's in
Comus, with only intermittent release into the Sabrina melodies:
the Christ of *Paradise Regained* is significantly static. The loss of
Comus's rod therefore reflects a wider poetic *loss* where there
might have been a *reversal*, while a rooted trouble persists.
Though profoundly Shakespearian, the later Milton shows a
rigidity which is also an opposite, if static, direction; as when
here the Spirit talks like Caliban while Comus and his wand recall Prospero (650-3). Shakespeare's power seems to derive from
trust in a vitality Milton rejects. Milton's substances are often

[1] It is discussed further in my *Christ and Nietzsche*, 134-5, 156. [1967]

Shakespearian, but they point differently. So, though the usual reading of *Comus* as a simple moral antithesis may miss the striking precision of its psychological penetration, its diagnosis may nevertheless be applied to hint a weakness behind Milton's own development.

Lycidas (1637), short as it is, presents more problems than we can properly discuss here. Milton's early work plays on a conflict of the pagan-sexual with the Christian-ethical. *Lycidas* is therefore interesting in its attempt at friendly association of the two pastoral traditions, ecclesiastical and literary, in one poem.[1] There is a clear personal cry questioning the wisdom of losing amorous joys with Amaryllis and Neaera through the high seriousness of a poetic temperament that may be allowed to illuminate the problems raised by *Comus* and *Paradise Lost*. Exquisite Spenserian melodies and flowery description do not cohabit very happily with the thunderous St Peter. Learned references are perhaps too thickly clustered without context enough to create the interest they demand. Personification of the Cam is of doubtful success, but the use, as in *Comus*, of a river-symbol is interesting in reference both to Spenser and to later English poetry. The main theme of death by water has fascinating analogies. Exquisite in parts and valuable as a whole, *Lycidas* reads rather as an effort to bind and clamp together a universe trying to fly off into separate bits; it is an accumulation of magnificent fragments. The elegiac interest has pregnant moments in the association of human immortality with the natural process of sunrise; of Heaven with 'nuptial song'; and in hint of some creative purpose within human disaster.

II

In *Paradise Lost* (pub. 1667) Milton attempts at once a rational cosmology and an epic of powerful action. Either alone would be hard and the artistic combination is yet harder. That such an attempt written from an age of political and religious conflict should result in a magnificent failure does no discredit to

---

[1] The coming together of these two traditions in *Lycidas* was well stated by E. K. Chambers during an excellent account of pastoral poetry in his introduction to *English Pastorals* (Blackie and Son, London; undated). [1967]

the author, though certain confusions in conception and design must be nevertheless related to Milton's poetic life-work. The subjective conflict of *Comus* is the main irritant behind the creation of *Paradise Lost*. There is little real change, though we watch a slow strangulation of one of the two contestants. Twenty years of political activity have made slight difference. Poetry works from a deeper and more personal level than that; and personality is not readily altered.

The central fortunes of Adam and Eve constitute the heart not of this poem alone but of Milton's work as a whole. Their connubial joys are emphasized with a deliberate repudiation of wrong-thoughted ascetic idealisms. Milton's 'puritanism' must not be misunderstood:

> Nor those mysterious parts were then conceal'd,
> Then was not guilty shame, dishonest shame
> Of nature's works, honour dishonourable,
> Sin-bred, how have ye troubled all mankind . . .
> (IV. 312)

Like D. H. Lawrence, Milton attacks primarily a lustful or unduly mentalized development of sexual energy, as well as many sophisticated and respectable pleasures, indeed the whole chivalrous and idealistic approach:

>   Not in the bought smile
> Of harlots, loveless, joyless, unindear'd,
> Casual fruition, nor in court amours,
> Mix'd dance, or wanton mask, or midnight ball,
> Or serenade, which the starv'd lover sings
> To his proud fair, best quitted with disdain.
> (IV. 765)

In strongest opposition we have marriage–love and its permanent physical rights. Those who think of abstention from sexual intercourse in terms of 'purity' and 'innocence' are 'hypocrites' or ranged with the devil (IV. 744–9). The Fall is therefore carefully shown as inducing a peculiarly *mental* lasciviousness, and my discussion here might be compared with the contrast of Orsino's with Viola's love in the third chapter of my *Principles of Shakespearian Production* (enlarged 1964 as *Shakespearian Production*). The forbidden fruit acts as an intoxication, till Adam and Eve 'swim in mirth', each casting 'lascivious eyes' (IX. 1008–16) on the other. There is an unpleasant, heavy humour:

> If such pleasure be
> In things to us forbidden, it might be wish'd
> For this one Tree had been forbidden ten.
>
> (IX. 1024)

There are 'glances' and 'toys' of 'amorous intent', raising in answer 'contagious fire', till they retreat to a shady spot for 'love's disport' and 'amorous play' (IX. 1034–45). There is a newly self-conscious enjoyment. It may be significant that intercourse takes place now by daylight, a thought relevant to Lawrence's emphasis on the dark unconscious in matters sexual. That the increase in pleasure is entwined with a nasty humour and lasciviousness suggests that the pleasure occurs in close relation to a sense of sin.[1] The final stage is an awakening to shame at nakedness; followed by wrangling and the birth of evil passions; leading finally to evil in the natural and animal world.

Yet the peak, as it were, of *mental* enjoyment – we are discussing something more subtle than physical intercourse – was so intense that it was given divine associations. Some glow of exquisite sensation is touched beside which the joys of innocence are 'flat' and 'harsh' (IX. 987). Milton skilfully allows a doubt as to whether the delight is real or fanciful (IX. 788–9), but it is definitely involved in thoughts of 'godhead' and the 'divine' (IX. 790, 986).[2]

[1] C. S. Lewis's interpretation of Spenser's Bower of Bliss in terms both of metallic imagery and a sense of the lascivious (p. 10 above) may with profit be brought to bear on Milton's poetic psychology and imagistic trends; see p. 42. It must have helped my present essay, which may however also be related to my early handling of *Othello*, which I called 'the most Miltonic thing in Shakespeare', in *The Wheel of Fire*. [1967]

[2] Milton is correctly interpreting the profound psychology of Genesis whereby the forbidden knowledge of good and evil is related to god-like status.

The experience is to be distinguished from straight sexual desire with consummation, and the fantasies concerned may take various 'perverted' forms. The problem has been handled by Pope (*Essay on Man*, II and III) and Nietzsche (*Thus Spake Zarathustra*, 22, 79) and given what may be a near-final clarification in the doctrine of John Cowper Powys. See on Powys *The Saturnian Quest*, 119–20 and 125–7. On others, see *Laureate of Peace*, reissued as *The Poetry of Pope*, 50–2 and 178; *Christ and Nietzsche*, 136–7 and v throughout, especially 163; *The Starlit Dome*, 302–3; *The Christian Renaissance* 1962, 273–4 and (referring to *Comus*) 276. Compare also the passage from *The Reason of Church Government* quoted on p. 113 below (discussed also in *Christ and Nietzsche*, 215 note). Pope's line 'How glowing guilt exalts the keen delight!' (*Eloisa to Abelard*, 230) makes a crisp definition. [1967]

This baffling complex of the divine and shameful is the heart of both *Comus* and *Paradise Lost*. Nor has any writer more closely and fearlessly approached it. Shakespeare has a sonnet (129) describing something of the sort. but he never gets close up, never pushes inside, content rather to speak in terms of those various passions here shown as derivative, or shadowing such psychic contradictions through light wit or sympathetic humour (see p. 32 below, note). In so far as Shakespeare speaks seriously, there is never this agonizing and final dependence of the divinely pleasurable on the ethically repellent. Milton is perhaps the closer psychological realist, as Marlowe is a closer realist than Lyly; yet those who fearlessly attempt such realism risk fogging their art. The pleasure is, in itself and at the *moment of impact*, a positive; and no later results must, to the poetic intelligence, be allowed to distort its essence. Milton is forced on to a rejection of human culture comparable with that of Tolstoy and Lawrence. This complex of divine pleasure and sinful shame so truly objectified at the climax of his greatest poem is also subtly at work throughout its philosophy and technique. There is a final rejection of some authentic positive to avoid inroads of some ugly lasciviousness. Horror at indignity, at the ludicrously shameful, in human nature works at the back of the Miltonic repressions: hence the emphasis, noted above, on an ugly humour. The Shakespearian alternative seems to be a *complete acceptance*, creating next harmonious works of art that nevertheless do not attempt such naked disclosures of subjective experience, clothing it in more respectable habits such as dramatic themes of murder, direct physical lust outside the marriage bond, warlike ambition, jealousy, and so on, sometimes with accompanying and purifying comedy. Milton is almost too honest. He brings into the full glare of daylight inward experiences perhaps better left in half-obscurity until a deeper solution is reached. For that instant of exquisite pleasure he describes, though its content may seem and indeed prove both evanescent and dangerous, was nevertheless a spark struck from some significant opposition, some contact of shivering delight with the very dynamic of creative life more ultimate than good or evil; though each of these may seem to be involved in an inextricable and hopeless tangle, as they are in God's creation. The swing-over from pleasure to intense reaction in itself proves nothing, and may succeed the most sanctified forms of conjugal intercourse. Now, in recording this little psychic drama from the negative aspect I believe Milton negates the dynamic of human life at its origin. He writes from a deep awareness of *fallen* human, and other, nature, which is poetically fatal. The results are, in Milton and our society as a whole, a denial of the specifically vital with a corresponding emphasis on the mechanical leading to ethical confusion. The provisional mental acceptance required may well appear dangerous and perhaps all but impossible for any sensitive and refined personality: which may explain why genius is rare. I say 'mental acceptance', for where actions are concerned respect for society and all the usual ethical values must normally come into force. Shakespeare, as I have noted, does not regard naked desire as fit even for artistic comment without a certain translation, at once an enlarging and a weakening of it, into more conventional forms: of these he next aims to distinguish fairly clearly the good from the evil, prior to that artistic sanctifying of all essences in the completed whole which corresponds to the acceptance conditioning his start.[1]

There is in Milton a clash of forces: an all but irrepressible sensuousness is clamped down. The lascivious-divine (remember Cleopatra was 'riggish'; *Antony and Cleopatra*, II. ii. 248) fights a battle to the death with an iron ethical will. Some force partly divine is rejected and cast out, like Satan: from which thought we may pass to the power-symbols in *Paradise Lost*.

The down-thundering of the Son of God 'gloomy as night' on the rebel host (VI. 746–66) is one of the supreme things in our literature. Nowhere is Milton's love for the semi-mechanical so nobly projected as in that winged and eye-blazing chariot. It lives and moves, as his natural phenomena do not: it 'rowls', it 'bickers'. It belches 'smoak' and 'pernicious Fire' (pp. 154–7 below). Yet is the image Christian? True, the Son is specifically opposing guns and militaristic inventions, and Milton claims to

[1] See my Prefatory Notes, also 'The Shakespearian Integrity' (p. 242 below, note). Shakespeare writes of men as from a consciousness *above* fallen humanity; Milton of God and the universe as from a consciousness within the Fall. Both ways hold value. Our best resolution of the antinomy lies in the doctrine of John Cowper Powys. See pp. 30, 113, 242, notes. For Adam's 'knowing good by evil' see *Areopagitica* (Columbia ed., IV. 310–11). [1967]

have advanced beyond the crudities of heroic and martial poetry
(IX. 1–47); the chariot slays with eyes, suggesting a spiritual
victory; and the narrating angel expressly warns us that he is
translating things heavenly into earthly terms. The Son's spectacular arrival on the scene of battle may be felt to reflect, and
there are touches which suggest it, Christ's spiritual victory of
the New Testament after ages of insoluble conflict. Yet that
victory was one of love, which here becomes 'pernicious fire'.
The normal discrepancy between outward expression and inward meaning in literature is driven to a jarring discordance,
the best Christian emotions being negated. In his dealings with
man, the Son is nearer the true Christ; indeed, somewhat milder
than that incisive, penetrating, and uncompromising figure
shadowed in the Gospels. But Adam and Eve after the Fall are
so pathetically weak and so eminently excusable that divine
tolerance is scarely tested, whereas when pitted against an
enemy of comparable stature the heavenly authorities are ruthless. In the surface fiction the difference appears one not of good
against evil but purely, as Satan says (I. 258), of force. There is
however a fine repudiation of militarism in *Paradise Regained* (see
p. 120) pointing to Pope and Byron (for Pope, *Imitations of Horace*,
Satires, II. i. 23–8, 73–5; for Byron, pp. 247–8 below).

The difficulty becomes more confusing when we turn back to
the early books. Milton's later treatment of Satan cannot obli-
terate the first impact. It is *unnecessarily* heroic. Probably the
poet started by determining to make a rebel strong enough to
resist the Almighty, little guessing how fatally easy his task was
to prove:

> What though the field be lost?
> All is not lost; the unconquerable will,
> And study of revenge, immortal hate,
> And courage never to submit or yield . . .
>   (I. 105)

Satan loses nothing in our eyes by the 'immortal hate', since
that is for him the convincing emotion, whereas God and the
Son are not given equally strong Christian tonings. Moreover,
the apparent futility of Satan's determination – although, of
course, he does in part succeed – serves to increase the heroism.
Armed force can only become effectively heroic in our era on

one condition: that it be felt as tragic. Compare the regular treatment of kingship or soldiership being overthrown by some more spiritual power in Shakespearian tragedy with the attempt to create a non-tragic yet heroic fiction in Marlowe's *Tamburlaine*; Shakespeare's Henry V being only saved, if at all, by religious backing. So Satan becomes a profoundly satisfying figure, into whom Milton injects large parts of himself, including his own political fortunes and that indomitable will and lack of humility that rings in his iron verse. Satan is as a Cromwellian chieftain who 'darts his experienced eye' (i. 568) with unbroken pride down the lines of his vanquished host; a born leader offering himself to danger for the public good. His countenance has human and tragic dignity:

> . . . his face
> Deep scars of thunder had intrench'd, and care
> Sat on his faded cheek . . .   (i. 600)

'Deliberation' and 'public care' engrave the forehead of Beelzebub (ii. 303). Such phrases transmit a specifically communal feeling not found elsewhere. The parliament of fiends is a parliament of noble, fallen, yet dauntless men: the intuition, at this moment, is Byronic. How well this suits the advance of man to maturity after the irresponsibilities of youth:

> Farewell, happy fields
> Where joy for ever dwells. Hail horrors, hail
> Infernal world, and thou profoundest Hell
> Receive thy new possessor: one who brings
> A mind not to be chang'd by place or time.
> The mind is its own place and in itself
> Can make a Heaven of Hell, a Hell of Heaven.
> What matter then if I be still the same,
> And what I should be, all but less than he
> Whom thunder hath made greater?
>   (i. 249)

However the poet may try from time to time to right the balance with an ethical comment, an underlying and insistent, if unintended, personal sincerity shatters the surface fiction. In this act of creation Milton *is* Satan, himself engaged in making a poetic heaven out of a social, political, and maybe a religious, hell. Insight and honesty together create a figure touched with that mysterious tragic aura, that wholeness and infinity, so much more poetically impressive than the harsher glories of victory. There is moreover, and in consequence, a unity of protagonist with setting, an organic plant-and-soil relation, for lack of which Heaven is uninteresting. In Hell material power is truly heroic, because tragic, as in Shakespeare. It is defined by means of its failure; and something other shadowed, yet not directly expressed, and certainly incapable of expression by Milton's theology, in terms of the forces vanquished. The first two books exist in a different dimension from the rest, and nothing which those say can hurt them.

This grandeur of conception is maintained in Satan's meeting with Sin and Death (ii. 629–870). The first is Satan's daughter, the birth from his head suggesting the mental origin of evil; the second, fruit of a further incestuous union. A certain semi-sexual element is integrated into Satan's ambition, similar to that complex shadowed by the total impact of *Macbeth*. He confronts the loathly figures like Macbeth before the Weird Sisters, the protagonist's human integrity in both fictions contrasting proudly with the subhuman and absurd evil that is nevertheless in part its own (compare also Byron's *Manfred*, p. 196 below). So Satan towers: and indeed his vast size, imaged to fine effect, seems to symbolize an assertion similar to that embodied by Swift in *Gulliver's Travels*; both Swift and Milton probably felt themselves to be channels of gigantic, though thwarted and unrecognized, power. As his story develops, Satan becomes more distant, our subjective sympathies transferring to Adam and Eve, the soliloquy in Book iv (32–113), which recalls the prayer-conflicts of Shakespeare's Claudius and Angelo, marking a transition from heroic integrity to self-conflict. Our admiration is recaptured during his first sight of Eve (iv. 358–92) with its generous and noble emotions. When eventually he slips into the serpent of Genesis and finally, in Book x, becomes one, the process is both necessary and blasphemous: the logic being schematic only and imaginatively incoherent.

The story of Satan is a universalization of the Fall of man. The story spirals in and down to earth after the first grand introduction, and there is an intended relation of the one fall to the other. The figures of Sin and Death suggest a sexual element; the serpent carries it on; and the later gorging of Hesperian fruit which turns to ashes completes the analogy. Moreover, just as the determination of Satan and the unforgiving wrath of God present an indomitable force repressed by an omnipotent and irresistible control, so in the sexual-lascivious matter generally the Miltonic scheme presents, it would seem, a repression rather than a sublimation of instinct. The 'unconquerable will' (I. 106) is felt on both sides. When Milton suggests that it is 'in our will to love or not' (V. 539) he speaks what is half truth and half most dangerous fallacy. Somewhere there is a failure in acceptance, in generosity, in elasticity, in humour; together with an implied critical rejection of nature, especially of those undignified lascivious instincts of which Milton feels most ashamed. A cosmic poem cannot develop correctly under so rigidly ethical a compression.

Here are some of the tangles. Satan and his followers suggest man's own nobly tragic destiny; the 'truth, wisdom, sanctitude, severe and pure' (IV. 293) of Adam and Eve indicate rather a future perfection than an original innocency, the words denoting spiritual victory, not happy inexperience; while the thundering Messiah is scarcely expressive of a love-conquest. Again, this sequence of Hell, Eden, and triumphant Messiah might be taken to shadow a progress from tragedy through purgatorial wisdom to vision of established divinity. Now I doubt if these are legitimate 'ambiguities' – I borrow the word from William Empson's valuable *Seven Types of Ambiguity* – since they tend to contradict rather than expand the surface meanings; as though the poet were trying to string out in a story-sequence impressions that might have been less logically but more precisely ordered. Moreover, not only do the iron bands of the design bulge dangerously under the upheaving emotional force of Satan's tragic grandeur, but passages concerning the Deity sag. Expostulation of his own blamelessness before the Fall, asserting predestination ('which had no less prov'd certain unforeknown'; III. 119) in the very act of its denial, is surely neither good theology nor sound philosophy. The Son, regarding his enemies simply as Death and Hell, follows up all signs of compassion in his Father, who nevertheless, while praising the Son's graciousness, emphatically returns (III. 330-3) to specific images of condemnation, as though himself not getting the point and thinking still on a more primitive plane. The sending of Raphael on a long embassy of warning known to be fruitless in order to throw full responsibility on man (v, Argument; also 243–5) is considerate neither to the angel nor to Adam and Eve. The traditional redemptive mechanism in terms of payment, from the start a dangerously rigid expansion of a Pauline metaphor, can seldom have seemed more arbitrarily unconvincing than in Milton's treatment. You would often almost suspect an ironic intention did you not know its impossibility in a poem explicitly written with the rather presumptuous aim of justifying God against human charges.

When Adam meditates on the strangeness of the Deity's ways, every phrase rings far truer than the trite arguments of admitted self-blame which seem rather unconvincingly inserted. Relevant passages occur at x. 720–844, where God's 'justice' is felt to be inexplicable, and xi. 497–511; and one might adduce *Samson Agonistes*, 300–25, 358–60, 667–704. Some burning resentment is being sternly, yet not quite successfully, bridled. The central fact of evil is, as I have remarked, insecurely defined; as in *Comus*, where the magical cup corresponds to the forbidden fruit here, and both to Satan's ambition which is felt as – to quote Dryden's *Absalom and Achitophel* – 'a spark too much of heavenly fire'. The Deity's conditions are acutely questioned (iv. 515–26). The temptation of Eve is deliberately made overwhelmingly convincing (ix. 679–732) through the miraculous presentation of a talking, rational and beauty-recognizing snake, grown newly human through tasting the forbidden fruit. Eve is carefully made to sin through obedience to a semi-divine ambition, self-persuaded that God could never repudiate such an act. The tree has 'sacred fruit' (ix. 924), it is of 'divine effect' (ix. 865), lifting the mind 'to Godhead' (ix. 877; see also ix. 790), inducing a pinnacle of consciousness intuitively recognized as high:

> but I feel
> Far otherwise th' event, not Death, but Life
> Augmented, open'd eyes, new hopes, new joys,
> Taste so divine, that what of sweet before
> Hath touch'd my sense, flat seems to this and harsh.
>
> (ix. 983)

Partly in loyalty to her, Adam eats too, and they 'swim in mirth', fancying they feel

> Divinity within them breeding wings
> Wherewith to scorn the earth.
>
> (IX. 1010)

This 'mother of science' (IX. 680), this fruit of 'sciental sap' (IX. 837) is hallowed, and the sin partly exists in its desecration (IX. 903). The baffling alinement of intuitive positives with the supremely evil is in the Marlovian tradition, directly un-Shakespearian, and vital to our understanding of Milton. This paradox is presented in naked distinctness. It is both profoundly human and yet profoundly unsatisfying; and, when expanded to epic magnitude, reveals the provisional nature of its realism.

Apart from all questions of structure and levels of meaning, an untenable philosophy emerges. The static and sculptural quality of Milton's nature-imagery, together with his mechanized cosmology, all constitute a rejection of the specifically vital. This tones with his attitude to sinful instincts which in turn leads to a rejection of women. The passages are striking (IX. 1182–6, X. 137–56, X. 867–908, XI. 628–32). In *Paradise Regained* Satan does not confront Christ with feminine allurements because he considers them beneath such a man's notice (II. 153–234). *Samson Agonistes* is a massive tirade against feminine wiles and guiles. Though evil comes through, or at least in close association with, lust in *Paradise Lost*, what positive hopes are hinted have no erotic relation. Here Milton draws apart from Dante and Shakespeare, and the New Testament too, itself fertile in erotic imagery positively toned. Angels, we are assured, know sexual intercourse in Heaven (VIII. 614–29), but the passage is slight, and it is never sexual intercourse, as such, that most bothers Milton, but rather the consciously lascivious instincts of the mind, together with the dangers of feminine domination. Yet creative thinking must be sex-flooded; risks Milton will not accept may condition a final imaginative integrity. Through loathing of the lascivious he performs a dual rejection. He stands for the proud and critical, rather than the interpretative, humorous and gentle approach to the baffling complex of foulness and divine pleasure entwined in the human consciousness. He lets evil express itself in ugly and heavy humour twice, in Adam directly after the Fall and in Satan's and Belial's mockery of the opposing angels after the success of their artillery (VI. 609–27), but although he may assert 'smiles' to be a distinguishing mark of human reason (IX. 239–40) he cannot apply a sympathetic Byronic humour, perhaps the most valuable approach, to the solution. He is therefore barred from natural and cosmic sympathy, repudiating the knowledge of good and evil together, considering the one to be bought too dear at the cost of the other. The blindness so nobly treated in his poetry becomes a cruelly apt symbol of another opacity. The sun to him is 'dark' (*Samson Agonistes*, 86) in more senses than one, and his great invocation to light (*Paradise Lost*, III. 1–55) takes on new pathos from such a reading. No natural scenes are more vitally projected in Milton than the burning lake of Hell and the bottomless vacuities of Chaos: wherein only is he properly at home.

The repressed instinct is eventually soaked up into the repressive will, which becomes all-powerful; yet, since there is now nothing for it to control, lacks purpose, and so looks about for something to destroy. Milton's most faultlessly organized work is probably the granite-like and deadly sincere *Samson Agonistes* (pub. 1671), with a theme, forecast in *Paradise Lost* (IX. 1059–62), which exactly dramatizes his thesis concerning woman in terms of a story ruthlessly dedicated to a pre-Christian conception of physical force and bloody destruction in the name of God. Where such force is positively forbidden by his story – as in *Paradise Regained* (pub. 1671) – the result is static. The New Testament supersedes the ten negatives of the Decalogue by two positives, but Milton reduces it to negation by isolating and expanding the temptations. He compasses violent force and frigid virtue, but does not blend action *with* passivity to project Shakespearian or Byronic figures of creative power. His Christ is actionless, the poem expressive of a frozen and paralysed will to good. There is, certainly, a more positive message in terms of 'reason': and for an admirable appreciation of this I would point to Charles Williams' *Reason and Beauty in the Poetic Mind*. But there is little love in Milton's later work. He is moreover untrue to himself and his own peculiarly academic genius, his Christ logically now rejecting Greek literature with scorn (*Paradise Regained*, IV. 221–364) and ratifying the placing of the Hellenic in Hell (p. 139). The elements of nature are themselves now under the dominion of evil spirits (*Paradise Regained*, II. 124). All is forced by Milton's dogmatic position, and intellectually coherent; yet it remains at the opposite extreme from Shakespeare. Milton writes of angels, Christ, and God from a consciousness saturated in the knowledge of sin; whereas Shakespeare, or Milton in his creation of Satan in Books I and II, sanctifies sin by writing of it from a god-like understanding.

III

No important poem can be satisfactorily analysed in terms of its ideological scheme alone. Yet, when we turn to inspection of Milton's more sensuous achievements, we find a balance of excellences and limitations corresponding to those inhering in the intellectual and emotional structure.

The descriptions of Eden tend to harden and solidify what is more properly flexible and yielding. The divine profusion is supposed to go beyond nature (IV. 207–8), but instead falls short of it. A certain aestheticism insists on translating the natural into terms of human artistry, so that we find an excessive luxuriance presented in terms of a stony, carven, immobility. Though Milton deliberately asserts the rule of nature as opposed to art in his Eden (IV. 242), his poetry here and elsewhere does not substantiate the claim. We have too many 'arbours' and 'alleys', with phrases such as 'floury roof' (IV. 772) and 'verdurous wall' (IV. 143); plants are 'gay enamell'd' (IV. 149); nature is seen pictorially, from without, sapless and static. The manner has its delights, as in the exquisite description of the nuptial bower:

> the *roof*
> Of thickest covert was *inwoven* shade
> Laurel and myrtle, and what higher grew
> Of *firm* and fragrant leaf; on either side
> Acanthus, and each odorous bushy shrub
> *Fenc'd up* the verdant *wall*; each beauteous flower,
> Iris all hues, roses, and jessamine
> Rear'd high their *flourish'd* heads between, and *wrought*

> *Mosaic;* underfoot the violet,
> Crocus, and hyacinth with rich *inlay*
> *Broider'd* the ground, more colour'd than with stone
> Of *costliest emblem.*   (IV. 692)

I italicize significant words. Nature is approached through
feeling for artistic design: its life is that neither of nature nor of
divine purpose, but of static art. Elsewhere, outside Eden, we
meet the ornate humanizing of

> Forth flourish'd thick the clust'ring vine, forth crept
> The smelling gourd, up stood the corny reed
> Embattl'd in her field: add the humble shrub,
> And bush with frizzl'd hair implicit.   (VII. 320)

In Eden the plan certainly intends to show nature as humanly
hospitable, and as we watch Adam and Eve wondering 'whether
to wind the woodbine round this arbour' (IX. 215) we attend
the beginnings of human civilization. But one cannot quite
credit Milton with a full awareness of the problems he raises. In
the rough approaches to Eden, a sylvan slope is called a 'woody
theatre' (IV. 141), while in one of the wilder districts expressly
compared to an Indian forest we find

> a pillar'd shade
> High overarch'd and echoing walks between.
>   (IX. 1106)

'Echoing' is a deliberate falsification, though the image as a
whole undoubtedly realizes the weightiness intended. Nature is
continually felt in three dimensions, with depth as well as outline; in Milton's own not exactly fortunate word for the moon
(VII. 357), it is 'globose'. There is a tactile pleasure and a
jewelled richness: dew-drops are pearls (V. 744), trees 'gemm'd
their blossoms' (VII. 325), fruit is 'burnish'd with golden rind'
(IV. 249), the Tree of Life bears 'vegetable gold' (IV. 220). We
are not surprised to hear stage thunder rolling through the
'dark aerial hall' (X. 667); to be told the earth itself is founded
in a 'glassy sea' (VII. 619); or to find the air in its translucent
purity called 'pure marble' (III. 564).

Such phrases do not argue a lack of natural enjoyment. They
spring rather from an almost too greedy desire that translates the
vital into plastic terms the more surely to possess it; a desire to
capture and eternalize each essence in statuesque permanence.

It is a poetic idolatry. I agree with E. M. W. Tillyard's general emphasis on Milton's sensuousness, and would point to C. S. Lewis's discussion of lust as (i) uncreative and (ii) related to metal-work imagery *imitating* nature in his analysis of Spenser's Bower of Bliss (p. 10 above). Milton's rich and weighty luxuriance resembles that of Keats. Like Keats, Milton engages the reader in the allurements of exquisite smell and appeal to the taste. The flowers breathe 'morning incense' from 'earth's great altar' (IX. 192–7). The sanctity attributed to nature by later romantic poets is found in Milton's Eden before the Fall. There is naturalistic ritual. Adam offers 'sweet-smelling gums and fruits and flowers' from 'grateful altars' (XI. 323–7). The best scent-passage shows Satan's arrival welcomed by 'odoriferous' airs and 'native perfumes' lengthily compared by the poet to scents blowing from 'the spicy shore of Araby the blest' (IV. 153–65) to ravish the senses of mariners at sea. The forbidden fruit has 'ambrosial smell' (IX. 852). Milton sets himself to realize an earthly paradise through use of smell; though again, when the visiting angel's sense is struck by 'groves of myrrh', 'flowering odours', 'cassia, nard and balm' (V. 292), an overstress of literary associations exerts a hardening influence detracting from the primal sweetness. Eden's pleasures are rich to the taste, a sense catered for continually in Milton's poetry. We have 'nectarine fruits' with 'savoury pulp' (IV. 332–5), draughts from a 'milky stream' (V. 306), 'juiciest gourds' (V. 327). Eve's preparations of hospitality for their angel guest are lusciously described (V. 331–49). This sense in sinful extreme is symbolically central in both *Comus* and the 'sensual appetite' (IX. 1017–24, 1129; XI. 514) of *Paradise Lost*; and later (XI. 472–3, 529–30) the dangers of intemperance are shown among the evils in store for mankind; and a magnificent feast is among the temptations of *Paradise Regained* (II. 337–77). Whatever the limitations of Milton's impressionism, his use of smell and taste is probably more abundant than that of any English poet but Keats, who directly follows, while revitalizing, the Miltonic emphasis.

The 'smell' and 'taste' impressions are not, however, so thickly massed as my quotations drawn from various books suggest, and there is a heavy preponderance of legendary and mythological learning with lists of proper names in the earlier

introductions to Eden which blend well enough into the arti-
ficialized nature. The total result is rather too academic to be
satisfying. Moreover a quite different and more realistic nature-
poetry occurs, describing the approach of evening, which I
shall discuss later (p. 56), so that there is scarcely a unity of
impression. With this reservation, we may suggest that the
heavy tangle of ensnaring smells, rich tastes, literary learning,
and luxuriant if immobile and sculptural vegetation with which
we are confronted is slightly too sophisticated and might have
been more appropriately placed in Heaven, with Eden left in
naked purity like Adam and Eve.

From this luxuriant Eden-bed of perfumed and colourous
description – for there is colour, too, in description of fruits and
sky, especially the 'purple and gold' (iv. 596) of sunset – there
springs once fine praise of 'wedded love' in a fashion worthiest
of the highest heaven:

> Here love his golden shafts employs, here lights
> His constant lamp, and waves his purple wings,
> Reigns here and revels.   (iv. 763)

This may be grouped with the best of my other recent quotations – I am making an abstraction from a wide area and the
massed effects are not exactly Milton's – to suggest a vital
richness which might more widely have been trusted and ex-
ploited. Nor does this passage really suit the innocent purity of
Adam and Eve or the description of nightfall. The literary,
aesthetic and religious-ritualistic phrase-colouring draws nearer
to Pope's *Eloisa to Abelard* and Keats's *Ode to Psyche*, witnessing to
perceptions fusing the human and the divine that might have
saved Milton from certain infertile directions and barren conclusions as well as proving the true, because creative, antagonist to his lascivious evil. See the lovely blend of movement
and stillness; the wealth, warmth and colour suggested in
turn; the exquisite entwining through alliteration of sovereign
dignity with an un-Miltonic merriment in 'reigns' and 'revels',
the regal association being so much more apt and effective here
than in Adam and Eve's 'naked majesty' (iv. 290). The passage
accepts, uses, and transcends Milton's own native and admirable sensuousness to the full. It burns steadily, illuminating
a path that does that not point to *Paradise Regained*.

It is sad to turn from this to the mirthful elephant performing to amuse Adam and Eve with his 'lithe proboscis' (iv. 346). There are, perhaps fortunately, few striking references to animals in Milton. Animal grandeur is his main success, as in the preying tiger changing 'oft' his 'couchant watch' (iv. 405), or the swan who

> with archèd neck
> Between her white wings mantling proudly, rows
> Her state with oarie feet.   (vii. 438)

As with vegetation, human associations recur in 'state' and 'oarie'. Fish swim with 'skulls' (vii. 402), watching their food in 'jointed armour' (vii. 408); here fishes are of metal and the leviathan stretches like a 'promontory' (vii. 414). Birds rise from the ground with a 'clang' (vii. 422); but when a flock 'wedge their way', making an arrow-head formation of their 'airy caravan' (vii. 425–8), the same mannerisms attain a certain charm. One cannot say as much for the beasts in procession 'cowering low with blandishment' before Adam, nor for the birds who stoop each 'on his wing' as they pass (viii. 350–1). Vegetation and animals alike are often fitted into arbitrary and variously unsuitable schemes of association or behaviour.

So much that Milton touches tends to exist in stony separation. We have little sense of any underlying spirit informing each woodland mosaic, tendril elaboration or fruity rondure, while his animals are slightly mechanical. There is a tactile, outward pleasure, but less in-seeing, none of those lightning exploitations of Shakespeare and Byron focusing that whole and vital universe of which they are felt to be authentic parts. In those everything exists for what is greater and beyond itself. Milton's nature has no such underlying and informing spirit. His wider universe therefore tends to go by machinery: it is for the most part mathematical and mechanic.

Heaven's gate turns on 'golden hinges' framed by the 'sovereign architect' (v. 255). God is a designer, a mathematician, setting out on the business of creation with a pair of 'golden compasses' (vii. 225). Fine images occur of the earth spinning noiselessly 'self-balanc'd' (vii. 242) on her 'soft axle' (viii. 165); and though such circling mechanisms suit well enough the mysterious and ordered harmonies of the cosmic scheme, the trick is driven too far. 'The wheel of day and night' (VIII. 135) is a good phrase for our own world, but there is less value in Milton's rather over-precise explanation of the revolving light-and-dark mechanisms in Heaven (VI. 4-12). This at least maintains the mysterious harmony of the circular, and there is much talk elsewhere of orbs, spheres, centres; but the tendency does not stop there. We are confronted by words such as 'eccentric', 'oblique', 'parallel', 'triform', 'quaternion', 'rhomb', 'cone', 'sextile, square, and trine and opposite' (x. 659), 'cubic phalanx' (VI. 399), 'mighty quadrate' (VI. 62). Mystic circularities form only one element in a universe composed as often of obliquities and angularities, an exact reverse of the Dantesque scheme where all is imaginatively subordinate to the circular, to an ultimate harmony. There is no ultimate harmony about Milton's cosmic structure: his universe cannot be felt as an organic whole. Though the bridge built by Sin and Death is scarcely impressive, yet the poet, whilst superficially deploring the intention, is yet characteristically abased in admiration of the 'wondrous art pontifical' (x. 312) that goes to its construction, since his love for all such arts of solid fabrication exists at a deeper and more poetic level than any ethical contrasts. This bridge, the stairs let down from Heaven, and the other 'passage' to earth beneath (III. 510-43), the sun as a compendium of jewels (p. 47 below), all make for a universe of separate detail and linear connexions without either organic heart or sense of mass. Shelley's *Prometheus Unbound* has a far greater cosmic mass, though its parts are less weightily globed; his Caucasus weighs more than Milton's metal sun. No central cosmic energy is tapped. Energy is mechanic rather than natural, reaching terrific explosive force in the heavenly war with the 'hollow cube', 'devilish enginry' (VI. 552-3), and 'iron globes' (VI. 590) of the rebel angels, clearly to be despised yet opposed by something not altogether dissimilar in the grasped bomb-like 'thunders', electric poisoned-rayed chariot-eyes and 'pernicious fire' of the Son of God riding to battle 'gloomy as night' (VI. 832). There are the 'rapid wheels' of the games in Hell (II. 532). As early as the *Nativity* ode, Milton showed a love for cars and urns similar to that of Keats: stars are 'golden

urns' of light (VII. 366). Anything metallic takes his eye; his
is a polished, burnished, almost a brazen universe. 'Celestial
armoury' (IV. 553) is no mean part of the Heavenly equipment.
The astronomer's 'glaz'd optic tube' (III. 590) sums our impressions. The smooth finish and workmanlike glint of the
Miltonic mechanisms are indisputable, but his universe is unconvincing. Our earthly visual experience and whatever of
religious insight we possess both demand some ultimate enclosing circularity, some all-inclusive harmony, such as Dante's;
or some vast and massive life, as in Shelley. Milton's cosmology
is different; his scientific, geometrically oblique, and mechanical
emphasis misses alike cosmic mystery, cosmic mass, and cosmic
harmony. There is slight sense of a single whole and slight feeling
for inner significance.

Paradise Lost contains, as does *Paradise Regained* too, brilliant
architectural descriptions – one of the finest I shall quote later
– and often aims to express itself through elevations. Eden is on
a mountain, Satan alights on Mount Niphates. Mountains
blend into architectural splendours, as when the gate of Eden is
described as partly an inaccessible and overhanging 'craggy
cliff' but partly also a smooth 'rock of alabaster pil'd up to the
clouds, conspicuous far' (IV. 543). Satan has a

> royal seat
> High on a hill, far blazing, as a mount
> Rais'd on a mount, with pyramids and towers
> From diamond quarries hewn, and rocks of gold . . .
>   (V. 753)

God sits on a 'flaming mount' (V. 598; V. 640). Lifting and
brilliant masses excite the eye, as when Satan sees Heaven as

> a kingly palace gate
> With frontispiece of diamond and gold
> Embellish'd, thick with sparkling orient gems
> The portal shone.   (III. 505)

Our world is compared to the view of a man seeing from a
mountain-top 'some renown'd metropolis with glistering spires
and pinnacles adorn'd' (III. 549), gilded by the morning sun.
And yet these isolated excellences scarcely build the marvels
intended: each seems strangely small in the vast spaces. The
jasper courtyards and pearly floors of Heaven stare a little

coldly. Jewels and glittering buildings need close human associations to render them fertile symbols. Our recent examples are not even cathedral-images or temple domes; they aim not at the sublime, Milton's safer territory, but at the brilliant and the scintillating, which is an insecure province of Milton's mind. True, the move from ideal nature in Eden through mountains to architecture, as in the Eden gate just noticed, and thence to City-of-God symbolism in Heaven is a usual development, as in Coleridge's *Kubla Khan*; and the poem as a whole uses it. My complaint is that the cosmic or Heavenly brilliance is not informed by the necessary emotions: it lacks eros-force and nature-force. The two 'brazen mountains' in Heaven (VII. 201) are significant. The weakness is clear in Milton's description of the sun on his 'meridian tower' (IV. 30), a phrase pathetically detracting from, whilst trying to inform, our sense of a vast supremacy, reducing an expansive radiance to a journey on stilts. Elsewhere he describes it in terms of glowing iron, 'potable' gold, silver, carbuncle, chrysolite, ruby and topaz (III. 592–612). Nothing is sacred to his concretizing and metallic technique. Set beside this barbaric and amazing conception the greater mystery and truth of Keats's 'evident' god (*Hyperion*, I. 338) and Byron's 'burning oracle of all that live' (*Sardanapalus*, II. i. 15) and you see the difference. The continual emphasis on jewels serves no better by itself to establish the cosmic or the divine than the almost burdensome references to power and regality. The sun and moon are given regal connations; God, his Son, and Satan possess them in turn; Adam and Eve enjoy 'naked majesty' (IV. 290); and the swan has her 'state' (VII. 440). Instances are everywhere. Milton's poem abounds in images of materialistic splendour.[1]

There are moments when the divinely high might seem to be

---

[1] It is a question of over-emphasis and arbitrary use. Jewels and crowns are correct symbols of the 'spiritual' in contrast to the 'natural': for jewels see *Christ and Nietzsche*, 194, note, and *The Christian Renaissance*, 1962, 288–90 (on Wilde). Here, as in his solidified imagery and descriptions of non-poetic arts, Milton labours to control his vast and intransigent action by an excessive and premature eternalizing of detail. For more successful 'eternalizings', see my references above in this note and pp. 216–18, 240–6, 252–4, on Byron; also the two sections entitled 'Symbolic Eternities' in *Laureate of Peace* (reissued as *The Poetry of Pope*) and *The Starlit Dome*; and my essay '*Timon of Athens* and its Dramatic Descendants' in *Shakespeare and Religion* (1967). [1967]

c

celebrated becomingly, even admirably, in terms of light and perfume. The light-invocation at the start of Book III is justly famous, but when during the colloquy between the Father and Son we hear that 'while God spake ambrosial fragrance fill'd all Heaven' (III. 135) we see how little the ideological content helps the impressionism, since the Deity's sentiments are scarcely ambrosial. Milton's artistic confusion is especially clear in Heaven, where a greater poetic honesty would have given his God only sublime and awful associations. However, a fine passage of angelic adoration (III. 344–71) has an exquisite use of solids. The most usual difficulty in realizing the highest radiance, the attainment of solidity, is necessarily no hardship to Milton. The angels cast down their 'inwoven' garlands of 'amaranth' and 'gold', till the pavement shining 'as a sea of jasper' is 'impurpled with celestial roses'. Amaranth, we are told, is an 'immortal flower' set by the Fount of Life and River of Bliss that rolls her 'amber stream' through Heaven. The imagistic fusion is admirable, for here we expect an idealized approach. Music accompanies. The trouble is that such glimpses of Heaven never sufficiently dominate. The scattered effects are less striking than my grouped selections suggest, and without a close marshalling of similar images no weightily spatialized significance can be realized. Of Hell and Eden we are given long consecutive descriptions, and a mental structure has time to establish itself; but one tends to visualize Heaven as small, tucked away in the top left-hand corner of Milton's universe; a little swirling vortex of music, circular grouping, and garlands, together with some disturbing theology, apart from the empty vastnesses, confused geometry, and insecure mechanisms of the main action. In contrast to the disasters outside, since the activities of Heaven tend to fail, the praises and harping sound a trifle forced.

The truth is, *Paradise Lost* not only presents a cosmic disharmony, which is its explicit theme; but further is in itself disharmonious, and therefore as a *whole* artistically fallacious. Though parts are superb, it is nevertheless designed from that very consciousness which art exists to replace.

I turn shortly to an inspection of Milton's 'style' in the narrower sense.

His best phrases have their own peculiar, slightly assertive, excellence. There are many effects of traditional belief, folk-lore and actual observation, but they are earth-born rather as nuggets earth-mined, with mould lingering about the edges but no fibrous, rain-sucking roots. Milton has often been accused of offending against the genius of our language;[1] his vocabulary tones with his nature-imagery in its premature solidification, its clasped and finished, created yet uncreative, beauties. The massed classical learning and abstruse Hebraic or Egyptian mythological references, together with a heavily Latinized syntax and word-choice, make the poetry remote. Yet there is a subtle variation in colour-perception; the mechanical and scientific imagery is often softly toned; there is little of the musty, the cobwebbed association, as in Webster's *The Duchess of Malfi*, and as little of the harsh ordinary surfaces of daily affairs. Nor are there, for all the striking kinship, the naïve, glaring, and unblended effects of Marlowe. Milton is Shakespearian in his depth, richness and – on the level, that is, of language and imagery – his refusal to be dominated by a discordant world. He goes farther than Shakespeare: every phrase and image comes out saturated from the habitual feeling of one romantic and scholarly mind. The poetry is personal, and because personal a little unyielding and hard, and however deeply burnished, however lustrous, a little esoteric in its appeal. Often his phrase-magic tends, instead of tapping our subconscious recollections, to force on us rather his own abstruse and learned enthusiasms. But all his relics burn newly in the act of presentation, and in his finest passages there is no obscurity, no impediment to an immediate response, while even his more personal and irritating mannerisms exert a peculiar fascination, his worst faults having exercised a wide, if dangerous, influence. Whatever our adverse criticism, this is certain: Milton's mind is dominating at every instant, and that mind is a storehouse of coffers and caskets weighty with the most rich and glamorous substances.

A mental, and often metallic, domination characterizes Milton's verbal music. His sounds match his images. Especially

1 I was thinking primarily of J. Middleton Murry's *The Problem of Style*, v. [1967]

in Hell, where the clash of forces is extreme, the quintessen-
tially Miltonic most powerfully declares itself:

> Him the Almighty Power
> Hurl'd headlong flaming from th' ethereal sky
> With hideous ruin and combustion down
> To bottomless perdition, there to dwell
> In adamantine chains and penal fire
> Who durst defy the omnipotent to arms.
>
> (I. 44)

Clanging stresses re-enact the cataclysmic event. The lightly
vowelled 'flaming from th' ethereal sky' gives swift falling and
the assured ease of victory; followed by the held-up agony of
'combustion'; the remorseless stresses of 'bottomless' and 'perdition'; with inevitable and unending security of doom in the
riveting and levelled weight of the last line but one. In such
clangours Milton is surely the world's master.

Here, and in all such, and many other, passages there is a
heavy reliance on 'm's and 'n's, especially in combination with
't's, 'g's, and 'd's. There are the 'fens' and 'dens' in a passage
to be quoted shortly. Read the following aloud, stressing all
nasals:

> The Stygian counsel thus dissolved; and forth
> In order came the grand infernal peers,
> Midst came their mighty Paramount, and seem'd
> Alone the antagonist of Heaven, nor less
> Than Hell's dread Emperor with pomp supreme,
> And God-like imitated state; him round
> A globe of fiery seraphim inclos'd
> With bright imblazonry, and horrent arms.
> Then of their session ended they bid cry
> With trumpets' regal sound the great result:
> Toward the four winds four speedy cherubim
> Put to their mouths the sounding alchemy
> By herald's voice explain'd: the hollow abyss
> Heard far and wide, and all the host of Hell
> With deafening shout, return'd them loud acclaim.
>
> (II. 506)

The consonantal nasal and brazen note throughout the first
eight lines develops into description of actual trumpets resounding and shouts echoing. Favourite Miltonic words such as

'firmament', 'empyrean', 'adamant', illustrate the general tendency; and proper names, 'Blind Thamyris and blind Maeonides', Phineus (III. 35–6), Sion, Aonian (I. 10, 15), Aspramont, Montalban (I. 583). There is a metal clangour in what we tend to feel as the specifically Miltonic. This we can associate with his Latinisms, Latin being probably heavier in such sounds than English. We do not get the nasal note always; it is especially strong in Hell, for obvious reasons, but always the poetry might, I think, be termed 'consonantal'. This is in part the key to the gong-like effect of Milton's verse, its metallic yet mysterious reverberations sending echoes wandering in the cathedral-lofts of the mind. Vowel-colour may often be powerful, but in Milton's later work it is often sternly compressed, the aural solids suggesting a clamping down of mental control on an expanding sensuousness. The Keatsian warmth occasional in *Paradise Lost* has to fight for itself against this domination. We may remember the almost Spenserian fluidity and luscious music of the flowery passage of *Lycidas*, and the names 'Amaryllis' and 'Neaera'. Yet even when speech is thin and pale there may be a nasal tone, as in the exquisite 'Chineses' driving their 'cany' wagons with the 'wind' (III. 438–9); or again, when soft and fluid, as in

> Lethe, the river of oblivion, rolls
> Her watery labyrinth
> (II. 583)

and

> Then feed on thoughts that voluntary move
> Harmonious numbers; as the wakeful bird
> Sings darkling, and in shadiest covert hid
> Tunes her nocturnal note.   (III. 37)

In *Paradise Lost* nasality seems stimulated by, while also assisting, any fine exuberance. Such passages do not thereby lack authenticity. The repressing power assimilates and finally *is* the instinct repressed; and Milton's grandest passages hold, as passages, the essence of greatest poetry. In them Milton's poetry is utterly itself, the peculiarly metal tone conditioning an organic utterance.

Not only does the control of emotional substance lead to a peculiarly effective organ-voiced music that is new, but the

paragraph-technique suggests a unique self-possession in metrical and rhythmic patterning. The lovely lines on the nightingale just quoted are a precise record of ultimate loneliness, of
musical and metrical harmonies brought to birth in dark
mental solitude; and I suggest that we may feel these technical
subtleties almost as a separate quality of Milton's mind,
brought to bear on a discordant world. One cannot safely
argue any extra degree of conscious design. Twice in *Paradise
Lost* Milton asserts the spontaneity of his art.[1]

There is a studied variation of pause. Clauses play against the
line-unit with peculiar effect. Line or paragraph repetition may
be happily used, as in Eve's loving address to Adam (iv. 634–
56). Repetition of rhythm with differing phrase-content or
repetition of word or phrase with changed line-position and
syntactical stress are employed with extreme aural subtlety:

> where peace
> And rest can *never* dwell, hope *never comes*
> That *comes* to all.   (i. 65)

Here, of three parts, number one is linked to two while two is
linked to three. This 'linkèd sweetness', to recall *L'Allegro*'s
lines on song-music, is a typical trick. Technical resource does
not stop there, and a variety of interweaving patterns may
inform the paragraph-texture:

> Thus roving on
> In confus'd march forlorn, th' adventurous bands
> With shuddering horror pale and eyes aghast
> Viewed first their lamentable lot, and found
> No rest: through many a dark and dreary vale
> They pass'd, and many a region dolorous,
> O'er many a frozen, many a fiery, alp,
> Rocks, caves, lakes, fens, bogs, dens, and shades of death,
> A universe of death, which God by curse
> Created evil, for evil only good,
> Where all life dies, death lives, and nature breeds,
> Perverse, all monstrous, all prodigious things,
> Abominable, inutterable, and worse
> Than fables yet have feign'd or fear conceiv'd,
> Gorgons and hydras and chimeras dire.   (ii. 614)

[1] I might better have written 'inspiratory source'. The key passage is at ix. 20–47,
especially 20–24 and 46–7, expanding i. 1–26 and iii. 37–40. [1967]

Notice the nasalized word-music; the use of vowel-colour for atmospheric effect in 'forlorn', 'lamentable', 'dreary', 'dolorous'; the careful and varying arrangement of pauses; internal rhyme ('fens' and 'dens') and alliteration; and the monosyllabic group set against polysyllables five lines later. Especially note the continual slowing-up of pace by pauses, by a monosyllabic line, or by chiasmus; and how the chiasmus of 'created . . . evil, evil . . . good' links on to 'life dies, death lives'. Movement evolves out of movement, there is a continual circling back and then again a drawing out, like a soft substance drawn out stringily; it is a spiralling labyrinthine movement. We are reminded of the mazy Echo song and other labyrinthine suggestions in *Comus* (pp. 23–4 above) and of the lines in *L'Allegro* on words fitted to music

> with many a winding bout
> Of linkèd sweetness long drawn out,
> With wanton heed and giddy cunning,
> The melting voice through mazes running;
> Untwisting all the chains that tie
> The hidden soul of harmony. (139)

Such technique is to resolve impossible antinomies: the 'linkèd sweetness' – even here there is a hint of metal – is to unloose, untwist the other heavier chains.

In *Paradise Lost* Milton sets his technical mastery to dominate a discordant world. That the poem's aural qualities may be related to his love of music has already been suggested, though with reference rather to the 'music' as against the 'sense' of separate passages, by T. S. Eliot in his 1936 'A Note on the verse of John Milton' (included in *On Poetry and Poets*). In *New Bearings in English Poetry* F. R. Leavis has referred to Milton's creation of a verbal music 'outside himself', and in *Revaluation* has written of 'effects analogous to those of music' in the *Comus* Echo song. Music is to Milton almost a material, a creative, force. He introduces *Paradise Lost* by complaining that rhyme has no 'musical' delight, and saying that he prefers blank verse with 'the sense variously drawn out from one verse into another'; the perfect comment on his technique and one which renders the *L'Allegro* music-relation especially clear, 'drawn out' occurring in both passages. The harmonies of Milton's verse are to this extent related to his musical interests. By the

'giddy cunning' – notice the *conscious* suggestion in 'cunning' –
of this mazy circling, this convolution and involution, the interweaving of cadences, he would resolve those other 'wandering
mazes' of 'Providence, Foreknowledge, Will and Fate' (II. 559):
compare the relating of music to 'necessity' in *Arcades*. That
frustration is a general meaning of mazes and labyrinths in
ancient magic and myth has been shown by my brother
W. F. Jackson Knight in *Cumaean Gates*.[1] Life's difficulties, as
in *Comus*, are to Milton especially labyrinthine; and no wonder,
considering the critical complexities his work forces on us. Sin
leads to 'mazes' of self-conflict (x. 830) and 'paths indirect'
(xi. 627). The resolution is to come, as in the Echo song and
final dance in *Comus*, through a 'victorious' (974) maze-tracing.
Here, as there, there is a linear and geometrical quality in the
complicated rhythmic designs. Leavis speaks of the 'ritual'
movement of Milton's verse; and Eliot actually uses the phrase
'mazes of sound'. My analysis indicates the justice of both
terms, though I should not develop either to an adverse criticism
of the passages concerned.

The maze is in Milton a symbol with both evil and good
directions. The serpent is used by the Devil to approach Eve
like a tacking ship (IX. 510–18), curling a 'wanton wreath'; it
lies in 'mazy folds' (IX. 161), making a 'labyrinth' (IX. 183). A
river may flow with 'serpent error' (VII. 302) or 'mazy error'
(IV. 239). The maze may be a symbol of harmony. The
Heavenly company delight

> In song and dance about the sacred hill,
> Mystical dance, which yonder starry sphere
> Of planets and of fix'd in all her wheels
> Resembles nearest, mazes intricate,
> Eccentric, intervolv'd, yet regular
> Then most when most irregular they seem.
>
> (v. 619)

This is the harmony which Milton's cosmic machinery in
Paradise Lost does not itself attain, though that envisioned by
Comus, with its 'wavering morris' (*Comus*, 116) of elements,
certainly does; and so too, very often, does the *verse-technique* of

---

[1] *Cumaean Gates* is now reissued with *Vergil's Troy* as part of a volume entitled
Vergil: Epic and Anthropology, edited by John D. Christie.

Paradise Lost, matching its own ritual against the labyrinths of cosmic evil. The whole poem meanders, from Hell to Heaven, Heaven to Earth; retracing its steps in time, then going ahead again, like Adam and Eve, with 'wandering steps and slow' (xii. 648). Scene and subject may change in a single book. The final transmutation of Satan and his crew to serpents (x. 504–47) is paralleled by the whole poem's move from dramatic thickness to narrative tedium at the end. It is melodic, serpentine, rather than symphonic: so is the verse-structure, recalling the meandering Eden rivers or the 'watery labyrinth' (ii. 584) of Lethe. I would point to the essentially *thin* structure of *Paradise Lost*, its lack of mass and weight, to be related to the poet's excessive love both of the pictorial arts already noticed and also of music and rhythmic and verbal mastery as things in themselves to be applied, with a corresponding failure to achieve an harmonious alinement of energies in the action. Many separate passages of superb rhythmical precision and outline may be truly and finely organic, but such subtleties on the plane of language cannot in a poem of action by itself harmonize a disrupted world. Verbal music is in the whole an imposition on Milton's wider material. The result is too often a thin, wavering time-stream rather than a created world. Rhythmic and verbal modulation work to remedy a weakness in organization. This is how Milton becomes in places our most perfect poetic 'technician' while failing as a 'maker' in the wider sense. He tries to do by verbal art what verbal art by itself cannot do.[1]

Milton's love of grand sounds finds scope in *Paradise Lost*. Trumpets and shouts in Hell resound and reverberate in the gloom (ii. 515–20); there are arms 'clashing' with 'shock' of 'horrible discord', and 'madding wheels' of 'brazen chariots', in the Heavenly war (vi. 205–14); the 'steadfast empyrean' shakes to the thunderous onslaught of the Son (vi. 833). Through the echoing of 'a shout that tore Hell's concave'(i. 542) sound gains mysterious overtones and is given architectural reference. Hell

---

[1] Compare Byron's *Cain*, where a successful organization of thought and action is transmitted through a bare language of no pretension which might be called 'transparent' or 'dull' according to our taste. In Byron's development *Cain* however corresponds really to *Paradise Regained*, where Milton's style is unadorned. Pope, Milton and Byron all show similar developments from the ornate to the simple. [1967]

'scarce holds' the 'wild uproar' of the Satanic games (II. 541).
Next the harmonies of song

> Suspended Hell, and took with ravishment
> The thronging audience.   (II. 554)

There is the hymning of God's angels in Heaven, elaborately
described; the story of the Creation to the sounds of spheral
music; the hush of an Eden night with the 'solemn bird' (IV.
648) so loved since *Il Penseroso*, softly melodious, till 'silence'
itself is 'pleased' (IV. 604). The tendency is so obvious that to
name more instances is unnecessary: the poem is built expressly of brazen clangours and dulcet harmonies. In such
terms the Miltonic powers attain their maximum nobility. Behind
the conception lies the desire to transmute the one to the other.

We have discussed as separate, spatial and temporal, entities
(i) the richly metallic and architectural and (ii) the musical
interests of *Paradise Lost*. Certain fine images and certain exquisite technical units have been inspected; yet both the archi-
tectonics and the massed music of the whole have been found
unsatisfying. I next attempt to define my meaning more closely
by examining two large movements where the spatial and
temporal elements co-exist in organic fusion, each being now in
separation no more than abstractions from the space-time
complex of epic or dramatic poetry; that is, action and atmosphere, movement and solidity, are felt as interdependent.

IV

I have already noticed and directly or by implication both
praised and criticized some of the richer and more colourful
descriptions of Eden. But in certain passages where we are to
feel throug the human experiences of Adam and Eve, there
is a quite different accomplishment. I start with the beautiful
description of evening:

> Now came still evening on, and twilight grey
> Had in her sober livery all things clad;
> Silence accompanied, for beast and bird,
> They to their grassy couch, these to their nests
> Were slunk, all but the wakeful nightingale;
> She all night long her amorous descant sung;
> Silence was pleas'd; now glow'd the firmament
> With living sapphires: Hesperus that led

The starry host, rode brightest, till the Moon
Rising in clouded majesty, at length
Apparent queen unveil'd her peerless light,
And o'er the dark her silver mantle threw.

(IV. 598)

Every word contributes to a close realization. There is an exact wedding of Milton's mind and manner to the mysterious nature of a *living* universe: one does not ask that his manner be changed, only that it shall be fitted, subdued, to his matter; and here it is so fitted. Though the stars are 'sapphires' note that they are 'living' ones: and this blend of the pulsing *with the solid* is all but the supreme excellence, as Keats knew, in any poetry. Life breathes from the description. There is a soft, almost unnoticed, movement within the stillness. The interrelation of stars, Venus, and the Moon is precisely graduated. 'Clouded majesty' is far from a loose phrase, with its feeling for low-lying evening mists: the first vague and atmospheric abstraction 'majesty' is subtly balanced against the clarity of 'apparent queen', which leads further to the decisive action of 'unveil'd', and so on to accomplished victory in 'peerless'. The vowellings of 'apparent' match both the gliding and silent ascendancy and its expansive splendour. 'Silver mantle' in the last line is faultless as 'sober livery' earlier. A certain levelling, almost muffling, of nature's particularities is needed for dusk; and an unearthly, almost deathly, yet magic transmutation for the moonlight. The verbal technique is in closest relation to its subject-matter as a whole; the music is the music of organic perception. Finally, see the unerring realization and Shakespearian felicity in 'silence was pleased'. The nightingale's song in its traditional quality is there, together with the very mystery of darkness, of otherness, of nothingness charged with a presence. This very thought is the concern of Eve's question a little later concerning the stars, so beautiful while men sleep. When Adam answers,

Millions of spiritual creatures walk the earth
Unseen, both when we wake and when we sleep . . .

(IV. 677)

those beings are of a different and more convincing order than Milton's usual angels. They are continuous with the nightingale, their 'celestial voices' sounding from 'hill' and 'thicket'; they grow from a soil, an atmosphere, already realized. Eve's speech on the wondrous beauties of creation has an unforced feeling for nature's sap and fertility, as in 'fragrant the fertile earth after soft showers' (IV. 645), that Milton's more decorative phrases lack. 'Soft' is a repeated word. Adam tells (IV. 659–73) how the stars' 'soft fires' exert an 'influence' on earth with their 'stellar virtue' irrespective of their visual glory, and his statement exists in and enriches a traditional, esoteric, wisdom that Milton for the most part appears to neglect. He is working at the essence of creation's unseen energies instead of copying, with a view to possessing, its miracles of design. Set, for example, his convincing equation of the sun and moon with masculine and feminine principles of existence (VIII. 150–2) against his description of the sun in terms of valuable metals (p. 47 above); where again we have an important contrast.

These last Eden passages cohere with a natural coherence depending on deepest insight. We are aware of an organic whole where each unit is at once dissolved as a unit and made infinite as a constituent part. Consider how jarring here would be one of Milton's abstruse scholarly and exotic references. My point is, not that his 'cassia, nard, and balm' (V. 293) are necessarily bad poetry and his damp earthy fragrance good, but that the latter is perfectly placed in the story and exquisitely mastered, whereas the former was not. Much of the tangle of scents, 'nectar' (IV. 240) streams, and sculptural luxuriance lavished on his Eden earlier – and my close grouping of quotations tended to establish a more organic selection than Milton's own – might be far more appropriate among the amaranth and jasper of Heaven, which needs all the poetic assistance available. Finally, this new and finer atmospheric recognition in Eden, itself a kind of love, comes in association with, and blends delicately into, the *human* love of Adam and Eve: the two are interdependent. The fusion is dramatic, the thoughts and feelings of Adam and Eve both growing from and contributing to their setting:

> But neither breath of morn when she ascends
> With charm of earliest birds, nor rising sun
> On this delightful land, nor herb, fruit, flower,
> Glistering with dew, nor fragrance after showers,

Nor grateful evening mild, nor silent night
With this her solemn bird, nor walk by moon,
Or glittering starlight, without thee is sweet.
(IV. 650)

See how simple the vocabulary, a mere list of nouns and adjectives: there is no straining at all. It is significant that Milton accomplishes this reserved excellence in terms mainly of evening, fertilizing rain and earthy scents. These are nearer the orthodox Christian emotion of *agapé* than to that of the unrestful sweetness of *eros*, which is to be felt rather in association with spring, bird-song and roseate dawn, the province of Shelley's *Prometheus Unbound*. Byron's ironic phrase 'that indecent sun' (p. 259 below) points the distinction neatly.

In the early scenes in Hell power-images attain an excellence comparable to the nature-excellence just noticed. This was a glimpse of nature as we know it islanded in a morass of nature exotic and ideal; it is the same in Hell; Hell is real, a convincing experience is transmitted and there is little pedantry. Images rise from depths, soaked in emotional suggestion, possessing an aura of indefinable magic:

. . . and what resounds
In fable or romance of Uther's son
Begirt with British and Armoric knights;
And all who since, baptiz'd or infidel,
Jousted in Aspramont or Montalban . . .
(I. 579)

How it burns with a steady consonantal and darkly glinting worth, and with what feeling for virile and heroic action. An especial vagueness overspreads the historic conceptions of the early books, while a glamorous geography makes the inhabited globe one wide romance. All ages of legend and myth pass, like 'gorgeous Tragedy' in *Il Penseroso* 'sweeping by' in 'sceptred pall', the muffled tramp of their hosts waking the inmost recesses of the poet's blindness; while the 'dim suffusion' (III. 26) of the setting at once darkens and enriches. It is the same with light. No scintillating extravagance of the later books holds half the integrity, the essential power, of that image of Satan's diminished glory:

. . . as when the sun new ris'n
Looks through the horizontal misty air

> Shorn of his beams, or from behind the moon
> In dim eclipse disastrous twilight sheds
> On half the nations, and with fear of change
> Perplexes monarchs . . .   (I. 594)

What vistas of human and ancient history are suggested; and how constant is the reference to monarchy. All that is kingly, noble, and glamorous here nerves Milton's genius to its most consummate achievement. His jewels are never more potent than when felt embedded in the depths of Hell:

> This desert soil
> Wants not her hidden lustre, gems and gold.
> (II. 270)

'Hidden lustre'. The glittering realms and crystal battlements of Heaven have less poetic weight than the more humanly warm and darkly glowing emblems of Satanic sovereignty:

> High on a throne of royal state, which far
> Outshone the wealth of Ormus and of Ind,
> Or where the gorgeous East with richest hand
> Showers on her kings barbaric pearl and gold,
> Satan, exalted, sat . . .   (II. i)

The darkness ennobles and softens, lending significance and mystery. Each image blends into its setting with no hardness of outline. Of the persons in the poem Satan alone enjoys this same vagueness, this aura of mystery, which is also an emotional and poetic precision. When he leaves Hell, he takes it with him for a while, matching his dark virility against the mainly castrated glories of Milton's other universe. No mountain, no towering edifice or cosmic height, in the later books is so vast as when he stands

> Like Teneriffe or Atlas unremov'd.
> (IV. 987)

Not only do those proper names themselves exert lines of force drawn from well-known historic or mythological associations often lacking to the more abstruse references elsewhere, but the human and dramatic significance with which they are fused makes them to exist in another dimension from the poetically lighter, more trivial, if more Heavenly, elevations. In Hell all is both weighty and mysterious; dark and glamorous; Satanic and yet royal. The weightiness is one with human personality, human destiny, summed in the royalty of Satan. No such royalism as Milton's ever burned through the poetic phrase: less inward and spiritual than Shakespeare's, the sense we receive of a premeditated and assured pomp, of symbolic potency and legendary magic, plays on certain territories unexplored and undesired by him. It has the Shakespearian dignity and depth joined to the barbaric colour of Marlowe.

Here Milton writes, as in the Eden passages I have praised, of a real world, a self-consistent world, a world of experience; and it is a tragic world. Those symbols of wealth and domination that tend to sully both his nature and his Heaven, here, in a more humanistic setting, attain sublimity. Felt as tragic, they are sublime; they achieve their whole being, and that is why the darkness ennobles. Milton's true experience is one of tragedy, the sun itself, in the passage recently quoted, becoming more authentic in this mode.

As his astringent sex-philosophy seems to be impelled by an excessive sensuousness, so Milton's love of sovereignty and power as things in themselves cohabits with a necessary rejection. Shakespeare sees his kings as part of a wide, natural, human and divine context, never expecting too much from them; but Milton is in this regard a grand pagan, and half knows it; and so his barbaric splendours are most convincing when most condemned, with a condemnation that yet enhances their essential glory. In Hell Milton buries the whole heroic past of the race, its intellectual and artistic achievements, its ambition and greed, its courage and futility; and the requiem is his noblest poetry. The effort to create a corresponding grandeur for Heaven from the materials already and in part rightly repudiated is necessarily unconvincing, as Dante's love-perfumed rose-path and the tingling dawn of Shelley's *Prometheus Unbound* are not; while conversely Dante would never allow the imperial though shadowy splendours of Milton's Hell. Milton as a poet never really penetrates beyond tragedy and *Samson Agonistes* is the fitting conclusion to his life-work. His best nature-poetry is toned for the mood of *Il Penseroso*, not *L'Allegro*. At the extreme, subnatural energies create a fiery lake, a 'burning marl' (1.296) and cavernous immensity in Hell that can challenge the sea of Byron or the mountains of Wordsworth. These early books are, if a reasonable allowance be made for Milton's love of academic reference, perfectly organic: they, action and atmosphere alike, exist in vassalage to a single quality made of both, a single music. They are imaginatively compact.

In so far as we view the whole poem expansively, we find a Milton who too often loves kingly titles, jewels, and fine architecture as things in and for themselves, while showing less rich and architectonic a realization of those spiritual energies to be poetically ordered. Therefore the poem's massed wonders never quite accumulate in the right directions, the stresses go wrong; their weight as often retards as assists the movement, leaving the poem, for all its first gathered momentum, variously forceful and sluggish.

The poet also seems to be more fascinated by the musical than is proper for a poet, who should find his music implicit in the, or his, created world, whose deepest harmonies should be a derivative of harmonious ordering. Music should flow from, not be applied to, the creation; just as pleasure, though the proper result of poetry, should not be its considered aim. But the Miltonic music, whether in rhythmic subtleties or metallic resonance, together with the use of actual music-references, corresponds to the poet's offering of architectural descriptions or nature described in terms of human arts of design, rather than a poetic architecture. He tends to rely too heavily on non-poetic arts.

The weakness is in the emphasis and the nature of the reliance. If less assertive and dominating each weighty elaboration, each curve of modulated skill, would contribute mass and music to the whole; and in that whole the spatial and the temporal, the architectural and the musical, would exist not in separation but in interdependence.

In two short passages these twin arts are explicitly Milton's descriptive theme, exquisitely blended as in the famous passage of *Il Penseroso* (155–66) to become, if we so wish to regard them, objective symbols of an ultimate reality. Here is the first.

The fallen angels start building in Hell. They are led by

Mammon who, we are told, even in Heaven loved best, rather like Milton himself, its pavement riches of 'trod'n gold':

> by him first
> Men also, and by his suggestion taught,
> Ransack'd the centre, and with impious hands
> Rifl'd the bowels of their mother earth
> For treasures better hid.   (I. 684)

That may be: but what would Milton's poem be without them? So the labour starts:

> A third as soon had form'd within the ground
> A various mould, and from the boiling cells
> By strange conveyance fill'd each hollow nook,
> As in an organ from one blast of wind
> To many a row of pipes the sound-board breathes.
> Anon out of the earth a fabric huge
> Rose like an exhalation, with the sound
> Of dulcet symphonies and voices sweet,
> Built like a temple, where pilasters round
> Were set, and Doric pillars overlaid
> With golden architrave; nor did there want
> Cornice or frieze, with bossy sculptures graven,
> The roof was fretted gold . . .   (I. 705)

How dark the gold burns; how much nobler, more weighty, and deeply signifying, is this building than any outside Hell. Observe the 'organ' comparison and the soft, 'dulcet' music: weight and intangibility cohere. The vast structure is raised to, or by, music, as in *Kubla Khan*,[1] and may be allowed to symbolize either Milton's whole attempt in *Paradise Lost* or his achievement in Books I and II. The universal creation in Book VII is weaker. There music certainly *follows* divine action, but mystery is all but reduced to mechanism.

Recall again my two instances of perfected creation in *Paradise Lost*, where scenic atmosphere and the fiction of human feeling and speech in the one, or strong action in the other, exist in mutual enrichment and organic indissolubility: nightfall in Eden, and Hell. What seems to be happening there?

---

[1] The fusion of the architectural and the musical is, on various levels, central to poetic art. See again 'Symbolic Eternities' in my study of Pope (p. 47 above, note), wherein I quote Byron's line on St Peter's 'all musical in its immensities' (*Childe Harold*, IV. 156).

In creation a moment may come when suddenly all units cease to exist except as parts of a whole which softens and interpenetrates all its parts; separate pieces no longer stand out, but cohere; a myriad details move in one direction, in obedience to a single artistic purpose; while most weighty substances become miraculously light as a feather. Action and atmosphere make one architecture, one music. Now note the exquisite manipulation of mass, sound, and movement in our second passage:

> Then straight commands that at the warlike sound
> Of trumpets loud and clarions be uprear'd
> His mighty standard; that proud honour claim'd
> Azazel as his right, a cherub tall:
> Who forthwith from the glittering staff unfurl'd
> Th' imperial ensign, which full high advanc'd
> Shone like a meteor streaming to the wind
> With gems and golden lustre rich imblaz'd,
> Seraphic arms and trophies: all the while
> Sonorous metal blowing martial sounds:
> At which the universal host upsent
> A shout that tore Hell's concave, and beyond
> Frighted the reign of Chaos and old Night.
> All in a moment through the gloom were seen
> Ten thousand banners rise into the air
> With orient colours waving: with them rose
> A forest huge of spears: and thronging helms
> Appear'd, and serried shields in thick array
> Of depth immeasurable: *anon they move*
> *In perfect phalanx to the Dorian mood*
> *Of flutes and soft recorders . . .* (I. 531)

Notice the metal-throated sounds, the solid wealth of imperial and warlike colour, with rich gems, dusky-mantled, burning in darkness; the simultaneous and instinctive shout reflecting a communal unity, repeated in the simultaneous advance of ensigns and spears. It is all of a piece, this 'thick array', this 'depth immeasurable'; defined, yet infinite; solid, yet composed of a number of individual lives, like the Eagle and the Rose in Dante's *Paradiso*. See also how, after the marshalling of forces, the squared masses, as by a natural flowering, move in easy yet disciplined movement, weighty phalanxes light as a feather, to the tune of expressly 'soft' music.

This is precisely how we would wish Milton's *whole epic structure* to accumulate mass and move. Instead, the reverse holds: its design, as a whole, is tenuous, its movement heavy. Significantly, the massive harmony is here apprehended in terms of military discipline as opposed to Dante's supernaturalistic organisms, the mighty Eagle and wondrous Rose made of myriads of lives in the *Paradiso* (XVIII, XIX, XXX, XXXI); significantly, too, the scene is in Hell. Only the early books show a fusion of poetic density and human action in organic stability and interdependence. Only on the 'burning marl' of Hell do we find at once strong action, depth of protagonist personality, communal reference, and a convincing density of imaginative atmosphere. Those books only are at once poetic and dramatic.

My whole complaint may be reduced to the statement that Milton writes an epic from an age and thought-scheme demanding a more dramatic technique. Heroic narrative is concerned mainly with material or external action, as drama with spiritual conflict. Milton attempts to express the latter in terms of the former. The myth is falsified by too precise an elaboration. The steady loosening of grip in the move from a dramatic opening to a graphic middle and on to a flat conclusion in the panoramic views of future history reflects the essential weakness. But the very faults of such a poem, at such a time, are a part of its statement. Milton's rejection of nature and human instinct leads to a final infertility in *Paradise Regained* (pub. 1671) and *Samson Agonistes* (pub. 1671), though *Samson* has its own peculiar greatness. Meanwhile he has imposed the 'sounding alchemy' (II. 517) of his private architectural visions and organ harmonies, his dreams of sovereignty and power, on a communal and universal chaos. If these had been less dominating, if the poetic will had been less unbending, there would have been no *Paradise Lost* at all. That ironside strength of the seventeenth-century imagination that he shares with Browne and others, the gun-metal and blue-black glint of phrase, here compresses both a Renaissance humanism and a psychological and cosmic exploration that lesser, more purely 'religious', writers ignored. If we praise Satan at the expense of the completed epic – the choice is partly ours, and we cannot have it both ways – that is only because we have in him a record of greater value: that is, a dramatization of Milton's own heroic, and tragic, self. His work is a superhuman effort that becomes, to use a phrase from his lines on Shakespeare, 'marble with too much conceiving'. With one foot in the age of Shakespeare and the other in the age of Bunyan, he stands across the centuries as a Colossus – of stone; or rather like those impressive monoliths in Butler's *Erewhon*, or the ruins of Norman Abbey in Byron's *Don Juan*, on which the winds of nature harp an inhuman and unnatural music.

ADDITIONAL NOTE, 1939: MARLOWE[1] AND MILTON

The sexual in both writers is approached through a subtle feeling for its complex fascinations. It is at once self-conscious and self-contradictory, as in Eve's

> Coy submission, modest pride
> And sweet reluctant amorous delay.
>
> (*Paradise Lost*, iv. 310)

Compare this from *Hero and Leander*:

> Treason was in her thought,
> And cunningly to yield herself she sought,
> Seeming not won, yet won she was at length,
> In such wars women use but half their strength.
>
> (ii. 293)

The finely aesthetic may blend with connotations of sin: Gaveston's description of visual delights to tempt Edward (*Edward II*, 51–72) being of a similar order to Milton's conception of Comus, and his poetry. Here and in the second part of *Hero and Leander* there is strong feeling for human nakedness, with reference to both excellence and shame: this recurs in *Paradise Lost*. Luxuriant and exotic Hellenic or other embellishments such as Milton uses in his Eden ('cassia', 'nard', 'nectar', fruit of the Hesperides) to thicken his sensuous atmosphere are Marlovian in tendency. There is in both an inflaming of the eye and mind, an aesthetic greediness, which has, at least in

---

[1] See also, for Marlowe, *The Sovereign Flower*, 215–17; *The Golden Labyrinth*, 54–9.

Edward II, a corresponding ethical reaction. Elaborations of human artistry, interior decorations, all rich appearances, please both.

The two poets share strong military enthusiasms. The tendency is materialistic. The flash of steel in Marlowe corresponds to deeper burnishings in Milton, but both are grandly metallic. Gorgeous state and rich jewels support themes of barbaric self-assertion. Royalism is glamorous and lust for power – 'A god is not so glorious as a king' (*1 Tamburlaine*, II. v. 57) – unbounded.

More complex are the intellectual ('spiritual' would not quite fit the case) adventures that engage both. Tamburlaine's lines on the ranging human intelligence, 'still climbing after knowledge infinite' (*1 Tamburlaine*, II. vi. 64), correspond closely to Satan's

> this intellectual being,
> These thoughts that wander through eternity.
> (*Paradise Lost*, II. 147)

Marlowe's thirst for mental satisfaction is paralleled by the probing soliloquies of Satan and Adam, and the latter's insistent questionings of Raphael. Aspiration is a key-theme in both poets, leading to similar theological challenges, in Tamburlaine and Satan; while Faustus's dissatisfaction concerning the justice of divine law is a forecast of many Miltonic passages. Compare, too, Mephistophilis'

> Hell hath no limits, nor is circumscrib'd
> In one self place, for where we are is Hell . . .
> (*Doctor Faustus*, 553)

with Satan's 'Which way I fly is Hell; myself am Hell' (*Paradise Lost*, IV. 75). The cosmic (sky, sun, stars, spheres) bulks heavily in both, though remaining rather 'literary'. Both poets enjoy references of bookish learning and proper, especially geographical, names. Their qualities are reflected in their verse: the regularized anvil-ring of the one holding kinship with the more varied but gong-like harmonies of the other.

There is correspondingly a weakness in treatment of earth. Marlowe is poor in earthy or arboreal images; in Milton such are, apart from the exceptions which we have noticed, nearer artefact than insight. Neither, normally, touches their life. With this goes an uneasiness with women: here Marlowe is definitely weak, Milton hostile. A strong sense of the vicious gives us the 'hot whore' incident in *Doctor Faustus* (572–90), balancing the Miltonic emphasis of 'venereal trains' in *Samson Agonistes* (533). Both poets use the words 'wanton' and 'lascivious' for key incidents (*Paradise Lost*, IX. 1014–15; *Doctor Faustus*, 573). Milton shows no kindly humour but only an ugly mockery, as in his lines on 'Eremites and Friars' in the Paradise of Fools (*Paradise Lost*, III. 474–97) and Satan's words on the effects of his gun-powder (VI. 607–29); paralleled by the sadistic fun of *Tamburlaine*, the horse-play of *Doctor Faustus* and the cruel farce of *The Jew of Malta*.

All this leads to an un-Shakespearian scheme of association. Aesthetic positives are ranged together beside lascivious and perverted lusts, all being pitted against the Christian ethic. Mephistophilis brings Homer and Helen to Faustus: Milton is forced into a similar position (p. 124). The conflicts are identical, though Marlowe finally tilts the balance one way and Milton the other. No synthesis supervenes; we are left with the respective and one-sided victories of aestheticism and ethic in *Hero and Leander* and *Samson Agonistes*. Neither poet writes pure tragedy in the Shakespearian sense. The epilogue to *Doctor Faustus* underlines its morality-structure; Edward II is a pathetic example rather than a tragic hero; and the chorus of *Samson Agonistes* helps to set the action in an ethical, though not narrowly didactic, framework.

Lyly and Shakespeare pursue different courses; or perhaps start from a different psychic structure altogether. There is far less poetic enjoyment of the aesthetic and the barbaric. Nature is given greater rights. Human love is more real and more inwardly conceived; so is kingship. The terms of the Miltonic sensuous-ethical conflict do not for Shakespeare exist in such vivid abstraction. He shows a complete absence of fascination with human nakedness, while nevertheless using it, for a more inwardly conceived purpose, with a greater essential power than Marlowe or Milton in *King Lear* and *Timon of Athens*. Marlowe and Milton are more normal than Shakespeare – I take their sexual and other confusions to be widespread – and certainly more masculine, but their art is the less perfect, too often itself torn asunder by the conflicting tendencies it aims to master; though the Byronic synthesis – forecast, perhaps, by parts of Marlowe's *Hero and Leander* – shows a solution to be possible.

Milton's similarity to Keats is equally important. I find myself in agreement with Tillyard's emphasis in *The Miltonic Setting*, though my own argument would be differently developed.

III
Chariot of Wrath:
on Milton's Prose and Poetry

This essay is a shortened and tidied version of the second and third chapters, with two paragraphs from the fourth, of my book *Chariot of Wrath: the Message of John Milton to Democracy at War*, 1942. My quotations from Milton's prose, originally drawn from the old Bohn edition, are now given numerical references to *The Works of John Milton*, New York, Columbia University Press, 1931-4, to which my final numerals in each reference bracket apply. 'Volume III' is divided into two volumes, so that, e.g., 'III. i. 5' designates the first volume of the third volume, page five. I follow mainly the Bohn edition for the English rendering of Milton's Latin in *The Defence* and *Second Defence of the People of England*.

I. CROWN AND CHRIST

I

From a period of political disorder stand out the life and work of John Milton. They are, like their national setting, disjointed. In this period of fracture Milton's prose and poetry act as an X-ray: they both record the agony and forecast recovery. The ideas and energies thrown up during the civil disruption of which Milton is the living voice are pointers towards an understanding of the inward mechanisms of the British Constitution; just as, by study of the forces in play during the world-conflict of our own time, we may begin to feel a new civilization in process of creation, struggling for birth.

During peace drama is the proper vehicle for poetic accomplishment; in time of war, epic. Written in a time of civil war, Milton's greatest work, like Vergil's, has affinities with both. He regarded himself as a national prophet. He wrote a *History of Britain* (1670) wherein he says that his intention is to

raise a knowledge of ourselves both great and weighty, by judging hence what kind of men the Britons generally are in matters of so high enterprise; how by nature, industry, or custom, fitted to attempt or undergo matters of so main consequence.

(III; X. 103)

His considered ambition, expressed in *The Reason of Church Government urged against Prelaty* (1641) is

that what the greatest and choicest wits of Athens, Rome or modern Italy, and those Hebrews of old did for their country, I, in my proportion, with this over and above, of being a Christian, might do for mine. (II. Intro.; III. i. 236)

His early purpose was to write a national epic. I quote from Mark Pattison's *Milton* (1923; orig. 1879):

In 1638, at the age of nine and twenty, Milton has already determined that this lifework shall be a poem, an epic poem, and that its subject shall probably be the Arthurian legend:

May I find such a friend . . . when, if ever, I shall revive in song our native princes, and among them Arthur moving to the fray even in the nether world, and when I shall, if only inspiration be mine, break the Saxon bands before our Britons' prowess. (XIII)

The quotation is a translation of Milton's Latin verse. This thought of British and Saxon opposition forecasts our present conflict. That may be of slight enough significance; but it is important to observe how Milton's work is rooted in thoughts of kingly valour and national mythology. He speaks of himself wondering 'what king or knight before the conquest might be chosen in whom to lay the pattern of a Christian hero' (*Reason of Church Government*,[1] II. Intro.; III. i. 237). He searched among 'lofty fables and romances, which recount in solemn cantos the deeds of knighthood founded by our victorious kings, and from hence had in renown over all Christendom' (*Apology for Smectymnuus*, 1642; title abbreviated; III. i. 304). Milton's thought turns naturally to 'kings'. In his conclusion to *The Reason of Church Government* he writes of 'that huge dragon of Egypt, breathing out waste and desolation to the land', and, thinking of the episcopate, continues:

Him our old patron St George by his matchless valour slew, as the prelate of the garter that reads his collect can tell. And if

---

[1] For Milton's prose, after each first reference I use where convenient abbreviated titles.

our princes and knights will imitate the fame of that old champion, as by their order of knighthood solemnly taken they vow, far be it that they should uphold and side with this English dragon; but rather to do as indeed their oath binds them, they should make it their knightly adventure to pursue and vanquish this mighty sail-winged monster, that menaces to swallow up the land, unless her bottomless gorge may be satisfied with the blood of the king's daughter, the Church.

(II. Concl.; III. i. 275)

The Church is the 'king's daughter', part of the total sovereignty; and in his *Of Reformation touching Church Discipline in England and the Causes that hitherto have hindered it* (1641; II; III. i. 54), Milton couples the 'monarchy of England' and that of 'Heaven' as both alike insulted by prelacy.

Milton feels English chivalry as a militant yet Christ-serving force. His nationalism is Messianic; to him England, or Great Britain, is a Messiah-nation, and he its prophet. England had 'this grace and honour from God',

to be the first that should set up a standard for the recovery of lost truth, and blow the first evangelical trumpet to the nations, holding up, as from a hill, the new lamp of saving light to all Christendom.   (*Reformation in England*, 1; III. i. 5)

The British are a chosen people: God 'hath yet ever had this island under the special indulgent eye of his providence' (*Animadversions upon the Remonstrant's Defence against Smec-tymnuus*, 1641; iv; III. i. 145). The thought beats throughout Milton's political writings.

'An elaborate song to generations' was planned by Milton as a thank offering to Providence for the inspired and God-guarded fortunes of Englishmen (*Animadversions*, iv; III. i. 148). Instead he was to write *Paradise Lost*, honouring the deeds not of the Messiah-nation, but of Messiah himself. His original plan of an Arthurian epic gave way to the more profound conception. Yet *Paradise Lost* remains the foremost, some would say the only, epic poem in our literature. It seems that the poetic genius of Great Britain tends instinctively to counter the epic and heroic with religion; and of this instinct Francis Berry's *The Iron Christ* (included in *The Galloping Centaur*) is a magnificent modern development. It is as though we as a nation cannot feel epically without the religious backing that Shakespeare's Henry V regarded as essential. This is one meaning of *Paradise Lost*. After the composition of his earlier poems from the ode *On the Morning of Christ's Nativity* to *Comus* and *Lycidas*, and before his return to great poetry in *Paradise Lost, Paradise Regained*, and *Samson Agonistes*, Milton engaged in his series of virulent prose-works on matters of ecclesiastical and political controversy. In them are revealed the conflicts of the hour, but the arguments at issue are not out of date. Though our own problems are not quite those of Milton, they are far from dissimilar, and many of our quotations, if applied today, will be found, with a reasonable expansion of meaning, strictly relevant.

Milton's life and work turn on a basic opposition of Christian virtue against pagan lust. Though there is opposition rather than synthesis, and more battling than peace, and though Milton shows little signs of learning to love his enemies, yet his pagan forces are given the respect which their dangerous insistence deserves, while Christian virtue enjoys pride and power. There is no facile sanctimony nor any easy solutions. Today, on a vast scale – though no vaster than that which Milton dreamed in *Paradise Lost* – we watch this same conflict engaged across the world.

The office of poet rightly concerns the actions of nations. To Milton they are interdependent, as at the opening to Book 11 of his *History of Britain*:

> For worthy deeds are not often destitute of worthy relaters: as by a certain fate, great acts and great eloquence have most commonly gone hand in hand, equalling and honouring each other in the same ages. 'Tis true, that in obscurest times, by shallow and unskilful writers, the indistinct noise of many battles and devastations, of many kingdoms overrun and lost, hath come to our ears. For what wonder, if in all ages, ambition and the love of rapine hath stirred up greedy and violent men to bold attempts in wasting and ruining wars, which to posterity have left the work of wild beasts and destroyers, rather than the deeds and monuments of men and conquerors? But he whose just and true valour uses the necessity of war and dominion not to destroy, but to prevent destruction, to bring in liberty against tyrants, law and civility among barbarous nations, knowing that when he conquers all things else he cannot conquer Time or Detraction,

wisely conscious of this his want, as well as of his worth not to be
forgotten or concealed, honours and hath recourse to the aid of
eloquence, his friendliest and best supply; by whose immortal
record his noble deeds, which else were transitory, become fixed
and durable against the force of years and generations, [whereby]
he fails not to continue through all posterity, over Envy, Death,
and Time also victorious.   (*History of Britain*, II; x. 32)

Tyrannic lawlessness is of age-old acquaintance on this earth
and no monopoly of the twentieth century. Milton's mind,
ranging over history, here asserts the short-lived triumphs of
destructive force; but literature he sees as guardian and im-
mortalizer of worthy deeds; which is right, for the spirit of poetry
lies close to those best ideals for which Milton laboured, and
both are of Christ. It is therefore no chance that Britain, for so
long precursor among the nations of religious liberty and
political justice, should have shown herself also pre-eminent in
letters. Cromwell and Milton together incarnate the genius, in
its sterner attributes, of Great Britain.

II

The reign of Charles I shows a rapid diminution of kingly
authority, starting with the *Petition of Right* presented to Charles
by Parliament in 1628. The petition was followed in 1629 by
the *Three Resolutions*, fruit of a struggle between the Puritans and
the High Church party for control of the English Church.
Charles thenceforth attempted to govern without calling Parliament at all. At this time the keenest contention centred on the
episcopate, that is, the institution of bishops in the Church of
England, which claimed to be both Catholic and Protestant
and stood central between Papists and Puritans. Throne and
Church were mutually interdependent. The breaking point of
Charles's rule without a Parliament came when he attempted
to enforce on Scotland the English prayer book. The King
prepared for war, but the English showed little enthusiasm and
in 1640 the King again summoned Parliament. This parliament, existing in various forms for twenty years, won the name
of the *Long Parliament*. A victory was thus attained for the
Puritan cause. As for Milton, Sir Herbert Grierson comments:
'For him the meeting of the Long Parliament had been what

CHARIOT OF WRATH 75

the entry of Henry VII into Italy had been for Dante. It was to inaugurate a "reformation of reformation" in Church and State' (*Cross Currents in English Literature of the Seventeenth Century*, 1929; VIII).

And yet Milton was no ordinary Puritan. He could never have been that. It is difficult to imagine the author of those colourous lines on church interiors and organ music in *Il Penseroso* (pp. 19, 21–2 above) belonging to a party which objected to the stained glass and carvings of the great cathedrals, and the music and ceremonial of church ritual. Yet so it was, and so it remains throughout Milton's life and work: an apparent incompatibility of reasoned argument and emotional predilection. In this juxtaposition of opposites lies the secret of his perennial fascination. The opposing elements might, no doubt, have been less starkly contradictory, but any less degree of inclusiveness would have left him a secondary figure. His attack on idolatrous externals is an aspect of his insatiable drive to the essence, but that essence he reclothes, again and again, in splendid adornment. We find an analogy in his approach to kingship.

Though destined to achieve a European fame for his defence of the execution of Charles, Milton's anti-episcopal pamphlets are the work of a fervent royalist. His first, the *Reformation in England*, discusses the compromise with Catholicism in the reigns of Henry VIII, Edward VI and Elizabeth, and argues that episcopacy holds no authority from primitive Christianity. That he should have contrasted 'the transparent simplicity of truth as one finds it in the Gospel with the tangled forest of theological argument and interpretation' (J. H. Hanford, *A Milton Handbook*, 11) is scarcely strange, since such contrasts are the burden of prophetic literature throughout the ages and might be called the prerogative of genius in a wide sense; as when Milton refers to Christ's attack on 'the prelatical pharisees' (*Apology for Smectymnuus*; III. i. 314). But in this age, when a whole section of the community was shortly to share, or at least claim, this prerogative – which is perhaps a way of defining the revolutionary impulse – it is remarkable to find so pulsing a royalism as Milton puts forward. The Prelates, he says, have been false to 'our Great Charter' and those who 'wrested' British liberties from the 'Norman gripe' (*Reformation in England*, II; III. i. 57), but his respect for the throne, for the majesty of state incorporated in a royal person, is at this period (1641) unimpaired. It is in the wrong done to royalty that he couches his indictment of the lesser office of bishop:

> Have they not been told of late to check the common law, to slight and brave the indiminishable majesty of our highest court, the lawgiving and sacred parliament? Do they not plainly labour to exempt churchmen from the magistrate? Yea, so presumptuously as to question and menace officers that represent the king's person for using their authority against drunken priests?
>
> (*Reformation in England*, II; III. i. 58)

The inherent majesty of law and the sanctity of parliament are felt as consummated in 'the king's person'. Milton is before his time; he writes as though our constitutional monarchy were already the established and recognized expression of national concord; and with that ideal in view must we understand all his work. From the start he thrills to a mysticism within royal authority comparable with the more sedate convictions of Burke:

> This is the sum of their loyal service to kings; yet these are the men that still cry, The king, the king, the Lord's anointed! We grant it; and wonder how they came to light upon anything so true; and wonder more, if kings be the Lord's anointed, how they dare thus oil over and besmear so holy an unction with the corrupt and putrid ointment of their base flatteries; which while they smoothe the skin, strike inward and envenom the life-blood.
>
> (*Reason of Church Government*, II. Concl.; III. i. 277)

The accent is uncompromising.

Milton's loathing of the episcopacy is a loathing of what he considered idolatrous paganism and spiritual tyranny. His life's work turns about an opposition not very dissimilar from that dividing the world in our time. It is easy, in the atmosphere of religious tolerance all Christian communities, whether Catholic or Protestant, expect today, to forget those horrors of religious compulsion from which Milton's England strove to liberate mankind. The episcopacy raises in him, and for almost identical reasons, the horror aroused in us by the totalitarian states of modern Europe. A passage from Milton's *Second Defence of the People of England* (1654) illustrates his direction:

> We approve no heresies which are truly such; we do not even

tolerate some; we wish them extirpated, but by those means which
are best suited to the purpose – by reason and instruction, the only
safe remedies for disorders of the mind; and not by the knife or
the scourge, as if they were seated in the body.   (VIII. 179)

To what extent Milton's ecclesiastical opponents were guilty
and the Puritan party guiltless of such excesses need not here
too deeply concern us. We should however mark closely Milton's
(i) attacks on the prelacy and (ii) acknowledgement of majesty.

It is sometimes asserted that Milton believed in the separation
of Church and State. Such a separation may be from time to
time suggested, but to assert this as Milton's considered end is
no satisfactory judgement. In the *Reason of Church Government*
the Church is spoken of as 'the king's daughter' (II. Concl.;
III. i. 275). The problem is complex and much of Milton's
thinking given to its solution:

> That which can be justly proved hurtful and offensive to every
> true Christian, will be evinced to be alike hurtful to monarchy;
> for God forbid that we should separate and distinguish the end
> and good of a monarch from the end and good of the monarchy,
> or of that from Christianity.
>
> (*Reformation in England*, II; III. i. 38)

Both in prose and poetry Milton is always striving for synthesis.

No major writer can remain content without such a striving,
for, since Church and State are objective aspects of twin functions of the human being, to remain content with their separation in the body communal is as dangerous as contentment with
anything less than personal integrity. Milton's writings are a
record of a continual disintegration and the will to reinstatement. The power released by the breaking of traditional forms
flows out, as blood from a body, and the fiery essence rages,
searching for a new home. 'Through all these stages', writes
Mark Pattison, 'Milton passed in the space of twenty years –
Church-Puritan, Presbyterian, Royalist, Independent, Commonwealth's man, Oliverian' (XI). This follows the comment:

> When he wrote his *Reason of Church Government* (1641), he is still
> a royalist; not in the cavalier sense of a person attached to the
> reigning sovereign, or the Stuart family, but still retaining the
> belief of his age that monarchy in the abstract has somewhat of
> divine sanction.   (XI)

Milton's royalism goes perhaps even further and deeper than that, nor is it ever fundamentally denied. In his anti-prelatical pamphlets he considers the priesthood to be a danger to the king, questioning his 'supremacy' and daring to consider itself 'independent and unsubordinate to the crown' (*Reformation in England*, II; III. i. 58); while in playing with worldly power the Church is an 'ass bestriding a lion' (that is, humility aping power), becoming itself dangerous as a 'dragon', the images of lion and ass being the culmination of a laboured analogy to which we shall return (*Reason of Church Government*, II. iii; III. i. 253). Later, in the *Defence of the People of England* (1651), angered at Charles's support of the bishops, Milton asserts that kings have even less right than they to 'lord it over the Church' (ix; VII. 463). Though virtue has been here transferred from regal office to revolutionary action, essential sovereignty, the lion-voice of authority, is not really being denied. In different forms it reverberates through Milton's life-work. In this deeper sense, which is the sense in which the Crown is today a potent symbol, Milton remains in essence a royalist to whom we may resort for a deepening of our own convictions.

No party contented him for long. As we watch his succession of disillusions, summed in the famous line 'New Presbyter is but old Priest writ large' (p. 102 below), and his confident manner of attack with no hint that his latest attack is anything but final, we may question whether he has any positive goal in view at all. We may even half-subscribe to Dr Johnson's mordant conclusions in his *Lives of the Poets* that Milton simply hated 'all whom he was required to obey'. That would be unfair, which is not to say that it is totally untrue. It is part only of the picture, that part which Shakespeare drew in the earlier speeches of Cassius in *Julius Caesar*; but Milton far more closely resembles Brutus. He, like Brutus, was serving an ideal, not merely, like Cassius, at least as Shakespeare's Caesar saw him (I. ii. 208), resenting the power of a greater than himself. We might say that he rejects authority wherever he finds it lodged in anything or anyone smaller than himself. His attacks on the prelacy arise from a basic Christian impulse towards religious freedom together with an intolerance of the formalism and idolatry, the spiritual inertia, that in all ages are ready to ally themselves with lust and cruelty. He has a superb conviction of his own righteousness:

> But when God commands to take the trumpet and blow a dolorous or a jarring blast, it lies not in man's will what he shall say, or what he shall conceal.
>
> (*Reason of Church Government*, II. Intro.; III. i. 231)

He has as much right to his passionate aversions as had Isaiah. He admits himself to be 'transported with the zeal of truth to a well-heated fervency' (*Animadversions*, Preface; III. i. 107), and defends the violence of his invective and his use of questionable language in controversy by alluding to similar examples in the words of Luther and Christ, advancing a defence of passion and doctrine (see p. 113 below, note) of sublimation (*Apology for Smectymnuus*; III. i. 312–15). His vices of intolerance and disdain can be considered negative aspects of the one positive drive within; and this is a drive of high spiritual power that if sympathetically understood will throw his many rejections, which finally include criticism of Cromwell himself, into perspective. Our enquiry, then, must consider in what precisely the Miltonic power consists. It has many aspects, good and evil; but, for the next part of our discussion, I ask that we consider it in close reference to ideals of (i) kingship and (ii) liberty. In both Milton is beyond his day, finding in consequence a difficulty of expression in any but negative terms, themselves radiating from the central negative act of Charles's execution.

III

The Civil Wars, starting in 1642, came to an end with the defeat of Charles in 1648 and his execution in 1649. Meanwhile Milton had turned against the Presbyterians and alined himself with the Independents, who had now over-ruled the Parliament and taken possession of the government. Directly after the King's execution his pamphlet *The Tenure of Kings and Magistrates* appeared, and this was followed by *Eikonoklastes*, both in 1649; *The Defence of the People of England* (in Latin) in 1651 and the *Second Defence of the People of England* (also in Latin) in 1654. In all these he strongly supported the action of Cromwell, under whom he now held office, having been in 1649 appointed

D

to the post of Secretary for Foreign Tongues to the Council for State.

The result was not happy. Milton endured a disillusion similar to that recorded a century and a half later in Coleridge's ode *France*. In a 'Digression'[1] in his *History of Britain* he describes, in the year 1670, how the revolutionary cause 'had armies, leaders and successes to their wish; but to make use of so great advantages was not their skill'. Liberty, so long desired, has been won, but no good comes of it:

> For a parliament being called, and as was thought many things to redress, the people with great courage and expectation to be now eased of what discontented them, chose to their behoof in parliament such as they thought best affected to the public good, and some indeed men of wisdom and integrity; the rest (and to be sure the greatest part) whom wealth and ample possessions, or bold and active ambition (rather than merit) had commended to the same place, when once the superficial zeal and popular fumes that acted their new magistracy were cooled and spent in them, straight every one betook himself (setting the commonwealth behind, and his private ends before) to do as his own profit or ambition led him. Then was justice delayed, and soon after denied: spite and favour determined all: hence faction, then treachery, both at home and in the field: everywhere wrong and oppression, foul and dishonest things committed daily or maintained in secret or in open.   (x. 318–19)

This condemnation may deepen our understanding of Satan in *Paradise Lost*. The paragraph describes a recurring pattern in human affairs.

Such events are as eruptions. Seething energies thrust and challenge the crust of society, willing its removal and destruction to make place for themselves, the scalding lava solidifying quickly to a new, and harder, surface. But the analogy must not be pressed too far; something is accomplished. The established order which is overthrown, though itself an order and in its degree good, falls through not being good enough; either not sufficiently powerful or not sufficiently liberal to contain the basic energies. Such a process is evident on a vast scale today. Hitler is a world-revolutionary, and one cannot deny him a certain affinity to Cromwell. Both conform roughly to the type

---

[1] In the Bohn edition this 'Digression' appears at the opening of Book III. [1967

of Marlowe's Tamburlaine and Napoleon, men who ruthlessly override ethical objections, considering themselves the scourge of God. Of Cromwell's trust in imaginative reality Middleton Murry writes:

> It shaped itself in him as a watching of events for 'mercies' and 'evidences' and 'dispensations'; as a self-less self-submission to the creative process of events.   (*Heaven – and Earth*, x)

Joan had her 'voices', and Hitler, according to Hermann Rauschning, trusts his astrologers. Sir Herbert Grierson has called attention (*Cross Currents etc.*, as above, VIII) to Carlyle's rhapsody on Cromwell in his *Oliver Cromwell's Letters and Speeches*:

> An armed Soldier, solemnly conscious to himself that he is a Soldier of God the Just – a consciousness which it well beseems all soldiers and all men to have; – armed Soldier, terrible as Death, relentless as Doom; doing God's judgements on the enemies of God.

Carlyle's phrases fit Milton's warring Messiah in *Paradise Lost*.

Such leaders do not consider themselves wicked. They are the implements of forces greater than themselves, which they do not themselves understand, and which they attribute to God. In *The Tenure of Kings and Magistrates* (1649) Milton writes of 'justice' and 'victory' as 'the only warrants through all ages, next under immediate revelation, to exercise supreme power' (v. 4). 'Human power' used to execute, 'not accidentally but intendedly, the wrath of God upon evil-doers' may be either 'ordinary' (i.e. presumably according to law) or 'if that fail extraordinary' (v. 7). Notice his reservations: his trust is in power *with goodness*. 'Success', he says, 'neither proves a cause to be good, nor indicates it to be bad; and we demand that our cause should not be judged by the event, but the event by the cause' (*Second Defence*; VIII. 185). The same thought is found in *Eikonoklastes*, with however the reservation that 'in a good cause success is a good confirmation' (xxviii; v. 307). Milton is labouring at a central human problem. Though he admits that 'who in particular is a tyrant cannot be determined in a general discourse', he yet asserts his condemnation of any ruler 'by whose commissions whole massacres have been committed

on his faithful subjects', and who bears responsibility farther
afield for destruction of 'whole' cities and countries: 'Be he
king, or tyrant, or emperor, the sword of justice is above him'
(*Tenure of Kings and Magistrates*; v. 6–7). Again, 'Not mortal man
or his imperious will, but justice, is the only true sovereign and
supreme majesty upon earth' (v. 40).
We are jerked above all normal political terms of reference.
Great Britain today fights, we say, for freedom; and yet our
liberty was won by Cromwell, a Hitler-type. Hitler certainly
thinks he, or Germany, is fighting for liberty too. In any conflict
each side fights for liberty. But there are infinite varieties of
liberty; the term can be understood on many different planes;
and the difference between Cromwell and Hitler can only be
analysed with reference to categories involving Christian, or
some similar, doctrine. To fight for liberty as a universal principle is a higher act than to fight merely for one's own. The
early thrusts of Protestantism, being revolutionary, show in both
Luther and Cromwell analogies to Nazi Germany. All revolutionary action feels itself working in transcendence of law,
almost in disregard of right and wrong, at least in their accepted
senses. Nevertheless there may be a difference of direction not
readily to be defined: subversive action can lift upwards, or it
can drag down. Among the political upheavals of post-Renaissance Europe Great Britain's internal revolution stands pre-
eminent in its claim to Christian support.

Cromwell is Britain's man of destiny. He set himself a piece
of work, and did it. He was master of the self-control Milton
rates so high, and no arbitrary, self-willed tyrant. He was, says
Sir Herbert Grierson, 'compared with Milton, a conservative',
and finally worked 'to substitute accepted authority for the rule
of the sword' (*Milton and Wordsworth*, 1937; VII). Though
Cromwell would not himself take the crown, his life was
dedicated to a more subtle royalty. He fought, says Middleton
Murry, for all men's right to 'immediacy with God':

> Immediacy with God meant naked contact with the source of all
> sovereignty, the everliving fount of all honour, the day-spring
> from on high that made men kings.   (*Heaven – and Earth*, x)

Again:

> For in that world – that forgotten, but once terribly living world

– immediacy with God and equality before Him have one ultimate meaning: that all men who have that immediacy and
equality are themselves Kings, by right divine.

(Heaven – and Earth, x)

This is the doctrine implied by our present constitutional
monarchy, aiming as it does to give equality while preserving
the royalistic essence. In this deeper sense both Cromwell and
Milton are conservative.

Though Milton's attitude to kingship after the execution of
Charles appears to have undergone a change from his first
royalistic fervour, the inconsistency is superficial. Kingly government was, he says, in the Old Testament repudiated by
Samuel and is always ready enough to degenerate into pride
and tyranny *(Defence of the People of England,* ii; VII. 89–91).
This is the limit of his generalized attack, and elsewhere he is
more sympathetic to the idea of royalty. In the full stride of his
Second Defence he addresses the 'most noble Queen of Sweden'
with deepest humility and with a respect for her 'magnanimity' in having read with 'incredible impartiality', and even it
seems approval, things in Milton's first *Defence* that might '*seem
to be levelled*' against her own 'rights and dignity'; thus bearing
'royal evidence' to Milton's 'integrity' and the truth that he has
'not written a word against kings, but only against tyrants'; so
that her 'greatness of soul' renders her the object of his 'homage',
'veneration' and 'love' *(Second Defence;* VIII. 103–5). The essence
of royalty is not denied; and the royalty of David, whose kingship resulted from the non-observance of Samuel's warning
(1 Samuel, viii. 11–19), burns central in Milton's political,
national and religious imaginations. Charles has forfeited his
title to kingly respect: that is all. He has become a 'tyrant', the
living opposite, like Shakespeare's Richard III and Macbeth,
of true royalty. On this Milton insists:

> For a tyrant is but like a king upon a stage, a man in a vizor and
> acting the part of a king in a play; he is not really a king.
>
> *(Defence,* Preface; VII. 17)

Just as the bishops had offended against Milton's religious
idealism, so Charles had offended his conception of royalty.
Both he sees as assuming a power which they do not rightly

possess. It is his life-long devotion to some more greatly conceived sovereign power, a devotion witnessed by the weight and
lustre of royalistic imagery throughout his prose and poetry,
that gives point to his attack on Charles:

> If I inveigh against tyrants, what is this to kings? whom I am far
> from associating with tyrants. As much as an honest man differs
> from a rogue, so much I contend that a king differs from a
> tyrant. Whence it is clear that a tyrant is so far from being a king,
> that he is always in direct opposition to a king.
> *(Second Defence*; VIII. 25)

It is no simple matter of authority as against the people. A king
may well be a blessing: 'How great a good and happiness a
just king is, so great a mischief is a tyrant' (*Tenure of Kings and
Magistrates*; v. 18–19). We are involved in complex issues of
right and wrong:

> The murder of a king and the punishment of a tyrant are not the
> same thing; but do differ, and will for ever differ, as long as sense
> and reason, justice and equity, the knowledge of right and wrong,
> shall prevail among men.   *(Second Defence*; VIII. 93)

A king is no more free to do as he pleases than anyone else, and
only remains truly king while he has a sense of moral responsibility.

We may group Milton's ideas on sovereignty in an ascending
scale from populace to divinity as follows:

(i) He considers 'that a commonwealth is a more perfect
form of government than a monarchy' and 'in the opinion of
God himself better for his own people' (*Defence*, ii; VII. 77).
Whatever of divine sanction a king may claim, that same sanction can be invoked in the people's cause: 'Be this right of kings,
therefore, what it may, the right of the people is as much from
God as it' (*Defence*, ii; VII. 113). The people themselves have
sovereign rights.

(ii) Good rulers have always been aware of this: 'Every good
emperor acknowledged that the laws of the empire and the
authority of the senate was above himself; and the same principle and notion of government has obtained all along in
civilised nations' (*Defence*, iii; VII. 167).

(iii) Such obedience is a traditional characteristic of British monarchy: 'For as the king of England can do no wrong, so neither can he do right but in his courts and by his courts; and what is legally done in them shall be deemed the king's assent, though he as a several [i.e. separate] person shall judge or endeavour the contrary; so that indeed without his courts, or against them, he is no king. If therefore he obtrude upon us any public mischief, or withhold from us any general good, which is wrong in the highest degree, he must do it as a tyrant, not as a king of England, by the known maxims of our law' (*Eikono-klastes*, xi; v. 176).

(iv) These conclusions are dictated by Christianity: 'Christians either must have no king at all; or if they have, that king must be the people's servant. Absolute lordship and Christianity are inconsistent' (*Defence*, iii; vii. 159). But this higher allegiance again involves the royal essence: 'I did not insult over fallen majesty, as is pretended; I only preferred Queen Truth to King Charles' (*Second Defence*; viii. 139). These are separate pieces chosen from long passages of discursive argument, but they show the general direction and range of the argument. Milton is finding it impossible to maintain any real distinction between the religious and the secular orders, and kingly absolutism is being invaded by Christianity. The constitutional monarchy of Great Britain is fundamentally a Christian creation.

Milton's argument in the *Defence* relies on a series of references drawn from thought and history in the ancient and modern world, with especial and detailed historical reference to the development of the British constitution in particular. He sees Britain as having through the centuries established a political freedom in advance of continental custom, and his *Defence*, written in answer to the continental scholar Salmasius, typifies the recurring political challenge, corresponding to that outlined in Tennyson's plays, of Britain to European tyranny: 'Since we are as free as any people under heaven', he writes, 'we will not be imposed upon by any barbarous custom of any other nation whatsoever' (*Defence*, xii; vii. 533). In the Puritan revolution the English have battled better than others against evil; this they did 'under the light of better information, and favoured by an impulse from above', the whole enterprise being characterized by a 'grandeur of conception and loftiness of spirit' which 'merited for each individual more than a mediocrity of fame'; and so Britain will 'hereafter deserve to be celebrated for endless ages, as a soil most genial to the growth of liberty' (*Second Defence*; VIII. 9). Such was the 'renown and everlasting glory of the English nation', he says,

> that with so great a resolution, as we hardly find the like recorded in any history, having struggled with, and overcome, not only their enemies in the field, but the superstitious persuasions of the common people, have purchased to themselves in general amongst all posterity the name of deliverers: the body of the people having undertook and performed an enterprise, which in other nations is thought to proceed only from a magnanimity that is peculiar to heroes.   (*Defence*, i; VII. 63)

To Milton the contest is one of righteousness against pagan superstition, while the people as individuals are felt as having behaved as heroes. The people have shown themselves royal in action: they have incorporated the royalty they slew, or rather only rose to such an action through instinctive allegiance to an eternal principle of which any one human king is at best a transitory symbol.

Milton believes that his countrymen have accomplished an action of world-wide importance. A tyrant 'is not only our enemy, but the public enemy of mankind' (*Second Defence*; VIII. 197). Addressing Cromwell, he writes:

> Revere also the opinions and the hopes which foreign states entertain concerning us, who promise to themselves so many advantages from that liberty which we have so bravely acquired, from the establishment of that new government which has begun to shed its splendour on the world, which, if it be suffered to vanish like a dream, would involve us in the deepest abyss of shame; and lastly, revere yourself; and, after having endured so many sufferings and encountered so many perils for the sake of liberty, do not suffer it, now it is obtained, either to be violated by yourself, or in any one instance impaired by others.
> (*Second Defence*; VIII. 225–7)

Milton himself has worked 'to defend the dearest interests not merely of one people, but of the whole human race, against the enemies of human liberty, as it were in a full concourse of all the nations on the earth' (*Second Defence*; VIII. 19). England has been proved a saviour among nations; a Christ-like force, setting free the nations, as Christ sets free men, from shackles; and it is an honour to belong to God's 'saints', whose royal business it is to 'overcome those European kings, which receive their power, not from God, but from the beast' (*Eikonoklastes*, xxviii; v. 306).

IV

'Liberty' and 'freedom' are treacherous quicksands. It is easier to attack tyranny than to define liberty. Liberty did not mean to Milton what it means to us. In fact, every individual means something different by the term. We all want different sorts of freedom, and when gained liberty proves often disappointing. It needs genius or saintliness to attain any real and enduring freedom, and such freedom is independent of political control; or so at least one might contend. We must therefore approach Milton's arguments with circumspection.

Milton is no democrat in the twentieth-century understanding of the term. 'In all Milton's writings', observes Walter Raleigh (*Milton*, 1915; 58), 'there is no trace of the modern democratic doctrine of equality.' Milton puts the issue clearly:

> For nothing is more agreeable to the order of nature, or more for the interest of mankind, than that the less should yield to the greater, not in numbers, but in wisdom and in virtue. Those who excell in prudence, in experience, in industry and courage, however few they may be, will, in my opinion, finally constitute the majority and everywhere have the ascendant.
>
> (*Second Defence*; VIII. 153)

Notice the words 'wisdom' and 'virtue'. Or, as phrased in *Paradise Lost*:

> Unjustly thou deprav'st it with the name
> Of servitude to serve whom God ordains,
> Or Nature; God and Nature bid the same,
> When he who rules is worthiest, and excells
> Them whom he governs. This is servitude
> To serve the unwise . . .
>
> (VI. 174; see also 179–81)

Such 'wisdom' and 'virtue' are themselves to be related, and Milton does so relate them throughout, to the only real freedom. Meanwhile some are better without too much liberty, being not fit for its exercise. Such 'vicious' men may well constitute 'the majority of the citizens' and the good should not then be deterred by 'smallness of numbers' (*Second Defence*; VIII. 177). Again:

> Liberty hath a sharp and double edge, fit only to be handled by just and virtuous men; to bad and dissolute it becomes a mischief unwieldy in their own hands: neither is it completely given but by them who have the happy skill to know what is grievance and unjust to a people and how to remove it wisely; what good laws are wanting, and how to frame them substantially, that good men may enjoy the freedom which they merit, and the bad the curb which they need.   (*History of Britain*, 'The Digression', see p. 80 above, note; X. 324)

Questions of good and evil are primary, and only in such terms can true liberty be discussed:

> For, should the management of the republic be entrusted to persons to whom no one would willingly entrust the management of his private concerns? . . . Are they fit to be the legislators of a whole people who themselves know not what law, what reason, what right and wrong, what crooked and straight, what licit and illicit means?   (*Second Defence*; VIII. 247)

Freedom and virtue are interdependent:

> It is not agreeable to the nature of things that such persons ever should be free. However much they may brawl about liberty, they are slaves, both at home and abroad, but without perceiving it; and when they do perceive it, like unruly horses that are impatient of the bit, they will endeavour to throw off the yoke, not from the love of genuine liberty (which a good man only loves and knows how to obtain), but from the impulses of pride and little passions . . . For, instead of fretting with vexation, or thinking that you can lay the blame on any one but yourselves, know that to be free is the same thing as to be pious, to be wise, to be temperate and just, to be frugal and abstinent, and lastly, to be magnanimous and brave; so to be the opposite of all these is the same as to be a slave; and it usually happens, by the appointment, and as it were retributive justice, of the Deity, that that people which cannot govern themselves, and moderate their passions,

but crouch under the slavery of their lusts, should be delivered up
to the sway of those whom they abhor, and made to submit to an
involuntary servitude. It is also sanctioned by the dictates of
justice and by the constitution of nature, that he who from the
imbecility or derangement of his intellect, is incapable of govern-
ing himself, should, like a minor, be committed to the government
of another; and least of all should he be appointed to superintend
the affairs of others or the interest of the State. You, therefore,
who wish to remain free, either instantly be wise, or, as soon as
possible, cease to be fools; if you think slavery an intolerable evil,
learn obedience to reason and the government of yourselves; and
finally bid adieu to your dissensions, your jealousies, your super-
stitions, your outrages, your rapine and your lusts. Unless you
will spare no pains to effect this, you must be judged unfit, both
by God and mankind, to be entrusted with the possession of
liberty and the administration of the government; but will rather,
like a nation in a state of pupilage, want some active and cour-
ageous guardian to undertake the management of your affairs.

(Second Defence; VIII. 249)

Besides this we might set Milton's Sonnet:

> I did but prompt the age to quit their clogs
>   By the known rules of ancient liberty,
>   When strait a barbarous noise environs me
> Of owls and cuckoos, asses, apes and dogs.
> As when those hinds that were transform'd to frogs
>   Railed at Latona's twin-born progeny
>   Which after held the sun and moon in fee.
> But this is got by casting pearl to hogs;
> That bawl for freedom in their senseless mood,
>   And still revolt when truth would set them free.
>   Licence they mean when they cry liberty;
> For who loves that, must first be wise and good;
>   But from that mark how far they rove we see
> For all this waste of wealth, and loss of blood.

And this, from *Paradise Lost*:

>   Yet know withal,
> Since thy original lapse, true Liberty
> Is lost, which always with right reason dwells
> Twinn'd, and from her hath no dividual being:
> Reason in man obscur'd, or not obey'd,
> Immediately inordinate desires
> And upstart passions catch the government
> From reason, and to servitude reduce

Man till then free. Therefore since he permits
Within himself unworthy powers to reign
Over free reason, God in judgement just
Subjects him from without to violent lords;
Who oft as undeservedly enthrall
His outward freedom: tyranny must be,
Though to the tyrant thereby no excuse.
Yet sometimes nations will decline so low
From virtue, which is reason, that no wrong,
But justice, and some fatal curse annext
Deprives them of their outward liberty,
Their inward lost . . .   (xii. 82)

Those 'upstart passions' Milton knew in himself. Though sub-
limated into denunciatory invective they from time to time
take on an almost repellent colouring, bearing witness to the
tumultuous energies, for good or ill, seething within. His attack
on tyranny is the more valuable for his own temptations towards tyrannic domination: he knows what he is talking about.
Throughout his life he works to heave over this power within
towards the creative and the good, as he sees it; the attempt
involving both a hatred of all other tyrannies and a recognition
that tyranny is to be countered not alone by cries of 'freedom'
but still more by the power of 'right reason' and the light of
Christian truth.

Middleton Murry points out that Cromwell's army itself
fought not for political but for religious equality (*Heaven – and
Earth*, x); and to Milton the king-worshipping people 'are an
inconstant, irrational and image-doting rabble' (*Eikonoklastes*,
xxviii; v. 309) whose pity at Charles's fall is 'no true and
Christian commiseration' but 'levity and shallowness of mind'
(*Tenure of Kings and Magistrates*; v. 3). Freedom is to be equated
with harmony of being, a state of personal integrity in which the
opposition of energy and ethic ceases to exist. This is what
Milton meant when in his *Apology for Smectymnuus* he says that
'he who would not be frustrate of his hope to write well hereafter in laudable things, ought himself to be a true poem'
(iii. i. 303). Such harmony of being Milton scarcely reveals in
either his life or his work, but he realizes the existence of a
soul-state mainly independent of politics:

I had leisure to turn my thoughts to other subjects; to the pro-

motion of real and substantial liberty; which is rather to be
sought from within than from without; and whose existence
depends, not so much on the terror of the sword, as on sobriety
of conduct and integrity of life.   (*Second Defence*; VIII. 131)

Which is certainly the ideal for individual, nation, or world.

Such 'integrity', though it can scarcely be advanced by its
political context, can, failing the highest spiritual achievement,
most certainly be so hampered. Political and religious freedom
is not so much a value itself as a preliminary to realization of
value; and, if at any point it ceases to assist man's truest good,
it may, as our recent passages suggest, be withdrawn. It might
seem, in spite of what he says in *Areopagitica* (pp. 102–3 below),
that to Milton liberty was freedom to do right and find the
truth, but not freedom to do wrong and follow falsehood. This
may seem a poor sort of freedom, but a similar paradox characterizes St Paul's claim that his message transcends without con-
tradicting the Judaic 'Law'. Such doctrines force the conclusion
that true psychic liberation results in right action, but that false
freedoms may masquerade as true. The problem converges on
the sacrificial death of Christ: to St Paul it is this, the Cross of
Christ, that blasts open the way for the higher state, and which
alone renders such emphasis on freedom valid. Milton's thought
is similar:

> Christian liberty, purchased with the death of our Redeemer, and
> established by the sending of his free Spirit to inhabit in us, is not
> now to depend upon the doubtful consent of any earthly monarch.
> (*Eikonoklastes*, xiii; v. 207)

'Inasmuch', says Milton in his *Christian Doctrine*,[1] 'as it was not
possible for our liberty either to be perfected or made fully
manifest till the coming of Christ our deliverer, liberty must be
considered as belonging in an especial manner to the Gospel
and as consorting therewith' (I. xxvii; XVI. 153). We may con-
clude that, failing a Christian or some equivalent centre, concentration on political freedom as an end in itself is likely to
prove infertile, if not disastrous.

The pitch of revolutionary experience whereby religious

---

[1] Milton's *De Doctrina Christiana* was not published in his lifetime. The text was
discovered in 1823 and published in 1825. In this work Milton applies to the New
Testament the method of spatial interpretation on which my own literary studies
have been based. [1967]

fervency and patriotic ardour were temporarily fused could not be maintained. It was dependent on a period of nobly conceived action, and the action being completed there followed a reaction. Church and State had been by Milton distinguished in his *Reason of Church Government*. If the Church, he there maintained, were truly humble in imitation of Christ's riding into Jerusalem on an ass, she would become, like Christ himself, a lion of strength; but in so far as she makes lion-like power and secular authority her aim, she will be ridiculed as an ass (II. iii; III. i. 252). The revolution, however, shattered this distinction, which was quite inconsistent with the dictatorial powers arrogated to itself by the Puritan party in the name of religion. Separate categories were temporarily fused; *and this fusion, in which both existed in a molten state, threw up an heroic figure, the super-king Cromwell, in whom the miraculous was incarnate*, and on whom Milton, who was certainly not prone to hero-worship, lavished the riches of a passionate idealization:

> For while you, O Cromwell, are left among us, he hardly shows a proper confidence in the Supreme, who distrusts the security of England; when he sees that you are in so special a manner the favoured object of the divine regard.
>
> (*Second Defence*; VIII. 219)

Again, 'the title of king', he writes, 'was unworthy the transcendent majesty of your character' (*Second Defence*; VIII. 225); a paradox beautifully illustrating the innate royalism of Milton's thought. This is nevertheless followed by the warning:

> You cannot be truly free unless we are free too; for such is the nature of things, that he who intrenches on the liberty of others, is the first to lose his own and become a slave.
>
> (*Second Defence*; VIII. 227)

Both ruler and subject attain freedom in proportion as they acknowledge allegiance to some greater royalty to which they are both in their respective stations subject. 'Cromwell', writes J. H. Hanford, 'never became an open champion of that complete religious freedom for which Milton hoped' (*Handbook*, revised 1936, 11). No man in high office could for long have satisfied Milton's uncompromising demands, and thenceforth Church and State again diverged in his thinking. Milton's life reads as a series of disillusionments in attempt to quench his tormented thirst for an impossible perfection. The hour when Church and State had been merged in a greater unity, of which Cromwell was the *majestic* embodiment, passed.

In *A Treatise of Civil Power in Ecclesiastical Causes* (1659) Milton argues that Christ's kingdom is spiritual and that the attempt to regulate it by external force can do only harm. He quotes John, xviii. 36: 'If my kingdom were of this world, then would my servants fight, that I should not be delivered to the Jews.' On this he comments:

> This proves the kingdom of Christ not governed by outward force, as being none of this world, whose kingdoms are maintained all by force only; and yet disproves not that a Christian commonwealth may defend itself against outward force, in the cause of religion as well as in any other, though Christ himself, coming purposely to die for us, would not be so defended.   (VI. 22)

Difficulties remain, but the distinction between outward force and spiritual power is clear.

And yet Milton, having once known under Cromwell the ecstasy of transcendence, cannot rest content with such a distinction. Nor can any great thinker do so. To distinguish absolutely Church from State, which is soul from body, is a living, or dead, contradiction of the principle of the Incarnation. Christ represents a fusion of the divine and the earthly: therefore in him somehow the total good rests. This total good can only provisionally be defined in personal and inward terms, and Christianity was from the start a communal religion aiming at creation from mankind of the Body of Christ.

Milton was no democrat; his royalistic instincts were ineradicable; so was his religious fervour. Parliament and even Cromwell eventually failed him, and he was inevitably driven towards arguing for a state ruled by Christ. One must recognize the prophetic and dynamic cast of his royalistic thinking: he had his eye on the essence, not merely the man, from the start. No man, he says, may assume absolute monarchy on earth but the Son of God (*Defence*, v; VII. 279), and such a Christ-rule is the logical conclusion of his various discontents. In *The Tenure of Kings and Magistrates* he had, in 1649, written:

> Therefore he who is our only King, the Root of David, and whose kingdom is eternal righteousness, with all those that war under

him, whose happiness and final hopes are laid up in that only just
and rightful kingdom (which we pray incessantly may come soon,
and in so praying wish hasty ruin and destruction to all tyrants);
even he, our immortal King, and all that love him, must of
necessity have in abomination these blind and lame defenders of
Jerusalem; as the soul of David hated them, and forbid them
entrance into God's house, and his own. (v. 57)

In all the manifold twists and turns of Milton's thinking the
sovereign essence is never lost, but runs as a gold thread throughout his arguments. His bitterness towards tyranny is one with
his craving for true royalty. Now, in 1660, when the Puritan
cause was dying and the Restoration itself an impending cert-
ainty, he composed – the title is not intentionally ironic – *The
Ready and Easy Way to establish a Free Commonwealth.*

Milton's 'beliefs', writes Walter Raleigh (*Milton*, 61), 'inclined
more and more, in two points at least, to the tenets of the newly
arisen sect of Quakers – to a pure spiritualism in religion, and
the complete separation of Church and State'. The separation
is not so complete as that. That Milton never shared 'their'
(i.e. the Quakers') 'horror of war' is true: poetically at least
war is one of his main joys. But the reference to the Quakers,
whose principles included a refusal to take oaths, certainly
recalls the analogy I have already drawn between Milton and
Shakespeare's Brutus. Here is Brutus on oaths:

> Swear priests and cowards and men cautelous,
> Old feeble carrions and such suffering souls
> That welcome wrongs; unto bad causes swear
> Such creatures as men doubt – but do not stain
> The even virtue of our enterprise,
> Nor the insuppressive metal of our spirits,
> To think that or our cause or our performance
> Did need an oath. (*Julius Caesar*, II. i. 129)

This breathes the very spirit, even to the slur on priests, of
Milton's political idealism. Both Milton and Brutus are at once
studious and brave. Both repress love and dedicate themselves
to a high-minded severity. Milton recaptures the very accents
of Brutus' Forum speech: compare 'For who is there, who does
not identify the honour of his country with his own?' (*Second
Defence*; VIII. 7) with, 'Who is here so vile that will not love his

country?' (*Julius Caesar*, III. ii. 35). The Puritan in the one matches the Stoic in the other. Raleigh's passage continues: 'The model of the Church he sought in the earliest records of Christianity, and less and less even there; the model of the State in the ancient republics. All subsequent experience and precedent was to him a hindrance and a mischief' (*Milton*, 61). Milton draws many direct analogies from ancient Rome for his purposes. Such is the intellectual context of his *Ready and Easy Way*.

Even here, the ascetic, other-worldly purity is not maintained. However much he tries, and in spite of his commentators' insistence on this Church and State separation, he cannot, in the depths does not wish to, reject the idea of sovereignty. His scheme is simple: no government comes nearer to the 'precept of Christ' than a 'free commonwealth' where the 'greatest' are public servants (VI. 120). The implied doctrine resolves, as Milton himself notices, the former paradox of kingship whereby a king was properly a 'servant' of his own subjects (*Defence*, iii; VII. 145, 157, and see 271–3). Power is therefore to exist in a permanent council of experienced men, chosen originally by the people (VI. 126). Milton does not approve changes in this council, nor once it has been formed any popular checks, for if we look back on such commonwealths in the ancient world, 'the event tells us that these remedies either little availed the people, or brought them to such a licentious and unbridled democratie, as in fine ruined themselves with their own excessive power' (VI. 130). The equal dangers of a tyrannic oligarchy are less obvious to him. He admits the convenience of a monarchy to some nations, while fearing its reinstatement in England (VI. 137). His Council is admittedly a second-best, and the best takes monarchic shape with Christ as King:

> The grand council being thus firmly constituted to perpetuity, and still, upon the death or default of any member, supplied and kept in full number, there can be no cause alleged, why peace, justice, plentiful trade, and all prosperity should not thereupon ensue throughout the whole land; with as much assurance as can be of human things, that they shall so continue (if God favour us, and our wilful sins provoke him not) even to the coming of our true and rightful and only to be expected King, only worthy as he is our only Saviour, the Messiah, the Christ, the only heir

of his eternal Father, the only by him anointed and ordained since the work of our redemption finished, universal Lord of all mankind.   (VI. 133)

This strong flight of the imagination constitutes a refusal to separate Church from State, flowering from a lively will to synthesis. We must remember, as Milton elsewhere remembers, Christ's supposed descent from a human king, David. Milton is working his way to a transfiguration of royalty. Starting with the old kings of England, leaving acceptance of the throne of Charles for the other sovereignty of the people of England and 'the transcendent majesty' of Cromwell, his royalistic imagination comes to rest in Christ.[1]

The council and commonwealth are suggested as temporary expedients whilst the true Sovereign delays. Now since the goal remains itself royalty, and since the main function of the council is to further the coming of that royalty, we might replace Milton's system to our advantage by one preserving within it, at least shadowily, that splendour towards which it gropes; and Milton's tormented thinking points towards the constitutional monarchy of a later day, whereby the royal essence is preserved within a living personality dramatically prefiguring the greater royalty which we await.

Milton's attacks are best understood within the context of futurity. With the justice of his charges against King Charles, set out in detail in his *Defence* and throughout *Eikonoklastes*, we need not be concerned. It is scarcely fair to judge individual persons by the standard of that richer political understanding which the civil disturbances of the seventeenth century served to establish. Milton had that richer understanding from the start: he is always assuming what is implicit in Britain's history. No more sensitive appreciation of our British system was ever penned than this, written in 1641:

There is no civil government that hath been known, no not the Spartan, not the Roman, though both for this respect so much

[1] Or perhaps, better, 'in the Messiah', the Hebrew of Milton's favourite term being often more naturally suited to his arguments than the Greek 'Christ'. For the problems inherent in Milton's Hebraic Christianity see Harold Fisch, *Jerusalem and Albion*, 1964, 163–4; and for an attractive account of Jesus as the expected Messiah, Hugh J. Schonfield, *The Passover Plot*, 1965. [1967]

praised by the wise Polybius, more divinely and harmoniously
tuned, more equally balanced as it were by the hand and scale of
justice, than is the commonwealth of England; where, under a
free and untutored monarch, the noblest, worthiest, and most
prudent men, with full approbation and suffrage of the people,
have in their power the supreme and final determination of
highest affairs. Now if conformity of church discipline to the civil
be so desired, there can be nothing more parallel, more uniform,
than when under the sovereign prince, Christ's vice-gerent, using
the sceptre of David, according to God's law, the godliest, the
wisest, the learnedest ministers in their several charges have the
instructing and disciplining of God's people, by whose full and
free election they are consecrated to that holy and equal aristocracy.   (*Reformation in England*, ii; iii. i. 63)

The passage, with its reference to a Messianic kingship, recalls
our recent quotation from *A Ready and Easy Way*, but whereas
there a 'free commonwealth' was considered a temporary ex-
pedient in preparation for a distant reign of Christ, here the
different elements are compactly held in organic harmony.
This is the whole from which all Milton's political arguments
are drawn as so many emphases of its several parts. Though he
is at pains in the *Defence* to distinguish king from parliament,
sometimes even asserting that 'every good king accounts either
the senate, or the people, not only equal, but superior to himself by the law of nature', and that 'a king is what he is for the
people only, not the people for him'; yet even here, and of
course strongly elsewhere, he disclaims any respect for the
judgement of the 'rabble' (vii; vii. 377, 389, 393). The desirable
end is a balanced harmony in which 'the name and power of a
king are very consistent with a power in the people and the law
superior to that of the king himself', while 'a kingly government, both in name and thing, may very well subsist even
where the people, though they do not ordinarily exercise the
supreme power, yet have it actually residing in them, and exercise it upon occasion' (vi; vii. 349, 353). In the *Apology for
Smectymnuus* he blames his adversary for distinguishing king
from parliament so as to make 'two bodies of one', and reproves
him for insulting the 'high and sovereign court of parliament',
that is, the 'king with all his peers', the 'inviolable residence of
justice and liberty', by the 'monkish' name of 'convocation'

(III. i. 331, 333). We have to return to the *Reformation in England* for the perfect statement:

> We know that monarchy is made up of two parts, the liberty of the subject and the supremacy of the king.   (II; III. i. 56)

Where the 'king', as a person, is only part of the total sovereignty which is at once the soul, and whole, of the nation.

This splendour Milton later felt to have been desecrated. In his *Brief Notes* on Dr Griffith's Sermon (1660), he asserts that Saul, David, and David's race 'which ended in the Messiah', from whom, he says, 'no kings at this day can derive their rule', are to be distinguished from later monarchs (VI. 155). Again, in his *Defence* (ii; VII. 109) he distinguishes David's posterity appointed by both God and the people from all other kings appointed by the people only: but since the people of England are themselves to Milton specially favoured by Providence, there is perhaps the less difference. Milton's insistent questioning drives towards the one possible solution: 'Who knows not', he says (*Tenure of Kings and Magistrates*; v. 36) that 'the king is a name of dignity and office, not of person?' Such a recognition allows re-entry to the most solemn associations. Scorn is poured on modern 'vice-gerents or deputies of Christ'[1] (*Second Defence*; VIII. 7). That on the one side; but on the other a realization that, as Christ exists potentially for and in every man, so the Crown itself is a communal and even a personal possession, an objective symbol of the super-self in each subject:

> But if every good man, as an ancient sect of philosophers magnificently taught, is a king, it follows that every bad one is, according to his capacity, a tyrant.   (*Second Defence;* VIII. 27)

This insight into the royalty of the individual, high or low, is the central wisdom of both Shakespeare's humanism and our own crowned democracy, existing by all the most sacred and 'life-blood laws' that are 'the holy covenant of union and marriage between the king and his realm' (*Reformation in England*, II; III. i. 57). Milton's political writings were given to a deepen-

---

[1] Milton is here using sarcastically royal phrases that were in common use (cp. p. 1 above), corresponding to Dante's contention in *De Monarchia* that the Emperor is to be regarded as the representative of Christ and the Pope of St Peter. See *The Golden Labyrinth*, 25–6; also *Shakespeare and Religion*, 22–3. [1967]

ing of Great Britain's understanding of her developing system, of whose royal centrality he remains one of our noblest exponents. Milton *is* the British Constitution in its battle for self-realization.

V

We do wrong to Milton's greater prose passages to limit our analysis to their 'thought', however accurate our inspection: they are too majestical for that, and too vital. Nor will even that strain of royalistic fervour, as powerful in revolt as in acceptance, by itself and in isolation open, except to a most sympathetic understanding, his inmost treasure. 'Words', writes Milton, 'must be conformable to things, not things to words' (*Defence*, vi; vii. 353). Words and symbols are little more than flotsam on the heaving swell of a great writer's passionate experience, though that passionate experience can to some extent be re-fashioned in us by attention to his words. The various expressions must be felt dynamically as aspects of a greater, a more rounded, whole.

The Puritan revolution stands central in Milton's drama, acting on him as the French Revolution on Wordsworth, or the Cross of Christ on St Paul. Such experiences have one characteristic in common: a claim either formulated, as with St Paul, or implied, as in Wordsworth's *The Borderers*,[1] that good and evil as usually understood have been transcended, a claim which the mass-effect of Milton's prose work, apart from the relevant separate passages, may be supposed to be asserting. From this consciousness rises the related assertion of political liberty, which, though at times of revolution it may be easily debased, becomes necessarily in the soul of genius an aspect of that subtler and transcendent freedom announced by St Paul; a freedom dependent, as Milton remembers (at *Eikonoklastes*, xiii; v. 207, the passage has already been quoted), on the Cross of Christ. That Milton and Wordsworth should have suffered disillusion is less strange than that men of their intellectual calibre should have pitched expectations so high; though such optimism was certainly in St Paul also, and appears an inevitable symptom of the

---

[1] The dangerous thought-excursions of this drama may, with due caution, be related to Wordsworth's experiences in France. [1967]

central experience. Only in terms of that experience may the details of controversy be assessed. St Paul's epistles and Milton's pamphlets correspond in point of close intellectual argument and wealth of scholarly resource tumbled out helter-skelter in service to a more than intellectual wisdom in whose comparison their authors realize them to be the language of childhood: hence the intolerance and asperity born of an infuriating disparity between author and reader. 'I did not insult over fallen majesty, as is pretended; I only preferred Queen Truth to King Charles' (*Second Defence*; VIII. 139): which is, with the necessary changes, St Paul's point too.

In the New Testament the Law, being negative, is superseded by positive power; in *Christian Doctrine* (I. xxvii; XVI. 135) Milton quotes St Paul (2 Corinthians, iii. 7) to prove the Decalogue a 'ministration of death'. What is this new power? Neither in St Paul's epistles nor Milton's various pamphlets, which grapple with a similar difficulty, is there any clear definition. That is always the trouble: details of the 'law' can always, in any age or any section of human affairs, for the New Testament opposition is archetypal of many, be satisfactorily defined; the creative antagonist never. We can follow all Milton's distinctions of Church from State with ease, but what Cromwell, or the God-given energies of the English people in revolution, meant to him is a matter of inexhaustible and indefinable fascination. Such events are goodness, and they are power: that is all the definition available. In them the physical order is irradiated with divine meaning. Distinctions of Church and State are dissolved into a dynamic unity in which the conventional terms scarcely apply, but since strong action is now involved the more energic and power-bearing principle assumes royal precedence:

> For truth is properly no more than contemplation; and her utmost efficiency is but teaching: but justice in her very essence is all strength and activity; and hath a sword put into her hand, to use against all violence and oppression on the earth. . . . We may conclude, therefore, that justice, above all other things, is and ought to be the strongest; she is the strength, the kingdom, the power, and *majesty* of all ages. Truth herself would subscribe to this, though Darius and all the monarchs of the world should deny. (*Eikonoklastes*, xxviii; v. 292–3)

Often 'truth' in Milton, as in the New Testament, transcends 'contemplation', meaning rather an alinement and direction of the total personality, when it necessarily includes 'justice', which itself might be called 'truth in action'; which is, again, royalty. When truth becomes operative physical energy assumes divine significance. Poetry is therefore necessary, or a myth. The main task of poetry is to fuse goodness with power, and this fusion transcends legal categories. Milton, though often a keen contestant for 'law' in other forms, puts the main antithesis crisply:

> For the imperfect and obscure institution of the Law, which the apostles themselves doubt not oft times to vilify, cannot give rules to the complete and glorious ministration of the Gospel which looks on the Law as on a child, not as on a tutor.
>
> (*Reason of Church Government*, I. iii; III. i. 195)

Milton is arguing that Church government should be patterned on the Gospel, not on the Law: it is an old, and ever-new complaint. Organized Christianity often seems, and usually is, a retrogression from Gospel to Law; and since moreover the complaint is also levelled in terms of episcopal usurpation of secular rule (p. 115 below), we can almost expand the distinction to an equation of the Law with secular administration; which returns us to the root opposition in Milton's thinking, which ever flies as a moth to a candle at this thought-destroying paradox of Crown and Christ.

This paradox the Puritan revolution aimed to resolve: truth was to enter politics. This 'truth', which Milton sometimes calls 'right reason', corresponds to 'faith' in St Paul's epistles or the Church fathers and to 'imagination' as conceived by Coleridge and Shelley. When outward expressions are taken as themselves the substance rather than the shadows of Truth, Milton, like St Paul and others of kindred vision, becomes angry. Down through the ages persists this unhappy conflict of creative truth and constricting organization. Milton turns against his own party at once when he feels the greater liberty and truth of Christ to be jeopardized:

> Because you have thrown off your prelate lord,
> And with stiff vows renounc'd his liturgy
> To seize the widow'd whore plurality
> From them whose sin ye envied, not abhor'd,

Dare ye for this adjure the civil sword
　To force our consciences that Christ set free,
　And ride us with a classic hierarchy
Taught ye by mere A. S. and Rotherford?
Men whose life, learning, faith and pure intent
　Would have been held in high esteem with Paul
　　Must now be nam'd and printed heretics
　By shallow Edwards and Scotch what d'ye call.
But we do hope to find out all your tricks,
　Your plots and packing worse than those of Trent,
　　That so the Parliament
May with their wholesome and preventive shears
Clip your phylacteries, though balk your ears,
　　And succour our just fears,
When they shall read this clearly in your charge,
New Presbyter is but Old Priest writ large.
　　　　　　　(*On the New Forcers of Conscience*)

A supreme value is in question.

Milton's gospel transcends politics, though political questions may be involved. It moves between man's noblest wisdom and divine inspiration, along the territory regularly traversed by works of poetic and religious genius. Among his prose-works one essay stands out with a unique positive power and coherence: the early *Areopagitica* (1644), a plea against the censorship of books. The generally accepted pre-eminence of this particular essay is natural, since Milton's message is here less immediately political than literary, though within that term a deep and long-range political wisdom is implicit.

Here he is writing in the cause of that subtle and furthest human development, its flower-like unfurling, which all great books, the New Testament at their head, aim to advance:

> And yet on the other hand, unless wariness be used, as good almost kill a man as kill a good book: who kills a man kills a reasonable creature, God's image; but he who destroys a good book kills reason itself, kills the image of God, as it were, in the eye. Many a man lives a burden to the earth; but a good book is the precious life-blood of a master-spirit, embalmed and treasured up on purpose to a life beyond life. (IV. 298)

As always the attack acts in service to a supreme positive. Milton will risk many evils rather than hamper the growth of a single good. Highest virtue, freedom's end, is thereon dependent:

> I cannot praise a fugitive and cloistered virtue, unexercised and unbreathed, that never sallies out and sees her adversary, but slinks out of the race, where that immortal garland is to be run for, not without dust and heat. (IV. 311)

Notice the strength of the athletic and physically vital imagery.

A good book is one with Truth and therefore Christianity in its inmost and widest, non-technical, Pauline sense, and all are 'virtue' or 'reason'. 'Truth' in writers of genius must often be read less as intellectual correctness than as truth of being, a right orientation of life in its wholeness, as when Pope in his *Essay on Man* (III. 306) says of religious Faith, 'His can't be wrong whose life is in the right'. Truth is invulnerable provided only state control does not stifle it:

> Who ever knew Truth put to the worse in a free and open encounter? (IV. 347)

Again, with Truth as a clear synonym for Christ as the incarnate *logos* or wisdom of God:

> For who knows not that Truth is strong next to the Almighty? She needs no policies, nor stratagems, nor licensings to make her victorious; those are the shifts and the defences that error uses against her power. (IV. 348)

This Truth must not be rigidly circumscribed; she 'may have more shapes than one'; and the 'Christian liberty' of which St Paul boasts, whereby a man may observe or break a received prohibition equally 'to the Lord' (IV. 348), is to be fought for and preserved.

This blazing Truth, which is the God-empowered Messiah potent in Book VI of *Paradise Lost*, has come to strong young life in England, or Britain, whose people are the honoured vehicle of a divine force:

> Lords and Commons of England, consider what Nation it is whereof ye are and whereof ye are the governors: a nation not slow and dull, but of a quick, ingenious, and piercing spirit; acute to invent, subtle and sinewy to discourse, not beneath the reach of any point the highest that human capacity can soar to. Therefore the studies of learning in her deepest sciences have been so

ancient and so eminent among us, that writers of good antiquity and ablest judgement have been persuaded that even the school of Pythagoras and the Persian wisdom took beginning from the old philosophy of this island . . .

Yet that which is above all this, the favour and the love of Heaven, we have great argument to think in a peculiar manner propitious and propending towards us. Why else was this nation chosen before any other, that out of her as out of Sion should be proclaimed and sounded forth the first tidings and trumpet of Reformation to all Europe? . . .

Now once again by all concurrence of signs, and by the general instinct of holy and devout men, as they daily and solemnly express their thoughts, God is decreeing to begin some new and great period in his Church, even to the reforming of Reformation itself. What does he then but reveal Himself to his servants, and as his manner is, first to his Englishmen; I say as his manner is, first to us, though we mark not the method of his counsels and are unworthy? Behold now this vast City: a City of refuge, the mansion house of liberty, encompassed and surrounded with his protection; the shop of war hath not there more anvils and hammers waking, to fashion out the plates and instruments of armed Justice in defence of beleaguered Truth, than there be pens and heads there, sitting by their studious lamps, musing, searching, revolving new notions and ideas wherewith to present, as with their homage and their fealty, the approaching Reformation; others as fast reading, trying all things, assenting to the force of reason and convince-ment. What could a man require more from a nation so pliant and so prone to seek after knowledge? What wants there to such a towardly and pregnant soil but wise and faithful labourers, to make a knowing people, a nation of Prophets, of Sages, and of Worthies? We reckon more than five months yet to harvest; there need not be five weeks; had we but eyes to lift up, the fields are white already.   (IV. 339–41)

That is the England in which Milton puts his faith.

And here is his vision of the nation rising as one man in her truth-born, sovereign might:

Methinks I see in my mind a noble and puissant nation rousing herself like a strong man after sleep, and shaking her invin-cible locks. Methinks I see her as an eagle muing her mighty youth, and kindling her undazzled eyes at the full midday beam, purging and unscaling her long-abused sight at the fountain itself of heavenly radiance; while the whole noise of timorous and flocking birds, with those also that love the twilight, flutter about,

amazed at what she means, and in their envious gabble would
prognosticate a year of sects and schisms.   (IV. 344)

Of this imagined splendour I shall have more to say hereafter:
in it a semi-pagan virility, an eagle and leonine magnificence
unmatched in our literature, burns. That a passage, quoted
later (pp. 115–16), of similar scope and tone from *The Reason
of Church Government* had referred this same Samson-figure to the
British throne shows how exactly the nation itself is in the
Areopagitica felt to be fulfilling the most expansive function of
what Milton understands by sovereignty. Distinctions of Church
and State become childish and unmeaning abstractions beside
the living muscles of the Messiah-nation, roused.

II. WAR IN HEAVEN

I

Milton thinks in terms less of ideas than of energies, and where
we remark any apparently static impressions, such as those of
sovereignty or the Messianic order, they will be prophetically
charged. His poetry, as Francis Berry once remarked to me, is
characterized pre-eminently by *power*. He is our supreme expo-
nent of power, in all its grades. We might accordingly expect a
clarity in terms of his later poetry not found in the tumultuous
succession of prose pamphlets. Yet his poetry is also confusing.
We can however bring knowledge of the prose to its understanding, and from these two, together with remembrance of
Milton's political and national experiences, attempt a general
synthesis.

The Restoration saw the ruin of Milton's hopes. His life-work
had crashed. He was now blind. Few great men in history have
faced so grim a disillusion, and at an age when many, after
youthful struggles, have attained comparative happiness and
the satisfaction of fame. In his old age Milton was plunged into
infamy. His life was in danger. He wrote *Paradise Lost, Paradise
Regained*, and *Samson Agonistes* (pub. 1667, 1671, 1671).

In these we shall expect former energies to be still function-
ing. Art is seldom totally discontinuous with a man's daylight

thinking, and still less can great poetry be considered discontinuous with a life's chosen activity, itself continuous with those energetic sources which are the substance of such poetry. A readiness to bring to certain passages of Milton's later poetry remembrance of his prose writings is rendered the more necessary by the peculiar nature and difficulties of the works to be discussed. Of these *Paradise Lost* is the most difficult, and I accordingly notice it last, aiming to wind back to it from a discussion of *Samson* and *Paradise Regained*, taking the three in reverse order.

There is a further apology to be made. In turning from politics to poetry Milton moves from the ephemeral to the archetypal, from time to eternity. He is concerned less with particular than with general implications. We are therefore at liberty to draw freely any analogies that may present themselves between the conflicts exposed and the problems, especially the great world-conflict, of today.

Samson Agonistes reflects Milton's own story as surely as *The Tempest* reflects Shakespeare's. In it, to borrow a phrase from *Il Penseroso*, 'more is meant than meets the ear'. The hero has been betrayed into slavery among the Philistines by his Philistine wife: Milton's unhappy marriage to a lady of Royalist sympathies is suggested. Samson's present misery reflects Milton's at the Restoration both in his blindness and in his enslavement to an authority he repudiates. Suggestions of Milton's life story and that of the cause he worked for are clearly present. Samson corresponds to the people of Britain as Milton saw them: he is therefore an expression of the Miltonic royalty. The primary condition of that royalty is self-discipline, like that of Cromwell:

> ... for he was a soldier disciplined to perfection in the knowledge of himself. He had either extinguished, or by habit had learned to subdue the whole host of vain hopes, fears and passions which infest the soul. He first acquired the government of himself and over himself acquired the most signal victories; so that on the first day he took the field against the external enemy, he was a veteran in arms, consummately practised in the toils and exigencies of war.   (*Second Defence*; VIII. 215)

Such was Cromwell's 'almost superhuman virtue'. But, like

Milton's countryman, Samson has fallen from grace, miserably rendering up the sovereign secret of his God-given strength to the wiles of a treacherous and pagan woman. Milton's strongest revulsions are projected into Dalila, his deepest longings into the divinely ordained strength, weakened but recaptured, of Samson. In his *Reformation in England* he wrote of Becket's 'insolencies and affronts to regal majesty', while attacking bishops as having been a lasting trouble to 'our monarchy and monarchs' and continuing, 'Have they not been as the Canaanites and Philistines to this kingdom?' (II; III. i. 45–6). The relation of the Philistines to Samson is precisely that of the prelacy to the monarchy, that is the soul, of Britain. The old loathing of idolatry burning so fiercely through the anti-prelatical invectives is in *Samson Agonistes* directed against the Dagon-worshipping Philistines.

Milton's love of military impressions gives us a fine description of Samson's former warriorship:

> Can this be he,
> That heroic, that renown'd,
> Irresistible Samson? whom unarm'd
> No strength of man, or fiercest wild beast, could withstand;
> Who tore the lion, as the lion tears the kid,
> Ran on embattled armies clad in iron,
> And weaponless himself,
> Made arms ridiculous, useless the forgery
> Of brazen shield and spear, the hammer'd cuirass,
> Chalybean temper'd steel, and frock of mail
> Adamantean proof . . .   (124)

Such was this 'lion' among men. Milton's use of the lion-symbol has a similar psychic connotation, though with a more directly political reference, to that of Nietzsche in *Thus Spake Zarathustra* (1 and 80). The lion, we are told, symbolizes 'power, high authority and indignation' (*Apology for Smectymnuus*; III. i. 314); and it was used to signify the power of the State, the Church being contrasted, not all in disrespect, as the ass, in *The Reason of Church Government*, though Christ himself was necessarily a Samson-like power, a 'Lion of the tribe of Judah' (II. iii; III. i. 252), a phrase to be compared with T. S. Eliot's

> In the juvescence of the year
> Came Christ the tiger

in *Gerontion*. Such phrases witness an attempt to fuse virility with goodness, and point towards a realization, whether psychic or political, beyond normal categories.

Samson is taunted by Harapha, the Philistine champion, and, though himself blind, offers combat:

> Then put on all thy gorgeous arms, thy helmet
> And brigandine of brass, thy broad habergeon,
> Vant-brass and greaves, and gauntlet, add thy spear
> A weaver's beam, and seven-times-folded shield.
> I only with an oaken staff will meet thee . . .
>   (1119)

Accused by Harapha of trusting in some 'black enchantments', Samson records the true nature of his strength:

> I know no spells, use no forbidden arts;
> My trust is in the living God who gave me
> At my nativity this strength, diffus'd
> No less through all my sinews, joints and bones,
> Than thine, while I preserv'd these locks unshorn,
> The pledge of my unviolated vow.   (1139)

His strength is God-given, yet proudly physical, corresponding to the armed strength of the Cromwellian revolution. The analogy is pointed by Harapha's levelling of an accusation directly fitting the regicide party:

> Fair honour that thou dost thy God, in trusting
> He will accept thee to defend his cause,
> A murderer, a revolter, and a robber.
>   (1178)

To which Samson argues that his friendship to the Philistine conquerors had been genuine until their own crafty hostility undermined it. Samson reflects the Puritan Revolution and becomes almost Milton himself. His routing of Harapha has been compared to Milton's routing of the continental scholar Salmasius, in reply to whom his exulting defences of Charles's execution had been composed. The correspondence is striking:

> I was no private, but a person rais'd
> With strength sufficient and command from Heaven
> To free my country; if their servile minds
> Me their deliverer sent would not receive,
> But to their masters gave me up for nought,
> Th' unworthier they; whence to this day they serve.
>   (1211)

That is how Milton saw himself and also Cromwell.

Like Milton, Samson has grown up (633-40) under Heaven's 'special eye' (cp. 'ever in my great Taskmaster's eye' in Sonnet VII), 'abstemious' and destined to accomplish things 'above the nerve of mortal arm' (cp. 'things unattempted yet in prose or rhyme' at *Paradise Lost*, I. 16). For both Samson and Milton 'Israel's deliverance' is 'the work to which I was divinely call'd' (225). Or again, with a bitterness corresponding to Milton's own experience:

> But what more oft in nations grown corrupt,
> And by their vices brought to servitude,
> Than to love bondage more than liberty,
> Bondage with ease than strenuous liberty;
> And to despise, or envy, or suspect
> Whom God hath of his special favour rais'd
> As their deliverer; if he aught begin,
> How frequent to desert him, and at last
> To heap ingratitude on worthiest deeds?
>
> (268)

The word 'strenuous' defines, as once in Keats ('strenuous tongue' in the *Ode on Melancholy*), the arduous implications at its best of a conception usually associated with pleasure. To Milton liberty is dependent on inward discipline, and Samson's sin, not his menial slavery under the Philistines, is the 'true slavery' (418). Samson can assert that 'this gaol I count the house of liberty' (949), like Byron's 'eternal spirit of the chainless mind' considered 'brightest in dungeons' (in his *Sonnet on Chillon*), or Cassius' lines:

> Therein, ye gods, you tyrants do defeat:
> Nor stony tower, nor walls of beaten brass,
> Nor airless dungeon, nor strong links of iron,
> Can be retentive to the strength of spirit.
>
> (*Julius Caesar*, I. iii. 92)

Milton's work stands eminent within the literature of freedom from *Julius Caesar* to the poetry of the nineteenth century.

The Philistian lords express Milton's abhorrence of the Court party in London. They are pagan worshippers of Dagon, a 'Sea-Idol' (13) symbolizing license; and the main conflict 'twixt God and Dagon' (462) is also Milton's old conflict of Puritanism and the Prelacy. So they are described in revelry:

> While their hearts were jocund and sublime,
> Drunk with idolatry, drunk with wine,

> And fat regorg'd of bulls and goats,
> Chanting their idol, and preferring
> Before our living Dread who dwells
> In Silo his bright sanctuary . . .   (1669)

Idolatry and debauchery intermix:

> So Dagon shall be magnified, and God,
> Besides whom is no God, compar'd with idols,
> Disglorified, blasphem'd, and had in scorn
> By th' idolatrous rout amidst their wine.
>   (440)

Emphasis is laid on the aristocracy of the Philistines. Milton refuses his hero an aristocratic impressionism, reserving such for
his enemies, while enduing neither side with explicit royalty,
though the royal essence must be felt, as I have already suggested and shall argue again, within Samson himself. Against
this pack of debauched and idolatrous nobles and their supporters Samson in his blindness advances, with the assurance
that he will do

> Nothing dishonourable, impure, unworthy
> Our God, our Law, my Nation, or myself . . .
>   (1424)

There is, compactly, our contrast.

Samson bears a stoic fortitude; and here again we may be
reminded of Shakespeare's Brutus. The stoic spirit however is
not regarded as sufficient, and in a fine passage the Chorus points
the limitations of ancient philosophy, continuing with a bitter
plea to God:

> God of our Fathers, what is man!
> That thou towards him with hand so various,
> Or might I say contrarious,
> Temper'st thy providence through his short course,
> Not evenly, as thou rul'st
> The angelic orders and inferior creatures mute,
> Irrational and brute.
> Nor do I name of men the common rout,
> That wandering loose about
> Grow up and perish, as the summer fly,
> Heads without name no more remember'd,
> But such as thou hast solemnly elected,

With gifts and graces eminently adorn'd
To some great work, thy glory,
And people's safety, which in part they effect:
Yet toward these thus dignified, thou oft
Amidst their height of noon,
Changest thy countenance, and thy hand with no regard
Of highest favours past
From thee on them, or them to thee of service.
                                                    (667)

Milton, surely, is here thinking of his own past. The play carries a
load of bitterness which reasonings that God being himself Law
is incapable of injustice (300–14) scarcely alleviate.

Physical blindness drives in this pervading and personal 'sense
of Heaven's desertion' (632):

O dark, dark, dark, amid the blaze of noon,
Irrecoverably dark, total eclipse . . .
          *   *   *   *
Since light so necessary is to life,
And almost life itself, if it be true
That light is in the soul,
She all in every part, why was the sight
To such a tender ball as th' eye confin'd?
                                                    (80)

Milton feels light and sight as spiritual energies, and at his greatest moments makes less distinction between spiritual and physical action than any of our poets. Manoa groups sight and
strength together:

And since his strength with eyesight was not lost,
God will restore him eyesight to his strength.
                                                    (1502)

Samson's physical sight does not return, any more than it returned to Milton, whose universe, during his last years, must
have been dark indeed, resembling that of Shakespeare's Brutus:

I shall have glory by this losing day . . .
So fare you well at once; for Brutus' tongue
Hath almost ended his life's history:
Night hangs upon mine eyes; my bones would rest,
That have but labour'd to attain this hour.
                                    (*Julius Caesar*, v. v. 36)

With which compare:

> All otherwise to me my thoughts portend,
> That these dark orbs no more shall treat with light,
> Nor th' other light of life continue long,
> But yield to double darkness nigh at hand:
> So much I feel my genial spirits droop,
> My hopes all flat, nature within me seems
> In all her functions weary of herself;
> My race of glory run, and race of shame,
> And I shall shortly be with them that rest.   (590)

It is strange how often Milton's life and work make patterns prefigured in *Julius Caesar*. Brutus' relation with Portia, at its best, resembles that of Adam with Eve in the early parts of *Paradise Lost*, while Adam's fall through Eve, and still more clearly Samson's rendering up of his secret to Dalila, corresponds to Brutus' surrender to Portia's importunity. Brutus rashly trusts feminine weakness ('How weak a thing', admits Portia, 'the heart of woman is'; II. iv. 39) with knowledge of the revolution; while Samson should not 'have trusted to woman's frailty' (783) the secret of his God-given strength.

Samson's hair conditions his physical powers which he lost when Dalila learned from him their secret and acted accordingly. Hair, being emblematic of virility, may bear reference to the sexual centres: an intimate, private, and personal matter appears to be involved in this 'holy secret' (497). The relation to physical strength, 'this consecrated gift of strength' (1354), is close; and physical strength, under wisdom's guidance, is a major Miltonic delight. Samson is a 'glorious champion', the 'image' of God's 'strength' (705), like Messiah in *Paradise Lost*. With a striking image he curses himself

> Who like a foolish pilot have shipwrack'd
> My vessel trusted to me from above,
> Gloriously rigg'd; and for a word, a tear,
> Fool, have divulg'd the secret gift of God
> To a deceitful woman.   (198)

This admiration of hair contrasts with the opposite attitude of the 'roundheads'. The relation of Milton to the average 'roundhead' resembles that of Shakespeare's Timon to Apemantus, and points Milton's lonely preservation, through all his tempestuous political adventures, of the innate royalty defined in his *Reason of Church Government*, where he rates 'inward reverence' as secondary only to that divine *fire* in the heart which is the 'love of God'. This 'pious and just honouring of ourselves' corresponds to Nietzsche's emphasis on the importance of self-love throughout *Thus Spake Zarathustra* (discussed in *Christ and Neitzsche*, 165–6, 177–80, and see 196–8), where such self-reverence becomes almost an internal love-affair, a passionate self-communion. To Milton, as to Nietzsche (*Thus Spake Zarathustra*, 79, 'great and small streams'), this self-communion is 'the radical *moisture* and fountain-head whence every laudable and worthy enterprise issues forth':

> And although I have given it the name of a liquid thing, yet is it not incontinent to bound itself, as humid things are, but hath in it a most restraining and powerful abstinence to start back, and glob (*globe*) itself upward from the mixture of any ungenerous and unbeseeming motion, or any *soil* wherewith it may peril to stain itself. (II. iii; III. i. 260; italics mine as elsewhere)

Liquidity, like the strong sap of a flower, though itself differentiated from the 'fire' of the 'love of God', yet raises the natural man above the 'soil' to condition the globed circularity of his contact with the eternal.[1] Such is the way of spiritual power and personal sovereignty. Therefore Samson is a grand person, and his waving locks symbolize a leonine integrity treasured in a man's own heart, between himself and God, which must not be expended. Since the implied doctrine so closely resembles that of Nietzsche's *Thus Spake Zarathustra*, one may wonder to what extent Milton regrets not having dedicated himself to a Nietzschean chastity. Certainly Samson was a 'Nazarite' who

[1] Cp. 'radical humour and passion' as the 'mould' of 'virtues', *Apology for Smectymnuus*, III. i. 313 (p. 79 above). *Oxford English Dictionary* compares Milton's 'globe' to Emerson, address, Cambridge, Mass., 15 July 1838: 'the moral traits which are all *globed* into every virtuous act and thought'. 'Moisture' and 'liquid' may refer to lonely fantasy in activation of the sexual centres as raw material for spiritual sublimation: see *Thus Spake Zarathustra*, 5, 22, 79; discussed in *The Christian Renaissance* 1962, 273–4. With Milton's 'globe' compare Nietzsche's 'eternity' (*Thus Spake Zarathustra*, 60, 79; *Christ and Nietzsche*, 187–8). Compare Pope's emphasis on the rights of instinct together with his 'God within the mind' (II. 204) as a check in the *Essay on Man*, discussed in *Laureate of Peace*, reissued as *The Poetry of Pope*, 178 and see 49–52; Keats's *Ode to Psyche* as discussed at *Christ and Nietzsche*, 136, and *The Starlit Dome*, 301–4; and the masturbatory doctrine of John Cowper Powys, discussed in *The Saturnian Quest*, 119–20, 125–7. See p. 30 above, note. [1967]

'against his vow of strictest purity' had sought an 'unclean' bride (318), and was thence caught in the snare of her 'venereal trains' (533). This anti-feminine bias works powerfully in *Paradise Lost*; and again in *Paradise Regained*, Christ exemplifying the super-sexual strength.

The Miltonic power-impulse may be ugly, as in his more extreme prose violences towards opponents; in the assertion here that God has given to the man 'despotic power' (1054) over the woman; and in the Chorus' delighted hope that, Samson's strength being restored,

> He now be dealing dole among his foes,
> And over heaps of slaughter'd walk his way.
>
> (1529)

It can follow a bygone heroic tradition, when Manoa, hearing of his son's death, asks, queerly enough to our ears, 'What glorious hand gave Samson his death's wound?' (1581). And yet the key-passages of Milton's noblest work depend directly on his heroic sense; here his power-thrust finds justification, is, as it were, sanctified. Hence the suitability to his purposes of Samson's story, where the hero's strength symbolizes a universal elsewhere projected into royalistic impressions or thoughts of England as a nation. Adam was royal, with Eve as his subject, and he resembled Samson:

> His fair large front and eye sublime declar'd
> Absolute rule; and hyacinthine locks
> Round from his parted forelock manly hung
> Clust'ring, but not beneath his shoulders broad.
>
> (*Paradise Lost*, IV. 300)

Royalty is both a psychic principle and a political office, domination of woman by man corresponding to the rule of lust in the individual and mass-instinct in the community. Samson is both a right *noble* figure as an individual and a *national* embodiment:

> It shall be my delight to tend his eyes,
> And view him sitting in the house, *ennobled*
> With all those high exploits by him achiev'd,
> And on his shoulders waving down those locks,
> *That of a nation arm'd the strength contain'd:*
> And I persuade me God had not permitted
> His strength again to grow up with his hair
> *Garrison'd round about him like a camp*

Of faithful soldiery, were not his purpose
To use him further yet in some great service,
Not to sit idle with so great a gift
Useless, and thence ridiculous about him.
And since his strength with eyesight was not lost,
God will restore him eyesight to his strength.

(1490)

Which reads as a direct comment, from Milton's view, on Britain under the Restoration, recovery of 'eye-sight' corresponding to the later political readjustment.

A great poet rarely modifies his primary impressionisms, but rather, using them as constants, gears them to the changing world of his experience. Milton's intuition of God-given strength and God-ordained rule is such a constant. In the *Reformation in England* 'royal dignity' founded on 'justice and heroic virtue' is a mighty Samson-like strength, before which the *edifice* of priesthood must collapse like the Philistian palace; so the prelacy 'want but one puff of the king's to blow them down like a pasteboard house built of court-cards' (II; III. i. 47). Similarly at the conclusion to Book II of the *Reason of Church Government*, the British throne is equated with Samson in a fascinating passage where, by a poetic transposition which will assist our understanding of Messiah in *Paradise Lost*, the supernatural gifts of a mythical hero correspond to the superhuman powers and rights of the community:

I cannot better liken the state and person of a king than to that mighty Nazarite Samson; who being disciplined from his birth in the precepts and the practice of temperance and sobriety, without the strong drink of injurious and excessive desires, grows up to a noble strength and perfection with those his illustrious and sunny locks, the laws, waving and curling about his god-like shoulders. And while he keeps them about him undiminished and unshorn, he may with the jaw-bone of an ass, that is, with the word of his meanest officer, suppress and put to confusion thousands of those that rise against his just power. But laying down his head among the strumpet flatteries of prelates, while he sleeps and thinks no harm, they, wickedly shaving off all those bright and weighty tresses of his laws and just prerogatives, which were his ornament and strength, deliver him over to indirect and violent counsels, which, as those Philistines, put out the fair and far-sighted eyes of his natural discerning, and make him grind

in the prison-house of their sinister ends and practices upon him:
till he, knowing his prelatical razor to have bereft him of his
wonted might, nourish again his puissant hair, the golden beams
of law and right; and they, sternly shook, thunder with ruin upon
the heads of those his evil counsellors, but not without great
affliction to himself.   (ii. Concl.; iii. i. 276)

The description is coupled with thought of 'the whole body of
people in England': these two, crown and community, being
convergent, if not identical. The 'sunny locks' falling on 'god-
like shoulders' recall Adam. As elsewhere in Milton, so greedy
for aesthetic delights and gorgeous decorations, 'ornament' and
'strength' are close-allied, while a quality more spiritual is
symbolized by 'fair and far-sighted eyes'. The two categories
are interdependent. On this 'puissant hair' depend 'the golden
beams of law and right' which in their strength thunder down
on wrongdoers, like Messiah in *Paradise Lost* and Samson in
Samson Agonistes. Such fearful *light* is a consistent Miltonic impression, as in the great passage in *Areopagitica* describing the 'puissant' British nation as a Samson-figure, roused 'like a strong
man after sleep and shaking her invincible locks', compared
next to an eagle kindling 'undazzled eyes' at the sun-fountain
of 'heavenly radiance', while 'timorous and flocking birds'
flutter about, 'amazed' (iv. 344).

Samson Agonistes offers just such descriptions of appallingly
active, terrifying, virtue.

> Oh how comely it is and how reviving
> To the spirits of just men long oppress'd!
> When God into the hands of their deliverer
> Puts invincible might
> To quell the mighty of the earth, th' oppressor,
> The brute and boist'rous force of violent men
> Hardy and industrious to support
> Tyrannic power, but raging to pursue
> The righteous and all such as honour Truth;
> He all their ammunition
> And feats of war defeats
> With plain heroic magnitude of mind
> And celestial vigour arm'd,
> Their armories and magazines contemns,
> Renders them useless, while
> With winged expedition

> Swift as the lightning glance he executes
> His errand on the wicked, who surpris'd
> Lose their defence distracted and amaz'd.
>   (1268)

Again 'amazed'. This passage closely reflects the victory of Messiah in *Paradise Lost*.

Samson pulls down the palace on the assembled nobility of Gaza, striking them 'with amaze' (1645). In another passage (1687–1707) he is, like our Samson-figure in *Areopagitica*, an 'eagle' descending on weak birds, thundering down, again like Messiah in *Paradise Lost*; or a phoenix strength roused not merely from sleep, as in *Areopagitica*, but from death, becoming a symbol of Britain's future recovery from the death endured under the Restoration. Spiritual sight ('inward eyes') is again, as in the great invocation to Light in Book III of *Paradise Lost*, vivid:

> But he though blind of sight,
> Despis'd and thought extinguish'd quite,
> With inward eyes illuminated
> His fiery virtue rous'd
> From under ashes into sudden flame . . .
>   (1687)

'Virtue given for lost' rises like that 'self-begotten bird', the Phoenix.[1] The close inter-relation and national reference of these key-passages are important: we shall return to them in discussion of *Paradise Lost*.

II

Milton was a fighter; his every accent exults in power; but he was a Christian. In what senses can power be Christian? What exactly is to be done about those analogies of lion and ass in the *Reason of Church Government*? We have watched Milton's various prose attempts to relate secular to divine ordinance. The great passages in *Areopagitica* and *Samson Agonistes* elevating heroic strength are symptomatic of Milton's will to blend strong action with a Christian, or at least Hebraic, fervour. But had the

---

[1] For a discussion of the rising dramatic power of *Samson Agonistes*, see my treatment of the drama in *The Golden Labyrinth*. [1967]

Revolution itself used *Christian* methods? The problem is obscure. The blend of purity and power in action depends on a choice occasion, the rare moment, and difficulties remain. Their resolution had been attempted in Milton's *Paradise Regained*, presumably written just before *Samson Agonistes*. To understand *Paradise Regained*, concerned throughout with the temptations of Jesus before his ministry, we must respect the highly convincing arguments of Satan. Their reasoning is that by which we normally regulate national affairs. In contrast Jesus takes what seems a pacifist position, though he is far from mild. He appears as a static, resisting, and scornful figure. Beneath his passivity rages a volcano, fiery as Satan's, and both are aspects of Milton himself. The normal reading which excludes Satan from intellectual sympathy cannot be unreservedly allowed: we must forget, if necessary, the Gospels. Epic and drama reach out to total reality born of conflicting opposites, as in *Julius Caesar*, where a complex whole is created from the interaction of revolution and Caesarism. Any art-form is as a whole likely to carry a greater wisdom than can one term of the enclosed opposition; and this is eminently true of so balanced an opposition as that in *Paradise Regained*. It follows, perhaps, that Christ is not a suitable figure for inclusion in a work of art intended for a Christian audience, the Christ-consciousness being itself correspondent to that richer wisdom involving opposites which dramatic art conveys. That Milton's Christ includes Satanic elements of bitterness and resentment scarcely restores a satisfactory balance. Milton is attempting to incorporate the power-thrust into a Christlike calm, and success is perhaps impossible.

Jesus is, as always in Milton, given titles of secular authority. He is destined to appear 'in the head of nations' as 'their king, their leader, and supreme on earth' (I. 98), their 'great dictator' (I. 113). Such phrases aim to fuse heaven and earth with direct political reference. We are reminded of prophecies that he is David's successor. A messenger from God has foretold:

> Thou should'st be great and sit on David's throne.
>
> (I. 240)

The phrase is repeated at III. 153 and 373, and with fervour at

III. 383; and elsewhere. He is 'Israel's true king' (III. 441)
and 'endued with regal virtues' (IV. 98). In *Paradise Lost* Jesus'
descent from 'the royal stock of David' (XII. 325) was emphasized, and the approach in *Paradise Regained* is royalistic
through and through: one look from Christ's 'majestic brow'
would put the charms and wiles of woman, such as those
which entrapped Samson, to shame (II. 216).

Milton's Jesus is brave, heroic and innately royal; one born
for power. Satan accordingly tempts him by appealing to his
heroic qualities in a series of closely reasoned arguments that
repay attention.

The Fiend observes his 'amplitude of mind to greatest deeds'
(II. 139); he suggests that 'all thy heart is set on high designs,
high actions', while arguing that such demand 'great means of
enterprise', involving wealth which brings 'honour, friends,
conquest, and realms' (II. 410–22). Jesus answers with a fine
comment on the cares of kingship, echoing well-known Shakespearian passages (e.g. *Richard II*, III. ii. 155–77, and *2 Henry
IV*, III. i. 4–31). Though these are honourable burdens enough,

> Yet he who reigns within himself, and rules
> Passions, desires, and fears, is more a king;
> Which every wise and virtuous man attains:
> And who attains not, ill aspires to rule
> Cities of men, or head-strong multitudes,
> Subject himself to anarchy within . . .
> (II. 466)

To guide nations into truth, he says, is more 'kingly' than to rule.

Satan next urges the possibilities of conquest. Milton's main
poetic favourites are in turn involved. There was the gorgeous
banquet in Book II (II. 337–67), glittering wealth (II. 427), and
now war:

> Should Kings and Nations from thy mouth consult,
> Thy counsel would be as the oracle
> Urim and Thummim, those oraculous gems
> On Aaron's breast: or tongue of seers old
> Infallible; or wert thou sought to deeds
> That might require th' array of war, thy skill
> Of conduct would be such, that all the world
> Could not sustain thy prowess, or subsist

In battle, though against thy few in arms.
These God-like virtues wherefore dost thou hide?
                                        (III. 12)

Compared with the records of past heroes such as Alexander,
Cyrus, Pompey and Caesar, his years are already 'over-ripe'.
To which Jesus replies that all glory of 'empire' is merely a
short 'blaze of fame' won from the 'herd confus'd', whose
vulgar tastes follow convention (III. 43–56). He repudiates the
brutalities of militaristic ambition:

> They err who count it glorious to subdue
> By conquest far and wide, to over-run
> Large countries, and in field great battles win,
> Great cities by assault: what do these worthies,
> But rob and spoil, burn, slaughter, and enslave
> Peaceable nations, neighbouring or remote,
> Made captive, yet deserving freedom more
> Than those their conquerors, who leave behind
> Nothing but ruin wheresoe'er they rove,
> And all the flourishing works of peace destroy,
> Then swell with pride, and must be titl'd Gods,
> Great benefactors of mankind, deliverers,
> Worship'd with temple, priest and sacrifice;
> One is the son of Jove, of Mars the other,
> Till conqueror Death discover them scarce men,
> Rowling in brutish vices, and deform'd,
> Violent or shameful death their due reward.
>   (III. 71)

The truth of that passage we can appreciate. And yet is not
military prowess a primary Miltonic joy? Is it not the Messiah's
glory in *Paradise Lost*? and Samson's? Is not Milton's work
crammed to overloading with images of kingly might, and God
himself in *Paradise Lost* conceived on the analogy of a human
tyrant? This last objection seems to have occurred to Milton,
since Satan replies:

> Think not so slight of glory; therein least
> Resembling thy great Father: he seeks glory,
> And for his glory all things made, all things
> Orders and governs, nor content in Heaven
> By all his angels glorified, requires
> Glory from men, from all men good or bad,

> Wise or unwise, no difference, no exemption;
> Above all sacrifice, or hallow'd gift
> Glory he requires, and glory he receives
> Promiscuous from all nations, Jew, or Greek,
> Or barbarous, nor exception hath declar'd;
> From us his foes pronounc'd glory he exacts.
>   (III. 109)

The lines repeat the sarcastic argument of Salmasius, Milton's
opponent in the *Defence of the People of England*, that to the
Cromwellian party 'God may properly be said to be the king of
tyrants, nay, himself the worst of all tyrants' (*Defence*, ii; VII. 129).
The answer is obvious: that with God things are different;
but a doubt lingers.

The argumentative battle is stiff. Satan urges that, all questions of glory set aside, yet Jesus is apparently *destined* to reign:

> But to a kingdom thou art born, ordain'd
> To sit upon thy father David's throne.
>   (III. 152)

David's throne is now in powerful hands that, having won it by
'arms', will not readily let it go. Satan observes that the present
political situation is far from satisfactory. Judaea is a Roman
province; the Temple and the Law are being daily violated.
Does Jesus expect to win his right without a struggle? Such has
never been the way of things. 'Zeal' must seize its opportunity,
for 'duty' demands he 'free' his country from 'heathen servitude'. Surely, if his reign be prophesied, this is the road to fulfilment. Why then delay? – 'What can'st thou better do the
while?' (III. 154–80).

Every phrase recalls burningly Milton's own strenuous political engagements. His various political idealisms reaching out
to a demand for the reign of Christ as an earthly, not only a
spiritual, king, are recalled by Satan's arguments. Through
Satan Milton tries to persuade this adamantine Christ to
assume flesh and blood, to come down from his lonely pinnacle
of irrelevant righteousness, and reign.

The temptations recorded in the New Testament are used by
Milton for a specific purpose. The problems weighed are not
personal but national. What he finds uninteresting is slurred,

but questions of war, sovereignty, government and empire are given extended treatment.

Satan, after admitting that Jesus' village upbringing may put highest enterprise for the moment beyond him, with some poignant remarks, from the viewpoint of Milton's own political experience, on his secluded and provincial home life, offers him a vision of the 'monarchies of the earth' and full initiation into 'regal arts' and 'regal mysteries' (III. 227–50). Satan again gives Milton a fine poetic opportunity, and we are treated to a panorama of the empires of the world and the magnificence of Parthia in martial organization:

> He saw them in their forms of battle rang'd,
> How quick they wheel'd, and flying behind them shot
> Sharp sleet of arrowy showers against the face
> Of their pursuers, and overcame by flight;
> The field all iron cast a gleaming brown,
> Nor wanted clouds of foot, nor on each horn,
> Cuirassiers all in steel for standing fight;
> Chariots or elephants endors'd with towers
> Of archers, nor of labouring pioneers
> A multitude with spades and axes arm'd
> To lay hills plain, fell woods, or valleys fill,
> Or where plain was raise hill, or over-lay
> With bridges rivers proud, as with a yoke;
> Mules after these, camels and dromedaries,
> And waggons fraught with utensils of war.
>   (III. 322)

All prophecy, says Satan, presupposes 'means' to its fulfilment such as David himself certainly employed:

> Prediction still
> In all things, and all men, supposes means,
> Without means us'd, what it predicts revokes.
>   (III. 354)

We might compare the Bishop of Carlisle's words in *Richard II*:

> The means that heaven yields must be embrac'd,
> And not neglected; else, if heaven would,
> And we will not, heaven's offer we refuse,
> The proffer'd means of succour and redress.
>   (III. ii. 29)

Even if Jesus gained the throne by free consent, how, in such a world, with mighty empires on either side, could he hold it?

Satan suggests a political alliance with Rome's great rival, the Parthian empire (III. 357–69). Jesus' answer is fraught with high scorn of world-power and all its 'luggage of war', sign not of 'strength' but of 'weakness' (III. 401–2).

He is taken to a high tower and shown Rome in all its glory and wickedness. Milton revels in description of man's architectural and scientific achievements:

> There the Capitol thou see'st
> Above the rest lifting his stately head
> On the Tarpeian rock, her citadel
> Impregnable, and there Mount Palatine
> The imperial palace, compass huge, and high
> The structure, skill of noblest architects,
> With gilded battlements, conspicuous far,
> Turrets and terraces, and glittering spires.
> Many a fair edifice besides, more like
> Houses of gods (so well I have dispos'd
> My aery microscope) thou may'st behold
> Outside and inside both, pillars and roofs
> Carv'd work, the hand of fam'd artificers
> In cedar, marble, ivory or gold.   (IV. 47)

Satan discourses on the decadence and lust that now possess this gorgeous city:

> With what ease
> Indu'd with regal virtues as thou art,
> Appearing, and beginning noble deeds,
> Might'st thou expel this monster from his throne
> Now made a sty, and in his place ascending
> A victor people free from servile yoke?
> And with my help thou may'st; to me the power
> Is given, and by that right I give it thee.
> Aim therefore at no less than all the world,
> Aim at the highest, without the highest attain'd
> Will be for thee no sitting, or not long
> On David's throne, be prophesied what will.
>   (IV. 97)

Satan's reasonable arguments, based, as in his urging of the alliance with Parthia, upon the principles by which nations inevitably order their affairs, are totally unsuccessful. He is baffled; so are we; and so, I think, was Milton.

Satan's best effort involves literature, and here it is especially hard to accept the rejection judgement as final. Since Jesus seems, says Satan, of a contemplative disposition not addicted to action, his medium must be literature:

> Be famous then
> By wisdom; as thy empire must extend,
> So let extend thy mind o'er all the world
> In knowledge, all things in it comprehend;
> All knowledge is not couch'd in Moses' Law;
> The Pentateuch or what the Prophets wrote,
> The Gentiles also know, and write, and teach
> To admiration, led by nature's light.
>
>   (IV. 221)

This is Milton's own opinion elsewhere: his respect for pagan learning is witnessed by his prose and poetry alike, and we may recall his definition of a good book as 'the precious lifeblood of a master-spirit' in *Areopagitica*. We are given a lengthy disquisition on Greek culture. All this Jesus dismisses with scorn, preferring, if books be involved, the Hebrew prophets to 'all the oratory of Greece and Rome':

> In them is plainest taught, and easiest learnt,
> What makes a nation happy, and keeps it so,
> What ruins kingdoms, and lays cities flat,
> These only with our Law best form a king.
>
>   (IV. 361)

Milton, it must be noted, is thinking in terms not of the individual alone, but of 'nations'. Here he enlists Jesus' argument on the side of national health, but elsewhere his uncompromising rejections are scarcely *politically* tenable. The Biblical message is to Milton truth. But how can it be put into national and international practice? And if it be not practicable, is it not useless? That is our problem.

Satan's patience is exhausted:

> Since neither wealth, nor honour, arms nor arts,
> Kingdoms nor empire pleases thee, nor aught
> By me propos'd in life contemplative,
> Or active, tended on by glory, or fame,
> What dost thou in this world? (IV. 368)

Different as they may be in their outward form, Satan's arguments may yet be set beside such an impassioned plea as this from the *Animadversions*:

> Come forth out of thy royal chambers, O Prince of all the kings of the earth! Put on the visible robes of thy imperial majesty, take up that unlimited sceptre which thy Almighty Father hath bequeathed thee; for now the voice of thy Bride calls thee, and all creatures sigh to be renewed.   (iv; III. i. 148)

Through Satan, Milton might be said to express and half-condemn his own impatient demand for the perfect Christian order. Yet what is the purpose of Christ's incarnation if it sets up an inhuman, impossible, and hence irrelevant ideal – irrelevant anyway to all the affairs of government and national action to which Milton has devoted his life?

Nor is Satan convinced that Jesus is, in any unusual sense, the Son of God:

> To whom the Fiend with fear abash'd replied:
> Be not so sore offended, Son of God;
> Though Sons of God both angels are and men . . .
>   (IV. 195)

Again,

> Then hear, O Son of David, virgin-born;
> For Son of God to me is yet in doubt . . .
>   (IV. 500)

And he next wonders

> In what degree or meaning thou art call'd
> The Son of God, which bears no single sense;
> The Son of God I also am, or was,
> And if I was, I am; relation stands;
> All men are Sons of God; yet thee I thought
> In some respect far higher so declar'd.
>   (IV. 516)

Though orthodox doctrine had rated Christ as wholly divine, Milton himself made a compromise, regarding him as uniquely 'the Son', but firmly distinguishing him from God (*Christian Doctrine*; I. v; XIV. 176–357).

The theological problem is however of less importance here than the balanced opposition of New Testament ethics and international affairs.

I have made emphases for my purpose. There are naturally many passages drawing our sympathies away from Satan. We can, if we like, see Satan as one aspect of Jesus' own meditations in the wilderness, as elements which he acknowledges in himself and rejects, or surmounts. The desired end is an understanding of Christ as a *figure of power* not less but greater than military heroes and emperors, and of a wisdom surpassing pagan imaginations. Milton defines in terms of various rejections a Christ-personality that scarcely attains any positive conviction and is throughout cold, and whose negative, almost nihilistic, attitude contains the germ of the more destructive and culture-scorning actions of Puritanism. *Paradise Regained* is an honest facing of an all but insoluble difficulty: the disparity between spiritual perfection and political action, between high goodness and the necessities of dominion; between the Puritan revival and Renaissance exuberance; between Christian pacifism and the necessities of the sword. The opposing forces are developed to an extreme: in Satan and Christ an irresistible force meets an immovable object. The poem offers no synthesis. It never attains the unity given by those great passages in Milton wherein goodness and action are identified. Nor is there any interaction of opposing elements, as in Shakespearian drama, but rather a stark divergence.

Though he may sometimes define the perfect state as absolute freedom, Milton naturally thinks in terms of discipline. Jesus in *Paradise Regained* is a titanically conceived figure of self-discipline clamping down Satan in himself. Such are the beams on which Milton's life and art are crucified.

So Milton attempts to relate political action to the individualistic gospel of Christ; and, though he fails, the attempt is of unique importance. The dualism of individual and society, of God and Caesar, admits of no easy solution,[1] and yet Christian patriotism should be, somehow, possible. Elsewhere in literature an insoluble personal conflict is redeemed by submission of the whole personality to national service, as at the conclusion to Shakespeare's *Troilus and Cressida* and Tennyson's

---

[1] Byron's life and writing was given to the solution: see my *Lord Byron: Christian Virtues*, VI, 'God and Caesar'; also my *Byron and Shakespeare*, Index of Byronic Themes, 'Politics', 'Religion'. [1967]

Maud. Now Milton treasured for long his conception of Britain as a God-chosen people, a Messiah among the nations, and only in some such terms can the dualism of *Paradise Regained* be resolved. We can, if we like, create from certain scattered suggestions the only terms in which its pained opposition may surmount itself into a sense of purposive and Christlike action, not of an individual, but of a nation; that is, of the people of Britain.

Jesus at the start meditates on his own aspiration to 'victorious deeds' and 'heroic arts', on the possibility of rescuing Israel from the Roman yoke (or Britain from the Prelacy?); and next, in thoughts apt to Britain's destiny, on his desire to quell 'brute violence' and 'proud tyrannic power' over all the earth. He decides however that it is both more 'humane' and more 'heavenly' to 'conquer willing hearts' and to employ 'persuasion' rather than 'fear', or at least to *try this first*, utterly subduing only 'the stubborn' (I. 214–26).

Judgement is pronounced on Rome's emperor in striking phrases:

> I shall, thou say'st, expel
> A brutish monster: what if I withal
> Expel a Devil who first made him such?
> Let his tormentor conscience find him out,
> For him I was not sent, nor yet to free
> That people victor once, now vile and base,
> Deservedly made vassal, who once just,
> Frugal, and mild, and temperate, conquer'd well,
> But govern ill the nations under yoke . . .
>   (IV. 127)

Here Jesus appears no pacifist after all. In his *Christian Doctrine* Milton observes: 'There seems no reason why war should be unlawful now any more than in the time of the Jews: nor is it anywhere forbidden in the New Testament' (II. xvii; XVII. 411). Conquest and empire may, it would seem, be good. It is a question of direction. There are accordingly two ways in which Jesus may conquer the earth: (i) through the steady humanizing mission of a chosen people, and (ii) by a sudden and apocalyptic descent in power, like the onset of the Messiah in *Paradise Lost* armed with God's thunder. Here they are:

> What wise and valiant man would seek to free
> These thus degenerate, by themselves enslav'd,

> Or could of inward slaves make outward free?
> Know therefore when my season comes to sit
> On David's throne, *it shall be like a tree*
> *Spreading and over-shadowing all the earth,*
> Or as a stone that shall to pieces dash
> All monarchies besides throughout the world,
> And of my kingdom there shall be no end:
> Means there shall be to this, but what the means,
> Is not for thee to know, nor me to tell.
>
> (IV. 143)

Though there is no explicit mention of Britain, the speech need not be finally dissociated from Milton's ingrained conviction of her civilizing mission:

> Surrounded by congregated multitudes, I now imagine that, from the columns of Hercules to the Indian Ocean, I behold the nations of the earth recovering that liberty which they so long had lost; and that the people of this island are transporting to other countries a plant of more beneficial qualities, and more noble growth, than that which Triptolemus is reported to have carried from region to region; that they are disseminating the blessings of civilisation and freedom among cities, kingdoms and nations.
>
> (*Second Defence*; VIII. 15)

In our passage from *Paradise Regained*, the only definition of ratified power which the poem contains, the image chosen of a vast tree, is of Biblical origin; but that it is equally applicable to the *organic* growth of Great Britain's empire is shown by Shakespeare's earlier use of it to define England's expanding sovereignty in the national prophecy with which his life-work concludes:

> Wherever the bright sun of heaven shall shine,
> His honour and the greatness of his name
> Shall be, and make new nations. He shall flourish,
> *And, like a mountain cedar, reach his branches*
> *To all the plains about him.* Our children's children
> Shall see this, and bless Heaven.
>
> (*Henry VIII*, V. v. 51)

With this one can compare Milton's phrase in his *Reformation in England* on 'royal dignity, whose towering and steadfast height rests upon the unmovable foundations of justice and heroic virtue' (II; III. i. 47). Only in terms of Milton's conception of his native land as the chosen implement of God on earth have we a satisfying key to the meaning of *Paradise Regained*.

III

Paradise Lost is a poem of unresolved discords, its central conflict lingering after the supposed resolution has been asserted. There is a schematic unity in terms of divine overlordship and reason, but the Satanic energies, though clamped down, are not stilled. Though Milton's phrases are often stiff and his arguments dry with an unconvincing logic, underneath great energies seethe and for those we must watch and listen. Our reading cannot be a pure, artistic receptivity, as with Shakespeare. My usual method of neglecting considerations outside the statement of the art-form itself breaks down. That method I pushed as far as might be in my earlier essay, and its comparative failure argues the necessity of bringing to bear on our interpretation knowledge of Milton's life and work as a whole. Nor does the greatness of the conception, almost too great to be contained and therefore bursting its artistic bounds, stop properly among the problems of Milton's day: it speaks even more insistently to our own. *Paradise Lost* was composed between the political arguments of Milton's prose and the more settled *international* suggestion of his latest poetry; and we must here allow ourselves an interpretative freedom similar to, but even wider than, that which has already proved helpful in inspection of *Samson Agonistes* and *Paradise Regained*. That reference of the Miltonic problem to the future of Great Britain which we used to resolve the difficulty of *Paradise Regained* is of yet greater help among the complexities of *Paradise Lost*. Only so can its 'hateful siege of contraries' (IX. 121) be dispelled.

We must first observe two insistent emphases on (i) war and (ii) royalty.

Milton's poetry is less naturalistic than Shakespeare's. He is fond of human artefacts: buildings, machinery, scientific inventions. His poetic genuis is mathematical and his lines laden with scientific terms. Metals predominate and harsh clangours alternate with dulcet melodies in accompaniment of his epic story. His word-music is nasal, his poetic sounds brazen-throated, like a trumpet. Vast noises, often echoing as in a

great cavern or palatial hall, are frequent. There is an insistent
prepossession with violent, and often mechanically apprehended,
war.

Here are some samples. The 'din of war' clashes on 'sounding
shields' (I. 668); 'two black clouds' are imaged meeting 'with
Heaven's artillery fraught' (II. 714); Bellona, goddess of war, is
seen 'with all her battering engines' directed against 'some
capital city' (II. 923); Heaven is equipped with

> Celestial armoury, shields, helms, and spears
> Hung high with diamond flaming, and with gold.
>   (IV. 553)

War's more mechanic and explosive qualities fascinate Milton:

> Others to a city strong
> Lay siege, encamp'd; by battery, scale, and mine,
> Assaulting; others from the wall defend
> With dart and javelin, stones and sulphurous fire;
> On each hand slaughter and gigantic deeds.
>   (XI. 651)

Gun-powder is vivid:

> As when a spark
> Lights on a heap of nitrous powder, laid
> Fit for the tun some magazine to store
> Against a rumour'd war, the smutty grain
> With sudden blaze diffus'd, inflames the air.
>   (IV. 814)

Aerial warfare drops its approaching shadow over his page:

> As when to warn proud cities war appears
> Wag'd in the troubled sky, and armies rush
> To battle in the clouds, before each van
> Prick forth the aery knights, and couch their spears
> Till thickest legions close . . .   (II. 533)

The 'horrid confusion' and 'infernal noise' of mountains meeting
in mid-air in the Heavenly war (VI. 664–70) prefigure our own,
contemporary, horrors. Though Milton claims to pass beyond
the usual themes of heroic verse, considering himself 'not sedu-
lous by nature to indite wars', preferring the 'better fortitude
of patience and heroic martyrdom' to the 'long and tedious
havoc' of imaginary knights, and though he definitely asserts

himself to be 'nor skilled nor studious' in this sort of writing (IX. 25-47), the claim cannot, without severe qualifications, be allowed. He remains our greatest poet of warfare, and 'the brazen throat of war' (XI. 709) is, poetically, his delight.

Power surges in Milton. His encased, metallic cast of thought, the ironside battalions of his imagery, are the measure of the tumultuous energies to be controlled. War is power-in-action, and it is hard to imagine active power without conflict; but power accomplished and at rest will be imaged in royalistic symbols, and on these the emphasis is even heavier.

The poem is richly inlaid with splendours of gold, jewels, palaces and so on, and its every person is called, at one time or other, a king.

God is 'monarch in Heaven' (I. 638), 'Heaven's awful monarch' (IV. 960), 'eternal king' (III. 374), 'Heaven's almighty king' (X. 387), and the archangel Michael is invested with 'majesty' (XI. 232). The conception works independently of ethical distinctions: Satan after his fall is also a great 'prince' (I. 128), throned above his peers in 'royal state' (II. i), while his companion Moloch is a 'sceptred king' (II. 43), Death (personified) a king (II. 698) with a 'kingly crown' (II. 673), Night (personified) has a 'sceptre' (II. 1002), the fallen angels are 'princely dignities' who recently 'sat on thrones' (I. 359), and Hell itself an 'infernal empire' (X. 389). Adam and Eve enjoy 'naked majesty' (IV. 290) and Eve 'virgin majesty' (IX. 270). Light is 'sovereign' (III. 22). A repeated line is

Thrones, Dominations, Princedoms, Virtues, Powers,

as at X. 460. The Heavenly array is given resplendent description:

The empyreal host
Of angels by imperial summons call'd,
Innumerable before the Almighty's Throne
Forthwith from all the ends of Heaven appear'd
Under their hierarchs in orders bright;
Ten thousand thousand ensigns high advanc'd,
Standards, and gonfalons twixt van and rear
Stream in the air, and for distinction serve
Of hierarchies, of orders, and degrees;
Or in their glittering tissues bear imblaz'd
Holy memorials, acts of zeal and love
Recorded eminent.   (v. 583)

The poem presents a universe of princely powers, at peace or contending, hierarchies in order or disorder. It works up to a great passage (XI. 381–411) on the kingdoms of the world, the high-sounding proper names ranging from Cambalu and Samarkand to El Dorado and Peru. The ubiquitous sense of power and sovereignty relates to Milton's feeling for the innate dignity and aristocracy of the individual; though not, I think, as with Shakespeare, any individual whatsoever, but of any individual worth Milton's serious attention; an important reservation. These thick inlaid and weighty impressions may therefore be regarded as poetic asseverations of our main argument, asserting as they do if regarded in the context of Milton's life-work, that denial of any authoritative centre will always correspond precisely for good or ill to a new perpetuation, indeed reduplication, of the sovereign principle. Milton's imagery, quite apart from the story of *Paradise Lost*, is a living witness that a true democracy is only attainable in so far as it includes a widespread nobility and ever-present royalty, each his own soul-lord and hence in direct contact with the sovereign principle throughout Heaven and Earth.

We shall concern ourselves primarily with the clashing opposition of Satan and Messiah. Adam and Eve, whose fortunes I have already (pp. 29–32) reviewed, are here less directly relevant. Neither they, nor God himself, are energetic, power-carrying figures, as are Satan and Messiah, whose opposition is an eternal opposition, like that in *Paradise Regained*, only more epically and dramatically convincing. Of this opposition the civil conflict of Milton's day and even more directly our own World War, are reflections; and the relations I am to point are not arbitrary but intrinsic.

The surface meaning of *Paradise Lost* appears to suffer from the unnecessary grandeur of Satan.[1] Though a defeated rebel against God's omnipotence, he remains impressive:

> He above the rest
> In shape and gesture proudly eminent
> Stood like a tower; his form had yet not lost
> All her original brightness . . .   (I. 589)

---

[1] Since these words were written Milton's Satan has been revealingly studied by R. J. Zwi Werblowsky in *Lucifer and Prometheus* (1952). [1967]

His resolution in defeat has received general acclamation. No military imagination can fail to admire something in this 'dread' (1. 589) or 'great' (1. 358) 'commander', as we watch him inspecting his troops:

> Advanc'd in view they stand, a horrid front
> Of dreadful length and dazzling arms, in guise
> Of warriors old with order'd spear and shield,
> Awaiting what command their mighty chief
> Had to impose: he through the armed files
> Darts his experienc'd eye, and soon traverse
> The whole battalion views, their order due,
> Their visages and stature as of gods:
> Their number last he sums. And now his heart
> Distends with pride, and hardening in his strength
> Glories: for never since created man,
> Met such embodied force.   (1. 563)

He is as a Cromwell casting an 'experienced eye' over his ironside warriors. The comparison further complicates our understanding, for Satan is not merely dramatically impressive: his cause is, pretty nearly, Milton's.

Remembering how closely Samson's endurance of disaster reflects Milton's under the Restoration, we can scarcely deny a similar correspondence while listening to Satan:

> What though the field be lost?
> All is not lost; the unconquerable will,
> And study of revenge, immortal hate,
> And courage never to submit or yield:
> And what is else not to be overcome?
> That glory never shall his wrath or might
> Extort from me. To bow and sue for grace
> With suppliant knee, and deify his power
> Who from the terror of this arm so late
> Doubted his Empire, that were low indeed,
> That were an ignominy and shame beneath
> This downfall.   (1. 105)

The correspondence is exact: Milton likewise refused an easy compliance with the new regime. The Stuarts had known their 'empire' threatened recently by revolution. Satan, like Milton, bears a mind 'not to be changed by place or time':

> The mind is its own place, and in itself
> Can make a Heaven of Hell, a Hell of Heaven.

> What matter where, if I be still the same,
> And what I should be, all but less then he
> Whom thunder hath made greater? Here at least
> We shall be free: th' Almighty hath not built
> Here for his envy, will not drive us hence:
> Here we may reign secure, and in my choice
> To reign is worth ambition though in Hell:
> Better to reign in Hell, then serve in Heaven.
>   (I. 254)

Notice how closely in Milton freedom involves sovereignty. Freedom *is* self-discipline and therefore sovereignty. They cannot be contrasted, though one kind of sovereignty may be preferred to another.

Satan has revolted from God, and the analogy to Milton's life is driven home by the emphasis on God's tyrannic rule. We are moreover made aware of a jarring, discordant split, a fracture leaving us with God on the one side as an abstract, reasoning, theological voice and Satan, a typically Renaissance figure, on the other as a very human, flesh-and-blood revolutionary, in which unhappy divergence neither is his true self. The related conceptions of sovereignty and liberty are felt as tugging apart, and while this severance persists both suffer.

The broken unity is reinstated in Christian theology by a superpersonal Trinity of Beings; and yet, in *Paradise Lost* it is the begetting and enthroning of Messiah that starts the trouble. In Heaven the process is the exact opposite of what is supposed to happen later on Earth, but in both instances the Son plays a similarly central part. Satan's action is understandable. After an age of innocent and happy existence the Heavenly host suddenly has this sprung on them:

> Hear all ye Angels, progeny of Light,
> Thrones, Dominations, Princedoms, Virtues, Powers,
> Hear my decree, which unrevok'd shall stand.
> This day I have begot whom I declare
> My only Son, and on this holy hill
> Him have anointed, whom ye now behold
> At my right hand; your head I him appoint;
> And by my self have sworn to him shall bow

All knees in Heaven and shall confess him Lord:
Under his great vice-gerent reign abide
United as one individual soul
For ever happy: him who disobeys
Me disobeys, breaks union, and that day,
Cast out from God and blessed vision, falls
Into utter darkness, deep engulf'd, his place
Ordain'd without redemption, without end.

(v. 600)

Dissension had hitherto been unknown, with harpings and praise a universally enjoyed routine. Why then this sudden need for more 'bowing of knees' and the concluding threat? It is almost a challenge, where nothing but God's courteous consideration for his faultless subjects was needed. Satan bridles inwardly, as would Milton, and plots revolution.

Satan's arguments are advanced in reasonable terms. He does not object to 'orders and degrees' (such as those of Ulysses' speech in *Troilus and Cressida*), acknowledging that these and true freedom are interdependent, but objects to a slur on his own royalty, by the establishing of Messiah as an all-eclipsing king, different in kind rather than degree. God has introduced 'law' into a free, yet not undisciplined, society; he has himself *forced* the fall, not of man, but of angels. 'Less power and splendour' Satan could accept, but demands equality in freedom:

Will ye submit your necks, and choose to bend
The supple knee? ye will not, if I trust
To know ye right, or if ye know your selves
Natives and sons of Heaven possess'd before
By none, and if not equal all, yet free,
Equally free; for orders and degrees
Jar not with liberty, but well consist.
Who can in reason then or right assume
Monarchy over such as live by right
His equals, if in power and splendour less,
In freedom equal? or can introduce
Law and edict on us, who without law
Err not, much less for this to be our Lord,
And look for adoration to th' abuse
Of those imperial titles which assert
Our being ordain'd to govern, not to serve?

(v. 784)

The statement needs no apology, but the opposing argument of Abdiel must be compared. After the contention that God's ordinance cannot be questioned, since here the usual terms of political discussion do not apply, Abdiel continues:

> But to grant it thee unjust,
> That equal over equals monarch reign:
> Thy self though great and glorious dost thou count,
> Or all angelic nature join'd in one,
> Equal to Him begotten Son? – by whom
> As by his Word the mighty Father made
> All things, ev'n thee, and all the spirits of Heaven
> By him created in their bright degrees,
> Crown'd them with glory, and to their glory nam'd
> Thrones, Dominations, Princedoms, Virtues, Powers,
> Essential Powers, nor by his reign obscur'd,
> But more illustrious made, since he the head
> One of our number thus reduc'd becomes,
> His laws our laws, all honour to him done
> Returns our own.   (v. 828)

That is, though Messiah be our superior, his honour and his royalty are now ours: we can derive honour from his office. All hinges on the precise nature of Messiah's kingship; and our difficulty can be resolved by suggesting that whereas Satan sees Messiah as an absolute and arbitrary monarch, Abdiel, more correctly in view of the part he plays elsewhere in *Paradise Lost*, sees him rather as a *constitutional* sovereign symbolizing and sharing out the divine purpose or creative principle inherent in society; and, we may add, finally summing and redistributing the various personal royalties, 'essential powers', of his people. Whether this was God's original idea, or only to be found in Messiah's own eminently tactful understanding, very apparent in his speeches, may be questioned: certainly God's introductory words justified the Satanic view. Milton may here be felt groping towards a solution of his earlier paradoxes.

We are again reminded of Shakespeare's *Julius Caesar*. Before his assassination Caesar is an arbitrary tyrant whose verbose asseverations fail to hide an inward weakness, while the conspirators enlist our sympathy without failing to incur guilt. After the assassination, in the words of Antony, Caesar exists in a new, resurrected and royal, strength. These complexities

I have discussed in *The Imperial Theme*. *Richard II* shows a similar development. The difference is that between any actualization of kingship and the royal essence: by slaying the man the revolutionary finds that he has only fertilized the essence, which rises again invulnerable and invincible, since authority is a universal principle deriving from the source and author of creation, God. Milton actualizes God as an even more verbose and intolerable person than Shakespeare's Caesar, yet this does not excuse Satan's crime. In the history of England, the solution comes by way of a new conception of constitutional royalty; in *Julius Caesar* by the impassioned speeches of Antony and the 'spirit of Caesar' (III. i. 270; v. iii. 95; v. v. 17–19) awake after death; and in *Paradise Lost* by the splendour of the triumphant Messiah. In *Paradise Lost* Milton is dealing with eternal political realities, and to complain, as does Walter Raleigh (*Milton*, 128), that the basis of his divine cosmology is political is perhaps less valuable than to complain that the outward form of his political epic is religious. To Milton there is no final distinction between politics and religion: each involves the other.

The equivalence of Satan to the Puritan party is close. His own government in Hell is parliamentary, with full voice allowed to other leaders in Book II, where all express their opinions at length. 'Just right' and Heaven's 'laws' first constituted Satan their ruler, but next 'free choice' and his own merit in council and war have made his rule one of 'consent', and he takes pride in knowledge that disaster has made his position of all the most dangerous and therefore least enviable, himself standing as a 'bulwark' to protect his followers (II. 18–30). When occasion demands, he assumes further risk:

> Wherefore do I assume
> These royalties, and not refuse to reign,
> Refusing to accept as great a share
> Of hazard as of honour, due alike
> To him who reigns, and so much to him due
> Of hazard more, as he above the rest
> High honour'd sits?   (II. 450)

No remarks of Milton to remind us that Satan remains Satan can destroy these noble significances. The society of fallen angels

is one of 'firm concord' (II. 497) where that central characteristic which Milton in his plea for a Free Commonwealth in-
sisted should be basic to Christian government is superbly
realized: for here he who aspires to rule serves. God's reign in
Paradise Lost is one of Law, but the Satanic order one of free
'consent'. Satan's sense of innate worth is not ill-judged. He *has*
nearly all the finer human qualities, including sympathy for his
followers (I. 605-6) and bravery (II. 417-29). He has, too, a
tragic and Byronic (p. 194 below) dignity:

> . . . his face
> Deep scars of thunder had intrench'd, and care
> Sat on his faded cheek.   (I. 600)

A similar dignity is accorded Beelzebub in a passage further
emphasizing the human and political analogy:

> Which when Beelzebub perceiv'd, than whom,
> Satan except, none higher sat, with grave
> Aspect he rose, and in his rising seem'd
> A pillar of state; deep on his front engraven
> Deliberation sat and public care;
> And princely counsel in his face yet shone,
> Majestic though in ruin: sage he stood
> With Atlantean shoulders fit to bear
> The weight of mightiest monarchies; his look
> Drew audience and attention still as night
> Or summer's noon-tide air, while thus he spake.
> (II. 299)

Hell is peopled by beings of tragic wisdom and masterful resolve.

There is, however, another side. The fallen angels incorporate
also many of Milton's obvious aversions. All that horror of
paganism so vigorous in the anti-prelatical pamphlets may be
considered as included in this assembly of Satan, Beelzebub,
Moloch, Belial and the rest. Satan's glory is an especially pagan
glory:

> High on a throne of royal state, which far
> Outshone the wealth of Ormus and of Ind,
> Or where the gorgeous East with richest hand
> Showers on her kings barbaric pearl and gold,
> Satan exalted sat, by merit rais'd
> To that bad eminence.   (II. 1)

This paganism Milton's imagination fuses with certain striking characteristics of the Puritan party and the heroic but losing battle of his own political life-work. In such matters failure is, pretty nearly, sin, as Byron knew (*Marino Faliero*, III. i. 67–80), however worthy the intention; and we may remember how the ghost of Caesar, visiting Shakespeare's Brutus, introduces himself as 'Thy evil spirit' (IV. iii. 281). The analogy would be scarcely present in Milton's conscious thinking, if only since his judgement on prelates and tyrants was based on firm conviction that they were themselves disturbers of an existing harmony: tyranny in the lesser context becomes rebellion in the greater. Even so the correspondences are too telling to be dismissed. Milton as a poet is telling us more about himself and his life's work than he can be supposed as a man to have understood. He had in his prose 'the use' only of his 'left hand' (*Reason of Church Government*, II. Intro.; III. i. 235); that is, of deliberated and conscious thinking. Poetry, like royalty, exists in a dimension transcending, while including, political thought. The revolution, though an advance on Stuart absolutism, was nevertheless sinful in its insult to essential royalty – the precise nature of the insult being poetically defined throughout the great passages of Shakespeare's *Richard II* – and the balance was not for many years, indeed is not yet, restored, awaiting some richer understanding and development.

Of this discrepancy Milton's Satan is a symptom. He is a composite of both political parties in so far as they have lost contact with God. All is now levelled under a single condemnation. Milton has no doubt that Satan and his crowd deserve their fate, but they are not exactly 'devils'; they are great men; it is our own fallen world that Milton depicts. Satan's followers in Hell are shown rearing magnificent buildings, digging for gold, engaging in Hellenic games, song, dance and philosophic and even theological discussion. Man and his total culture are condemned in the manner of *Paradise Regained*, rather as Shakespeare dismissed Renaissance civilization in *Timon of Athens* and Tolstoy grew to scorn the noblest works, including Shakespeare. The Satanic party are mankind in its fruitless struggles; in them Puritan revolution and Episcopal idolatry, Cromwellian force and Stuart finery (suggested at I. 497–502), all are contained.

Or, looking to our own European War, they include the pagan virility of our foes and the democratic and parliamentary principles of our own cause. All this is Satan; and all are condemned.

Satan's root sin is 'pride':

> his pride
> Had cast him out from Heaven, with all his host
> Of rebel angels, by whose aid aspiring
> To set himself in glory above his peers,
> He trusted to have equal'd the most high,
> If he oppos'd; and with ambitious aim
> Against the Throne and Monarchy of God
> Rais'd impious war in Heaven and battle proud
> With vain attempt.   (I. 36)

He imitates divinity itself:

> High in the midst exalted as a God
> The apostate in his sun-bright chariot sat
> Idol of majesty divine, enclos'd
> With flaming cherubim and golden shields.
>   (VI. 99)

Elsewhere he has a 'royal seat' on a 'far-blazing' mount (V.753) and is a 'mighty paramount', 'Hell's dread emperor', enjoying 'pomp supreme' and 'God-like imitated state' (II. 508–11). In him a barbaric will to power burns fiercely, in which he resembles both Milton and his opponents as Milton saw them, the bishops and the Stuart tyranny; indeed, the whole unhappy conflict in its negative aspect. We are reminded of Shakespeare's last play, *Henry VIII*, where man's nobility and pride, in Buckingham, Wolsey and Queen Katharine, are set against the humility of Cranmer and subordinated to a sense of (i) the throne and (ii) divine grace. Wolsey at his fall compares himself to the ruined angels:

> Mark but my fall, and that that ruin'd me.
> Cromwell, I charge thee, fling away ambition;
> By that sin fell the angels; how shall man then,
> The image of his Maker, hope to win by it?
>   (III. ii. 440)

Now, just as these great persons to Shakespeare's final judgement exist properly only in vassalage to the Crown and thence to God, so Satan and his followers sin through their will to self-determination. They cry for liberty: but liberty without the higher allegiance is a barren cry. They are good democrats: but *democracy is not enough*. They are powerful: but they fall by a greater power.

The Satanic party is mankind without Christ, and God is human theology in miserable abstraction; as Pope saw, a 'school divine' (*Imitations of Horace*, 'To Augustus', 102). Neither is satisfying and their opposition is worse.

In his *Reason and Beauty in the Poetic Mind* (1933; 92) Charles Williams complained

> that the despair of Satan and the pathos of Adam and Eve are regarded as the important achievements of Milton's imagination, whereas in fact it is the transcending of that despair and pathos which is his sublimity.

I shall next develop, in my own, different fashion, this statement. Milton is to advance beyond all normal dramatic or epic categories. His poem after those early scenes in Hell must develop a transcendence *of at least equal power and conviction*, or its failure results. In this Milton succeeds, but the exact nature of his success has not received attention.

Transcendence has two aspects: it may be regarded as apocalyptic and outside time or as a long-distance futurity within the temporal succession. When a prophet announces the establishment of the Kingdom of Heaven, this may mean a sudden dispersal, as a cloud puffed away by wind, of all earthly realities whatsoever to reveal some greater structure; or it may mean a long and travailing process by which history is gradually transmuted into heavenly likeness. Both ideas are contained in a key-passage of *Paradise Regained* (p. 128). Now, since the main difficulty in *Paradise Lost* derives from the human warmth and political contemporaneity of the Satanic persons, we may next approach Milton's triumphant Messiah through a frank willingness to see in him the developing future of mankind, and especially of our own nation, so often already regarded by him as a Messiah-nation. The daring equation of the Messiah with Great Britain to which we were forced in *Paradise Regained* is now to be further developed. In this process a willingness to make transitions from Milton's poem to the great struggle of our own time will be of assistance, and I ask that the reader holds his critical judgement in reserve until the argument is concluded. My attempt is not irrational. In all great literature there is evidence of what Shakespeare in Sonnet 107 called 'the prophetic soul of the wide world dreaming on things to come', and it would be strange if Milton's greatest poem did not foreshadow the archetypal conflict in which Great Britain is today engaged.

We cannot use the World War to assist our understanding without some preliminary agreement as to its nature. I see Great Britain in the Renaissance era in which we live as having assumed the guiding office of the medieval Church. One system broke, and, church authority falling to a purely spiritual and personal level, political energies were undisciplined. International affairs are today pagan. Nevertheless Great Britain, without any conscious recognition, outside her greater poets, of this destiny, has on the whole laboured to curb lust for power and tyrannic ambition; she has on the whole maintained in the secular order that respect for law and the gentler and more chivalrous values which belong to the traditions of Christendom. There has been continual tension, as Tennyson in his three dramas realized, between the British conscience and Machiavellian Europe. Britain and her Empire are therefore uniquely placed as the bearers of a great and civilizing mission. This trust has rarely been acknowledged by her official spokesmen; its responsibilities have been feared and shirked; and even today, so great is the split between energies and religion that the claiming of a religious sanction for any action of far-reaching importance appears variously blasphemous or ridiculous. Even so, we may glimpse an unfurling design towards a world-order in whose creation Great Britain has for long played, and is again today playing, a central part.

That world-order is not yet established, but, daring as the statement must sound, I ask that we accept the following as a preliminary proposition: that on Great Britain and her succession of poet-prophets the Providential choice has elected to lay some great, vice-gerent, to use Milton's habitual phrase, responsibility, indeed sovereignty, under God; not unlike that wherewith the Son was installed in the speech which so infuriated Satan. This is no static proposition, but one utterly dependent on a deeper recognition and acceptance by Britain of the attendant duties than she has hitherto shown.

Revolution against an existing order requires energy. That energy was in Cromwell's army and characterizes Satan. To twentieth-century Germany it has seemed, rightly or wrongly, that a world-order existed, or was in process of becoming, in which Great Britain dominated in wealth and power; which was probably a truer reading of the world-situation than most British thinkers would have admitted. Germany has also tended to revolt from that mind-structure of medieval Christianity which Britain has tended to preserve. Mystical philosophers from Luther to Nietzsche have reacted with a superb energy against the static and conceptualized culture of the European tradition: in them burn the Renaissance fires from which the upspring of German militarism and will to domination is not to be finally dissociated.[1] Perhaps the best of all definitions of the Renaissance and the Medieval-Christian in clashing discord is offered by Marlowe's plays, which point unmistakably to Nazi Germany. *Tamburlaine*, with its hero's meteoric rise, Napoleonic sense of cosmic backing and strength of purpose melting opposition, all accompanied by a bullying and sadistic cruelty, enjoys in line after line the inmost thrill of a Hitler's predatory advance. *Doctor Faustus* shows Faustus *reborn* to new youth as a personification of the scientific, aesthetic and militaristic power-quests of the Renaissance in vivid conflict with medieval Christianity, rising to a shattering conclusion in which Christ's victory functions in the verse precisely as does Messiah's onset in the war of *Paradise Lost*. The Germanic source of the Faust-legend is significant. *The Jew of Malta* is toned, as *The Merchant of Venice* is not, to suit the Jew-baiting we have watched on the continent of Europe. The Marlovian conflict is, as I have elsewhere (pp. 66–9) shown, closely Miltonic, and the vivid correspondence of Marlowe's work to Nazi Germany suggests a line of thought valuable in our analysis of *Paradise Lost*. There is only one main conflict to focus: the upthrust and impingement of a Renaissance power-will – in her *Christopher Marlowe* Una Ellis-Fermor has well shown the importance of Machiavelli to Marlowe, who

---

[1] The thoughts of this paragraph are expanded throughout my study *Christ and Nietzsche* (1948), which I hope may in due course be reprinted.

F

introduces him to speak a prologue – against a Christian structure. This structure Great Britain is today defending. The
religious, yet still military, form of the Cromwellian revolution
was part of that defence; for there the revolutionary energy, so
often involved in 'sin' and 'evil' – a thought which bears on the
Cromwellian affinities of Satan – arose in alliance with full conviction of Biblical support. From this unique alinement much
of Great Britain's later authority developed.

Satan's sense of injustice under the enthronement of Messiah
as God's vice-gerent reflects Germany's view of Great Britain's
ascendancy. The danger to God's 'empire' closely resembles
that to ours (v. 718–29). Supposing we consider Satan after his
fall with 'dauntless courage' and 'considerate pride waiting
revenge' (I. 603) to correspond to Germany after the last war,
we have some attractive analogies. Satan, like Hitler, is wor-
shipped 'as a god' (II. 478). The concourse in the infernal
regions of fallen angels plotting revenge is not unlike a National-
Socialist gathering. In this dark place of 'fiery waves' (I. 184)
and 'burning marl' (I. 296)

> void of light
> Save what the glimmering of these livid flames
> Casts pale and dreadful,   (I. 181)

Satan's legions attend their leader like hordes of black-uniformed
Nazis gathered in their thousands by the illumination of inter-
lacing searchlights to hear Hitler speak at Nuremberg. The cries
of 'Sieg Heil!' thundering heroic resolution have their counterpart
in *Paradise Lost*. Satan, hardly able, like Nazi Germany, to believe
in his army's defeat and convinced that they must swiftly regain
their rightful place, has concluded a long speech (I. 622–62) with

> Peace is despair'd,
> For who can think submission! War then, war
> Open or understood must be resolv'd.
>   (I. 660)

And this is followed by

> He spake: and to confirm his words, out-flew
> Millions of flaming swords, drawn from the thighs
> Of mighty cherubim; the sudden blaze
> Far round illumin'd Hell: highly they rag'd

Against the Highest, and fierce with grasped arms
Clash'd on their sounding shields the din of war,
Hurling defiance toward the vault of Heaven.
(1. 663)

Remembering Satan's 'mighty standard' and 'imperial ensign'
streaming 'like a meteor' gold-emblazoned in a passage already
(p. 64) quoted, followed by a 'shout that tore Hell's concave'
and the further raising in the 'gloom' of 'ten thousand banners'
with 'orient colours' (1. 531–46), we can watch a modern poet,
writing of modern Europe, draw automatically on both Milton's
Paradise Lost and reports of the Nuremberg rally. I quote from
Francis Berry's poem *Spain, 1939: from Devon:*[1]

> In you lives a Fascist, and a Christ.
> Flares up the Fascist, when you thrill at midnight
> Rumble of artillery, or at harangue
> Conjuring pagan shouts in glimmering bannerdom . . .

How many a German, in the inter-war period, burning with a
sense of Providential injustice and cramped national energy,
must have endured Moloch's impassioned sense of constriction:

> No, let us rather choose
> Arm'd with Hell flames and fury all at once
> O'er Heaven's high towers to force resistless way,
> Turning our tortures into horrid arms
> Against the torturer. (11. 60)

So they meditate on invasion of Heaven, as Germany, at this
hour, plans conquest of Britain:

> The towers of Heaven are fill'd
> With armed watch, that render all access
> Impregnable; oft on the bordering deep
> Encamp their legions, or with obscure wing
> Scout far and wide into the realm of night,
> Scorning surprise. (11. 129)

Satan's various leaders, the violent Moloch, crafty Belial,
Mammon and Beelzebub, have rough counterparts in Hitler's
following.[2]

[1] First published in *The Wind and the Rain* for Spring, 1942, and now included in
his collection *The Galloping Centaur*, 1952. See my Prefatory Notes, above. [1967]
[2] God is envisaged as defending an ancient 'empire' against 'a foe' (i.e. Satan)
throned in 'the spacious North' (*Paradise Lost*, v. 723; and see I. 351). The geography

Two reservations are necessary. Admiration of Satan or Hitler must not preclude remembrance of the horrors involved. Milton deliberately equates his fallen angels with the evil practices of paganism, seeing Moloch as a

> horrid king besmear'd with blood
> Of human sacrifice and parents' tears.
>
> (I. 392)

So, too, the Hitlerian gospel – if the term be allowed – includes an appeal to the more ruthless, cruel instincts of man. Satan's 'eye' is likewise 'cruel' (I. 604). The affinity of Hitler's regime to ancient paganisms has been driven home in H. G. Baynes's *Germany Possessed*. 'It is undeniable', writes Dr Baynes, 'that the present division in Europe has to do with the pagan-Christian conflict within the soul of Christendom' (II. 75). Again:

> Hitler is proud of the title anti-Christ, and I doubt whether this is mere vanity on his part. He stands for criminality as a necessary implement of power, while the source of his inspiration is, admittedly, a daemonic pagan god. (III. 111)

Such statements wrong no one: Hitler himself, according to his own remarks as given in Herman Rauschning's *Hitler Speaks*, would not repudiate them.

Our sense of ethical superiority however must not obstruct our recognition of some authentic power both in Milton's Satan and in Nazi Germany; and goodness without power is quite as dangerous and far less interesting than power in dissociation from goodness. The Pharisaical cast of our own national self-righteousness, so different from the Cromwellian integrity, cannot pronounce an easy judgement. What to Satan seem 'deeds' of 'glory' are no whit disturbed by Michael's 'imperious' *ideas* of moral superiority (VI. 281–95). We must focus the power-thrust as an element in existence, shared variously by Cromwell and by Hitler. Within the Renaissance world this thrust is a necessary challenge. All new knowledge, says Nietzsche, has grown up with an evil conscience (*Thus Spake Zarathustra*, 56); certainly all revolution, in its degree, partakes of evil. There is

---

of the Heavenly war may be to this extent related both to Milton's proposed Arthurian epic (p. 71 above, 'Saxon') and to our own experience in the Second World War. [1967]

likely to be a day in the life of every great innovator on which
he must say 'Evil, be thou my good' (*Paradise Lost*, IV. 110); and
the dividing line between creative and destructive energy,
though often recognizable, is less readily defined. Now the
Cromwellian, Puritanical direction of the British people has
grown rigid; its intellectual armour is rusted; it has itself become
the established order of Great Britain, of Western civilization.
It has grown verbose as Milton's God. In Germany those paganisms which Milton found in the established Church and the
Stuart regime are, in their turn and in extreme form, in revolt
against the Puritanical tradition. Hitler is a grand-scale revolutionary, one, to adapt Dryden's line on Shaftesbury in *Absalom
and Achitophel*, 'resolv'd to ruin or to rule the state'; in which
he resembles Milton's Satan, the eternal prototype of revolution.

Let us pass to Milton's account later in his poem, which has
its own progressive logic independent of the supposed sequence
of events, of the war in Heaven. We have a conflict of an army
certain of their rectitude and divine backing with Michael, a
St George figure, at its head against Satan as protagonist of
pagan revolt. Our present world-conflict is, from the normal
British view, similar. Milton's description is magnificent:

> Now storming fury rose
> And clamour such as heard in Heaven till now
> Was never, arms on armour clashing bray'd
> Horrible discord, and the madding wheels
> Of brazen chariots rag'd; dire was the noise
> Of conflict; over head the dismal hiss
> Of fiery darts in flaming volleys flew,
> And flying vaulted either host with fire.
>
> (VI. 207)

The fight progresses with a see-saw action in 'even scale' (VI.
245). The good angels trust in God, the bad show skill in
mechanical warfare; whereupon the former answer by using
hills as missiles, a nature-symbolism pointing on to the mountains of the elemental war, which has also a contrast of mine-
folk and water to be compared with the Miltonic opposition,
in Goethe's *Faust* (discussed in *The Christian Renaissance*, 1962;
111). These symbolisms suggest an alliance of good and nature
against the will-to-power and explosives. The gunpowder is

Satan's idea, and his followers mingle 'sulphurous and nitrous foam', using 'subtle art' to reduce it to 'blackest grain' (VI. 512–15). The foe advances 'in hollow cube training his devilish enginry' (VI. 552). Here is the climax:

> Immediate in a flame,
> But soon obscur'd with smoke, all Heaven appear'd,
> From those deep-throated engines belch'd, whose roar
> Embowell'd with outrageous noise the air,
> And all her entrails tore, disgorging foul
> Their devilish glut, chain'd thunderbolts and hail
> Of iron globes, which on the victor host
> Level'd, with such impetuous fury smote,
> That whom they hit, none on their feet might stand,
> Though standing else as rocks, but down they fell
> By thousands, angel on arch-angel roll'd.
>
> (VI. 584)

The good angels' cause avails them nothing. Does strength depend not at all on virtue (VI. 114–26)? The rebel host sardonically enjoy their discomfiture; whereupon the good angels start hurling mountains.

This is the state of the battle before the advent of Messiah. It may, according to my scheme, be allowed to correspond roughly to our present world-conflict at the moment of writing (May 1941); a conflict of accepted good, trust in God, and certain natural alliances, against aspiring will-to-power and cunning use of mechanized resource. The Son of God now appears. The Son, or Messiah, is conceived as, normally, a figure of 'compassion' (III. 141), whose especial function is to blend, though the poem as a whole does not, mercy and justice (III. 407; X. 59), and to establish 'peace' between man and God (XI. 38). He is, more vividly than anyone else, a king. Angels must acknowledge his 'regal sceptre' (V. 813); he is 'our king, the great Messiah' (V. 687), a 'king anointed' (V. 661). That last phrase well defines his kingship. God, Satan, Adam, and Eve – and pretty nearly everyone else – possess either innate or actual sovereignty of some kind: God is an oriental despot, Satan a barbaric chieftain. But Messiah is more gentlemanly, more truly chivalrous, a person of mild disposition deliberately *made* king, and willingly though never desirously undertaking the sacred responsibility. His delicacy of perception is in advance of his Father's, and his rejection by the magnificent and power-impregnated Satan understandable: to Satan he must appear, as he comes near to appearing in *Paradise Regained*, an intolerable and usurping weakling. He reigns as an 'anointed' king, not in his own right but in his Father's, being 'heir' of God's 'might' (v. 717). Such is 'his great vice-gerent reign' (v. 609). And yet it is because 'love' in him predominates over 'glory' that he is deliberately exalted as 'anointed universal king' above 'thrones', 'princedoms', 'powers', and 'dominions' (III. 311–20). He is an incarnation of that royalty blending justice and mercy defined in Portia's speech in *The Merchant of Venice*.[1] He is also an especially *constitutional monarch* as an impersonal carrier of God's grace into the domain of secular action. He is God's 'word' (VII. 163), the creative principle. To him the earthly creation was delegated, and for it he went forth 'girt with omnipotence', 'with radiance crown'd of majesty divine', with 'sapience and love', and round his chariot numberless attendants, 'cherub and seraph, potentates and thrones', 'virtues, winged spirits, and chariots wing'd' (VII. 192–9). He is

> The King of Glory in his powerful Word
> And Spirit coming to create new worlds.
>   (VII. 208)

He is God's 'vice-gerent Son' (x. 56), on whose kingship the whole poem pivots.

His dealings with man are characterized by mercy, and despite his royal status he advances, as Milton in his *Ready and Easy Way* urged that all Christian rulers should, to lowly service, finding clothes for Adam and Eve after the Fall; and yet his central function in *Paradise Lost* is the assumption of God's thunderous terror in the Heavenly war. The juxtaposition of qualities in the one figure is important.

We left the good and bad angels at war. The good angels resemble Great Britain in that they have no further ambitions and are defending what they believe to be a God-supported order, though the righteousness of their cause profits little against explosives; while the others resemble our foes in point

---

[1] Defined also in Byron's *Sonnet to the Prince Regent on the Repeal of Lord Edward Fitzgerald's Forfeiture*: see *Lord Byron: Christian Virtues*, 287–8, and *Byron and Shakespeare*, 109, 336.

of heroic determination, mechanical expertise, a bold over-leaping of moral canons, and a partly justifiable sense of wronged worth in face of what they consider injustice. We must not under-rate the adversaries. Michael is a bloodless figure beside Satan, and nothing less than Messiah can prove victor over Satan's heroic virility. The dark powers are not readily dethroned, and no amount of reasonings or imaginative description of hieratic marvels, no, not God himself as a lordly voice or as defined in the great invocation to Light in Book III, can by themselves balance the heroic impact of Satan in Books I and II. Power and action can only be mastered by a greater power and a more strongly conceived action. So 'none but' Messiah 'can end' 'this great war' (VI. 702).

Messiah is the mighty prototype of that God-given power for which we as a nation tentatively pray; in which we half-believe, which we half-fear to trust, ourselves set between shame of unworthiness and fear of ridicule. Our right to claim this especial assistance is variously suggested by our knowledge of Shakespeare, Milton, Pope, Burke, Blake, Wordsworth, Coleridge, Byron, Tennyson, Hardy, Swinburne and Kipling; as well as many others of lesser stature. Each is a bearer of the Messiah-strength, but each we disclaim, if not by attack, certainly by neglect. Suppose however that what those poets witness directly or indirectly, by support or as with Byron by attack, as Great Britain's destiny were in truth ordained, that a divine force were awaiting our acknowledgement, then such a force would conform to Milton's fiction. In order to understand Messiah's onslaught and read Milton's account with a pulsating sympathy, to tune our minds to the moment when the 'golden sceptre' rejected turns to an 'iron rod' (V. 883), I suggest we dwell on any ruthless cruelties in man's history such as those described in Milton's sonnet *On the late Massacre in Piedmont*, 'Avenge, O Lord, thy slaughter'd saints':

> In thy book record their groans
> Who were thy sheep and in their ancient fold
> Slain by the bloody Piedmontese that roll'd
> Mother with infant down the rocks.

Similar brutalities have of late been widespread across Europe. Great Britain has since Milton's time consistently opposed violence and tyranny;[1] she has, more than any nation on earth, held in balance justice and mercy, the twin attributes of royalty in Portia's speech in *The Merchant of Venice* and of Milton's Messiah, though it must be confessed that Milton himself is a more convincing advocate of justice than of mercy. As the empire-passage of *Paradise Regained* (p. 127 above) asserts, sheer force may be necessary, if not in the individual's certainly in international affairs. Messiah's warring is a denial of pacifism. He corresponds more to the Crown than to the Church in our national system. One cannot argue that the whole incident is a 'spiritual' battle, since both parties are equally angelic, and the archetypal conflict has corresponded point by point to earthly wars.

Messiah fights not in his own right but as 'vice-gerent' of God. He is a figure of the same *genre* as our own, or any other Christian nation's, constitutional monarch understood as 'defender of the Faith'. He is that towards which such monarchy approximates, as is suggested by Milton's passages (pp. 97, 115; and see 93-6) on the British throne. Part of Messiah's merit is humble acceptance of and willingness to employ a force not properly his own. Two days God has allowed the battle's continuance; the third is to be the day of victory. He addresses the Son:

> Go then thou mightiest in thy Father's might,
> Ascend my chariot, guide the rapid wheels
> That shake Heaven's basis, bring forth all my war,
> My bow and thunder, my almighty arms
> Gird on, and sword upon thy puissant thigh;
> Pursue these sons of darkness, drive them out
> From all Heaven's bounds into the utter deep:
> There let them learn, as likes them, to despise
> God and Messiah his anointed King.
>   (VI. 710)

If Britain be, potentially, a Messiah-nation, she might receive that as a command. Next, in so far as she fights to establish a world-order, in which process she must as a nation temporarily

---

[1] We must, of course, compare her history with that of former *imperial powers*. Today, surveying man's record of cruelty to man *and animal*, I am less inclined to make firm distinctions between our own wickednesses and those of Hitler's Germany. [1967]

assume, indeed has already assumed, some sort of international sovereignty, let this be the pattern of her answer:

> Sceptre and power, thy giving, I assume,
> And gladlier shall resign, when in the end
> Thou shalt be all in all, and I in thee
> For ever, and in me all whom thou lov'st;
> But whom thou hat'st, I hate, and can put on
> Thy terrors, as I put thy mildness on,
> Image of thee in all things; and shall soon,
> Arm'd with thy might, rid Heaven of these rebell'd,
> To their prepar'd ill mansion driven down
> To chains of darkness, and th' undying worm,
> That from thy just obedience could revolt,
> Whom to obey is happiness entire.   (VI. 730)

One would, perhaps, prefer a different conclusion. The tendency to end a gracious speech on a vengeful note is undeniably Miltonic.

In order further to establish our equation of the action of *Paradise Lost* with Milton's prophetic nationalism, I point to his peroration to the *Reformation in England*, whose structure resembles that of our last quotation:

> And now we know, O thou our most certain hope and defence, that thine enemies have been consulting all the sorceries of the great whore, and have joined their plots with that sad intelligencing tyrant that mischiefs the world with his mines of Ophir, and lies thirsting to revenge his naval ruins that have larded our seas: but let them all take counsel together, and let it come to naught; let them decree, and do thou cancel it; let them gather themselves, and be scattered; let them embattle themselves and be broken; let them embattle, and be broken, for thou art with us.
>
> Then, amidst the hymns and hallelujahs of saints, some one may perhaps be heard offering at high strains in new and lofty measures to sing and celebrate thy divine mercies and marvellous judgements in this land throughout all ages; whereby this great and warlike nation, instructed and inured to the fervent and continual practice of truth and righteousness, and casting far from her the rags of her old vices, may press on hard to that high and happy emulation to be found the soberest, wisest, and most Christian people at that day, when thou, the eternal and shortly expected king, shalt open the clouds to judge the several kingdoms of the world, and distributing national honours and rewards to

religious and just commonwealths, shalt put an end to all earthly
tyrannies, proclaiming thy universal and mild monarchy through
heaven and earth; where they undoubtedly, that by their labours,
counsels, and prayers, have been earnest for the common good of
religion and their country shall receive, above the inferior orders
of the blessed, the regal addition of principalities, legions, and
thrones into their glorious titles, and in supereminence of beatific
vision, progressing the dateless and irrevoluble circle of eternity,
shall clasp inseparable hands with joy and bliss, in overmeasure
for ever.

One might well wish Milton had concluded there. But, as in
Messiah's lines, we are finally directed to the terrors of retribution falling on God's antagonists:

But they contrary, that by the impairing and diminution of the
true faith, the distresses and servitude of their country, aspire to
high dignity, rule, and promotion here, after a shameful end in
this life (which God grant them), shall be thrown down eternally
into the darkest and deepest gulf of hell, where, under the
despiteful control, the trample and spurn of all the other damned,
that in the anguish of their torture shall have no other ease than
to exercise a raving and bestial tyranny over them as their
slaves and negroes, they shall remain in that plight for ever, the
basest, the lowermost, the most dejected, most underfoot, and
down-trodden vassals of perdition.

(Reformation in England, II; III. i. 78–9)

The bitterness is uncompromising.

Such national assertions may to some prove repellent. But
my proposition that Milton's Messiah = Great Britain is no
static equivalence. I suggest a dynamic proposition that develops, or may develop, at least partial reality in so far as our
response is genuine. As we watch Milton taxing his mighty
poetic strength to present a divine force able to crush his indomitable Satan, we may glimpse part of mankind's futurity:
Milton's technical problem is the problem of world civilization.
The dark threats with which our last quotation concludes may
apply both to us and to our foes, to whatever is impure in either
cause. To what extent Britain at this hour deserves assistance
may be argued indefinitely. The challenge is here; my reasons
have been presented; and the great passage on Britain roused
in *Areopagitica* may with profit be remembered.

Messiah's God-empowered chariot is a transcendental conception deriving from Old Testament prophecy, but also incorporating and driving to the limit Milton's habitual fascination with the military and the mechanical. It is at once a super-tank and a super-bomber, forecasting contemporary inventions just as the Greek myth of Pegasus, or of Daedalus and Icarus, forecasts air-mastery in general.[1] Whatever we think, it remains a superb conception and one to which our own experience of mechanized war on land and in the air may serve as an approach. It appears with a rushing sound, like some gigantic, more than human, airplane of blazing and supernal fabrication:

> So said, he o're his Scepter bowing, rose
> From the right hand of Glorie where he sate,
> And the third sacred Morn began to shine
> Dawning through Heav'n: forth rush'd with whirl-wind sound
> The Chariot of Paternal Deitie,
> Flashing thick flames, Wheele within Wheele undrawn,
> It self instinct with Spirit, but convoyd
> By four Cherubic shapes, four Faces each
> Had wondrous, as with Starrs thir bodies all
> And Wings were set with Eyes, with Eyes the Wheels
> Of Beril, and careering Fires between;
> Over thir heads a chrystal Firmament,
> Whereon a Saphir Throne, inlaid with pure
> Amber, and colours of the showrie Arch.
> Hee in Celestial Panoplie all armd
> Of radiant *Urim*, work divinely wrought,
> Ascended, at his right hand Victorie
> Sate Eagle-wing'd, beside him hung his Bow
> And Quiver with three-bolted Thunder stor'd,
> And from about him fierce Effusion rowld
> Of smoak and bickering flame, and sparkles dire;
> Attended with ten thousand thousand Saints,
> He onward came, farr off his coming shon,
> And twentie thousand (I thir number heard)
> Chariots of God, half on each hand were seen:
> Hee on the wings of Cherub rode sublime
> On the Crystallin Skie, in Saphir Thron'd.
> Illustrious farr and wide, but by his own

[1] It would, I suppose, be in alinement with the tenor of my argument to compare this fearful contraption with the Hiroshima Bomb, discussed in my small 1946 book *Hiroshima*. [1967]

First seen, them unexpected joy surpriz'd,
When the great Ensign of *Messiah* blaz'd. . . .
(VI. 746)

In these superlative passages I preserve Milton's own spelling and capitals. Notice the impressions of eyes and light. Such is the inrush of divine energy supervening on purity and humility; and so Messiah sets out. Milton's description is complex. The chariot is composed of faces and multitudinous eyes, like the Eagle of Justice in Dante's *Paradiso* created by thousands of blessed lives, or his Rose-formation, signifying Christ's Church (references p. 65 above). There are, too, the 'ten thousand thousand saints'. Messiah's onset is more than personal: he wields a communal and more than communal power. In him is summed and surpassed all Milton's more national and political cravings for a Messianic victory. His attack is directly continuous with Milton's earlier work. It is foreshadowed in *An Apology for Smectymnuus*, where Milton is defending his polemical virulence:

> Zeal, whose substance is ethereal, arming in complete diamond, ascends his fiery chariot, drawn with two blazing meteors, figured like beasts, but of a higher breed than any the zodiac yields, resembling two of those four which Ezekiel and St John saw; the one visaged like a lion, to express power, high authority, and indignation; the other of countenance like a man, to cast derision and scorn upon perverse and fraudulent seducers: with these the invincible warrior, Zeal, shaking loosely the slack reins, drives over the heads of scarlet prelates, and such as are insolent to maintain traditions, bruising their stiff necks under his flaming wheels. (III. i. 313-14)

Just so, says Milton, 'Christ himself, the fountain of meekness, found acrimony enough to be still galling and vexing the prelatical Pharisees'.

Arrived on the battlefield, Messiah bids God's armies cease their lonely and indecisive striving:

> Stand still in bright array ye Saints, here stand
> Ye Angels arm'd, this day from Battel rest;
> Faithful hath been your Warfare, and of God
> Accepted, fearless in his righteous Cause,
> And as ye have receivd, so have ye don
> Invincibly: but of this cursed crew

> The punishment to other hand belongs,
> Vengeance is his, or whose he sole appoints;
> Number to this dayes work is not ordain'd
> Nor multitude, stand onely and behold
> Gods indignation on these Godless pourd
> By mee; not you but mee they have despis'd,
> Yet envied; against mee is all thir rage,
> Because the Father, t'whom in Heav'n supream
> Kingdom and Power and Glorie appertains,
> Hath honourd me according to his will.
> Therefore to mee thir doom he hath assig'n'd;
> That they may have thir wish, to trie with mee
> In Battel which the stronger proves, they all,
> Or I alone against them, since by strength
> They measure all, of other excellence
> Not emulous, nor care who them excells;
> Nor other strife with them do I voutsafe.
>
> (VI. 801)

We can relate that, as best we may, and as far as we dare, to our own cause. Now swiftly is launched this thundering poetic climax.[1]

> So spake the Son, and into terrour chang'd
> His count'nance too severe to be beheld
> And full of wrauth bent on his Enemies.
> At once the Four spred out thir Starrie wings
> With dreadful shade contiguous, and the Orbes
> Of his fierce Chariot rowld, as with the sound
> Of torrent Floods, or of a numerous Host.
> Hee on his impious Foes right onward drove,
> Gloomie as Night; under his burning Wheeles
> The steadfast Empyrean shook throughout,
> All but the Throne it self of God. Full soon
> Among them he arriv'd; in his right hand
> Grasping ten thousand Thunders, which he sent
> Before him, such as in thir Soules infix'd
> Plagues; they astonisht all resistance lost,
> All courage; down thir idle weapons drop'd;

[1] Nevertheless in reading aloud the climactic power will be best realized by a quiet awe-struck tone coming in at 'they astonish'd' and used thenceforward with suitable contrasts. In these mighty passages, on a task unattempted by, and probably beyond the powers of, other great poets, Milton's heavy-plated style attains justification. In *Christ and Nietzsche* (88) I wrote that he was 'only happy on a supreme occasion, like a knight in armour, lumbering on foot but at ease when mounted for the joust'. [1967]

O're Shields and Helmes, and helmed heads he rode
Of Thrones and mighty Seraphim prostrate,
That wish'd the Mountains now might be again
Thrown on them as a shelter from his ire.
Nor less on either side tempestuous fell
His arrows, from the fourfold-visag'd Foure,
Distinct with eyes, and from the living Wheels,
Distinct alike with multitude of eyes,
One Spirit in them rul'd, and every eye
Glar'd lightning, and shot forth pernicious fire
Among th' accurst, that witherd all thir strength,
And of thir wonted vigour left them draind,
Exhausted, spiritless, afflicted, fall'n.
Yet half his strength he put not forth, but check'd
His Thunder in mid Volie, for he meant
Not to destroy, but root them out of Heav'n:
The overthrown he rais'd, and as a Heard
Of Goats or timerous flock together throngd
Drove them before him Thunder-struck, pursu'd
With terrors and with furies to the bounds
And Chrystall wall of Heav'n, which op'ning wide,
Rowld inward, and a spacious Gap disclos'd
Into the wastful Deep; the monstrous sight
Strook them with horror backward, but far worse
Urg'd them behind; headlong themselvs they threw
Down from the verge of Heav'n, Eternal wrauth
Burnt after them to the bottomless pit.

(vi. 824)

On this, the most spectacular incident in *Paradise Lost*, perhaps
in England's, perhaps even – outside the Bible – the world's,
literature, commentary has remained strangely silent. Why?
Because, I think, a power-impregnated righteousness is as yet
alien to our thinking and outside our vision. As in *Samson
Agonistes*, the heroic action is symbolic of a vast *community* –
'numerous host'. An earlier passage, as so often, helps us:

A commonwealth ought to be but as one huge Christian person-
age, one mighty growth and stature of an honest man, as big
and compact in virtue as in body.

(*Reformation in England*, ii; iii. i. 38)

Messiah's onset is also, in 'floods', a nature-force. From this one
titanic conception of Christ in action the twin later themes of

Christian passivity in *Paradise Regained* and pre-Christian heroism in *Samson Agonistes* branch out: they are Milton's own further *interpretations* of this central event. Notice the terrible powers of (i) eyes and (ii) light.

Milton's obsession with light and eyes is fascinating, and may be compared with many passages on God and especially that famous invocation at the opening of Book III:

> Hail holy light, off-spring of Heaven first-born!

with its poignant references to Milton's own blindness and its noble conclusion:

> So much the rather thon Celestial light
> Shine inward, and the mind through all her powers
> Irradiate, there plant eyes, all mist from thence
> Purge and disperse, that I may see and tell
> Of things invisible to mortal sight.   (III. 51)

'Shine inward' corresponds to the 'inward eyes' of *Samson Agonistes* (p. 117 above). Light is power, as in this gem from the *Reformation in England*:

> Wherefore should they not urge only the Gospel, and hold it ever in their faces like a mirror of diamond, till it dazzle and *pierce* their misty eyeballs?   (I; III. i. 35)

So the 'multitude of eyes' ruled by one 'spirit' in our Messiah-description signifies an infinity of personal visions, as when a great nation finds its soul and is fired with a single purpose. *Vision* is opposed to the Machiavellian *plots* of Satan and his politicians. Light is conceived both inwardly and dynamically. It becomes a matter less of passive sensation than of will, in which the deepest centres of the personality are engaged.[1]

Should my comparisons appear rash, remember that they aim to penetrate an underlying experience to which surface fictions are subsidiary. Three great Miltonic passages present substantially the same experience in terms superficially (i) divine, (ii) human, and (iii) national. These are (i) the passage just quoted; (ii) the Chorus's victory-speeches in *Samson Agonistes* (pp. 116–17); and (iii) the great description of Britain roused

---

[1] Compare Coleridge's description of Byron: 'his eyes the open portals of the sun – things of light for light' (quoted John Drinkwater, *The Pilgrim of Eternity*, 259). For Byron and the Sun, see pp. 234–7, 259–61 below. [1967]

in *Areopagitica* (p. 104). These tower above the many unresolved oppositions of Milton's work. We have already (p. 152) reviewed a passage showing how closely Messiah's triumph corresponds to Milton's reading of Britain's destiny and another (p. 115) showing how Samson's golden locks were first employed to characterize 'the state and person of a king' in Britain's constitution. But our three main passages are further intertwined.

The '*puissant*' nation in *Areopagitica*, envisaged as a single being of active truth and virtue, is first a Samson-figure, a 'strong man' with 'invincible locks', and next an '*eagle*' 'unscaling her long abused *sight* at the fountain itself of *heavenly* radiance', and making '*timorous and flocking birds*' to 'flutter about', '*amazed*'. In *Samson Agonistes* (1687–1707) Samson, 'blind of *sight*', is illuminated 'with *inward eyes*' and 'his *fiery virtue* roused' comes as a dragon on '*tame villatic fowl*'; next as an '*eagle*' drops '*thunder*' on their heads; and becomes finally a *Phoenix*, symbol of resurrection, to be compared with the 'towering *eagles*' and '*Phoenix*' of *Paradise Lost*, v. 270–4, used in direct contrast to '*fowls*' in description of the archangel Raphael. In our other *Samson* passage (p. 116) concerned more directly with political and international affairs, the 'deliverer' defeats the 'brute and boisterous force of violent men', and armed with 'heroic magnitude of mind' and '*celestial vigour*' he sets at nought their '*ammunition*' and '*magazines*', attacking 'with *winged expedition* swift as the *lightning glance*'[1] so that the 'wicked', '*surprised*, lose their *defence*, distracted and *amazed*' at such God-given strength. In *Paradise Lost* the Messiah, into whom God's '*virtue* and grace' are 'transfused' (vi. 703), sets out in a *fire*-impregnated chariot full of *eyes* which 'glared lightning' (vi. 849), bearing God's sword on his '*puissant*' (vi. 714) thigh, with at his right hand victory '*eagle*-winged' (vi. 763), shattering God's foes with 'ten-thousand *thunders*' while 'they, *astonished*, all *resistance* lost' (vi. 836–8), finally driving them before him as 'a herd, or *timorous* flock' (vi. 856–7), like the 'timorous and flocking birds' of *Areopagitica*. The impressions of irresistible

---

[1] Compare the central importance of lightning and related imagery in Byron's poetry, discussed in my *Byron and Shakespeare*, 270–9; and see Index of Byronic Themes, 'Concepts and Symbols'; also pp. 192–4, 200 below. [1967]

might are identical. Many recur in the Samson-passage of the *Reason of Church Government* (p. 115 above), where emphasis on 'puissant' hair and blindness changed to 'the golden beams of law and right' in *thunderous* victory serves to characterize a royal British integrity. In his *Animadversions* Milton sees Christ as having put to shame the 'persecutors of the Church', and continues:

> . . . thou hast made our false prophets to be found a lie in the sight of all the people, and *chased* them with *sudden confusion* and *amazement* before the redoubled *brightness* of thy descending cloud, that now covers thy tabernacle.   (iv; III. i. 146)

Similar description is given the Long Parliament in the *Apology for Smectymnuus* (1642):

> Nor did they deceive that expectation which with the eyes and desires of their country was fixed upon them: for no sooner did the force of so much united excellence meet in one *globe of brightness* and efficacy, but encountering the *dazzled* resistance of tyranny, they gave not over, though their enemies were strong and subtle, till they had laid her *grovelling* upon the fatal block; with *one stroke* winning again our lost liberties and charters, which our forefathers after so many battles could scarce maintain.
>   (III. i. 337)

Milton's use of 'globe', as in that earlier quotation from the *Reason of Church Government* which we referred to Samson (p. 113 and note), to symbolize the greater kind of integrity so continually housing itself throughout poetry in imagery of domes and other circularities, corresponds to the crown in the political order. It is therefore by no arbitrary act of interpretation that I refuse any ultimate separation of the experiences involved and poetically transmitted in such passages, while relating all together to the integrity, which is the sovereignty, of Great Britain, itself legitimate part of the total prophetic significance. Let us regard once more the striking lines from *Areopagitica*:

> Methinks I see in my mind a noble and puissant Nation rousing herself like a strong man after sleep, and shaking her invincible locks. Methinks I see her as an Eagle muing her mighty youth, and kindling her undazzled eyes at the full midday beam, purging and unscaling her long abused sight at the fountain itself of

heavenly radiance; while the whole noise of timorous and flocking birds, with those also that love the twilight, flutter about, amazed at what she means, and in their envious gabble would prognosticate a year of sects and schisms. (IV. 344)

We may compare the 'amazement' of Satan's followers at *Paradise Lost*, I. 313, with the 'amaze' struck into 'jealous monarchs' by Fairfax's 'unshaken virtue' in Milton's sonnet *On the Lord General Fairfax at the Siege of Colchester*. Our various inter-relations will be clear. They are all fused and covered by the great passage in *Samson Agonistes* beginning 'Oh how comely it is and how reviving . . .' This passage (p. 116 above) serves to blend the Messianic victory of *Paradise Lost*, 'ammunition' and 'magazines' recalling Satan's explosives, with the cause of Great Britain in the World War.

Our contemporary analogy acts as a clarification. If this strangely potent Messiah is equated with the Christ of our religion, the imagination bridles at his ruthless warring; if he is not so equated, he is in danger of seeming a meaningless supernatural monstrosity with neither pagan nor Christian reference. Now the same difficulty presents itself in our study of national action, where even righteous warring seems a strange reflection of God's purposes on an un-Christlike earth. Though we cannot deeply believe in the Heavenly war, many troubles are settled once we make the national analogy, seeing *Paradise Lost* as a prophetic forecast of world-conflict. The function exercised by Messiah in Milton's poem is precisely that exercised today by the soul, that is the Crown, of Great Britain. In our unredeemed national existence the Crown of Britain cannot as yet claim complete Christ-likeness, and must engage in war, but it nevertheless exists in humble vassalage to Christ and thence God. Milton's Messiah, whom we need not equate directly with Christ, is pre-eminently princely; and he is God's warrior. We are, I think, forced to the equation: Milton's Messiah = the Crown of our constitutional monarchy. This crown-principle is not tyrannic, and is, as far as may be, creative – Milton's Messiah directs the creation of our world (p. 149) – preserving respect for other liberties, that is sovereignties, recognizing all such as equivalent powers in vassalage to Christ the overlord of earthly princedoms.

Milton's later work is far from easy and guilty of many discordances. Long parts are tedious. My own present interpretation has been, admittedly, something of a re-creation. I do not retract the strictures pronounced on *Paradise Lost* in my earlier essay, but the very faults there observed force the more generous and flexible approach. Adverse criticism of great literature must always remain provisional: where direct interpretation proves impossible, our method must be indirect. We have therefore turned on the poetry what we know of Milton's life and times, together with three centuries of national experience. We have watched his passionate imagination dwelling variously on the Throne of David, Britain, Messiah, truth and freedom, a strength golden-locked and an eagle and leonine heroism. The king of England, in a passage we have quoted (p. 97), is 'Christ's vice-gerent, using the sceptre of David, according to God's law' (*Reformation in England*, II; III. i. 63), just as Messiah is God's 'vice-gerent' and executor of his law in *Paradise Lost*. All Milton's impassioned reasoning for or against this or that form of secular or divine ordinance derives from his consuming desire to realize power with goodness and a union of freedom with dominion to create a national integrity and a national soul-energy that may in a flash resolve all 'sects and schisms', in one Christlike blaze expanding over all nations on earth the kingdom of righteousness.

IV
Swift

First published as 'Swift and the Symbolism of Irony' in
The Burning Oracle, 1939

Satire conditions Dryden's best work; in Pope it expresses a
final disparity; but in Swift it is congenital. His disappointed
ambition is of secondary and surface interest only. Psychological
guesses, if based on the works, can reveal little beyond the works
themselves; and if independent, not so much. Moreover,
whether or why Swift was neurotic concerns us less than why
his work seems to us important.

Therefore biographical analysis must remain tentative. On
the personal plane, I doubt if Swift's genius got so far as the
sex-thwarting sometimes suggested, since his fascinated disgust
of ordure seems to reveal an even more fundamental disorder;
but the cause may as well turn out a symptom even here. Pope's
own comprehension, his at the same time whole and therefore
holy intuition, forced a similar break. We may see Swift as a
giant among pigmies, the hideous disparity using neurosis as a
relief, and may suppose that, though he was politically am-
bitious, no material success would have removed a disease deep
as Hamlet's. As with Hamlet, blame cannot be apportioned
where the relation is so utterly disorganized and the time 'out
of joint', Pope's progress indicating as clearly as may be how
and why this was so. The friendship between them was natural:
they would, even when their work appeared outwardly most
dissimilar, have understood each other, as would Webster and
Lyly, negative and positive profundities of the same *genre* being
complementary rather than contradictory. Whether superhuman or subhuman – always a hard distinction – Swift clearly
felt himself isolated, and, with or without justice, considered
himself wronged. But his best work always either satirizes
abuses deserving attack, or throws into relief questions we are
significantly loath to ask. He has two directions: physical

nausea and intellectual scorn. The first perhaps deserves more serious attention than we feel disposed to give it, our reluctance itself marking an unconscious concern; and his intellectual attitude to Church and State, and the numerous problems involved, though it might, or might not, have derived from this, is certainly not unrelated to it. So from the centre outwards, from sensory and immediate human experience to the free range of a rational inspection over a wide communal front, ripples expand of bitterness and disgust. Reverential and heroic traditions are alike deflated.

Swift's prose is noted for control and reserve. He is a master of lucidity and understatement. The reading aloud of any long sentence of Scott's will probably involve you quickly in misplaced stresses: you need to know the end before you start. But you can slip through any long sentence of *Gulliver's Travels* without fear or forethought: there is a swift forward-flowing transparency. Though the experience may be one of disorder, the stylistic reaction is superbly ordered. Yet Swift's style, like Milton's poetry, may in its own fashion prove a barrier to understanding. Milton puts an opacity over his passionate meanings, cramming vizarded and plated helmets on each, while Swift's very lucidity may head off our appreciation from close concern with his more rich effects. The heavy symbolisms in thought and language of *Sartor Resartus* might seem utterly alien to anything in Swift, Defoe, or Addison, the difference appearing to supporters of 'plain prose' as a mark of necessary superiority in these last. But this is a most unfortunate judgement, since it is the very quality they share with Carlyle that raises such authors from 'journalism' and 'fiction' to the level of 'literature'. Addison's characterizing and peculiar strength lies in his adept handling of concrete symbolisms, and it is probably this rather than prose 'style' or profundity of sentiment that lifts his reputation above Steele's. *The Vision of Mirza* is an allegoric design; *The Golden Scales* has a precise symbolism briefly radiating a host of observations; and *The Dream of Judgement* is a powerful eschatological myth. There is human creation in the *Roger de Coverley* essays (for which, however, Steele holds part credit), and atmospheric description in *The Royal Exchange* and *Westminster Abbey*. Addison is a poet, a maker, first; a preacher second: we are brought to live his statement. So too *Robinson Crusoe* is not 'just a tale', nor any book of long renown ever was. By skilful use of his island and animals to replace men Defoe dramatizes loneliness: the adventures are charged with an inward, psychological, and spiritual meaning that might even be said to make contact with *The Tempest.* Both Addison and Defoe, however plain their prose, use it in service to a rich impressionism; and it is the same with Swift.

The Battle of the Books (comp. 1697; pub. 1704) is a highly allegorical affair, with a wealth of meaning struck from the opposition of ancient and modern literature. How exquisitely are the limitations of Swift's own day outlined in the comparison of spider and bee, the one exuding 'excrement and venom', the other 'honey and wax'. This neat antithesis of objective health and its reverse is widely valid, and covers Swift's own work, its envenomed self-exuded loathing as well as its fine balance and objectification in symbolic narrative. *A Tale of a Tub* (comp. c. 1696–7; pub. 1704) is similarly allegoric, developing a central clothes-symbolism, akin to that used by Carlyle in *Sartor Resartus,* in the coats left to the three sons Peter, Martin, and Jack, representing the Roman, Anglican, and Puritan obediances. Swift's ecclesiastical satire is comprehensive and the Anglican Church, though favoured, does not escape: in the appended 'History of Martin' Queen Elizabeth makes laws against the 'receipt books' of Peter from whom the greater part of her own 'dispensatory' was 'stolen'.

Throughout *A Tale of a Tub* skilful use is made of various concrete, often strongly physical, symbolisms: the shoulder-knots, gold lace, silver fringe (ii); the ludicrous descriptions of the visionary Aeolians and the unsavoury mechanisms of 'wind' (viii); the physical causes of madness, making tyrants go to war and philosophers compose systems (ix); the woman flayed, and the beau stripped (ix); the satirizing of Jack's use of the 'will' (i.e. Bible) for *all* occasions whether as nightcap or umbrella, and when 'taken short' his inability to find a suitable phrase, with dire results (xi); the section on 'ears' (xi); religions conceived as salves, powders, pills, plasters ('The History of Martin'). Especially powerful, after the dominating clothes-symbolism, which is at one point (ii) elevated into a universal symbol in the manner of Carlyle, is the use of food to satirize the Mass, as when Peter invites his brothers to a feast and gives them nothing but dry bread (iv). Food and clothes are primary simplicities which only the greatest literature, such as the New Testament and Shakespeare, endues with a consistent positive power. But Swift's more negative use of them is neat. The section on critics (iii) shows skilful irony entwined with references to asses, serpents, rats, wasps, vomit, and mud. In all this I point to the heavy reliance on sensory or other concrete suggestion to create a living action. Swift's narrative may seem colourless, but the materials within are not. The plainness consists rather in continual emphasis on noun and verb with little reliance on *qualifying* adjectives.

Gulliver's Travels (pub. 1726), however plain and realistic its surface, depends likewise on a symbolic, sensory-physical structure. It is in four parts. Parts I and II use people either dwarf-like or vast, and the logic within this imaginative structure repays exact attention. Compare with Shakespeare's and Milton's feeling for kingship this description of the tiny King of Lilliput:

> He is taller by almost the breadth of my nail than any of his court, which alone is enough to strike an awe into the beholders. His features are strong and masculine, with an Austrian lip and arched nose, his complexion olive, his countenance erect, his body and limbs well-proportioned, all his motions graceful, and his deportment majestic.   (I. ii)

And his proclamation:

> Golbasto Momaren Evlame Gurdilo Shefin Mully Ully Gue, most mighty Emperor of Lilliput, delight and terror of the universe, whose dominions extend five thousand *blustrugs* (about twelve miles in circumference) to the extremities of the globe; monarch of all monarchs, taller than the sons of men; whose feet press down to the centre, and whose head strikes against the sun; at whose nod the princes of the earth shake their knees; pleasant as the spring, comfortable as the summer, fruitful as autumn, dreadful as winter ...   (I. iii)

These rely for their satiric force on our knowledge of his size. His *pride* is felt to be absurd – we may compare Pope's hatred of pride – when we remember his pigmy physique. Yet size is only relative. The King of England viewed by a hypothetical creature much larger would appear correspondingly small, but so, for that matter, would the larger person in similar plight, as indeed Gulliver himself does in Book II, where it is clearly stated that the King of England must have suffered similar indignities had he been there. So a sequence of bigger and bigger people can be imagined indefinitely. Swift has therefore, in playing with size, said precisely nothing. But see what has happened: pride has been condemned, not by the author but by the reader. A new perspective reveals a truth which, once recognized, stands independent of any particular perspective: once the recognition is established, knowledge of the trick played on us will not invalidate it. Or we see that pride, so easily dethroned by an unreality, can only be so satirized since it depends on one. It is felt to be fundamentally a make-believe, whereas self-sacrifice, courage, simple good sense, are not; for all qualities in the book inherently praiseworthy do not appear invalidated at all. Something similar often happens in Byron's otherwise very different *Don Juan*. The judgements are all the time our own, a thought we shall return to in discussion of Swift's irony, Swift merely forcing them to daylight recognition. This recognition is not always bitter, and may touch pure humour, comparable with that of Pope in *The Rape of the Lock*, as when, in Part II, after Gulliver's elaborate and proud exhibition of nautical skill in a tank with Glumdalclitch's breath for wind, the girl, it is quietly and unobtrusively observed, hangs the boat on a nail to dry (v). The humour depends on recognition of a possible context in which any pride may appear funny. In Swift, such ludicrous events condition narrative power and sincerity, his admirable scheme leaving him nothing to do but the barest description of a simple *action*. Having the right nouns ready, he has only to attach the verb: the power of surface simplicity is fed from the symbolism beneath.

Reliance on direct sensory-physical effects is greater in Part II than in Part I. Especially interesting is Swift's use of small animals of a supposedly disgusting or absurd sort. The first Brobdingnagian he meets looks on Gulliver as 'a small dangerous animal' that may 'scratch' or 'bite', such as a 'weasel', and Gulliver himself fears that he may be dashed to the ground as 'any little hateful animal' a man has a mind to destroy; the man's wife screams on seeing him as 'at the sight of a toad or a spider'; and when the boy is to be punished for holding him up in the air by the legs, Gulliver intercedes, remembering a boy's natural mischievousness towards sparrows, rabbits, kittens, and puppy dogs (i). To him a cat is now three times the size of an ox. His fight with the two rats is satirically heroic and his pride ludicrous, especially when the maid picks up the dead one with a pair of tongs and throws it out of the window (i). He sleeps in a doll's cradle in a drawer (ii). They consider him a *splacknuck*. The child Glumdalclitch was once given a lamb which later went to the butcher and she fears that the same may happen to Grildrig (Gulliver); he is carried in a 'box' with gimlet holes to let in air (ii). The dwarf, in professional jealousy, drops him into a large bowl of cream, but, being a powerful swimmer, he survives; his legs are also wedged by this dwarf during dinner into a marrowbone 'where I stuck for some time, and made a very ridiculous figure'; flies, 'odious insects', trouble him, and he is admired for cutting them in pieces with his knife; fierce wasps steal his cake but he shows courage in attack and 'dispatched' four of them (iii). A spaniel carries him in its mouth to its master, tail wagging, but this was hushed up: 'And truly as to myself, I thought it would not be for my reputation that such a story should go about' (v). A kite swoops down on him, he falls into a mole-hill, breaks his shin by tumbling over a snail-shell; he fights a thrush that snatched a piece of cake from his hand, but the birds beat him off and return to hunt for 'worms' and 'snails'; he throws a 'thick cudgel' at a linnet, and, knocking it down, runs 'in triumph' to his 'nurse', but the bird recovers and causes great trouble; a frog gets into his boat and daubs his face and clothes with its 'odious slime' (v). Then there is the monkey catching and squeezing him and taking him on to the roof, feeding him with food from its own mouth, patting him when he will not eat (v). Such impressions culminate in the King's explicit statement about Gulliver's kind as 'the most pernicious race of little odious vermin that nature ever suffered to crawl upon the surface of the earth' (vi).

I apologize for this rather obvious list; but observe the emphasis on actions. Swift follows the Shakespearian tradition of nauseating animals, spiders, toads, monkeys, the experience being similar to that which Shakespeare projects into *Othello*. The comparisons aim at suggesting indignity and disgust, and the substance is to this extent non-rational, and of an immediate and sensory sort, however it may be used to blend with rational thinking. In contrast, we may point to Pope's more cosmic sympathy for all small life, and his apparent fondness for spiders, though he and Swift are one in their condemnation of pride: *Gulliver's Travels* drives to an extreme that sense of mankind's purely relative importance found in Pope's *Essay on Man*.

Sense-reaction may be specifically human, as when Gulliver in Lilliput puts out the fire burning the palace with his own water (I. v); in the emphasis on ordure in the same book (I. ii); and the descriptions of a meal and execution in Part II (II. iii, v). The most precise expression of such sensory feeling comes in the exquisitely devised Book IV. Book I is sometimes indecisive, as when the Lilliputians, usually reflecting European weaknesses, are suddenly made to present Utopian ideals of education and justice; and in Book II the King and his people, who stand for reason, justice, and intellectual precision, as in certain references to neat prose and learning, are also horrible, because large, examples of physical coarseness. The confusion perhaps is unavoidable; but Part IV, where none occurs, is the more perfect work. The author has found exact equivalents to his intuition in the Houyhnhnms and Yahoos. The choice of horses may be related to Swift's excretory prepossessions, since the scent of stables is strangely non-abhorrent to man. Consider this passage:

> The first money I layed out was to buy two young stone-horses, which I keep in a good stable, and next to them the groom is my greatest favourite; for I feel my spirits revived by the smell he contracts in the stable. (xi)

In contrast Gulliver is disgusted by human odours. The choice of horses as Swift's highest creatures shows how exactly the intellectual design is being dictated by a sensory, almost poetic, aversion. As for the Yahoos, they are nauseating beasts in human form, disposed (vii) to 'nastiness and dirt', and ironically defended in comparison with swine:

> I could have easily vindicated human kind from the imputation

of singularity upon the last article, if there had been any swine in that country (as unluckily for me there were not), which although it may be a sweeter quadruped than a Yahoo, cannot I humbly conceive in justice pretend to more cleanliness; and so his Honour himself must have owned, if he had seen their filthy way of feeding, and their custom of wallowing and sleeping in the mud.   (vii)

In the Yahoo physical and intellectual satire are beautifully at one. Gulliver's Houyhnhnm master tells how five of the Yahoos will quarrel violently over enough food for fifty, each wanting all for himself, and only failing to kill each other for want of human inventions; how they will dig with their claws for coloured stones, carrying them to their kennels and pining away if they be removed. As for drink, they suck a juicy root that goes to their heads:

> It would make them sometimes hug, and sometimes tear one another; they would howl and grin, and chatter, and reel, and tumble, and then fall asleep in the dirt.   (vii)

The physical is one with the moral satire. The hatefulness of the Yahoo form is emphasized together with its comparative uselessness and limitations in strength and speed, and subjection to cold and heat. The Yahoos hate each other because of 'the odiousness of their own shapes' (vii), and the human custom of the concealing by clothes of otherwise 'hardly supportable' human 'deformities' appears to Gulliver's master thoroughly wise. The Houyhnhnms

> had very imprudently neglected to cultivate the breed of asses, which were a comely animal, easily kept, more tame and orderly, without any offensive smell, strong enough for labour, although they yield to the other in agility of body; and if their brayings be no agreeable sound, it is far preferable to the horrible howlings of the Yahoos.   (ix)

Such a passage shows clearly how Swift's famous understatement and lucidity depend mainly on his first finding satirical-symbolic schemes so exactly suited that barest narration releases all the emotional force desired. No first-order writer is independent of sensory symbolisms, and Swift's striking realism and fine use of the active verb measure the madness of his tale.

Part IV repeats much of Parts I and II. The satire on European wars, politics, and professions generally is a more direct
reworking of similar substances in Part II, and the Utopian
suggestions in Lilliput are elaborately redeveloped in description of the Houyhnhnms. Rational simplicity is the keynote of
Swift's Utopia. No one lies, because language exists to convey
meaning, and opinions cannot differ since, where passions are
absent, truth, in so far as it is not unreachable, will be self-
evident, as in Pope's 'Truth breaks upon us with resistless day'
(*Essay on Criticism*, 212). Marriage is eugenically arranged with
no unnecessary play of emotions, there is no possessive fondness
for children, nor any distress at death of a relative, nor fear of
one's own, and the whole race is equally loved by all. Women
get the same education as males to avoid the error of entrusting
children to inferior beings. Notice how close this rational levelling is to (i) both Plato and the New Testament, and (ii) certain
ultramodern theories; but also how abhorrent it remains to the
more sensitive intelligences of the Christian tradition. This is no
place for an attempt at elucidation, but Swift's reasoning may
well appear rather as a facile retreat from emotions than as a
mastery and use of them; this is very different from Pope.

And yet Swift is scarcely a 'rationalist' or 'intellectualist' in
any modern sense. He desires a simple state of nature. Part III,
a rather less satisfying book in a different mode from the others,
shows how little he trusts man's scientific advances. Here, as
often in *A Tale of a Tub*, he is very modern, attacking all over-
intellectualization and a will-o'-the-wisp science, with an attack
which may be variously related to Marlowe's *Doctor Faustus* and
certain passages in *The Duchess of Malfi* before his day, as well as
Samuel Butler and D. H. Lawrence after. Hence the Laputians
and their need for 'flappers', their clothes decorated with suns
and moons, fiddles and flutes, food cut into geometrical shapes,
their passion for astronomy and music, clothes elaborately
constructed from scientific calculations and eventually turned
out ill-fitting, and absurd fears of planetary disaster (ii). Music
and mathematics go together, the most abstract of the arts with
the most abstract of the sciences, both being here considered by
Swift to be as irrelevant to human existence as abstruse theories
concerning the heavenly bodies. The thought often appears quite

modern, the Laputians' fear of the sun's going out corresponding with certain 'thermo-dynamic' arguments today that can
only be opposed by such non-scientific vitalisms as those of
Pope's *Essay on Man* or Shaw's *Back to Methuselah*. Swift certainly underestimates the potential advances and advantages of
science, but looking deeper we can recognize some profound
truths. When (iv) he sees the land of Balnibarbi uncultivated
and wantonly misused, and contrasts the general ugliness with
a fertile district that brings mockery on its owner, we may
suspect a dark reflection of that future mechanization which he
could not be expected to describe more closely. We have the
mad schemes of 'projectors', who plough by setting hogs to root
up laboriously buried acorns (v), aim at extracting sunbeams
from cucumbers (v), and spoil a good mill for ridiculous
theoretic proposals concerning a better that never gets built (iv).
Learning becomes mechanized, a kind of turnip-machine
rolling out sentences ready-made so that anyone can compose
fine books without 'genius or study', our recent mass-production
in books and education receiving a palpable hit. Church ritual
is satirized in the student who swallows a wafer bearing an
inscribed geometrical proposition with a view to assimilating
its truth (v). If there is any danger today that the evils of
science may out-speed its benefits, a fear most readily felt in
consideration of war, then the Swiftian prophecy is not all
jaundiced. Any great writer, being by definition one who senses
significant directions in his own age, tends inevitably to reflect
the future. So, whatever contemporary meanings may have
been intended by Swift's Floating Island (iii), we can also say
that aerial warfare is being foreshadowed; particular and general
implications, as so often in imaginative work, tending to coalesce. Swift's brilliant satire on European wars in *Gulliver's
Travels* should today receive an especial respect. In Parts I, II
and IV there are harsh criticisms, social, political and ecclesiastical; in Part III the criticisms are less subtle, jostling each
other somewhat chaotically, but the same tendencies are being
attacked. At Glubbdubdrib a vision of the Roman senate is
contrasted with modern assemblies (vii), and modern history
shown as a list of crimes (viii). The King of Luggnagg poisons
nobles by infecting the dust they are made to lick (ix), recalling

the stick-jumping and ribbons in Lilliput (I. iii). Church bap-
tism is satirized in the immortal Struldbrugs with the red spot
on their foreheads (x). Swift appears to have slight sympathy
for the mystical and the ritualistic, and it is difficult to see how
any defence of his fundamental orthodoxy can stand in face of
such writings. He appears rather as a sceptical humanist who
again and again tilts at Christian belief: the geometrical wafer
in Lagado (III. v); the wars of Big-Endians and Little-Endians
in Lilliput (I. iv); the burial upside down among the Lilliputians
in hope of resurrection the right way up (I. vi); together with
obvious analogies from *A Tale of a Tub*; all serve to establish his
scepticism. The Houyhnhnms have no religion.

Swift does not, normally, give any impression of actual
savagery. He writes as though well above his subject, with a
deadly ease and serenity of statement. Which brings us to his
famous irony: *A Modest Proposal* is only the most celebrated instance of a continual technique. Irony says one thing while
aiming to make the reader think its opposite, so that the reader
himself produces the required thought from his own mind. This
is, of course, the secret of persuasion in general of which rhetorical questions are the crudest, and irony the most concentrated,
form. Swift, by commenting on his carefully invented situations
with a quietly exaggerated respect to conventional values,
releases in the reader a sudden revulsion from those values.
What we call 'control' in any art is similar, being the technique
of leaving certain things out, the use of suggestion, relying on
the reader's, or in acting the spectator's, ability to do the rest.
It is therefore easy to see why lack of it may offend, though it is
equally clear that since few readers normally do their share, the
more violent artist may on occasion have as good a case as the
other. Pope seems to be aiming always at couplet-rhyme, his
thought not stressed, to be received almost by mistake with a
half-awareness, with the unfortunate result that we have taken
him at his face value. Jesus speaks in parable to awake, rather
than inject, the thought required, to release an automatic
recognition. All symbolism takes you to the threshold, no more.
Swift's irony is, compared with those, scarcely profound, nor
can it be missed, but its nature poignantly condenses a universal
truth: that to force people's minds may be less valuable than to

engage their co-operation; as when Dryden, by masking his attack on Buckingham through the character of Zimri, makes his audience itself perform the act of recognition before weighing its justice, which is by then already admitted. All this relates closely to Swift's use of sensory symbolisms: the one is allied with the other, mad schemes chosen which lend themselves to ironic comment; and as we have already observed, his use of size relies on raising judgements instinctive to the reader. Swift *proves* nothing. The general result is an especially powerful effect with an appearance of effortless ease that impresses with a sense of necessity and truth, and causes us to think the author an intellectual giant, though there is little close thinking, as such, in these works. He is not exactly an emotional giant either; and yet he certainly seems to be a giant of some sort. In Lilliput Gulliver's size may be taken to symbolize some Gargantuan sense of superiority, as perhaps the vast stature of Satan symbolizes Milton's; some wish-fulfilment in material terms of that ease and mastery he feels within him, yet can only attain in literature. It has been observed that in Brobdingnag we tend to see Gulliver as tiny, still identifying ourselves with the big people; which, if it be so, might reflect a similar identification in the writer. The cat and thrush we may see, for a short while, as vast, but not the men; though there are other possible reasons for this.

The richest negative profundities, Milton's Hell or Webster's charnel-mongering, are absent from Swift; and, perhaps, from Pope. A certain dark intensity is left unexperienced: Pope's *Dunciad* satirizes the mentally absurd, asses his symbol; Swift's Yahoos are ape-pigs, corresponding to a more physical disgust. Pope's appears the more healthy, and clearly, in view of his other work, the more just. Certainly Swift's concentration on ordure suggests a limitation. Three sense-complexes may trouble the growing human organism: ordure, sex, death. Two organic negations seem to enclose a positive, but the sequence, I think, exists. The first normally gets, and some would say deserves, slight attention, though we may remember that excretion is a miniature death in its expulsion of poisons, and that all sensory reactions to it hold interest in reference to death itself. Sexual troubles of one sort or another are the natural playground for adult agonies, and their solution seems to condition understanding of the final mystery. Much of our horror at death is, at bottom, a physical repulsion, and may be related to both the earlier stages. It seems that Swift, on this plane of analysis, was stuck at the first obstacle and we may suspect a corresponding limitation in his gospel. He is rather like Apemantus in *Timon of Athens*.

Nevertheless, his apparent suffering elevates him far above the more smug and contented satirists. Moreover, his symbolic schemes aim at a deeper, more emotional redirection, as I have shown, than would a more facile surface argument lacking sensory-appeal. He is not merely 'intellectual'; but his strong sense-aversions, which we may, in view of their overpowering emphasis, suppose to be, originally at least, troubling elements in his own life, are fundamentally a denial of the poetic essence, and it is to his credit that he so finely reversed that denial to poetic account. We can say either (i) that his psychological peculiarities prevented his finding a positive and dynamic pattern, and that his thwarted genius did the best it could, by wrenching nausea to prophetic standard; or (ii) that in this age of simultaneous respect to and repudiation of the heroic tradition such a man was best equipped for literary genius, since satire alone conditioned that entwining of symbol and story necessary to the greatest works. But our view must be measured against the comparable but different development of Pope. Though he is merciless to the main activities of Western civilization, Swift respects the heroic traditions of Greece and Rome; and this sympathy is reflected into his own narrative skill and even sentence-construction, wherein the best points are continually being made through lucid statements of action. Most great writers express somewhere or other the best possible unconscious commentary, whether critical or appraising, on their own work. Here is Swift's, from *The Battle of the Books*:

> For anything else of genuine that the Moderns may pretend to, I cannot recollect; unless it be a large vein of wrangling and satire, much of a nature and substance with the spider's poison; which, however they pretend to spit wholly out of themselves, is improved by the same arts, by feeding upon the insects and vermin of the age. As for us the Ancients, we are content with the bee

G

to pretend to nothing of our own, beyond our wings and our voice, that is to say, our flights and our language. For the rest, whatever we have got, has been by infinite labour and search, and ranging through every corner of nature; the difference is, that, instead of dirt and poison, we have rather chosen to fill our hives with honey and wax, thus furnishing mankind with the two noblest of things, which are sweetness and light.

The beautiful handling of the symbol contrasts strongly with Arnold's prostitution of it in *Culture and Anarchy*. Swift here glimpses, if insecurely, a positive human excellence not incomparable with Pope's; and his satire, like Pope's, is directed against an age poisoned by petty wrangling; it is satire against satire. If the medicine is strong, so was, or is, the disease. Moreover, though this passage may today be read as self-condemnation, its beautiful strength and precision of statement, relying almost entirely on concrete nouns and active verbs with scarcely an adjective to assist, range Swift in the company rather of those ancients whose art he describes.

ADDITIONAL NOTE

The Challenge of Genius

A review of *Jonathan Swift* by J. Middleton Murry in *The Yorkshire Post*, 26 May 1954

In Swift we find certain tendencies common to men of literary genius driven to an extreme which becomes, at the limit, unpleasant, if not repellent; and the study of him has an interest all its own. The problem of literary genius is one of the pressing problems of our time. Who, or what, are these disturbing giants? Why do we write books about them and build round them departments of learning? Wherein lies their peculiar, and abnormal, health?

Among those who have most steadily tried to gear our ordinary thinking to such abnormal figures Mr Middleton Murry holds an honourable place. One of his outstanding qualities, which on its first appearance proved a welcome contrast to the fashion of biographical denigration it superseded, has been his capacity for admiration, seen at its extreme, and perhaps at its best, in his hero-worship of Keats. Other of his

subjects have been figures so different as Shakespeare, Dos-
toievsky, Cromwell and Blake; and even when, as in his study
of D. H. Lawrence, he takes back with one hand what he claims
to be offering with the other, the hero-worship is there, even if
rather disconcertingly handled.

Mr Murry can certainly be confusing; and the reason is this.
While honestly trying to face the challenge of genius, he has
always been reluctant to depart too far from traditional
valuations in either religion or the psychology of sex. In the
sphere of creative writing his old antagonist in many a literary
conflict, T. S. Eliot, has taken, as we can see in retrospect, a
similar course: never did so original a writer appear to his
contemporaries so *safe*. But whereas Mr Eliot has always been
free to preserve a limited clarity by going his own way, Mr
Murry has had to interpret a number of talents whom he
genuinely admires but who nevertheless went theirs; and their
ways have not always been Mr Murry's or Mr Eliot's, or indeed
that of most respectable people today. Hence the confusion.

Mr Murry's new book is a work of wide reading, studious
care, exact thought, considerable insight and, from any normal
view, sound judgement. It is as sane a study of literary genius as
one could wish for; though whether sanity is the last word in
wisdom in expounding the significance of the insane – for all
true genius, and Swift's pre-eminently, contains a large element
of insanity – may be questioned.

Swift's relation to the politics of his day, and in especial his
strong convictions on the inter-relationship of Church and
State, are lucidly analysed, but we receive no strong impression
of his political importance; even with *The Drapier's Letters* we
are warned not to romanticize the undertaking, nor its results.
Though nothing is omitted, we are perhaps left with too light
an emphasis on Swift as a great liberator. Far more vivid is Mr
Murry's handling of Stella and Vanessa – significant names! –
in relation to Swift's spiritual pride and personal inhibitions;
and of his peculiar physical disgusts. Here the analyses, as far
as they go, are admirable.

Swift is one of those writers who lend themselves naturally to
Mr Murry's favourite method of combining literary analysis
with biography, and it is well done. *A Tale of a Tub* is neatly

characterized, though Mr Murry's wholesale denial of meaning within the iconoclasm of values its humour involves appears to go too far and might be valuably supplemented by Mr John Cowper Powys' work on *Rabelais,* probably the most exact statement of the 'transvaluation of values' carried by great humour on record. With *Gulliver's Travels* Mr Murry is, at his best, most revealing: the symbolism of the Houyhnhnms has never before been so admirably expounded. Good biographical use is made of Swift's verse, though its poetic strength is probably over-rated: Dryden's famous prophecy was surely justified.

Faced by so admirably conceived and carefully executed a work, adverse criticism may seem inept; but some awkward questions nevertheless force themselves forward. Though the fourth book of *Gulliver's Travels* can be criticized as the expression less of any spiritual, moral or rational valuation than of an instinctive and sensuous disgust, do not sense-impressions form a large part of what we call 'imaginative literature', and does not this, probably Swift's greatest achievement, derive its peculiar and appalling power from this very unreasoned, and unhealthy, disgust? Again, do not Swift's abnormal sexual relationships, together with his anti-feminine thrusts, chime only too well with aspects of Dante, Shakespeare's Sonnets, Milton, and others? Is it enough to show once again, as Mr Murry has already shown with Lawrence, that the redeeming power of love has been unjustly ignored? Had these men been sexually normal, would they have composed their greatest works? And should we still be writing books about them? What, then, is the secret of their enduring appeal? – of this strange *malaise* which proves more vital than health?

These questions Mr Murry does not answer. The inmost citadel of Swift's genius is not wronged, or slighted, but he does not pluck out the heart of its mystery; nor was it his purpose to do so. What he has done is to deploy the facts with strict adherence to the evidence and offer as good an interpretation of them as is possible within the boundaries of normality and good sense. It will be for others, should they choose, to delve deeper.

V

Byron: the Poetry

First published as 'The Two Eternities' in *The Burning Oracle*, 1939

I

A poet's work may often appear to contradict his life. With Lord Byron this is not so. He is, as a man, a vital embodiment of post-Renaissance poetry, a proud individualist asserting the primacy of instinct through an agonized self-conflict. His social sympathies are violently given to causes of liberty. He incurs charges of immorality. He lives what others so often write, leaving his native land as Timon leaves Athens. That insistent aspiration, that aristocracy of spirit, met with variously in fiction after fiction, is here incarnate: more, it is given, as in Shakespeare's plays, an outward formulation in aristocracy of birth. Such aristocracy may be used in poetry to materialize an inner, spiritual, royalty, as in *Tess of the D'Urbervilles*, and Byron is so much the more effective as a dramatic figure by reason of his title. His ingrained Shakespearian respect for tradition, for history, increases the agony and tension of revolt. He has weakness, and is tortured by a sense of sexual sin. The vice, weakness and nobility behind all high literary adventures are his, as a man.

How slight some famous poets might appear should we choose to scrutinize their apparent littleness, their failure to match in life the spectacular essences of their work. A slight shift of perspective and Wordsworth looks like an old maid; Coleridge becomes a not very pleasant blend of talkative don and dope-fiend; Keats an adolescent; Shelley a seraphic blur. But Byron has warm flesh and colour. His life itself falls into poetic and tragic form. Mediterranean coasts are perennially fertilizing forces to northern poetry. Italy floods the Renaissance and particularly the Shakespearian consciousness; poets from Chaucer and Milton to Browning and Lawrence have travelled there; and many have managed to die there, or thereabouts. But Byron does it all more superbly than any. In poetry Greece has for long been challenging our traditional Christian culture, an Olympian or Dionysian theology appearing as partners with the Christian. Liberty of spirit, mind, body, and community has been for centuries a pressing imaginative demand. Our dominant personal and communal poetic directions from Marlowe and Milton through Pope to Shelley, Browning, and Lawrence are related (i) to erotic instincts and (ii) to the cause of liberty. Byron suffers social ostracism and banishment for the one and death for the other. Incest, says Shelley, is a very poetical thing:[1] presumably since every act of artistic creation involves an incestuous union within the personality. Byron is suspected of it in actual fact. He dies fighting for the perfect sacrificial cause: the liberty of Greece. He lives that eternity which is art. He is more than a writer: his virtues and vices are those entwined at the roots of poetry. He is poetry incarnate. The others are dreamers: he is the thing itself.

His poetic work, our only present concern, is continuous with these impressions. He did not at first see himself as a poet, as an early preface shows; and when he did start writing in earnest, he favoured stories of colour and action. His human understanding is glamorous, his incidents well costumed. Piratical adventure mixes with passionate love; there is the flash of steel and smell of powder. His is a cruel, yet romantic, world where blood flows hot. It is objectively conceived. Byron can lose himself in creation of emotional shapes outside his direct experience. He will use a reverential Christianity for his purpose, but can with equal ease salute a dying Moslem in *The Giaour* with:

> But him the maids of Paradise
>   Impatient to their halls invite,
> And the dark heaven of Houris' eyes
> On him shall glance for ever bright.
> (739)

---

[1] 'Incest is, like many other incorrect things, a very poetical circumstance.' (To Mrs Gisborne, 16 Nov. 1819; quoted, *The Works of Lord Byron: Poetry*; edited E. Hartley Coleridge; IV. 100, note.) [1967]

This is a Shakespearian power; we find it in the impersonal historic interests of *Childe Harold* and Byron's love of peoples and places generally; the sense of a particular and honourable past lingers round each person or place he touches. He is sensitive to human tradition and culture; he is cosmopolitan and ex-traverted; and yet his tales also express a violent and recurring psychological experience whose mysterious depths of passion and guilt are variously hinted or revealed. To this I give my primary attention.

The Giaour (1813) is a powerful example. The inside of mental agony is revealed, the poetry piercing and twisting into its centre:

> The Mind, that broods o'er guilty woes,
>   Is like the Scorpion girt by fire;
> In circle narrowing as it glows,
> The flames around their captive close,
> Till inly search'd by thousand throes,
>   And maddening in her ire,
> One sad and sole relief she knows –
> The sting she nourish'd for her foes,
> Whose venom never yet was vain,
> Gives but one pang and cures all pain,
> And darts into her desperate brain . . .
>   (422)

The rhetorical tension is maintained with a never-failing grip: each word is charged, each sentence tight. What universes are here housed in the tiny yet deadly form of the scorpion; its own venomous nature makes its agony the more terrifying. The little drama symbolizes the horror, which is one with the energies, of biological existence; it gets at the very nerve behind ecstasy and anguish alike. Byron's in-feeling into animal life and energy is from the start distinctive. *The Giaour* is rich with it:

> Go, when the hunter's hand hath wrung
> From forest-cave her shrieking young,
> And calm the lonely lioness:
> But soothe not – mock not, *my* distress!
>   (1214)

He attributes sensitive nerves and minds to the animal creation, or may delight in its more lyric vitalities, as when he sees a butterfly

> . . . rising on its purple wing
> The insect-queen of Eastern spring
> (388)

being chased by a boy, and makes subtle comparison between this and love. Either the fleeting loveliness rises far above the 'panting heart', or, if caught,

> With wounded wing, or bleeding breast,
> Ah! where shall either victim rest?
> Can this with faded pinion soar
> From rose to tulip as before?   (410)

Notice the choice placing of a well-considered diction and the soft use of consonants. Stern as are his tales, Byron's poetry masters with equal ease a lyric grace and wrenching guilt: and through all burns deep sympathy for animals, often, like Alexander Pope's, for small ones; a sympathy one with his penetration to the central energies, the springs of action, in beast or man: the two are continuous.

The hero of *The Giaour* is typical of Byron's tales, a man in hell yet unbowed, a certain obscurity veiling the dark cause of his suffering:

> Wet with thine own best blood shall drip
> Thy gnashing tooth and haggard lip;
> Then stalking to thy sullen grave,
> Go – and with Gouls and Afrits rave;
> Till these in horror shrink away
> From Spectre more accurs'd than they!
> (781)

This ends a passage of towering satanic virulence, and its compressed explosiveness must surely win respect even from those whose direct response will be most impeded by the traditionally modelled, but pulsing, phraseology. Though the hero retires to a monastery where it 'soothes him to abide' for 'some dark deed he will not name' (800), he nevertheless 'looks not to priesthood for relief' (1207). The balance of irreligious passion against orthodox Christianity approaches in tone that of Pope's *Eloisa to Abelard*, while the rejection of religious assistance as powerless to ease the dark anguish and alter an inevitable course recalls *Doctor Faustus, Wuthering Heights,* and Byron's own *Manfred.* The close is subdued:

> I would not, if I might, be blest;
> I want no Paradise, but rest.
>
> (1269)

He would be buried with no record but a simple cross. The Moslem's hatred for the infidel is here burningly proud and fierce; but Christianity is also at the last reverenced. Such opposites of pagan fire and Christian gentleness are characteristically Byronic, and they are to be in poem after poem subdued, as here, to an eternal peace.

Perhaps Conrad in *The Corsair* (1814) is the finest of his early human studies:

> Lone, wild, and strange, he stood alike exempt
> From all affection and from all contempt . . .
>
> (I. 11)

The narratives tend to revolve on inward psychic, or spiritual, conflicts. Though Conrad is a pirate chief of stern and ruthless action, his is a deeply spiritual bitterness. His anguish is fearfully revealed:

> There is a war, a chaos of the mind,
> When all its elements convuls'd, combin'd,
> Lie dark and jarring with perturbed force,
> And gnashing with impenitent remorse . . .
>
> (II. 10)

The lines suit Macbeth; and though we may be reminded of Crabbe, the Byronic hero has a tragic direction not found in *Peter Grimes.* He is noble and Miltonic:

> His was the lofty port, the distant mien,
> That seems to shun the sight – and awes if seen:
> The solemn aspect, and the high-born eye,
> That checks low mirth, but lacks not courtesy . . .
>
> (I. 16)

No captive girls ever seduce his attention from his loved Medora. 'None are all evil' (I. 12), we are told; and at the core of his personality is a love, a 'softness' (III. 22); this word, or 'soft', recurring throughout Byron's work with the deepest central significance. In this same poem Antony is the 'soft triumvir' (II. 15). Conrad is however a grim figure, and his endurance whilst awaiting torture is given terrible poetic disclosure. Yet he refuses to save himself by a cowardly murder and is nauseated when a woman, Gulnare, does it for him. All horrors of his wide piratical experience or natural imagination are as nothing to that arising from this desecration of feminine gentleness. From none

> So thrill'd, so shudder'd every creeping vein,
> As now they froze before that purple stain.
>
> (III. 10)

The passage is most powerful, tracing territories explored in the conception of Lady Macbeth. The hero suffers originally through a determination to save women from his own piratical massacre: which, though perhaps irrational, is intensely Byronic. Frequently we come across such ruthless evil and cynical callousness enshrining a strangely soft, almost feminine, devotion. Conrad's heart 'was form'd for softness, warp'd to wrong' (III. 23). The poem's conclusion holds a reserved depth of feeling reminiscent of Pope. He finds Medora dead:

> He ask'd no question – all were answer'd now
> By the first glance on that still, marble brow.
>
> (III. 21)

Notice the strength of the simple statement 'all were answer'd now', and how that makes of one human death a vast eternity, almost an assurance. So

> his mother's softness crept
> To those wild eyes, which like an infant's wept . . .
>
> (III. 22)

Yet he is not sentimentalized. As in *Macbeth*, the poet dares to end with a condemnation, leaving the human delineation to plead its own cause:

> He left a Corsair's name to other times,
> Link'd with one virtue, and a thousand crimes.
>
> (III. 24)

The central complex of loneliness and cruelty is left undefined. The same figure recurs in *Lara* (1814). Though cold, ruthless and with a smile 'waned in its mirth and wither'd to a sneer' (I. 17), the hero is yet one 'with more capacity for love than earth bestows' (I. 18) on most men. The dark mystery shrouding his past is never lifted. Bryon's heroes, like Heathcliff and Captain Ahab, are personalities tugged by some strange evil between time and eternity.

The poetic vigour of each narrative, depending on choice and exact statement rather than abstruse analogy or magic sound, never fails. Subtle rhythmic variation may finely realize description, as this of a floating corpse, in *The Bride of Abydos* (1813):

> As shaken on his restless pillow
> His head heaves with the heaving billow.
> (II. 26)

Continually a fine thing is said as a way to realize some great feeling. Especially strong are the darkest moments, as 'I want no Paradise, but rest' (1270) and 'This brow that then will burn no more' (1313) in *The Giaour*. The decasyllabic couplets of *The Corsair* hold a similar force:

> Oh! o'er the eye Death most exerts his might,
> And hurls the Spirit from her throne of light.
> (III. 20)

Verbs play a major, often a dominating part, as in the remorseless beat of the line 'Eternity forbids thee to forget' (I. 23) from *Lara*. The diction accepts personifications of a vast yet simple and un-ornate kind, and traditionally poetic words of various sorts. These, as in Pope, are chosen to express a ready-made fusion of the particular and the general. The influence of Pope may be at times very obvious, too, in couplet-modulation, as – to take random examples from a wide field – in *The Corsair* (I. 11), and the lines beginning 'No danger daunts . . .' in *The Bride of Abydos* (II. 20). As in Pope, each word is exactly used but loaded with more than its natural maximum of force. The lines cry to be uttered and can be understood, if not fully appreciated, at once. The emotional precision is unerring, defined yet never metallic: like the twang of a taut string.

However perfect the control, the spiritual or physical energies

set in action are striking. Many fine animal creations are symptomatic of the Byronic mastery of the vital and the organic, as
in the wild Tartar horse of the later story *Mazeppa* (1819) with
in his limbs the 'speed of thought' (9), and the other thousand
with

> Wide nostrils never stretch'd by pain,
> Mouths bloodless to the bit or rein . . .
>
> (17)

Byron feels in and with the animal. There is the 'stately buffalo'
of 'fiery eyes' and stamping hoofs attacked by wolves in *The
Siege of Corinth* (1816; 23); the insect stinging to save its
property (compare the wren in *Macbeth*, IV. ii. 9), and the adder
seeking vengeance when trodden on, in *The Corsair* (I. 13–14).
The end of *The Prisoner of Chillon* (1816) provides perhaps the
best; where, after an eternity of dark imprisonment, the hero
has actually made such friends with the spiders of his dungeon
and so long loved the mice at their moonlit 'play' that he is
reluctant to leave; and I doubt if the whole range of Byron's
work provides a sweeter instance of his uncanny penetration
into the most secret chambers of a mind in agony and loneliness.
The moon in Byron has elsewhere such tragic associations. Continuous with these animal intuitions is the Shakespearian feeling
for human personality, characterized by ability and desire to
give vital action and project figures of – quite apart from their
ethical standing – innate dignity and blazing courage; and
women, including Gulnare in *The Corsair*, of an utterly instinctive, yet magnificent, devotion.

The tales are characterized by (i) vivid and colourful action,
and (ii) a recurring psychological conflict normally related to
some feminine romance-interest. We may get mainly action,
as in *The Bride of Abydos* and the nightmare frenzy of the ride in
Mazeppa; or mainly a psychological study, as in *Lara*. *The
Corsair* is probably the finest in its balance of both. The atmosphere of *The Giaour* is powerfully realized but the hero's remorse
seems disproportionate to the occasion. However, the central
guilt-complex may be better left without premature definition,
as in *Hamlet* and *Macbeth*. We can feel the poet aiming at a
story-action that fits his intuition, though once, in the tightly

woven and sustained power of *Parisina* (1816), a short plot is cleverly devised to condition the typifying mind-state of the Byronic hero, the story stopping where that begins. The perfect fusion of inward experience and active plot is never perhaps quite mastered. There is no deeply significant outer conflict, no clash of universal forces, unless the balance of religions in *The Giaour* might so qualify. Profundities are found in most searching human comment continually, but the action is not by itself profound. A bridge is needed; a conduit to flood the whole with some element of the hero's tragic power. The narratives are to this extent slightly inorganic in comparison with Shakespeare: they have a hero, but no heart. A field of dramatic meaning has not been generated; a psychological and spiritual study, however deep, cannot quite do this; and the incidents and persons accordingly lose generalized significance and stature, though we may receive a sense of some mysterious eternity at the close. Only a judgement most insensitive to the deadly marksmanship of Byron's peculiar excellences would stigmatize them as 'melodramatic'.

II

These tales of action and geographic colour are strung together by a central, personal experience. The human penetration, the revelation of mental suffering, is primary. *Childe Harold* (Cantos I and II, 1812; III, 1816; IV, 1818) is more consistently extraverted, though it has a similar twofold appeal, with, again, a separateness: nature-descriptions, however, serving towards a fusion, as I shall show. A series of meditations on places and events is given unity by the admittedly shadowy conception of Harold; that is, Byron. Yet, this looseness once forgiven, we are struck by the amazing vitality of the creation. Byron is the only poet since Shakespeare to possess one of Shakespeare's rarest gifts: that of pure artistic joy in the annals – after searching I can find no better word – of human action; in close association, moreover, with places. He feels the tingling nearness of any heroic past. Gray had something of this; so had Scott; and Hardy gets it in his *Dynasts* as a whole, perhaps, if not in the parts. This is a quality well beyond our contemporary sophistication. It is an ability to love, not mankind, as did Shelley, but men; and men, or women, of various sorts, places and times:

> Is it for this the Spanish maid, arous'd,
> Hangs on the willow her unstrung guitar . . .
>
> (I. 54)

Or, of Waterloo:

> And wild and high the 'Cameron's gathering' rose!
> The war-note of Lochiel, which Albyn's hills
> Have heard, and heard, too, have her Saxon foes: –
> How in the noon of night that pibroch thrills . . .
>
> (III. 26)

And this of the dying gladiator:

> He reck'd not of the life he lost nor prize,
> But where his rude hut by the Danube lay . . .
>
> (IV. 141)

He is fascinated with the persons of one scene or event after another. The scattered incidents are given a sincere unity by the autobiographical thread; this extraverted interest, almost love, being integral to the Byronic imagination.

The suffering behind every glamorous association is not forgotten. Historic excitement is often one with a condemnation of history; for a fundamental love of men is involved and history often cruel. For example:

> Ah, monarchs! Could ye taste the mirth ye mar,
> Not in the toils of glory would ye fret:
> The hoarse dull drum would sleep, and Man be happy yet!
>
> (I. 47)

The clang and fury of world affairs are shown in opposition to simple, often sensuous, joys. On the eve of Waterloo a 'heavy sound' of cannon breaks short the pleasures of the dance. Then are there

> cheeks all pale, which but an hour ago
> Blushed at the praise of their own loveliness;
> And there were sudden partings, such as press
> The life from out young hearts, and choking sighs . . .
>
> (III. 24)

I point not merely to verbal excellences, but to the impersonal, yet warm, sympathy with human instincts. So from 'Beauty's circle' the men are shown next in 'battle's magnificently-stern array'; and finally hurled, horse and rider, friend and foe, 'in one red burial' (III. 28). The fervour admiring courage and battle-finery is one with that which pities the transition from dance to slaughter. It is a total awareness of Shakespearian quality. Byron can start to describe a bull-fight in a glamorous stanza (I. 73) of steeds and spurs and ladies' eyes and pass on to give a poignant sympathy to the suffering of bull and horse in a 'brutal' sport. Though a similar sympathy is accorded the dying gladiator in Book IV butchered for Rome's enjoyment this sympathy does not preclude strong feeling for Rome's imperial greatness. The poet is aware of emotional opposites involving each other, or rather of a single emotion taking opposite forms of assertion and pathos; just as the agonized conflicts and evil passions of his heroes are somehow one with their instincts of chivalry and tenderness. The poet lets himself be, as it were, annihilated before each splendour and pathos in turn.

His feeling for human nobility past and present is also one with his acceptance of a traditional poetic diction. This repays our close attention. Few poets have accomplished so much effortless force in single lines, as, for example:

> Stop! – for thy tread is on an Empire's dust!
> (III. 17)

Or

> The spouseless Adriatic mourns her lord . . .
> (IV. 11)

Or

> Oh Time! the beautifier of the dead . . .
> (IV. 130)

The utterance is weighty yet carried easily: the thing said seems to be all in all, with no especial drive for original expression. The style here, as in the Tales, is finely assured, involving a use of words where the fusion of general and particular, philosophic meditation and objective description, has already been performed. No effort is expended on abstruse comparison or the jerking of word or image from its habitual use or associative value. Personifications and abstractions are frequent but never cloudy, denoting concepts generally accepted. The words are words of an adequate syllabic weight; words, as it were, tested in the past and found to ring true; words of poetic lineage. In the first two lines just quoted 'tread', 'dust', 'spouse', 'mourns' all strike me as examples of what might be called a middle diction, a workmanlike poetic, but not too poetic, manner. This may rise even to

> Their praise is hymn'd by loftier harps than mine
> (III. 29)

without loss of sincerity. We have strong nouns, plain, usually active, verbs, sentences cleanly turned out, well drilled, and marching to their purpose. No verbal magic is allowed at the expense of clarity. Byron's religious intuitions are based on a preliminary acceptance of the conventional, felt in the robust Johnsonian phraseology and thought of

> I speak not of men's creeds – they rest between
> Man and his Maker –   (IV. 95)

For the most part every accent is poetically distinguished, though none superlative; nor meant to be. But the thing said, or the object seen, may be of superlative grandeur, as in this, of Rome:

> The Niobe of nations! There she stands,
> Childless and crownless, in her voiceless woe.
> (IV. 79)

The sympathy with the present pathos of ruins cannot be detached from that acceptance of the one-time historic splendour which also chooses well-worn associations such as the splendour of 'nations', the awe of crowns, the traditional poetic appeal of a word such as 'woe'. Byron likes, as a poet, what is already warm with human contact. He injects into it his own vitality, whether in admiration or rebellion. He likes human society and its history; which is but a surface effect of that deeper infeeling into animal or human vitality that enables him to display both convincing action and a moving pathos.

And yet again he stands outside the world he writes of, balancing human purpose against human futility. *Childe Harold* is a lamentation in noble phrases over the widespread ruins of a dead chivalry and a dead tyranny. Byron is superbly conscious

of the whole of Europe. He sees it as one vast theatre of tomb-
stones, though at his touch the dead are temporarily raised, and
in the poetry there is no futility. He ranges across the centuries
accepting and cherishing a past or recent present which he
simultaneously repudiates and regrets. He hymns empires while
hating tyranny; recognizes the 'lion' in Napoleon whilst decrying servility to 'wolves' (III. 19); glories in patriot battlefields
though attacking the iniquities of wars by which monarchs
'pave their way with human hearts' (I. 42); at the limit, he
praises life whilst entranced by death. He is a militant pacifist,
exposing the fallacies of ambition (I. 42–4). The tragic notes are
his surest, the richer for the human excellences apprehended.
The whole poem is written from a vast eternity-consciousness
to which historic events, as events, are the negative symbols of
its expression. There is thus a very 'life' in 'despair', a mysterious
'vitality of poison' (III. 34). Particulars are vivid chiefly by
reason of their felt transience. Somehow their transience *is* their
eternity:

> Far other scene is Thrasimene now . . .
>
> (IV. 65)

Or, when we come to Rome, the mystery of time itself takes
ghostly form, entwined with infinite space and natural magic:

> But when the rising moon begins to climb
> Its topmost arch, and gently pauses there;
> When the stars twinkle through the loops of time,
> And the low night-breeze waves along the air
> The garland-forest, which the gray walls wear,
> Like laurels on the bald first Caesar's head;
> When the light shines serene but doth not glare,[1]
> Then in this magic circle raise the dead:
> Heroes have trod this spot – 'tis on their dust ye tread.
>
> (IV. 144)

The grandeur of Rome lives most in its ruins. After visiting the
Coliseum and wandering through memories of a dead empire
we come to St Peter's, which strikes from the poet both a magnificent religious fervour and subtle architectural appreciation
in living terms, characteristically, of the *human* mind unable to

---

[1] The word 'glare' jars. I have found it used elsewhere in this period with a
similar effect. Its tone seems to have changed. [1967]

take in the whole splendour with a single glance, yet at last distended to eternal comprehension; and end with the great invocation to the sea, imperial beyond all empires:

> Roll on, thou deep and dark blue Ocean – roll!
> Ten thousand fleets sweep over thee in vain . . .
>
> (IV. 179)

With what sureness are handled, as in Gray's *Elegy*, the noble
platitudes so often composing the greatest poetry. 'Assyria,
Greece, Rome, Carthage, what are they?' he asks (IV. 182).
Their life was conditioned by that spirit – he calls it 'freedom'
but perhaps we should give it a wider name – that alone can
preserve, without which they are dust. That spirit is reflected
by both (i) the poet's ranging consciousness, the 'eternal spirit
of the chainless mind' of his *Sonnet on Chillon* (1816), autobiographical soliloquy alternating with the scenic progress and
reaching its culmination in the great personal apologetic and
satiric outburst near the close (IV. 132–7); and (ii) the sea, unfettered by temporal law.

> Time writes no wrinkle on thine azure brow:
> Such as creation's dawn beheld, thou rollest now.
>
> (IV. 182)

This vast unfathomable and elemental power interlocks itself
with that humanism, that social and historic sympathy, so
strong in Byron.

Childe Harold has many elemental passages, together with a
continual swerve in comment from particular to general. My
remarks on diction do not say the whole truth. Often a metaphor
may start up with both surface flash and revealing depth, the
more vivid for the generally level style:

> And how and why we know not, nor can trace
> Home to its cloud this lightning of the mind . . .
>
> (IV. 24)

Natural immensities fill out wide areas of the later Cantos III
and IV, acting as a bridge between the hero and his world: his
own consciousness is shown as more akin to them than to the
human drama that was his first story. The process reflects that
dissociation found first in *Timon of Athens* and urgent since,
but no other poet of Byron's period shows a range of sympathy

sufficient to include both sides of the opposition. He invokes 'maternal Nature' (III. 46). The sea is felt as a freedom after stifling human contacts (III. 2), and that other vastness of mountains so weightily insistent in the imagination of his day is duly honoured:

> Not vainly did the early Persian make
> His altar the high places, and the peak
> Of earth-o'ergazing mountains . . .
>
> (III. 91)

Such an association may be related to the mountain poetry of Wordsworth and Coleridge. There are passages more finely detailed, more energy-striking than this: as that describing the roar and hell-cauldrons of a *Kubla Khan* mountain waterfall, the rising mist above, the ever-fertilized green turf, the peaceful river of the plain; and, as we look back, an Iris rainbow shot through the dreadful waters, still and brilliant above agonized distraction, like 'Love watching Madness with unalterable mien' (IV. 69–72): a line whose depth and fervency of tragic understanding shows the author to be potentially an artist of Shakespearian stature.

Often such a swift transition penetrates its mark with quivering intensity: Byron's nature-images are normally made to serve, or at least blend into, some human purpose. But they are also great in their own right: so we have 'shaggy summits' (IV. 73) where, when storm and darkness riot, there are flashes lovely as – typically – a woman's 'dark eye', when

> From peak to peak, the rattling crags among
> Leaps the live thunder! (III. 92)

'Live': a living ecstasy continually energizes Byron's work. He can also treat of mighty glaciers or the placid Rhone with immediate descriptive force. All such vast natural symbols objectify that in himself that demarks him from men's society. Any man 'who surpasses or subdues mankind' is as a mountain looking on the hate of those below (III. 45). He is himself a 'portion' of the nature 'around' him, rejecting the agonies of human society, finding life in natural kinship with the 'mountains, waves, and skies' as 'part' of his soul, and looking to death for cosmic freedom (III. 71–5). He knows the secrets of 'pathless

woods' and 'lonely shore' (iv. 178). They and their eternity are
the watch-towers from which he looks down on the rise and fall
of empires. Yet he never for long forgets man. 'I love not Man
the less but Nature more' (iv. 178) is no overstatement. All his
finest nature-impressions up-pile to blend with the supreme
human grandeur of Rome. His mind outdistances his companions, that is all: if he could put all of himself into one word,
that word were 'lightning' (iii. 97). The choice is exact; and
the image can be reversed. His brow, like that of his own Azo
ploughed by the 'burning share' of sorrow (*Parisina*, 20), may
metaphorically be felt as kin also to that of Milton's Satan
which 'deep scars of thunder had intrench'd' (*Paradise Lost*, i.
601); or the She-wolf of his own description, the 'thunder-
stricken nurse of Rome' whose limbs lightning has blackened
(iv. 88); or, best of all, the bust of Aristo 'doubly sacred' by the
thunder-flame that stripped it of its crown (iv. 41).

Though few poets show so instinctive a human insight, Byron
is being forced into the individualism of Wordsworth and
Shelley. Yet there is a difference. He assimilates, but is not
subdued by, the splendours of nature. He has been blamed for
lightly and theatrically making poetic gestures not deeply felt;
and it is true that certain lines in *Childe Harold* appear to merit
the charge. Sometimes the transition from the more Augustan
diction of the Tales, written before the latter Cantos of *Childe
Harold*, to a newly vital nature-imagery is not perfect. Byron
seems to gather in his new material with too sweeping a gesture,
too aristocratic a superiority: he takes it for his own, more
human, purpose. He is not, any more than Shakespeare, subdued to nature-mysticism; and yet he can, when he cares to, turn
it to a far finer, because more human, account, as in the image
of Love and Madness recently noticed, than any poet of his day.
He is always above, not below, his contemporaries. The others
rave over cataracts and mountains, and he too goes to mountains for inspiration. They serve him magnificently, probably as
a man, certainly as a poet; but they do not rank so importantly
with him as that other more Shakespearian vastness, the sea.
That, from *The Corsair*, which contains some fine sea-poetry, to
Canto ii of *Don Juan* (1819) and *The Island* (1823), is a permanent possession, whereas mountains affect him deeply only now,

in mid-career. No English poet has written more finely of the
sea, as in the rolling volumes – got by 'o'-sounds – of

> Thou glorious mirror, where the Almighty's form
> Glasses itself in tempests; in all time –
> Calm or convuls'd, in breeze, or gale, or storm,
> Icing the pole, or in the torrid clime
> Dark-heaving – boundless, endless, and sublime,[1]
> The image of eternity, the throne
> Of the Invisible; even from out thy slime
> The monsters of the deep are made; each zone
> Obeys thee; thou goest forth, dread, fathomless, alone.

> (IV. 183)

'The image of eternity': the concept pulses throughout Byron's
work. Contrast this with his great denunciatory and prophetic
passage (IV. 132–7) where he piles on the heads of mankind his
curse of 'forgiveness'; next strikes the exact note and manner of
Pope's satiric epistles ('petty perfidy', 'the small whisper of the
as paltry few', 'venom', 'reptile'); and finally asserts the undying
powers ('something unearthly') of his poetry to reassert his
rights. We can see how the two elements, objective human interest and lonely individualism, of the early narratives are
rending apart. Byron is torn between history and tragic insight,
mankind and lonely self-conflict, time and eternity. The disparity is bridged by sea and mountains, infinite expanse and
lifting mass, each at once symbols of both the natural and the
eternal.

III

The transition from *Childe Harold* to the dramas of spiritual conflict resembles Shakespeare's development at the turn of the
sixteenth century. The manner, too, changes. Augustan influence is no longer evident, though the basic vocabulary remains slightly traditional. Byron's style is now unassertive,
serving whatever his thought, imagery, or passion may require,
while maintaining his usual reliance on nouns, verbs, and clear
syntax.

---

[1] For the use here of a vertical emphasis in 'sublime' see my *Byron and Shakespeare*,
271. I refer the reader to that volume (especially 37–54, 271–6, 283–5) for a more
extended, and deeper, commentary on *Childe Harold* than that here presented.

The setting and action of *Manfred* (1817) are devised to express an intense spiritual conflict:

> It is an awful chaos – Light and Darkness –
> And mind and dust – and passions and pure thoughts
> Mix'd, and contending without end or order . . .
>
> (III. i. 164)

'I plung'd amidst Mankind', says the hero, after having been 'dashed back' into the gulf of his own 'unfathomed thought' (II. ii. 143); though the image might better have left him high and dry on a rocky eminence. The setting is mountainous and elemental – the Alps, cataracts, sun, and stars being interwoven with titanic spiritual drama. *Manfred* is a miniature *Faust*, with a greater intensity and condensation of spiritual issues and elemental impressionism. The two go together; the Witch of the Alps here is conjured from a cataract. The stage-directions – one involves a 'cataract', another a 'tower', and all of them, by implication, mountains – are explicit, building a height-symbolism to match the towering solitude of the protagonist. Manfred is in direct descent from earlier heroes. He has their peculiar guilt and proud isolation. 'I am not of thine order' (II. i. 38), he says to the Chamois Hunter. His spiritual aristocracy is yet more emphatic when he shows himself a greater than the spirits he calls up and refuses the Witch's help unless given unconditionally. She is his slave, not he hers: the thought recalls that innate because human sovereignty of Macbeth and Satan (p. 35 above) in similar situations. So, clogged by sin and a guilty horror, he yet challenges the presence of Arimanes himself, the god of natural creation, or some similar great, yet not final, divinity, such as Shelley's Jupiter, with a throne called a 'Globe of Fire'.[1] The attendant spirits realize that Manfred, who will not kneel, is of 'no common order' (II. iv. 52). There is an 'Infinite' beyond Arimanes and to that alone he is dedicated. This is to be reached not through nature but through *human personality*; so the figure of Astarte belongs to 'powers deeper still beyond' all natural splendours (II. iv. 76); and leaves even Nemesis 'baffled' (II. iv. 116). Manfred feels himself to be above men and spirits alike, bearing

[1] The mythology is Zoroastrian and Arimanes is Ahriman, the principle of evil, though here to be related less to human sin than to the negative aspects of natural existence on earth. [1967]

in his life 'what others could not brook to dream' (II. i. 78). He was not a ruler of men since he could not 'tame' his nature to their service; the crowd are 'mean', he a 'lion' among 'wolves' (III. i. 116–23). An inward and Timon-like profundity is shown scorning either the lower group-consciousness or any persons seen in objective unreality. There recurs the characteristically Byronic reservation: he has not been 'cruel' (III. i. 126). Whatever wild arrogance or intolerable sin torments the Byronic hero, there is, at the personality's core, a love, a softness.

Manfred is agonized by 'some half-maddening sin' (II. i. 31) like Conrad and Lara. Its 'uneradicable taint' (*Childe Harold*, IV. 126) possesses him. He knows a 'deep despair' which is 'remorse without the fear of Hell' (III. i. 70): the Byronic guilt is in Manfred given its final form. The mystery is deliberately embodied in a 'beautiful female figure' resurrected from the dead, at once a 'madness' and a 'mockery'. In her is yet hope of peace:

> I will clasp thee,
> And we again will be –   (I. i. 190),

The figure vanishes. She is later resurrected by Nemesis as 'Astarte'. Manfred addresses her:

> Can this be death? there's bloom upon her cheek;
> But now I see it is no living hue,
> But a strange hectic – like the unnatural red
> Which Autumn plants upon the perish'd leaf.
> It is the same! Oh, God! that I should dread
> To look upon the same – Astarte! – No,
> I cannot speak to her – but bid her speak –
> Forgive me or condemn me.   (II. iv. 98)

He would hear again 'the voice which was my music' (II. iv. 134), yet recalls some deadly sin between them. He sees blood,

> the pure warm stream
> Which ran in the veins of my fathers, and in ours
> When we were in our youth, and had one heart,
> And loved each other as we should not love,
> And this was shed . . .   (II. i. 24)

Yet she has been his guiding memory; he has searched for her in nature and man and not found her likeness. What is this memory of the years? – this

> . . . sole companion of his wanderings
> And watchings – her, whom of all earthly things
> That lived, the only thing he seem'd to love, –
> As he, indeed, by blood was bound to do,
> The Lady Astarte, his –   (III. iii. 43)

'Bound to' love her. Yet he himself called it 'deadliest sin' (II. iv. 123). She resembles the maternal figure of Keats's Moneta in *The Fall of Hyperion* (250):[1] before her he is as much child as lover. Elsewhere she seems a sister and he disclaims fathers and mothers in comparison. She is his own *double* in looks and soul but with 'gentler powers', and becomes a symbol not of passion so much as of 'pity, and smiles, and tears', raising his own 'tenderness' (II. ii. 112–14). She corresponds to Isabel in Herman Melville's *Pierre*. The specifically family emotion of identity with mother or sister is contrasted and entwined with the sexual passion of opposites. A union of the deep-rooted psychological principles has taken place on the sexual side of the balance, and there is a corresponding guilt, condemnation flashing from both sides; for these by nature fling apart and the union offends both in excess. Astarte embodies both a dual accusation and final synthesis, being a comprehensive deity of licence, fruitfulness and purity. She is both the great principle of cruel and tender purity that tortures man's sexual instincts, spurning them till they writhe under its heel; and the very aim and consummation of those instincts. The two Aphrodites as goddesses of love and lust, *agapé* and *eros*, the maternal-sisterly and sexual impulses, are in her swiftly unified, only to make of some uncanny heaven a too realistic hell. Though the love be a guilty love, like Eloisa's in Pope's *Eloisa to Abelard*, it is no cruelty nor love of cruelty but rather some passionate union with that first principle of softness and peace that sleeps at creation's centre. Remember how 'his mother's softness' crept even into Conrad's eyes, at sight of his loved one's death (p. 184 above). Manfred boasts that he has never quelled an enemy save in

[1] Compare also Astarte's 'bloom' that is yet 'no living hue' but a 'strange hectic' (p. 197 above) with Moneta's 'wan face' 'bright-blanch'd' by an 'immortal sickness' (*The Fall of Hyperion*, 256). [1967]

'just defence', and yet his 'embrace was fatal' (II. i. 86–7). Lust and sweetest tenderness are for Byron changing facets of one reality: that reality is Astarte. She embodies the lascivious-divine complex I have argued to be the disrupting force as well as the primary cause of Milton's poetry. His error was to read it as a static two-way sign-post statement, to submit to the point-ing accusation, instead of willing its transmutation into a single one-way dynamic symbol of movement from this to that; as a direction. The very creation here of Astarte is such a recognition and transmutation.[1]

The nature poetry of *Manfred* is both closely referred to the inward conflict and sublime in its own right: in the mountains and plunging cataracts, the moon rising on snows never trod by 'human foot' (II. iii. 2), the stars as a 'language of another world' (III. iv. 7), or the sun, magnificently invoked, as the idol of 'undiseased mankind' (III. ii. 5). See how substantial each in-human splendour remains through some human reference: there is a warmth, a close realism, that Shelley's *Prometheus Unbound* neither attains nor expects, felt also in the drama's closely real-ized persons, the Chamois Hunter and the Abbot. Moreover, even here Byron's close imaginative dependence on the past – the play opens in an old 'Gothic gallery' – his feeling for its living and speaking presence, is given expression in Manfred's meditation from his tower (III. iv. 1–41) on the ruins of Rome seen by moonlight. He recalls a grove that 'twines its roots' among 'imperial hearths', the moon's 'tender light' softening all and filling up 'the gaps of centuries',

> Leaving that beautiful which still was so,
> And making that which was not – till the place
> *Became religion*, and the heart ran o'er
> With silent worship of the Great of old –
> The dead, but sceptred, Sovereigns, *who still rule*
> *Our spirits from their urns.*

The italics are mine: the phrases go deep into the acceptances and revolts of Byron's work.

So among mountains and cataracts, beneath the stars of night

---

[1] Astarte may be supposed also to cover Byron's homosexual propensities and engagements. See *Lord Byron's Marriage*, 126. [1967]

or facing the 'glorious orb' of the sun, Manfred's tortured existence, that has inhabited arid deserts like 'the red-hot breath of
the most lone Simoom' (III. i. 128), reaches its end. Having rejected material ambition, not caring to be 'mighty' among the
'mean', willingly 'averse from life', refusing to be 'a living lie'
(III. i. 119–25) in the world of men, the world of Pope's satires,
he challenges death and all spiritual powers that may confront
him. The Abbot corresponds to the Old Man in *Faustus* and
Nelly in *Wuthering Heights*. Manfred puts him and his religion
aside though with a typically Byronic reverence: 'I do respect
thine order' (III. i. 154). There is strong meaning in Manfred's
refusal to abnegate his human sovereignty at the close. He will,
to borrow a phrase from Shelley's *Prometheus Unbound* (IV. 575),
neither 'falter nor repent'. The 'lightning' of his personal 'being'
that darts 'far' as any force of nature (I. i. 155) recognizes no
final authority in any religion of man. No hell can equal that
already in his mind, no accusation pierce keener than his own.
He fears no damnation – 'Must crimes be punish'd but by other
crimes and greater criminals?' (III. iv. 123) – but rather plants
his direction in a more single faith. The last spirit of guilt is
passed:

> Back, ye baffled fiends!
> The hand of Death is on me – but not yours!
> (III. iv. 140)

It is a proud and subjective trust, an assertion of some utterly
instinctive and innate royalty. *Manfred* is a tight compression
of essences primary in writer after writer from Marlowe and
Shakespeare onwards. It dramatizes a struggle to preserve intact
the faith of Pope against the faith of Milton. The preliminary
guilt is terrific:

> a tyrant-spell
> Which had its birth-place in a star condemn'd,
> The burning wreck of a demolish'd world,
> A wandering hell in the eternal space . . .
> (I. i. 43)

Such is the 'strong curse' binding his 'soul' (I. i. 47). Byron's
great importance rises from his battling honesty, the powerful

sexual thrust of his imagination, conjoined to intellectual awareness of all the issues involved.[1]

This recurring theme of guilt points naturally to the Biblical
legend of Cain, whose 'curse and crime' was one with Byron's
conception of his tragic hero as early as *The Giaour* (1058) and
mentioned also in *The Bride of Abydos* (II. 12) and *Manfred* (I. i.
249), and *Marino Faliero* (IV. ii. 56). Byron's respect for orthodoxy
was ingrained and he turns naturally to the traditional mythology of the Church, whose teaching he does, however, through
subtle dramatic suggestion nevertheless repudiate.

In *Cain* (1821) God's arbitrary – according to the Old Testament – law is balanced against a reasonable Lucifer, one
who

> dare look the Omnipotent tyrant in
> His everlasting face, and tell him that
> His evil is not good.   (I. i. 138)

We must translate the dramatic figures into *conceptions:* the Old
Testament conception of God-as-Law is therefore being attacked, no more. Lucifer makes out a good case. The Tree of
Knowledge was what it claimed to be and God's arbitrary rule
alone turned its enjoyment to sin. Lucifer claims never to have
tempted man[2] yet he himself would certainly have made them,
what the God of Genesis feared to make them, 'gods' (I. i. 203).
The reading of the Fall as an evolutionary ascent is by now,
though it was not in Byron's day, respectable Biblical interpretation; but if developed into a living ethic, the intended direction might still seem appallingly dangerous. Byron is grafting
the energies of Renaissance poetry on to Europe's traditional
religion; is relating Pope's *Essay on Man* to Biblical mythology;
and simultaneously throwing a shaft of light on to the Miltonic,
and our own, confusions by using Milton's own devil as an
admittedly, instead of insidiously, sympathetic figure. Lucifer,

---

[1] The implications of *Manfred* cover Shakespeare's progress from *Hamlet* to *The Tempest*: e.g., 'enlightener of nations' (III. i. 107) etc. for Hamlet against Claudius; dark magic and (II. i. 21–30) blood-guilt for Macbeth; return to nature for *Timon of Athens*; love and lust for *Antony and Cleopatra*; and good magic (defended at III. iv. 113–119) for *The Tempest*. See my *Byron and Shakespeare*, throughout. [1967]

[2] He insists that the tempter was simply, as Genesis records, the 'serpent' (I. i. 218–32). If we suppose a sexual reference we have a relation to the sexually impelled evils in Spenser and Milton. [1967]

like Goethe's Mephistopheles,[1] supports, if he does not instigate, man's quest of knowledge and life, regarding despair as a 'grovelling wish' (I. i. 292). What is sin? Is it to be arbitrarily defined from without, or has it an absolute and intrinsic quality? (I. i. 380). The discussion acutely concerns both sin, and death (I. i. 249–99).

The poem next (II. i) opens out to infinity as Lucifer takes Cain on a tour of inspection. The conception is daring but successful; aiming to exploit to the full that mysterious 'eternity' so insistent in Byron's tragic approach from the start through the medium of that eternity-symbol met in *Childe Harold*, as also in Shakespeare's *Timon of Athens*, the sea. Impressions of vast space and depth correspond to the mountains of *Manfred*.

Lucifer symbolizes the poet's ranging *imagination*, Pope's 'priestless muse' (Epilogue to the Satires, II. 234), guiding Cain through immensities without demanding any 'conditional creed' (II. i. 21). They first pass through 'beautiful and unimaginable ether' with 'multiplying masses' of 'still-increasing lights' in the 'blue wilderness' that sweep in 'unbounded revelry' through an 'aerial universe of endless expansion' (II. i. 98–109). Cain is 'intoxicated with eternity', yet when the earth looks a tiny spark only, Byron characteristically remembers insect-life:

> The little shining fire-fly in its flight,
> And the immortal star in its great course,
> Must both be guided . . .   (II. i. 130)

A poetic thought surely of higher importance than many a passage of more substantial phraseology. So they 'cleave the blue' (II. i. 144). The voyage is one over a 'gulf' (II. i. 22), clear as 'limpid streams' (II. i. 104), among worlds with 'enormous liquid plains' and 'floating moons' (II. i. 187–8). The glories of the 'empurpled night' (II. i. 179) begin to darken, and beyond space Cain is introduced to realms of death and phantoms, to the 'phantasm of the world' of which our world is a 'wreck' only (II. i. 152). It is fearfully dark, with 'huge dusky masses' (II. i. 181). The journey is thought of in terms of a typically Byronic conquest of dark fears. This past infinity is an extension

---

[1] Mephistopheles is however a more ambiguous conception who simultaneously assists and derides the hero's quest. [1967]

of his habitual fascination with the historic. Time and space are both as vast seas. They are now among 'swimming shadows' and 'floating' phantoms, once great and noble beings on a greater and nobler earth; 'mighty pre-Adamites' (II. ii. 31, 44, 359). There is an 'immeasurable liquid space of glorious azure' that 'looks like water', is 'of an ethereal hue' and is called 'the phantasm of an ocean' (II. ii. 178–83). Lucifer will not, or cannot, explain to Cain the exact nature of these deathly realms. 'Matter cannot comprehend spirit wholly'; there are 'many states beyond'; and it 'will seem clearer to thine immortality' (II. ii. 169–77).[1]

The thinking plays round the ultimate problems. The serpent-image, so frequent in Byron and correspondent to his strong feeling for sexual guilt, runs persistently throughout, and once attains gigantic proportion in the 'immense serpent' which 'rears his dripping mane' from out of the 'abyss' (II. ii. 190–3). The sexual act is cynically referred to by Lucifer as 'a sweet degradation', an 'enervating and filthy cheat' to lure man to procreation (II. i. 56). There is no facile emphasis on Biblical absurdity and simple solutions; the tangle gets more and more complex, as though the imagination may be stimulated but can never be satisfied by these dizzying mental excursions and deathly infinitudes: the one is cleverly shown as leading to the other.

The relation of these scenes to Cain's later crime obeys the same law as the presence in *Macbeth* of what I have called 'naked spirit' (*The Wheel of Fire*, enlarged, 264–5) in relation to evil. But in *Cain* the infinity of wondrous lights and blue depths and the crime that follows are less evil. Cain's is a kindly nature caught by a ruthless providence. His fall is referred to a laudable hatred of animal-sacrifice. Abel's sacrifice is accepted, his of fruits rejected. The sympathy is striking:

> *His pleasure!* What was his high pleasure in
> The fumes of scorching flesh and smoking blood,
> To the pain of the bleating mothers, which

---

[1] I omit a couple of my concluding sentences which appear to over-emphasize the fearsome quality of the adventure, preferring to leave the impressions quoted to speak for themselves. For the relation of Byron's 'Hades' to the etheric plane of Spiritualism, see *Byron and Shakespeare*, 308–9. [1967]

Still yearn for their dead offspring? Or the pangs
Of the sad ignorant victims underneath
Thy pious knife? Give way! This bloody record
Shall not stand in the sun, to shame creation!
(III. i. 298)

Earlier (II. ii. 153), explicitly at grips with the deepest problems of evil, Byron concentrates his challenge in terms of the suffering of animals: 'Did they, too, eat of it that they must die?' (for animals see *Lord Byron: Christian Virtues*, 3–16). Again:

I lately saw
A lamb stung by a reptile: the poor suckling
Lay foaming on the earth, beneath the vain
And piteous bleating of its restless dam . . .
(II. ii. 289)

It is given medicinal herbs and the mother all 'tremulous' licks its 'reviving limbs'. Yet why should it so have to purchase its 'little life' with 'agonies unutterable' (II. ii. 300–305)? Similarly with men: what, asks Cain, has man done to be considered guilty even before a crime? What need of any future 'atonement' (III. i. 87)? He rejects 'base humility' (III. i. 101) and hypocritical gratitude. His recent experience, the

Suns, moons, and earths, upon their loud-voiced spheres,
Singing in thunder round me
(III. i. 182)

have made him 'unfit for mortal converse'. His sister-wife Adah – again the sister-emphasis first met in *The Bride of Abydos* – remains, as so often do Byron's and Shakespeare's women, outside the hero's conflict; a figure of sweet simplicity and unquestioning virtue. She alone stands by Cain at the close. Their child is poignantly used to point a contrast of natural innocence with destiny's or God's unreasoning cruelty; to negate, we may suggest, those promptings of original sin that Byron has found so appallingly powerful within himself. Cain, like Manfred, will not submit. 'That which I am, I am' (III. i. 509). But he would willingly die to revoke his deed.

Heaven and Earth (1821; pub. 1823) dramatizes, rather lyrically, the sinful union of angels with humankind recorded in

Genesis; and may be allowed to symbolize from a different view that complex of lust and divine intuition so deeply rooted in Milton. Aholibamah asserts the equality of her own to an angel's love; her possession of a 'ray' at present 'forbidden' to shine yet originating from God; and her fearless welcome of her angelic lover even though his love coil round her 'like the serpent' (i. i. 103–28). We could have no clearer statement of our old complex from the positive aspect. Japhet, a typical Byronic spokesman, has also a more positive vision than Cain of a future paradise on earth, accepting the Christian terms of a 'Redeemer' coming first in pain and next in glory, and opposing this to the scoffing 'spirits' from 'the cavern' (i. iii. 205). He wills to believe in a final 'celestial mercy' (i. iii. 680) in spite of the shortly expected Flood. He cannot believe 'rage' to exist with 'justice' (i. iii. 762). But the 'implacable Omnipotent' (i. iii. 860) is found unalterable. The two girls are taken off by their angels (see *The Golden Labyrinth*, 234); a distraught woman is brought in to point Jehovah's cruelty; but another voice preserves a typical Byronic balance by accepting God's ways with unquestioning submission. The poem has in parts a more assured and positive direction than *Manfred* or *Cain*, while approaching a resolution of their conflicts. It contains some of Byron's finest nature-poetry on his trinity of favourites: sun, mountains, and sea. The circling rhyme-schemes and line-variation seem to mark an attempt at expression of an especially lyrical harmony, though the form is, finally, tragic.

On these three visionary dramas pivots a central transmutation which must be closely referred to the teaching of both Pope and Nietzsche's *Thus Spake Zarathustra*.

IV

The more spiritual energies in *Manfred* and *Cain*, not incomparable with those of *King Lear* and *Macbeth*, are in *Marino Faliero* (1821) and *Sardanapalus* (1821) active in more realistic plots. The realism is firm but within burn cosmic vision and intense thought. They may, respectively, be compared with *Coriolanus* and *Antony and Cleopatra*.

Though the royalist ideal central in Shakespeare had lost

prestige in Milton, Swift, and Pope, its essence persists, for various reasons, basic: aristocratic scorn of the mob in a dramatic hero may reflect less snobbishness than the assertion of individual personality against a group-consciousness. Byron's life was given to freedom and in pressing for a new *personal sanctity* he logically conceives a new *sovereignty*, dramatizing stories of (i) a revolutionary duke and (ii) a pacifist king. His deep interest in the story of *Marino Faliero*, recorded in his long preface and additional notes, where we watch a dramatist of Shakespearian calibre revealing the historical interest behind his work, is understandable; for it touches some of the most complex issues of post-Renaissance Europe, of which Byron, the revolutionary aristocrat, was a symbol.

This is the story. Marino Faliero, Doge of Venice, has served his people as a great general before advancement to the ducal office, and is now, in age, married to Angiolina, a young and high-minded wife. Steno, a youthful member of the decadent but all-powerful and oppressive nobility, writes an insult to Angiolina on the Doge's chair, and is given by his peers a purely nominal sentence. The Doge, who is both fiery in temper and deeply public-spirited, plots with his people to overthrow the nobility. The plot fails.

First, I offer a short description of Marino Faliero himself. His heroic service is emphasized, and also his original unwillingness to undertake supreme authority; though once having it, he has a deep sense of its dignity and honour. He is nearly eighty years old, but his passions are still youthful and his eye 'quick' and impatient (I. i. 13). Hearing of Steno's sentence his fiery temperament reveals itself in speeches of rising impetuosity. He would have the Saracens, Genoese, or Huns victoriously overrunning Venice, his passion falling to treasonable thoughts. Then, alone, he meditates on the ducal cap, seeing it as a gilded 'toy' with the 'thorns' but not the 'majesty' of a crown:

> How my brain aches beneath thee! And my temples
> Throb feverish under thy dishonest weight.
>   (I. ii. 265)

A Shakespearian kinship is preserved within the implications of a constitutional and limited monarchy. An essential falsity is defined by 'dishonest'. Later he expands on the mockery of his position as man and ruler:

> Begirt with spies for guards, with robes for power,
> With pomp for freedom, gaolers for a council,
> Inquisitors for friends, and Hell for life!
>
> (III. ii. 358)

He longs to 'free Venice' and 'avenge' his own 'wrongs' (I. ii. 316). The continuity of personal and general emotions is evident from the interview with Bertuccio (I. ii. 328–578) which leads to his association with the conspiracy; if his people could share his 'sovereignty' and both together master the 'aristocratic Hydra', he would at last rule. His agreement is skilfully motivated; Bertuccio, formerly a soldier, channels his sense of comradeship; and recollection of his son's death in battle is turned to thoughts of his people's 'filial' love. Them, not the senate, he served as a soldier. Left alone, he now, as conspirator, feels 'unworthy' of his ancestors and yet in terms of that very unworthiness he must have 'revenge' on baseness and create true freedom (I. ii. 579–97). The paradoxes are emphasized.

We heard from Angiolina (II. i. 18) that his passions go deep, everything wearing in him 'an aspect of Eternity'. He is a true successor to earlier heroes. His faults, his fiery and patrician passions, and a sense of honour so keen that it approaches a 'vice' (II. i. 109), are those naturally allied with his warrior past. The analysis might suit Coriolanus in Shakespeare: 'pride' (II. i. 104) is a fault in both. Angiolina urges her husband in vain to give Steno's fault the neglect its triviality merits, to dwell less on honour, and more on Heaven's charge of forgiveness. When his passion cools its place is taken by a deadly and a hated duty; his proposed betrayal of all honourable tradition appals him; his integrity refuses to call it anything but 'treason' (III. i. 56). Success will win the gratitude of posterity, but failure leave a record of baseness, a stern realism admitting that the quality of such actions appears to depend on their results (III. i. 67–78). The nobles' villainy itself forces the 'means' (III. i. 114–18). Yet again, asked whether all the nobles should fall, he answers

> Ask me not – tempt me not with such a question –
> Decide yourselves . . .   (III. ii. 296)

H

His eventual decision, tilted by remembrance of personal ingratitude, is for general massacre, though afterwards recollections of past social and military companionships crowd back
to make each proposed 'stab' a 'suicide' (III. ii. 472). The strange
magnanimity of a prince who risks all in plotting for his people
is set in contrast to the conventionally honourable 'tyrant' im-
pervious to remorse though he depopulate 'empires' rather than
punish a few 'traitors' (III. ii. 534). And yet, just as we are again
convinced, mention of Steno elicits two lines of unerring dramatic insight which reveal the personal resentment beneath:

> Man, thou hast struck upon the chord which jars
> All nature from my heart. Hence to our task!
>
> (III. ii. 540)

The balance of impure motive and revolutionary idealism is
maintained.

As action draws near, the Doge becomes calm:

> It was ever thus
> With me; the hour of agitation came
> In the first glimmerings of a purpose, when
> Passion had too much room to sway; but in
> The hour of action I have stood as calm
> As were the dead who lay around me . . .
>
> (IV. ii. 93)

In which there is a general truth which many will recognize.
The Doge determines to resign after the plot's consummation,
and meditates again on the wrongs and justice of his course.

When his expectations are reversed by the betrayal of the
conspiracy he bears failure with a stoic calm. At the trial he
recapitulates his original reluctance to take office and resentment at the nobles' insult, but remains proud and aloof:

> I deny nothing – defend nothing – nothing
> I ask of you, but silence for myself,
> And sentence from the Court!
>
> (V. i. 295)

Alone with Angiolina (V. ii. 15–41), he tells how a priest whom
he once struck prophesied that in maturity a 'madness' would
seize him at an age when 'passions' should properly 'mellow'

into 'virtues', Byron's respect for religion and uneasy relations with priests both finding here a natural home. The Doge sees his life as a 'maze' and his pride takes pleasure in yielding only to an over-ruling 'Power' greater than men's understanding (v. ii. 46, 72). At his final speech (v. iii. 26–104) he addresses 'Time' and 'Eternity', denounces Venetian vices, prophesies for the City a shameful future, and dies with a gesture as toweringly proud as Coriolanus.

The human delineation is Shakespearian; it has the same sense of destiny interwoven with penetration into the springs of human action, combining personal traits and general issues. The Doge could not exist in any other play; he and the action inform each other; the comments of others help to realize his personality. The dramatic texture is tight, and yet we also receive an insight into the man comparable to that which we have, not of our friends, but of ourselves. He is complete and individual, an honourable past and intimations of an undefined future lingering about the tragic conception.

Our quotations have witnessed to the verbal power. The language is reserved without any striving for an overlay of metaphor and image, every accent rising from the tense thought or smouldering passion concerned, every speech from the speaker's nature and the situation's demand. The utterance is transparent, yet weighty, the weight owing little or nothing to poetic tradition. Yet Byron's Augustan apprenticeship has served to winnow away all trivialities, leaving him free for an unfettered, yet well-sorted, diction that carries quiet profundities with Shakespearian ease, as in

> ... as yet 'tis but a chaos
> Of darkly brooding thoughts: my fancy is
> In her first work, more nearly to the light
> Holding the sleeping images of things
> For the selection of the pausing judgement.
> (I. ii. 282)

Continually comment strikes home into human psychology, into the human soul itself, as when the Doge remarks how, once bloodshed starts, 'the mere instinct of the first-born Cain' (IV, ii. 56) will render brutal those to whom such acts were recently abhorrent. When a speech catches fire the passion curves up like a wave, fierce as a crested snake:

> Yet for all this, so full of certain passions,
> That if once stirr'd and baffled, as he has been
> Upon the tenderest points, *there is no Fury*
> *In Grecian story like to that which wrings*
> *His vitals with her burning hands*, till he
> Grows capable of all things for revenge . . .
>
> (II. ii. 168)

The passion plays against the line-units, starting with a pointed intensity, relaxing to a swift parenthetic realism ('as he has been . . .') then towering steadily to the moment of striking ('his vitals . . . hands'), and next withdrawn, relapsing as an ocean breaker, at the close. It suggests and demands the vocal variation which is the life-blood of stage utterance. Such variation works continually to define passionate depth against colloquial changes, and is here, as in Shakespeare, carried into manipulation of scene-movement too. The Doge's early dialogue (II. i. 150–513) with Angiolina has a wavelike undulation, with, after extreme rhetorical fury, such a powerfully dramatic pause as

> What matters my forgiveness? An old man's,
> Worn out, scorn'd, spurn'd, abus'd . . .   (II. i. 266)

We hear the quiet voice and deeper note. Soon the passion again rises (at 'this blight, this brand, this blasphemy'), though not so high as at first. He is what he says, an old man, tired. 'Come hither, child . . .' marks a new movement. Such changes serve to make psychic disclosures; and both suspense and discovery are age-old dramatic tricks, the one preparing for, and the other reflecting, that depth-seeing and revelation of psychic dimensions, dark underground rivers or cloudy heights, that are the business of drama.[1]

Both surprise and discovery are frequent. We wait anxiously for the court's first judgement. The Doge's interview with Bertuccio is a cleverly devised partnership in dual unmasking;

---

[1] I do not deny that severe cutting would in practice be needed. The drama was not composed for the stage but for what Byron called 'a mental theatre' (To Murray, 23 Aug. 1821; *LJ*. v. 347). Nevertheless, its stage qualities are witnessed by Mr Roy Walker's notice of the Hovenden Theatre Club production in 1958; 'Unexpected merits of *Marino Faliero*', *The Times*, 21 May 1958. I quote from and discuss the notice in my article 'Byron as Poet'; see p. 263 below. [1967]

his subsequent appearance among the conspirators a powerfully staged surprise; and the development of his mental conflict
a gradual and ever more deep disclosure of tangles and emotions
as we feel him tearing out his own existence at its roots. A key-
incident is Bertram's discovery of the plot to Luigi. The whole
action is by way of being a half-paralysed struggle to overthrow
an invincible, though rotting, order; and one long suspense
waiting for the pealing of the great bell in Act iv. At the last,
the Doge works through a long and steadily rising invective to
die on as shattering a climax as we shall anywhere find. The
mind is both awakened by surprise and distended by suspense
to experience thoughts and emotions of profound subjective
importance. We are united to the action on a deeper level than
one of entertainment.

Though the style is in the main direct and unmetaphoric and
the whole most carefully constructed, yet the lucidity and care
obey an imaginative conception. There is a reserved play of
nature-imagery. Human actions are felt shading into comparisons from animal life, and we have a normal assortment: scorpion, silk-worms, viper, tiger, raven, wolves, eagle, geese, adder,
worm, dog, lion; and a lamb 'bleating' before a butcher (v. i.
393). These tone into the fierce and poisonous passions and
thoughts that are involved. More important are those directly
relating human society to organic nature. My next quotations
all occur in iii. ii, at the conspirators' meeting. The final massacre is to

> unpeople many palaces
> And hew the highest genealogic trees
> Down to the earth, strew'd with their bleeding fruit,
> And crush their blossoms into barrenness . . .
>
> (492)

The metaphor conforms to Byron's consistent awareness of the
present as grown from the soil of its own past. But the nobility
are also felt as a single insidious, living, body and to aim primarily at Steno is to 'lop the hand' rather than its 'head' (416).
To show mercy to any individual among them would be to give

> such pity
> As when the viper hath been cut to pieces,

The separate fragments quivering in the sun,
In the last energy of venomous life,
Deserve and have.   (26)

The extraordinary virulence and impact derive from a strong feeling for biological energy, which is paradoxically most intensely realized when both (i) dangerous and (ii) suffering destruction, as with the scorpion in *The Giaour*. Metaphors from natural organisms are vivid: all must die since it is the 'spirit' of the aristocracy that needs to be 'rooted' out, whereas one 'single shoot' of the 'old tree' would only 'fasten in the soil' and give rise to more 'gloomy verdure' and 'bitter fruit' (40–4). The passage recalls with an important difference a similar speech in Shakespeare's *Julius Caesar* (II. i. 162–5) and might be used as evidence, if any were needed, to rebut a charge of plagiarism in such Shakespearian reminders.[1] In political and social analysis *Marino Faliero* holds its own in comparison with Shakespeare's *Coriolanus* – both plays very similarly relate the social order to natural organisms – and it probably strikes more cleanly to the heart of our contemporary situation than any Shakespearian drama. How modern rings the Doge's asseveration that the 'present institutes of Venice' nourish a 'fatal poison to the springs of life' and all 'human ties' (316–18). Though the proposed deed may be only hideously fertilizing in Bertram's horrified thought of 'blood which spouts through hoary scalps' (67), another view may see the dead 'gathered' in to 'harvest' and reaped with a 'sword' for 'sickle' (263). All the nobles must die since

all their acts are one –
A single emanation from one body,
Together knit for our oppression.
(285)

As in *Julius Caesar* the act is viewed as a divinely appointed 'sacrifice' (532). The willed harmony-to-be is very subtly conceived not precisely as a living organism but, being still a dream in the mind only, as a work of art, a temple. Opposed to the decadent and decaying living death of the present order imag-

[1] There are many: see Samuel C. Chew, 'Shakespearean Echoes in *Marino Faliero*', *The Dramas of Lord Byron*, Gottingen, also Baltimore, 1915; App. III.
[1967]

ined as a 'monster of a state' and as a 'spectre' to be exorcised
with 'blood' is set the artistic vitality of a 'fair free commonwealth', a considered art-form with no 'rash equality' yet with
'equal rights',

> Proportion'd like the columns to the temple
> Giving and taking strength reciprocal,

where no part may be removed without infringing the general
'symmetry' (165–75). The old order was not truly an organism,
but a ghost only; and the new is only a planned symmetry with
ever so faint a suggestion of the artificial. The chances of a willed
social development remain problematical.

The balance of sympathies is just. We are continually caught
by an unexpected reverse of what we thought the play's 'thesis':
whereas the thinking is moving on a deeper level. Though the
action depends on our recognition that the nobility are a poor
lot; though they are imagined as 'a few bloated despots' (IV. ii.
87), and the Doge honestly thinks that he is helping to free the
'groaning nations' from an ever-tightening grip (V. i. 398), yet
they are shown at the trial as perfectly just, if austere and cold.
To them the Doge's treason is a crime of unprecedented wickedness comparable with 'earthquakes' and 'pestilence' (V. i. 491).
Their imputation of 'wild wrath and regal fierceness' strikes
home. They take pride in remembering what they consider the
Doge himself has forgotten, his own 'dignity', and in the order
of his punishment acknowledge their 'prince', so that he dies
in state (V. i. 556–75). The terms are, however, not really kind,
since the cruelly apt reference to 'dignity' must be intolerable to
so fiery-proud a temperament; and the Doge, himself sincere to
danger-point, has for long been bitterly sickened by that hypocrisy of respect of which this formal mockery is the last towering
example. We can perhaps strike a balance in terms of the Doge's
final speech (V. iii. 26–104), which it will do us no harm to
consider as levelled at ourselves. Though the nobles' original
dishonouring of the Doge in passing over Steno's lewd insult
may have been defensible in view of Steno's emphasized youth,
what virtues they possess are merely those of respectability, convention and the outward shows of rectitude, secreting vices cold
and dangerous. The Doge, at the point of death, levels his last

scalding and prophetic denunciation of future shame to Venice in the strikingly Lawrentian terms of

> Vice without splendour, sin without relief
> Even from the gloss of love to smooth it o'er,
> But in its stead, coarse lusts of habitude,
> Prurient yet passionless, cold studied lewdness
> Depraving Nature's frailty to an art . . .
>
> (v. iii. 85)

Their 'smiles' shall lack 'mirth', their 'pastimes' bring no pleasure; and so on, up to the shattering climax. But, meanwhile, we have lived through the mental territory of Pope's satires; just as Steno is a variation on Sporus.

The gloomy passions and shadowed thought throughout produce a dark impressionism. The word 'black' is insistent. Steno's deed is a public 'blackening' of the Doge's wife (II. i. 435); the nobles are men of 'black blood', their faults causing the 'black deeds' (III. i. 8, 58) of the rebels whose action, if a failure, will be written 'black' in the calumnies of time (I. ii. 593), the dark day itself being henceforth one 'black' in the calendar, though perhaps to be succeeded by days of brightness (IV. ii. 155). Here is a typical phrase:

> When you lie down to rest,
> Let it be black among your dreams . . .
>
> (I. ii. 244)

with a following suggestion of 'ill-omened cloud' obscuring the 'sun'. The play works up to a 'funeral marriage' and 'black union' (v. ii. 8). We have 'darkly brooding thoughts' (I. ii. 283), and hear of senators

> In dark suspicious conflict with the Doge,
> Brooding with him in mutual hate and fear.
>
> (III. ii. 378)

'Stifled treason' lurks in 'narrow places' and whispers 'muffled' curses to the night (IV. i. 224). The nobles' vices are 'gloomy' (III. ii. 345). Freedom is a sun (IV. ii. 245) and so is virtue (II. i. 397), but more emphatic here is the presence of 'souls obscured' (IV. ii. 244). The weather is gloomy, not violently tempestuous, since that would not suit its shadowed gravity, but rather sultry and ominous:

Doge: At what hour arises
The moon?
Bertuccio: Late, but the atmosphere is thick and dusky,
'Tis a sirocco. (I. ii. 569)

Later Lioni remarks that 'the cloudy wind' blowing from the Levant has subsided to leave the moon unobscured (IV. i. 25). The play is mostly in half-light. The Doge is at the 'twilight' of his life (I. ii. 315). Angiolina imagines Steno 'grovelling by stealth in the moon's glimmering light', and struck by conscience at 'every shadow' (II. i. 41), as he goes to his ugly deed. The Doge's fortunes are early seen

Now darkling in their close toward the deep vale
Where Death sits rob'd in his all-sweeping shadow.
(II. i. 502)

He naturally dwells on death. Quite early he hints of an impending doom to make the 'cemeteries populous' (II. i. 507), and later feels the 'destroying Angel' above Venice (IV. ii. 133), finely imagined as a swooping bird. When he and his companions are in their 'graves' will future generations, he wonders, revere those 'tombs' (III. i. 69)? Death and moonlight pervade the atmosphere. The moon dominates, not for romantic glamour, but rather for its steely pallor suiting the hard ethical precisions, cold vices and chaste virtues of the grave conception. The persons are touched by the ghostly finger of it, and walk near death.

As in Shakespeare's *Antony and Cleopatra* Enobarbus' description of Cleopatra on Cydnus and Cleopatra's dream of the cosmic Antony beyond death distil the drama's various tonings, so in *Marino Faliero* the imaginative atmosphere is concentrated and focused into two crystallizing scenes.

The first (III. i. 1–47) discovers the Doge alone by the Church of San Giovanni and San Paolo before which stands an 'equestrian statue'. It is a moonlit night.

His sense of guilt imagines the midnight bell pealing across the 'arch of night' to wake sleepers from hideous dreams of the

fate overhanging them. Then in weighted accents he addresses
the church, home of his dead ancestry, the building

> whose dim statues shadow
> The floor which doth divide us from the dead,
> Where all the pregnant hearts of our bold blood,
> Moulder'd into a mite of ashes, hold
> In one shrunk heap what once made many heroes,
> When what is now a handful shook the earth –
> Fane of the tutelar saints who guard our house!

He addresses the past which lives still in him. Two doges, his
'sires', rest there. He stands before them, sinks himself beyond
the transient moment to ask grace or condemnation of the
eternal. He would have the dead rise to people the dim aisles,
lending their 'high blood' and 'blazon-roll of glories' as witnesses to his integrity, even though in him their 'mighty name'
lies 'dishonour'd'. Such an intuition of the living dead, of the
past within the present, we find nowhere outside Byron, nor
anywhere else so noble a feeling for the ancestral honours of the
race; and both are one with the sacred building where those
dead rest. The Church is a symbol of eternity. The Doge would
draw strength and justification from the dead, share with them
his scarcely endurable responsibility. 'Spirits! smile down upon
me', he prays. His cause is theirs, their fame mingles into his,
and if he prospers he will make their city for ever 'free and immortal'. The religious and ancestral conception is so inevitable
in this context that we may too easily pass over its relation to
the historic eternity and religious reverence so important elsewhere in Byron. Here his deepest feelings are, as in Shakespeare, unobtrusive, within, not crowning, the action. The
Doge's soliloquy makes of the silent Church an actor.

After Bertuccio's entrance yet greater dramatic powers are
awakened through dialogue and the equestrian statue:

> *Bertuccio:* 'Tis not the moment to consider thus,
> Else I could answer. – Let us to the meeting,
> Or we may be observ'd in lingering here.
> *Doge:* We *are* observ'd, and have been.
> *Bertuccio:*   We observ'd!
> Let me discover – and this steel –

Doge: Put up;
                Here are no human witnesses: look there –
                What see you?
Bertuccio: Only a tall warrior's statue
                Bestriding a proud steed, in the dim light
                Of the dull moon.
Doge: That warrior was the sire
                Of my sire's fathers, and that statue was
                Decreed to him by the twice rescued city: –
                Think you that he looks down on us or no?
Bertuccio: My lord, these are mere fantasies; there are
                No eyes in marble.
Doge: But there are in Death.
                I tell thee, man, there is a spirit in
                Such things that acts and sees, unseen, though felt;
                And, if there be a spell to stir the dead,
                'Tis in such deeds as we are now upon.
                Deem'st thou the souls of such a race as mine
                Can rest, when he, their last descendant chief,
                Stands plotting on the brink of their pure graves
                With stung plebeians?   (III. i. 81)

I do not recall a more powerful instance of a stage-object used to share in, focus, and universalize the action. This is the play's heart. Notice that a statue, as so often in poetry, symbolizes the eternal.[1]

Such an opening towards the infinite applies, as we shall find also in *Sardanapalus*, to *both* sides of the dramatic conflict; while the cosmic symbolism of moonlight helps to bind the plot and realize a super-personal dimension. Our second example (IV. i. I–III) involves mainly spatial, as our first temporal, infinities. Lioni returns from a dance full of a foreboding that has chilled love-flirtations with deathly fears, turning the music to a 'knell'. At an open window he watches the night's expansive 'stillness' under a 'broad moon'. He meditates on social falsities, on age trying to appear young by artificial light and youth wasting its energies on misconceived attempts at pleasure. Feminine attractions and the whole 'dizzy' delusion of 'false and true enchantments', of 'Art and Nature' mixed, are recalled and probed.

---

[1] This dialogue is included with a number of other Byron passages in my tape-recording 'Byron's Rhetoric', published by Sound Seminars, 50 East Hollister, Cincinnati. [1967]

Contrasted are the moon, stars, waters, and buildings ghostly-sweet as vast 'altars' or ancient pyramids. Next he dreams of some true-love serenade in the moonlight, the phosphorescent plash of an oar, the twinkle of gondola lights. The moon, symbol of chastity, blends with a romantic integrity, but its steely truth is set against those social superficialities which the play condemns.

Later the Doge waits for the dawn that is to bring dark conspiracy to an open triumph:

> Will the morn never put to rest
> These stars which twinkle yet o'er all the heavens?
>
> (IV. ii. 71)

He is impatient for daylight action after our scenes of half-light indecisions, anxiously sensing a 'morning freshness' and noticing that the sea looks 'greyer', while his keener-eyed nephew thinks that he sees the dawn already 'dappling' the sky (IV. ii. 110). The suspense is breathless.

> Thou Day!
> That slowly walk'st the waters! – march – march on –
>
> (IV. ii. 138)

But no dawn can come to Venice: for that we must turn to *Sardanapalus*. The bell which he is waiting for indeed strikes; but the night of oppression and hatred is not to be lifted.

The great bell of St Mark's symbolizes an ultimate authority. Its use by the Doge, who alone can sound it, as the signal for massacre, helps at first to justify his right as sovereign to exert full power. He uses this 'last poor privilege' left him (III. ii. 248) to herald the last blow for justice. It is to strike 'at dawn' (III. ii. 389) and wake the city. The poetry is weightily charged with thought of the 'sullen huge oracular bell' which 'knells' only for a 'princely death' or a 'state in peril', pealing 'bodements' (IV. ii. 182–6). This is to be its 'awfullest and last' office, and one which is, precisely, 'oracular'. The bell with all its traditional and royal associations becomes the voice of those eternal dead to whom the Doge prayed; but it falls instead as a condemnation, throwing its balance against the Doge. It overhangs the action, oppressive and awful, and may be referred to that other earlier irony of the Doge's guilty but prophetic fancy of a great bell rousing the city from dreams of conspiracy (III. i. 1–7). The stage effect when at last it strikes should be overpowering. Angiolina alone expresses an ultimate righteousness. Her original attitude to Steno's fault was one of pity or scorn, almost unconcern. To her shows and words mean nothing, substantial values are everything. 'What is virtue', she asks, 'if it needs a victim?' (II. i. 57). She is undisturbed by slander. To desire even 'justice' proves that you prefer a name to a quality (II. i. 66). No 'base passions' rule her, no image of a younger lover than the Doge ever entered her head. When told that others are less pure-minded she replies:

> It may be so. I knew not of such thoughts.
> (II. i. 132)

She is not even interested. She urges the Doge to Christian forgiveness and is herself a personification of uncompromising Christian idealism, pointing a solution beyond the mazed troubles and vices of the rest; but when at the Doge's trial (v. i. 407–65) the remorseful Steno asks for a Christian's compassion, her severe temperament shows a doubtfully Christian refusal of compromise. She refers to her previous unconcern while remarking that some, like the Doge, cannot so easily remain unaffected by 'shadows' and are troubled by unreal conflicts; and in them resentment becomes a fault, especially at that sternest test of greatness, an insult to a 'proud name' and 'pinnacle' of honour. An 'insect' may hurt beings of a higher order. She recounts examples from history of communal disaster brought on by questions of personal honour; and even such a thing as Steno has now

> put in peril
> A Senate which hath stood eight hundred years,
> Discrown'd a Prince, cut off his crownless head,
> And forg'd new fetters for a groaning people!
> (v. i. 445)

Her icy integrity levels all – Doge, Senate, and Steno – in a level, critical judgement, like the steely fluid of moonlight washing away both shadows and colours, to level all under the one pallid gaze. The attack recalls Pope's in the Horatian Satires and Epistles. Images of reptile and venom have elsewhere been

applied to Steno, and within our view of the whole action
Angiolina's speech may serve as a clarification of Pope's satiric
fury. The play's statement narrows down to condemnation of
such sexual superficialities as those of Shakespeare's Lucio in
Measure for Measure and Pope's Sporus in his *Epistle to Arbuthnot*,
just as that in our own thinking which makes them possible, and
they are aspects both of their creators and of ourselves, might be
named the root evil of our culture. Her words are cold and hard:

> Nothing of good can come from such a source,
> Nor would we aught with him, nor now, nor ever:
> We leave him to himself, that lowest depth
> Of human baseness. Pardon is for men,
> And not for reptiles – we have none for Steno,
> And no resentment: things like him must sting,
> And higher beings suffer; 'tis the charter
> Of Life. The man who dies by the adder's fang
> May have the crawler crush'd, but feels no anger:
> 'Twas the worm's nature; and some men are worms
> In soul, more than the living things of tombs.
>   (v. i. 455)

The clever pauses and metrical disruptions, the mastery of the
colloquial, the reserved dignity and purity of winnowed diction,
joined to scorn more scalding because less involved in the object
than even Pope's, witness Byron's powers in maturity.

Angiolina's relentless and almost cruel perfection will not
serve as a final Byronic solution, though his enduing of a feminine figure with an idealized distinction is normal. The specifically sexual is here under a cloud. The Doge boasts of his mastery
of such instincts even in youth (II. i. 313); Angiolina leaves even
Shakespeare's Isabella behind in chastity; and their marriage
arrangements, carefully described, do not appear to have been
romantic. Here fiery pride is a lesser fault than sexual licence,
and Lioni's repudiation of the dance integral to the conception.

The conspiracy fails through the personal feelings of Bertram,
whose Byronic softness is distinguished from cowardice (III.
ii. 45–57). Destiny exposes the revolution's inorganic weakness
through Bertram's inability to crush *personal* gratitude. The
Doge himself has to fight his own nature, crushing memory of
his former comradeships among the aristocrats to be destroyed
in the approaching massacre. We can feel pressing through the

play's structure an implied pattern where the sexual and soft personal emotions might *together* reach some solution. The chaste fervours of Angiolina are not all attractive, blending with the play's moonlit and dawnless quality, while a fine speech of the Doge's on virtue (II. i. 379–98) has all the severity of *Comus*. Angiolina's scorn of Steno may be contrasted with her earlier unwillingness that his 'young blood' (II. i. 241) be shed. She does not compass the Christian compassion which Steno so pathetically asks in a speech (v. i. 398–406) exemplifying Byron's Shakespearian generosity of dramatic balance. There is an alternative possible alinement of values which Byron was to exploit in *Sardanapalus*; this will be flooded by the sun; transfers sexual enjoyment to the more positive side of the conflict; and presents not a revolutionary but a pacifist sovereign. Which is the more Christian? The Doge's deep meditations tremble on the brink of a solution:

Oh World!
Oh Men! What are ye, and our best designs,
That we must work by crime to punish crime?
And slay as if Death had but this one gate,
When a few years would make the sword superfluous?
(IV. ii. 166)

From the view of eternity man's attempts at justice are childish; and yet this failure has its own, tragic and eternal, sanction:

That moment would have changed the face of ages;
This gives us to Eternity.   (IV. ii. 275)

But again, had the plot succeeded, would not a better Venice have matured? Byron clearly (e.g. in Note C of his Appendix) means us to realize that the Doge's final prophecy of a shameful future for Venice has been fulfilled. Does success or failure define the quality of a deed? Or does the quality determine the deed's ultimate success? Perhaps the plot was, ultimately, successful, in so far as its whole nature, including the judgement of St Mark's bell as its condemnation, receives a full though tragic understanding. Our next play, *Sardanapalus*, directly projects the eternal values into single, positive action. It is accordingly simple where *Marino Faliero* was complex, and bright where that was dark.

The Byronic conflicts achieve an all but final resolution in *Sardanapalus* (1821). The hero is a king sternly criticized for lax rule and sensuous indulgence; Sardanapalus gives his brother-in-law Salamenes authority to crush a rebellion which nevertheless through the king's clemency ultimately succeeds. A powerful love-force is present in the person of Myrrha, a Greek slave for whom Sardanapalus has left his own wife. After showing extreme though futile bravery, he dies with Myrrha on a lighted pyre. As in *Antony and Cleopatra* a relaxation of sexual ethic ranges a fiery eroticism with other positive values against efficiency and war.

Sardanapalus is not rashly idealized. He enters (I. i) to 'soft music'

. . . effeminately dressed, his head crowned with flowers, and his robe negligently flowing, attended by a train of women and young slaves.   (I. ii; direction)

Salamenes hates the 'lascivious tinklings' of his attendant music and the 'reeking odours of the perfumed trains' (I. i. 29, 38). He accuses the king of 'sensual sloth' and lack of 'virtue' (I. ii. 70, 89), despising his 'feasts', 'concubines' and 'lavish'd treasures' (I. ii. 234). The king is called an 'effeminate thing', 'silkworm', and '*she* Sardanapalus' (II. i. 95, 87, 404). He himself admits having 'wasted down' his 'royalty' (IV. i. 276). Salamenes' faithfulness has in contrast a manly strength:

> I will not see
> The blood of Nimrod and Semiramis
> Sink in the earth, and thirteen hundred years
> Of Empire ending like a shepherd's tale.
>
> (I. i. 5)

References to ancestry are even more continual here than in *Marino Faliero*. The rebels would extinguish 'the line of Nimrod' (IV. i. 378). Nimrod and Semiramis are quoted to shame the king. They symbolize respectively the chase and war, which Salamenes equates with (i) health and (ii) glory, while disgusted that his king takes part in neither (I. i. 24–6). 'A line of thirteen ages' comes to an end with Sardanapalus' fall (III. i. 234).

Nevertheless the hero makes out a good case. When confronted by the example of Semiramis in leading her people as far as the Ganges and returning unvanquished with only twenty guards, he has a powerful answer:

Sardanapalus:	And how many
	Left she behind in India to the vultures?
Salamenes:	Our annals say not.
Sardanapalus:	Then I will say for them –
	That she had better woven within her palace
	Some twenty garments, than with twenty guards
	Have fled to Bactria, leaving to the ravens
	And wolves, and men – the fiercer of the three,
	Her myriads of fond subjects. Is *this* Glory?
	Then let me live in ignominy ever.
	(I. ii. 131)

To him she was only 'a sort of semi-glorious human monster' (I. ii. 181). He realizes that he might quite easily have himself shed blood 'in oceans' till his name became a 'synonym of death', at once 'a terror and a trophy' (I. ii. 402–5). He has however ruled differently. He has not 'decimated' his people with 'savage laws', or 'sweated' them to build pyramids, but instead pursued civic ambitions, founding cities:

> What could that blood-loving beldame
> My martial grandam, chaste Semiramis,
> Do more, except destroy them? (I. ii. 230–40)

His motto 'Eat, drink, and love; the rest's not worth a fillip' (I. ii. 252), though it may at first shock us, sinks deeper as you meditate it; and set against his ironic picture of a trophy raised over fifty thousand dead makes one pause. His aim is that all, not only the privileged, should be happy (I. ii. 265). He has aimed to lessen 'the weight of human misery' and not increase it (I. ii. 264). He loathes 'all war and warriors' (I. ii. 529) and prefers the pleasure that 'sparkles' at a feast to all 'Nimrod's huntings', or 'my wild Grandam's chase in search of kingdoms' (III. i. 5). His logic is often witty:

Myrrha:	Look to the annals of thine Empire's founders.
Sardanapalus:	They are so blotted o'er with blood, I cannot.
	But what would'st have? The Empire *has been* founded.
	I cannot go on multiplying empires. (I. ii. 547)

He is simultaneously aware of his limitations. Salamenes is as 'stern' as he 'heedless', and since he realizes that 'slaves' may deserve to feel a 'master' (I. ii. 387), he gives his brother-in-law authority to crush the suspected insurrection. Sardanapalus lacks that particular hardness so often conditioning virtue and efficiency. He can regard his supporters as 'better men' than himself (II. i. 291), but a consciousness of royalty also renders him proudly independent of the 'vile herd', in either their 'noisy praise' or their 'noisome clamour' (I. ii. 341-3), and a superb confidence rings in his threat to prove himself more fierce than 'stern Nimrod' conjured from his 'ashes' (I. ii. 373) should his people insist on brutality of rule and refuse their potential humanity.

He is a man of unpractical enlightenment beyond the super-stitions of his day. When the Greek Myrrha shows surprise at his actually enjoying, like Cassius, a thunderstorm that strikes others with awe, and says how she herself respects all such portents as 'auguries of Jove', he replies:

> Jove! – ay, your Baal –
> Ours also has a property in thunder,
> And ever and anon some falling bolt
> Proves his divinity – and yet sometimes
> Strikes his own altars.   (II. i. 549)

Notice the clever touches in 'your Baal' and 'property'.

Sardanapalus shamelessly 'blasphemes the worship of the land' (II. i. 236) and shocks the priest Beleses. To him the stars are most wonderful when unsullied by religious connotations:

> Oh! for that – I love them;
> I love to watch them in the deep blue vault,
> And to compare them with my Myrrha's eyes;
> I love to see their rays redoubled in
> The tremulous silver of Euphrates' wave,
> As the light breeze of midnight crisps the broad
> And rolling water, sighing through the sedges
> Which fringe his banks: but whether they may be
> Gods, as some say, or the abodes of Gods,
> As others hold, or simply lamps of night,
> Worlds – or the lights of worlds – I know nor care not.
> There's something sweet in my uncertainty
> I would not change for your Chaldean lore.
> Besides, I know of these all clay can know
> Of aught above it or below it – nothing.

I see their brilliancy and feel their beauty –
When they shine on my grave I shall know neither.
                                      (II. i. 252)

Such an immediate contact with a living universe is set against
the horror of being 'sermonised' and 'dinn'd' with memories of
'dead men', 'Baal', and 'Chaldea's starry mysteries' (II. i. 249).
We are aware of the faults of priestcraft, traditional superstitions, and ancestral domination. Salamenes accuses Beleses of
'smooth words and juggling homilies' (II. i. 232), and even
Arbaces sees in him 'a subtle spirit' of more 'peril' than a
'phalanx' (II. i. 388). Priests have 'codes', mysteries, and 'corol-
laries' of right and wrong too tortuous for a 'plain heart' to
understand (II. i. 379–82). Sardanapalus says that the gods
never themselves speak to him except through the priests, and
then usually for some 'addition to the temple' (I. ii. 545). Yet,
with all this, there occurs one powerful and typically Byronic
example of respect to religious office when Sardanapalus,
meeting Beleses in battle, is reluctant to dip his hands in 'holy
blood' (III. i. 274). There is evidence of the priest's magic insight: his prophecy proves true, suggesting, as happened in
Marino Faliero (pp. 208–9), an almost superstitious feeling of
the Church's invisible power, however the enlightened hero may
enlist our immediate sympathies. Our response to him is usually
direct. When the overflowing Euphrates breaks its bulwark and
strikes awe into Pania, Sardanapalus answers curtly: 'I can
forgive the omen, not the ravage' (v. i. 198). He repudiates con-
ventions and superstitions in the cause of a health, sanity and
realism that his opposers cannot understand.

    Simultaneously effeminate and exceptionally brave, he ap-
pears even to himself a paradox.

                My gentle, wrong'd Zarina!
        I am the very slave of circumstance
        And impulse – borne away with every breath!
        Misplac'd upon the throne – misplac'd in life.
        I know not what I could have been, but feel
        I am not what I should be . . .
                    (IV. i. 329; and see II. i. 489)

His very truth to central impulses makes him a continual
enigma. He is not really effeminate. He indeed analyses the
dangers of the feminine temperament, how it may become

'timidly vindictive' to a 'pitch of perseverance' beyond masculine passion (II. i. 587); and talks of a mother lion 'femininely' raging 'because all passions in excess are female' (III. i. 379–81). Yet again Myrrha speaks some exquisite lines on the feminine element behind all man's activities, the earliest and the latest troubles of his existence being nursed by maternal or some other feminine gentleness (I. ii. 509–15). Our hero, poet-like, may be called bisexual, joining man's reason to woman's emotional depth, while repudiating the evil concomitants. Sardanapalus is to this extent rightly to be designated, as is Semiramis (I. i. 43), a 'Man-Queen', with no condemnation of effeminacy. There is evidence of a womanly streak in the incident of the looking-glass (III. i. 163–5),[1] but directly afterwards he shows a resounding soldiership. The battle teaches him a simple thing, the value of water as opposed to wine, the contrast suggesting an advance beyond the sensuous. 'All the gold of earth' could not repay 'the pleasure' of this water (III. i. 360). The plan demands that he should show himself to lack nothing of that manliness characterizing his inferiors in vision. Though astounding everyone by his efficiency and valour when tested, his scorn of military glory persists:

> *Salamenes:*   This great hour has prov'd
>   The brightest and most glorious of your life.
> *Sardanapalus:* And the most tiresome.   (III. i. 342)

His arms are 'toys' (III. i. 165), the sword-hilt hurts his hand (II. i. 194), his throne is uncomfortable (III. i. 339). He mocks the baubles of respectability. He is 'inscrutable' (III. i. 319). He is Byron's 'superman'.

Like the Duke's in Shakespeare's *Measure for Measure*, his clemency, however unwise, is conscious and purposeful:

> To love and to be merciful, to pardon
> The follies of my species, and (that's human)
> To be indulgent to my own.   (I. ii. 276)

This, not glory, is the only 'godlike' thing about him. The execution of rebels would leave him no sleep (II. i. 497). His virtues are felt to be one with his sins which 'have all been of the softer order' (IV. i. 398). He is of 'softer clay' than his rock-like

---

[1] The incident makes us think of *The Scarlet Pimpernel*. Perhaps the Baroness Orczy's hero was in part modelled on Byron's. [1967]

brother-in-law (II. i. 522), our 'soft sovereign' (III. i. 311). His first entrance was heralded by 'soft music'. The word is an *Antony and Cleopatra* favourite: Antony was the 'soft triumvir' in *The Corsair* (II. 15). Sardanapalus aims to avoid piling burdens on a mortality already overweighted, and to set instead an example of 'mild reciprocal alleviation' (I. ii. 353) of life's agonies, to make his 'inoffensive rule' an 'era of sweet peace 'midst bloody annals' (IV. i. 511). That is 'the sole true glory' (III. i. 11) and the only victory he has ever coveted (IV. i. 504). 'Bloodshed' is a 'mockery' and no 'remedy' against evil (II. i. 467) and conquest no 'renown' (IV. i. 505). Idealized romance in 'Grief cannot come where perfect love exists' (II. i. 599) blends into the wider implications of 'I seek but to be loved, not worshipp'd' (III. i. 36) and that into a pastor-like concern and a desire to convert the realm 'to one wide shelter for the wretched' (III. i. 42).

Whatever the exact prophetic statement intended, its erotic basis is undeniable. Such thoughts as 'My very love to thee is hate to them' and 'I cease to love thee when I love mankind' from *The Corsair* (I. 14) have matured to a wider unity. Love's 'devotion', though it makes him faithless to his wife, comes on him like a 'duty' (IV. i. 339). The softness of which we hear so much is a duty, as in a wider context it is felt to be a strength. 'I have loved and lived', he says, and 'my life is love' (I. ii. 400, 406), empires being nothing to that one central fire he would express; hence his desire for a rustic life apart from the 'falsehood' of his 'station' (I. ii. 448–52). He asks Myrrha to define that 'unknown influence' and 'sweet oracle' of love that makes wordless communion between him and her:

> *Myrrha:*   In my native land a God,
> And in my heart a feeling like a God's,
> Exalted; yet I own 'tis only mortal.
> (I. ii. 424–30)

Like Sean O'Casey today Byron entwines his positive statement with a fearless eroticism:

> I would not give the smile of one fair girl
> For all the popular breath that e'er divided
> A name from nothing.   (I. ii. 338)

A more tranquil, Wordsworthian, experience is elsewhere
shadowed, though still in association with 'errors' of a gentle sort:

> If I have err'd this time, 'tis on the side
> Where error sits most lightly on that sense,
> I know not what to call it; but it reckons
> With me ofttimes for pain, and sometimes pleasure;
> A spirit which seems plac'd about my heart
> To count its throbs, not quicken them, and ask
> Questions which mortal never dar'd to ask me . . .
>
> (II. i. 524)

This is a state of listening passivity: Sardanapalus is conceived
as, in essence, a saint. 'If then they hate me, 'tis because I hate
not' (I. ii. 412) he says. He shows a profound insight elsewhere
(IV. i. 312–18) in discussion of ingratitude, noting that kindness
often raises its reverse while those on whom one has no claim
'are faithful'. Unwise or not, Sardanapalus is the 'king of peace'
(III. i. 18). His courage is that of warrior, king, and martyr in
one. He forgives 'royally' (II. i. 338), yet fights 'like a king'
(III. i. 200). His is an innate royalty:

> Methought he look'd like Nimrod as he spoke,
> Even as the proud imperial statue stands
> Looking the monarch of the kings around it,
> And sways, while they but ornament, the temple.
>
> (II. i. 352)

'Sway' is earlier contrasted with 'subdue' (I. ii. 144). A Biblical
and Shakespearian use of royalty enlists the splendours of an
outworn value to establish poetically a new. Sardanapalus
refuses a plain helmet for one lighter and more regal against all
advice given on grounds of practical utility and danger of
recognition by the rebels, with the shatteringly royal phrase:
'I go forth to be recognised' (III. i. 143). He would quell
rebellion with spiritual, not merely martial, authority. His
bounty to his followers after disaster is golden as Antony's. His
sublime confidence and scorn of compromise recalls the New
Testament drama. He is, as was Christ, alone in his instinctive
royalty:

> *Sardanapalus:* This is strange;
> The gentle and the austere are both against me
> And urge me to revenge.

Myrrha: 'Tis a Greek virtue.
Sardanapalus: But not a kingly one.[1]   (II. i. 578)

At the herald's infuriating message after the final defeat he
first, in a flash of anger, determines to execute swift punishment;
but, being implored in the name of a herald's 'peaceful' and
'sacred' office, replies, with a New Testament echo blending
into a delicate irony:

> He's right – Let him go free – My life's last act
> Shall not be one of wrath. Here, fellow, take
> This golden goblet, let it hold your wine,
> And think of *me*; or melt it into ingots,
> And think of nothing but their weight and value.
>   (v. i. 335)

When early in the action his friends kneel to him as a god, the
conception is pagan; but when at the last his soldiers throng
round 'kissing his hand and the hem of his robe' (v. i. 400;
direction) we have been trained to a deeper insight.

Byron's careful balance of sympathies counteracts the danger
of an excessive idealism. Against the hero, Salamenes stands out
with a manly and conventional strength demanding respect,
his allegiance unaffected by his sister's wrongs. As in Dryden's
All for Love the hero's sexual fault is emphasized by the actual
entry of his wife and frequent mention of his children; though
it is also suggested that no king of normal instinct can be bound
by a state marriage (I. ii. 213–17). Zarina is beautifully drawn,
and at his interview with her Sardanapalus seems to recognize
a value and a virtue beyond him, while forseeing the remorse
which attends on 'a single deviation from the track of human
duties' (IV. i. 433). The old Byronic guilt is not quite exorcized,
and the personal conception of Sardanapalus not left as an
absolute; for that we must consider the whole play, conclusion
and all. Myrrha, the Ionian slave and Sardanapalus' mistress,
has a peculiar importance. Her devotion puts the historical and
cultural connotations of Greece at the hero's feet; frequent
Greek references contribute richness to the impressionism.
Myrrha serves as a critical standard, meditating on the meaning

---

[1] Compare Byron's *Sonnet to the Prince Regent on the Repeal of Lord Edward Fitzgerald's Forfeiture* which I have discussed in *Lord Byron: Christian Virtues*, 287–8, and
Byron and Shakespeare, 109, 336. [1967]

of her love for so strange a man and variously relating his weaknesses and nobility to her native traditions. Both Zarina and
Myrrha rank high among Byron's succession of fine women.
Throughout we have a happy blend of nature and romantic
humanism. The hero is 'crown'd with roses' (I. i. 34), refuses to
crown himself 'with a single rose the less' (I. ii. 312) whatever
dangers are afoot, prefers a cottage with Myrrha and 'crowns
of flowers' to his kingdom's 'dull tiara' (I. ii. 451), and equates
his fall to that of a 'pluck'd rose' (I. ii. 605). The bee gathering
'honey' from 'wholesome flowers' only is contrasted with mankind's ability to transmute evil to good (IV. i. 321). A tempest
may be a metaphor for social conflict (I. ii. 282), though Sardanapalus loves actual tempests as a pleasing variation (II. i.
543). His strength is compared to a 'twilight tempest' thundering from out a hot summer's day (III. i. 317). The suffusing
tone is summery, as in the 'gay pavilion' thought of as the king's
'summer dotage' (II. i. 124), and 'the big rain pattering on the
roof' (III. i. 65). The moon breaks through in 'brightness' after
storm (III. i. 142), and the king's 'silk tiara' and 'flowing hair'
are seen making 'a mark too royal' in its 'broad light' (III. i.
204-6). Beleses points to the 'earliest' and 'brightest' of the
stars

which so quivers,
As it would quit its place in the blue ether.
(II. i. 64)

There are Sardanapalus' star-lines already (p. 224) quoted.
The heavens are alive, bending down and speaking alike to
saintly king and plotting priest. The priest reads their hiero-
glyphic meanings, but Sardanapalus feels rather an exact coincidence of the cosmic on the human. His flowery banquet

> Shall blaze with beauty and with light, until
> It seems unto the stars which are above us
> Itself an opposite star . . .   (I. ii. 556)

The most indicative and compact of all minor impressions here
is that of a 'crimson' blush on Myrrha's cheek

> Like to the dying day on Caucasus
> Where sunset tints the snow with rosy shadows . . .
> (I. ii. 42)

or that of her arms 'more dazzling with their own born white-
ness' than the sword-steel she brandishes (III. i. 395).
Brilliances abound. We have 'glittering spears' (II. i. 46), a
sword that shall 'out-dazzle comets' (II. i. 68), Sardanapalus'
mirror 'of polish'd brass' from India (III. i. 146), his diadem'd
helmet (III. i. 131), the 'golden realm of Ind' (I. ii. 151), 'all the
gold of earth' (III. i. 360), a 'golden reign' of peace (IV. i. 516),
Nimrod's chalice as a 'golden goblet thick with gems' (I. ii. 159),
the 'golden goblet' and other golden treasure at the close (V. i.
337). Especially beautiful is Sardanapalus' thought of himself
as a poor miner and Zarina as a 'vein of virgin ore' which he
may discover but not himself possess, though it 'sparkles' at his
feet (IV. i. 344–9). These bright impressions of rosy nature and
sparkling heaven blend with the wider action and its royal
centre, with music and the feasting, and the 'immortal' wine,
its 'soul' so deeply praised (I. ii. 173–6); and the drama's fiery
conclusion.

The use of impressionism and stage symbolism, the music,
garlands and banquet and their interruption by thunder, the
comments thereon and the rising Euphrates, are Shakespearian.
We are often close in feeling and phrase-reminiscence to Shakespeare, but *Sardanapalus* has its own, independent, life. It has
both surface clarity and metaphysical depth. It is not one of
those many would-be poetic dramas where you cannot, to
borrow a phrase from *Julius Caesar* (II. ii. 40), 'find a heart
within the beast'. I point next to the negative and positive
pulses of that heart, which relate respectively (i) to the ancestral
taboos against which the hero is fighting, and (ii) to that cosmic
radiance of which his life is conceived as a spontaneous expression.

The negative extreme is given in Sardanapalus' nightmare
in Act IV. We start with Myrrha's lines (IV. i. 1–23) spoken over
the sleeping Sardanapalus after the battle, which may be compared with Lara's unrestful sleep (*Lara*, I. 12–14) and the
happier sleep-lines in *Don Juan* (II. 147–8, 196–7); all fine
examples of Byron's Shakespearian ability to blend human
exactitude with ultimate mystery. In *Sardanapalus* the 'God of
Quiet' is felt as brother to Death, as in Shakespeare (e.g.
Macbeth, II. iii. 83). Myrrha watches the 'play of pain' on her

lover's features; exquisite nature-imagery supports human description, the 'sudden gust' that 'crisps' the 'reluctant' mountain lake, the blast ruffling autumn leaves. Sardanapalus' dream concerns (i) Nimrod the Hunter, and (ii) Semiramis the fighter. These two, founders of his Assyrian empire, represent traditional values and suggest the ingrained fear of ancestral authority whose weight so often masquerades as conscience. They oppose respectively Byron's sympathy with the sanctities of animal and human life. They may be equated with the 'ancestral voices prophesying war' of Coleridge's *Kubla Khan*. Sardanapalus, we are told, had not used his 'bow' and 'javelin' for years, not 'even in the chase' (I. ii. 316–20). Now, yet half in his dream, he cries:

> Hence – hence –
> Old Hunter of the earliest brutes! and ye,
> Who hunted fellow-creatures as if brutes!
> Once bloody mortals – and now bloodier idols,
> If your priests lie not!   (IV. i. 27)

Both are 'bloody'. He awakes to find their opposite: Myrrha, symbol of pure, sexual, passion. It is a move from death to life: 'I've been i' the grave – where worms are lords.'

He had, like Byron's Cain, seen 'a legion of the dead'. The Nimrod of his dream had a 'haughty, dark, and deadly face', with a quiver of 'shaft-heads feather'd from the eagle's wing'. The scene was a guest-hall and Sardanapalus invited his ancestor to fill the cup between them; he then filled it and offered it himself, but the vast figure with changeless expression refused the convivial joy, preserving a deadly immobility. He next turns to face Semiramis. She is a more gruesome figure: bloody, withered, 'sneering' in 'vengeance' and 'leering' with 'lust'. The entwining of sexual suggestion with cruelty is symbolized by her goblet 'bubbling o'er with blood', the sadistic connotation being similar to that of the Fountain running with blood in Flecker's *Hassan* (v. i). There is another goblet whose contents are left undefined. Other figures are there, but none of them eat or drink, being conceived as deathly contrasts to festivity and health.

Sardanapalus felt himself turning to stone, yet still alive and breathing. There was a 'horrid sympathy' between these dead and the living; the nightmare figures are made of the negative elements of the 'Byronic hero' as Sardanapalus of his gentleness, and a state is outlined of living death, apart from both Heaven and Earth. At length the lips of the two ancestors smiled. At this extremity a 'desperate courage' infused Sardanapalus' limbs and, fearing no longer, he laughed 'full in their phantom faces'. He grasped the hunter's hand, which melted away. There is here a reconciliation; the man at least looked a 'hero', but the woman was less easily mastered. She attacked him with 'noisome kisses', and spilled both goblets till their 'poisons' flowed round him, while he shrank as if he were the son who slew her for 'incest'. Loathsome objects cluster. He is dead, yet feels; buried, yet raised; consumed by worms yet purged by flames; wither'd in air yet – the rest is vague save that he searches for Myrrha and awakes to find her beside him.

The reaching of a positive beyond death by relegating death's realisms to a dream state is a clever mechanism resembling the purposive structure of Flecker's *Hassan*.[1] A similar progress through death is found in Keats's *The Fall of Hyperion* (see p. 198, note); and the hideous figure here might be compared with that of Keats's *La Belle Dame sans Merci*. The dream is loaded with suggestions of incest and cruelty, and may be related variously to the domination of ancestral authority, to an over-emphasis of power-instincts to the exclusion of sexual health, and to sadism. Semiramis is a 'homicide and husband-killer' (iv. i. 180). Nimrod comes off better, but every time he is called 'hunter' there is blood-insinuation. The death-impressions are icily sculptural, suggesting a forbidding eternity: 'If sleep shows such things, what may not Death disclose?' (iv. i. 53). The answer can only be in terms of a corresponding awakening or some vast apprehension of cosmic life hinted by Myrrha's reply:

> The dust we tread upon was once alive
> And wretched.   (iv. i. 65)

This, then, is the drama's negative heart. Its dramatic placing is apt since Sardanapalus has been fighting and shedding blood. To this the leers and sneers and welcomings hold an obvious

[1] For my study of *Hassan* see *The Golden Labyrinth*, 337–40; at greater length, *The Wind and the Rain*, II. 3; Winter 1944. [1967]

reference, just as the Weird Women get at Macbeth after a bloody battle. Myrrha sees it as 'mere creations of late events'. It is that, and more. Afterwards, the king reports how his ancestors have been trying to '*drag me down* to them' (IV. i. 176).[1]

For the positive heart: to Byron the Sun is all but God, as in the opening of Canto III of *The Corsair*. His early tales are set in sun-warmed regions. *Manfred* has an interesting invocation, close to the sun-worship in *Cymbeline*, and central to an understanding of Byron's mind and work:

> Glorious orb! the idol
> Of early nature, and the vigorous race
> Of undiseas'd mankind, the giant sons
> Of the embrace of angels, with a sex
> More beautiful than they, which did draw down
> The erring spirits who can ne'er return.
> Most glorious orb! that wert a worship, ere
> The mystery of thy making was reveal'd!
> Thou earliest minister of the Almighty,
> Which gladden'd, on their mountain tops, the hearts
> Of the Chaldean shepherds, till they pour'd
> Themselves in orisons! Thou material God!
> And representative of the Unknown –
> Who chose thee for his shadow!   (III. ii. 3)

The Sun's sacred life is related to a past golden age. It is 'chief star', and 'sire of the seasons', alone making earth 'endurable'. The 'inborn spirits' of man still have a 'tint' of it. It has psychological influences and associations. To Byron-Manfred the sun-qualities of 'life and warmth' have been of a 'fatal nature'. Arimanes, grand divinity of nature,[2] is throned on a 'globe of fire' (II. iv).

Sardanapalus concentrates powerfully on the Sun. As with the Moon in *Marino Faliero*, the Sun here covers both sides of the human conflict, though with subtle differences in conception.

[1] In my essay 'Shakespeare and Byron's Plays' (*Shakespeare–Jahrbuch*, 95; 1959) I wrote: 'It is more than a dream, being conceived, like Cain's excursion among the phantoms, as a meeting with the dead who are said to lose some of their death in order to make contact with a mortal who in sleep has lost some of his life' (IV. i. 125–7). The impingement of the one dimension on the other is exactly, and according to the spiritualistic sciences of today correctly, handled. [1967]

[2] Perhaps rather 'terrible' than 'grand'. Arimanes, 'Prince of Earth and Air', is nature in its more fearsome aspects. See p. 196 above, note. [1967]

It is associated with worship of Baal, the orthodoxy of the realm. The priest Beleses watches its setting (II. i. 1–36). He searches for its meaning, would read the 'everlasting page' of this 'true Sun', this

> burning oracle of all that live,
> As fountain of all life, and symbol of
> Him who bestows it . . .
>
> (II. i. 15)

His understanding is superstitious in comparison with Sardanapalus', but he has his own wisdom too. Why, he asks, must the Sun's 'lore' be limited to 'calamity'? Why not herald a day more worthy its own 'all-glorious burst from ocean'? Why not a 'beam of hope' to replace omens of 'wrath'? He talks of fear and sacrifices. His religion is negative, but in terms of it the sun is felt as a dominating force. Its red setting appropriately gilds this scheming revolutionary. We watch it, as it were, deserting its worshipper: 'While I speak, he sinks – is gone'. The speech concludes with an equation of sunset and death. Later Beleses is shocked at the king's disrespect for Chaldea's 'starry mysteries' (II. i. 251). Yet Sardanapalus has, as we have seen, his own way of worship, and his particular approach, at once erotic, aesthetic, and agnostic, is covered by our second sun-incident, in Act v. Two great sun-symbolisms thus frame the central storm and nightmare movements of Acts III and IV.

The Sun's second appearance (v. i. 1–58), as the tragic conclusion approaches, is not a sunset, but a sunrise, and is to be imaginatively related to the spiritual victory of Sardanapalus and his love. Myrrha and Balea are at a window. Storm has broken the night's loveliness; even so, the contrast in nature was beautiful; but what, asks Myrrha, of that other human storm of dark passions? What dawn-fire, what resolution, can rise on that? As in Shakespeare and Pope (*Essay on Man*, I. 155–60), the human-tempest analogy is precise. The dawn is splendid:

> And can the sun so rise,
> So bright, so rolling back the clouds into
> Vapours more lovely than the unclouded sky,
> With golden pinnacles and snowy mountains . . .
>
> (v. i. 9)

Dawn makes heaven a glorious replica of earthly forms. This sun-splendour is related to the 'soul' of man. It 'dwells upon', 'soothes', and 'blends into' the 'soul'. Sunrise and sunset are the 'haunted epoch' of 'sorrow and love' (the word order, unless chiasmus is intended, seems a slip). Both are needed for spiritual insight: they are 'twin genii' that 'chasten' and 'purify', more sweet than 'boisterous joys', and build palaces for choice souls to possess peacefully apart from, while enduring, the agonies of existence. 'Pain' and 'pleasure' are 'two names for one feeling' surpassing speech, like some *Kubla Khan* dome above antinomies, a unity 'which our internal, restless agony' would 'vary in the sound'. She describes the super-consciousness which all poetry aims to create. She speaks with the dawn streaming in on her, flooding her with gold. She, knowing, like Shakespeare's Antony, that she may not see its rising again, regrets having not felt more of the 'reverence' and 'rapture' due to that power which keeps earth living though mortals die. She almost becomes a 'convert' to Baal. Once, says Balea, repeating the golden age reference of *Manfred* (p. 234 above), the Sun reigned on earth. Myrrha prefers him in heaven, where he sways more powerfully than any 'earthly monarch', each ray more potent than empires, the thought relating to Sardanapalus' preference of love to earthly kingdoms.

The Sun is here our supreme reality. Balea calls it, surely, a god. Myrrha answers that her own, Greek belief is the same: yet she thinks it rather the abode of gods than itself one of the 'immortal sovereigns', repeating Sardanapalus' conception of the stars. The meaning of all this goes far beyond my transcription. The rising, flooding, sunlight increases with developing stage dialogue: it is all dramatically active. The usual poetic association of royalty, sun, and love[1] becomes a personified association, since Myrrha is the play's love-force. The moving

---

[1] I was thinking of Shakespeare. Sun and Love are associated in the Sonnets and at *Love's Labour's Lost*, IV. iii. 27, 334 ('eagle'), and *Twelfth Night*, IV. iii. 1; and in the Sheep Shearing Scene (IV. iii) of *The Winter's Tale*; sun and royalty at *Richard II*, III. ii. 36–53, and *Henry VIII*, III. ii. 416; love and royalty in the Sonnets and at *The Merchant of Venice*, III. ii. 176–84, and *Troilus and Cressida*, III. ii. 36–9. The moon is, however, a more usual association for the mysterious glamours of sexual love, and Byron's confident association of such love with the sun both here and in *Don Juan* marks an advance. See the *Crown of Life*, 102, and *Byron and Shakespeare* 244. [1967]

dialogue adds wonder to wonder till the blaze shuts out the world, dissolving it in light which Myrrha can no longer face (v. i. 57–8). The sun all but equals the divine, though with a reservation, felt also in *Manfred* where Arimanes on his globe of fire is not all-powerful over the protagonist. The human, for Byron, must to this extent preserve its integrity as against nature: hence the sense of the stars earlier and the Sun here as the 'abode' of more human gods rather than themselves divine.

The Sun accordingly dominates in twin rhythms of evening and morning – and the order is important – associated with the two sides of the conflict; but more directly with Myrrha, the love-centre, to whom the king earlier compares the stars. A golden haze aureoles the central action of battles, storm and nightmare, the sun blazing from each side. When there is next more battling and tragic failure, the movement dissolves into a sovereign nobility as the lovers die on their sacrificial pyre, loaded with frankincense and myrrh, the throne its 'core'. This is as a sunrise, a 'leap through flame into the future' (v. i. 362, 415). Sardanapalus had wanted the *future* to 'turn back and smile' on his reign (iv. i. 514). He now addresses his ancestors, bearing home to them the insignia of his lost empire through the 'absorbing element' of fire. His faults have been great, but he writes his name on the memory of centuries:

> Time shall quench full many
> A people's records and a hero's acts;
> Sweep empire after empire, like this first
> Of empires, into nothing; but even then
> Shall spare this deed of mine . . .
> (v. i. 442)

The blazing palace shall be more firmly established than Egypt's pyramids. A torch from Baal's shrine 'lights' the lovers 'to the stars' (450), in an embrace of 'commingling fire' (471). The orthodoxy of the realm contributes to the sacrifice.

Sardanapalus is less complex than *Marino Faliero*, but the simplicity is integral to its demanding monistic vision and the equating of dawn-fire with human tragedy not easy to probe though obvious to the view. The drama marks a resolution of former conflicts and corresponds to *Antony and Cleopatra* in the

Shakespearian sequence; though its purity of diction and lucidity of symbolism contrast with Shakespeare's more masked
effects. What is implicit in Shakespeare is continually here, as
often in *Marino Faliero* also, explicit. The ritual-conclusion is a
purposeful 'sacrifice' (v. i. 281), Myrrha pouring a libation to
the gods and Sardanapalus drinking a formal farewell to his
pleasures. There is also a certain plastic quality about the
whole, supported by references to sculpture and visually
descriptive passages of persons, the most striking that of
Myrrha in battle with 'her nostril dilated from its symmetry'
(iii. i. 386–400), and in stage-pictures, to be differentiated
from Byron's earlier more inward and energic, non-sensuous,
effects, and corresponding to similar emphases throughout *Don
Juan*.

    Sardanapalus alines a non-moral eroticism with a Christian
idealism, and the transference is pivotal. Though the purpose
forces a subtle humour and a tragic conclusion its positive
alinements might be said to dramatize eternity in action: and
that is why the play has a certain stillness, a plastic quality.
Energy and eternity coalesce and we are aware less of conflict
than of *essence*. It belongs to the feeling-world of *Don Juan*
which shows throughout a penetration not so much of energies
as of essences expressed in terms of visual description and references to spatial art.[1]

V

Don Juan was started in the year 1818 and continued, canto by
canto, till 1823.

    The occasional flamboyance of *Childe Harold* derives from its
too aristocratic temper, using traditional forms and invading
contemporary territories like a monarch. *Don Juan* carries this

---

[1] Byron's final emphasis on spatial arts had its antecedents in the sculptural
descriptions of *Childe Harold* iv and the architectures and equestrian statue of
Marino Faliero, where once (ii. i. 388–9) a poet's dream-god in marble-chisel'd
beauty contrasts as an image of sexual appeal, resembling in this the Apollo
Belvedere of *Childe Harold* (iv. 162), with the drama's prevailing sobriety. The
sculptures of *Childe Harold* iv and *The Prophecy of Dante* (comp. 1819) are discussed
in *Byron and Shakespeare*, 48–50. [1967]

peculiar superiority farther. The poet deliberately asserts his own, technical, supremacy:

> Prose poets like blank-verse, I'm fond of rhyme,
> Good workmen never quarrel with their tools . . .
>
> (I. 201)

Continually he allows some dissyllabic or trisyllabic word to set him a seemingly impossible task, arousing our pleasure by his comic resource. In his Satires Pope used a free play of self-dramatization, and in *Don Juan* the composing poet is the poem's real hero. In long digressions he discusses his own satiric and humorous approach, and the charges brought against him of immorality and irreverence. The widest social implications of poet-become-satirist interest Pope; but, though Pope's ground is covered, Byron is less concerned with the negatives of satire than with the positive of a new erotic and comoedic gospel. This we shall now discuss and in the process observe certain recurring and related tendencies: (i) visual and statuesque descriptions; (ii) correspondences with Shakespeare, especially in his final period; and (iii) further variations on the imaginative concept of 'eternity'.

The tempest-wreck and parching agony of Canto II leading up to the island romance of Juan and Haidée recall *The Tempest* and *The Ancient Mariner*. Haidée's innocence has points of similarity to Perdita's in *The Winter's Tale* or Miranda's in *The Tempest*. The essence of immediate love excluding tradition, forethought, and social complexity, is here distilled. It is as though through an attunement basic to the dream-desires of our race child innocence were incorporated into sexuality.

The imagery tends to show the whole incident as dewy and dawn-suffused. Haidée's cheek is not only 'rosy' as a sunset-tinted sky but when meeting the morning 'face to face' on her way to Juan she is flushed with 'headlong blood' (II. 118, 141). The physical is lit, as in Shakespeare's *Venus and Adonis*, by an inward emotional flame. Again:

> For still he lay, and on his thin worn cheek
> A purple hectic play'd like dying day
> On the snow-tops of distant hills; the streak
> Of sufferance yet upon his forehead lay,

I

Where the blue veins look'd shadowy, shrunk, and weak;
And his black curls were dewy with the spray . . .

(II. 147)

The inmost self is felt physically, the physical inwardly and all
but cosmically, and sensuousness alined with tragic feeling. A
natural simile recalls Shakespeare's impressions of tragic youth
in his early Histories (e.g. *3 Henry VI*, II. ii. 115; v. v. 62-7;
Richard III, I. ii. 249; I. iii. 178; see *The Mutual Flame*, 109-10):

like a young flower snapp'd from the stalk,
Drooping and dewy on the beach he lay . . .

(II. 176)

Haidée breathes over Juan's mouth as the 'sweet south'
upon a 'bed of roses' (II. 168). There is an emphasis on Juan's
nakedness, his 'so white a skin' (II. 129), and even later they are
together 'half-naked, loving, natural, and Greek' (II. 194). All
blends with the purity of naked sea and sand, the rosy evening
with one star like an 'eye' from a living universe (II. 183).
Delight and loving-kindness are one. Haidée comes on Juan
sleeping, and stops: 'for sleep is awful' (II. 143). Both *Lara* (I. 29)
and *Sardanapalus* touch sleep's mystery (p. 231 above); here no
joy on earth is felt equivalent to that of watching over what
you love 'sleeping', helpless, unconscious, somehow most
utterly itself when its whole self, all past actions and passions,
are 'hush'd into depths beyond the watcher's diving', like
'death without its terrors' (II. 196-7). The watcher's emotions
find a tranquillity unknown in the thrust and parry of wakeful
intercourse: the eternal essence is captured, out of time. The
intuition is tragic. As so often, Bryon treads the knife-edge
between the spiritual and the physical, eternity and time. This
delicate balance characterizes also our human descriptions.
Haidée's cheek is called 'transparent' and 'warm'; of 'pure dye'
like 'rosy' twilight; illuminated by its inner pulse, the blood-
flame. She is also 'fit for the model of a statuary', though
surpassing any 'stone ideal' wrought by a 'chisel': the statue-
thought getting at her eternal essence of beauty, felt as timeless (II. 114-19). Description is visual yet deep; aiming to
capture an essence, not to inaugurate action. Haidée's ten-

derness suffuses the story, her love flowers from a maternal care
deeper than desire. Juan is her 'infant' (II. 143),

> Fair as the crowning rose of the whole wreath,
> Soft as the callow cygnet in its nest . . .
>
> (II. 148)

Her voice is a 'warble' (II. 151); they are young birds (II. 190).
She bends over him 'hush'd as the babe upon its mother's
breast', still as a drooping willow or calm ocean depth (II. 148).
The maternal blends into the sexual, both bathing innocently
naked (II. 172) and talking a private language like birds (IV.
14). Haidée comes to love without thought or sense of sin (II.
190-3). Their 'pure hearts' mingle the feelings of 'friend, child,
lover, brother' into a 'sweet excess' ripe for death, being rather
'spirit' then 'sense' (IV. 26-7).[1] She is 'Nature's bride' and
'Passion's child' (II. 202). The 'mountain-crescent' and 'rosy'
sky, 'glittering' ocean, purple twilight, and the waves plashing
(II. 183-5), condition and impregnate their romance. Their
kisses are kindled from 'above', controlled by a cosmic power
beyond both (II. 186), they cling naturally, as 'swarming
bees', their hearts 'flowers' and 'honey' (II. 187). The stars burn
as 'nuptial torches' to shed 'beauty upon the beautiful', they are
hallowed by their own emotions, Ocean their witness, and
Solitude their priest (II. 204). They are alone within a magic
universe and feel their 'life could never die' (II. 188). It is
because their love is timeless that their clinging forms a
sculptured 'group', an eternal essence (II. 194). 'Each was an
angel and earth paradise' (II. 204). Haidée bends over Juan as
an angel over one lately having died 'in righteousness' (II. 144):
she is his Beatrice. We are pointed to love's 'mystic' art (I. 106),
something 'celestial' (III. 5), a perfect beyond-sin consummation, carefully conditioned, but potentially at least human, and
negating Milton's Fall; which, through intuition of an erotic
centre in unity with those gentler instincts that our religious
mythology isolates, suggests an inclusion and an absolute that
challenge orthodox Christianity.

Byron knows what he is doing, the antithesis being often
phrased. Juan even in church turned to images of the Virgin

[1] This last sentence replaces my original, though the reference IV. 26 was there.
For love's tragic plenitude see *Byron and Shakespeare*, 57-66; also 32. [1967]

rather than 'grisly saints' (II. 149). Eden is in Byron's mind
(II. 189, 193), and commentators who reduce Dante's Beatrice
to 'theology' (III. 11) given an ironic reference. That Haidée
should have no thought of marriage (II. 190) is necessary. In
Eloisa to Abelard (88: and see 73–90) Pope's Eloisa rates the
position of mistress above that of wife, since such poems –
Shakespeare's *Antony and Cleopatra* is another – aim to isolate an
essence unplaced in orthodox hierarchies.[1] Byron works round
and round the problem: since love cannot be a 'devil', yet is
clearly a god, we must have it for 'god of evil' (II. 205). He
remarks, in the manner of John Lyly's *Alexander and Campaspe*,
how it has both subdued greatest heroes and made philosophers
(II. 205–7). Though not necessarily lasting – Juan has forgotten
Julia (II. 208) – love remains a superconsciousness and a
cosmic insight, an admiration of 'nature's profusion' exceeding
adoration of a lovely 'statue'; a 'fine extension of the faculties',
starry in origin and 'filter'd through the skies' (II. 211–12).
Byron is as conscious as the Shakespeare of *Romeo and Juliet* of
the relevant criticisms. The romance is varied by stern or
humorous realisms, as when Zoe cooks eggs whilst Haidée
plays the angel (II. 144). Feeding underlines physical necessity.
Ironic moral viewpoints are offered, with an honest distinction
of the romance from marriage-permanencies. Fragility is
love's essence, one with that very value for which Byron feels so
deep a reverence (XIV. 94). From an uncompromising honesty
and a narrative as objectively conceived as any in English
the 'burning tongues' of a speechless wonder interpret 'nature's
oracle' of 'first love' (II. 189) in revelation of feelings 'universal
as the sun' (II. 167).

[1] The matter is lucidly stated in Dryden's *Amphitryon*: see *The Golden Labyrinth*,
132. A dynamic value seems to be involved, defined in Pope's 'How glowing guilt
exalts the keen delight!' (*Eloisa to Abelard*, 230), corresponding to Byron's compact
'ambrosial sin' (*Don Juan*, I. 127). The mental twist which Spenser and Milton
show desecrating natural instinct (pp. 10, 30–2 above) is by these others regarded
as a positive constituent, forecasting Nietzsche's drive for a value beyond good and
evil at once depending on and transcending morality in *Thus Spake Zarathustra*. For
the nature of Shakespeare's rather different and yet also positive approach to this
centre see my essay, 'The Shakespearean Integrity' (*The Sovereign Flower*, IV; included in *Shakespeare Criticism, 1935–60*, ed. Anne Ridler, World's Classics).
   For practical purposes the adventure, which may involve dangerous perversion,
is probably best confined to fantasy, according to the teaching of John Cowper
Powys, explained in *The Saturnian Quest*, 119–20. See pp. 30, 32, 113, notes. [1967]

There are two eternities: one or death and dark otherness, variously kind or cheerless; and one of perfect consummation in time, of the temporal become timeless, shot through with the eternal, by love. Both will tend to expression in terms of stillness, or motion subdued to stillness. Milton's motionless and sculptural imagery is an extreme development of eternal cravings, a too eager will to impose eternality on time. A dark eternity has often in Byron overshadowed energies and conflicts; but *Sardanapalus* projects bright eternity, and so does the Juan and Haidée romance in *Don Juan*.

Starting with nature and instinct, the narrative passes to an emphasis on many arts of barbaric finery recalling passages of Marlowe and Keats.

We are now (III. 61–73) in a world of 'fair slaves', carvings, tapestry, an 'ivory inlaid table'; ebony, crystal, marble, porcelain; gorgeous carpets of pictorial design; splashes of colour, gold, crimson, blue; fine dresses (Haidée's particularly) and extravagant foods and drink; as well as ritual sacrifice (III. 32), dance (III. 30), and song. Earlier description has been visual and naturalistic but now the poetry becomes more richly ornamental. The move would be dangerous were Haidée, herself plastically described (III. 71–2), not still central to make the 'atmosphere' alive (III. 74). The plastic or ceremonious expresses a timeless, flame-vital essence. The balance is precarious, as is the human story it accompanies, where all this revelry is felt treading a precipice before disaster. Desire is often a greedy craving to render permanent what is more properly a fleeting delight: and hence the poetic temptation of a facile reliance on static arts. Here lust is not in question; but the solidification of any winged vitality may be dangerous in life or poetry and the many statuesque essences in *Don Juan* need, and get, a fine delicacy of presentation. The magnificence touches Keats's *Lamia* as the earlier love-warmth *The Eve of St Agnes*. 'Burning Sappho' in the song 'The Isles of Greece' lives for a moment vivid within this setting of 'classical profiles and glittering dresses' (III. 33), but Byron knows that 'there is no sterner moralist than Pleasure' (III. 65) and is not confined to any limited Hellenism or limited eroticism. Sense-extravagance matures into the quietude of the 'Ave Maria' stanzas, the lovers facing the 'rosy flood' (III. 101) of evening, hour at once of 'love' and 'prayer' awaking reverential thoughts of Virgin and Son. Byron pauses to assert his faith: such pictorial images are too true for fiction (III. 103). His worship is not less than orthodox but greater, like Pope's, expanding to the 'great Whole' (III. 104). Soft thoughts of the young bird under its parent's wing and the child at its mother's breast lead to a typically Byronic, maternal, gentleness: noting how, even at Nero's death, 'some hands unseen strew'd flowers upon his tomb' (III. 109).

Haidée's story closes pathetically. She dreams of a cave of 'marble icicles', the 'work of ages' on its 'water-fretted halls' where her tears 'froze to marble' as they fell (IV. 33). It is perhaps an ancestral accusation from the other eternity. She awakes to stand 'pale' and 'statue-like' (IV. 43) before her father, who is remorseless. There follows a reworking of the heroine's madness in *Parisina*. Her head droops in death 'as when the lily lies o'ercharged with rain' (IV. 59); she lies, for a while, like Juliet, untouched by 'corruption', like the 'exquisitely chisell'd' marble of an unchanged Venus 'for ever fair', or those sculptured groupings of 'eternal' agony where 'energy' is, and yet is not, 'life' (IV. 61). Such sculptural eternities relate both to Keats's *Ode on a Grecian Urn* and Hermione's statue in *The Winter's Tale*, and recall the coincidence of the eternal on time handled in Byron's descriptions of sleep. The romance, despite the poet's often lightly objective approach, is mainly Haidée's, and seen through her eyes, as with Venus in *Venus and Adonis*. No English poet more closely than Byron approaches Shakespeare's darkly inward penetrations and fierce conflicts; but another Shakespearian gift is his too, a sense of the delicate yet fine texture of physical personality, the supreme value yet 'fragile mould' of 'the precious porcelain of human clay' (IV. 11). Haidée and Juan are its personifications.

Though the Juan-Haidée romance is saved from over-sensuous dangers by its tragic conclusion, the poem itself advances among such dangers with an easy mock-prudery:

> I therefore do denounce all amorous writing
> Except in such a way as not to attract.
>
> (v. 2)

We now leave Keats for the despotic barbarism of *Tamburlaine*. We meet slaves and human beings sold like cattle, a 'Circassian' girl 'warranted virgin' (IV. 114) going for fifteen hundred dollars. When bought for the Sultana's craving, Juan is taken (V. 45–56) to a 'noble palace' with a fine hall and 'marble fountain' and through an 'enormous room without a soul', the phrase recalling Pope's view of such extravagances in his *Moral Essays* (IV) and being perhaps relevant also to some of my strictures on Milton's architectural exploits: Byron himself notes that such unsocial interiors may do well enough for a church (V. 59). There is an explicit further criticism of the masonic and the architectural, and more ornaments embarrassing nature with art (V. 63–4); gorgeous divans, sofas it seems a sin to sit on, 'glittering galleries' and 'marble floors', carvings of 'gilded bronze', a gate of 'pyramidic pride', and in short so much perfume and dazzle that you can make nothing of it, as with certain Western falsities, 'bad statues', and so on (V. 85–94). Such is Byron's setting for the Sultana Gulbeyaz' lust. She is visually projected: her cheeks' flush comes 'blood-red' as clouds in 'sunset' (V. 108) and in temper she is an 'embodied storm' (V .135). Her own desire is visually prompted, as when she 'eye'd' Juan 'o'er and o'er' (V. 107) on his arrival. Her dressing of Juan in woman's clothes for safety has interesting reference to the poem's continual admiration of an almost feminine beauty in its hero. Descriptions of persons are aesthetic and pictorial, Gulbeyaz rising like Venus 'from the wave' (V. 96). Her final fury is staged in a room rich with 'porcelain', vases, pearl, porphyry and marble, to the sound of warbling birds (VI. 97–8), recalling Spenser's Bower of Bliss. The 'heart's dew of pain' stands out on her forehead 'like morning's on a lily'; she is a 'pythoness'; dramatic postures are locked in statuesque poetry as the poet sees her head 'hung down' and one hand drooping all 'white, waxen, and as alabaster pale', and ends by wishing himself a painter with 'colours' and 'tints' at his service (VI. 105–9). But however plastic the approach there is no devitalizing: strong poetic life burns in every sculptural phrase, the imagery moreover relating dynamically to the aesthetic and sensuous atmosphere required. Sexual feeling is strong throughout the amusing incidents, in Gulbeyaz'

246 POETS OF ACTION

'Christian, canst thou love?' (v. 116) and Juan's having to go to bed with Dudú, and her resulting 'dream' (vi. 75-7). Pageantry in the harem is formal, almost ritualistic, yet also humorous, as when the Sultan arrives with his eunuchs 'black and white' and train a 'quarter of a mile' long (v. 146); or Juan is led off with the crowd of harem girls, 'lovely Odalisques' (vi. 29),

> with stately march and slow,
> Like water-lilies floating down a rill . . .
> (vi. 33)

The girls Lolah, Katinka, and Dudú are softly and luxuriantly felt and yet may also be seen sculpturally as in Dudú's 'Attic forehead' and 'Phidian nose' (vi. 42). One girl smiling in sleep is given an exquisite nature-comparison (vi. 66), while another is seen 'statue-like and still' like a 'frozen rill' (vi. 68). The tendency is persistent, growing from the will to project essence rather than energy.

The massed formations of barbaric splendour and lustful sexuality blend into Gulbeyaz' passionate revenge. Their potential dangers are recognized. Byron is including, judging, and in his own way purifying, that area of aesthetic yet morally dubious sexuality found in Spenser, Marlowe and Milton.

Juan's adventures at the Court of Catherine of Russia are the occasion of some happy descriptions. Throughout the poem dress receives an emphasis. Here the hero is given a brilliant uniform and stockings

> uncurdled as new milk
> O'er limbs whose symmetry set off the silk . . .
> (ix. 43)

Nature is improved by 'art'. He is placed 'as if upon a pillar' for our inspection like, in a phrase of light yet pungent satire, 'Love turn'd a lieutenant of artillery'. He is a 'Cupid', 'blushing and beardless'; angelic, yet with an 'eye' and 'turn of limb' promising erotic adventures; indeed, a 'most beauteous boy' (ix. 45, 47, 53). A Pygmalion statue-reference occurs at ix. 51; and a *Hamlet* reminder of Mercury poised 'on a heaven-kissing hill' at ix. 66. The femininity of Sardanapalus and Juan is interesting. Juan's 'features' suit feminine attire (v. 115) and

his complexion varies from blush-warmth to pallor and tears
(v. 117) like Gulbeyaz' (v. 124). In his Juan Byron is deliberately
creating less a male agent than a bisexual essence. Observe that
the hero is passive; the energy is in Byron's approach.

The poem might be divided into (i) amatory adventures and
(ii) militaristic and social satire. These do not quite correspond
to what I have called the two 'eternities', since the darker of
those is nobly tragic and war is here presented mainly as a
stupid evil. Plastic imagery, which we have seen first as a
glowing expression, and next as a more artificial accompaniment, of desire, and shall find later as grave monuments of a
dark but noble past, is, in these war scenes, absent. Strong
action tends to negate such impressions. It is often the business
of literary art to transmute crude action by aesthetic ratification
and poetic form, but in this poem of essences war-action,
regarded as the destruction of essence, is left naked and unadorned.

Byron sees his satire in the tradition of Falstaff's (VII. 21).
'The noble art of killing' (VII. 58) goes on for 'cash and
conquest' (VII. 64). A couplet may remind us of Pope (*Imitations of Horace*, Satires, II. i. 23-8, 73-5):

> Bombs, drums, guns, bastions, batteries, bayonets, bullets;
> Hard words, which stick in the soft Muses' gullets.
> (VII. 78)

Homer's descriptive art may outreach us but we leave him far
behind in brute 'fact' (VII. 81). A warlike hero is merely a
'butcher in great business' (VII. 83). 'Common fellows' are
left to 'shriek for water' (VIII. 11) while attention is given to a
prince. We are forced to look on

> the all-white eye
> Turn'd back within its socket . . .
> (VIII. 13)

After all

> War's a brain-spattering, windpipe-slitting art,
> Unless her cause by right be sanctified.
> (IX. 4)

Byron's pacifism is never absolute: if the cause be truly noble a
battlefield may well be 'holy ground' (VIII. 5). In general he

opposes war to Christianity: Catherine is ironically called a
'Christian' empress (VII. 64), her army 'Christian' soldiery
(VIII. 37), and carnage itself 'Christ's sister' (VIII. 9). Byron's
feminine sympathies are antagonized as 'babe and mother'
shriek to Heaven (VIII. 69). For

> The drying up a single tear has more
> Of honest fame, than shedding seas of gore.
>
> (VIII. 3)

War can be ranged easily enough against Christian emotions,
but Byron is equally concerned to involve the sexual. Like
Swift he describes official decorations, and compares them to
the purple of 'the Babylonian harlot' (VII. 84), neatly switching
convention's sexual disapprovals into horror of war's slaugh-
terous decorum.

Though Don Juan fights, like Sardanapalus, finely, yet he
remains 'feminine in feature' (VIII. 52) and ever 'hated
cruelty' as all do 'until heated' (VIII. 55). 'Sovereigns', not
human nature, inculcate the arts of war-lust (VIII. 92). A life
close to nature is contrasted with the bloody 'joys' of 'civilization' (VIII. 61–8). The pains of national glory are in Shakespearian manner balanced against the peasant's simple content
(IX. 14, 15). Juan rescues Leila, a child with

> A pure, transparent, pale, yet radiant face
> Like to a lighted alabaster vase.
>
> (VIII. 96)

This is perhaps the most exquisite of all our vital yet plastic
images, recalling the flame-lit personality of Haidée and other
impressions of blushes and facial light. In these war scenes it
stands solitary and pathetic as the child herself amidst the
carnage. Juan saves Leila, a child 'parentless and therefore
mine' (VIII. 100). 'One life saved' is a greater deed than all
the 'fame' ever sung for heroism (IX. 34). Byron delights in the
child's refusal to be converted although three Bishops get to
work on her (X. 55–6). He has a sympathy with the Moslem
faith, and the siege of Ismail provides a neat antithesis of
ruthless Christianity and brave Turkish defence. The Khan's
dying son sees 'bright eternity' flashing like 'ceaseless sunrise'
where houris are mixed with angels in one 'voluptuous blaze'

(VIII. 115), phrases compactly illustrating the transition of erotic brilliance into the eternity-concept which is the poem's heart. The old Khan himself has a noble death (VIII. 116–19). We end with the comic emphasis on the good Russians' chastity when sacking the city, their content with slaughter and comparatively little raping, and a remark on the disappointment among certain ladies 'of single blessedness' (VIII. 131; *A Midsummer Night's Dream*, I. i. 78) whose minds had been preparing for the worst.

Byron's satire is both humorous and religious, aiming to make us 'ponder what a pious pastime war is' (VIII. 124). It develops into a denunciation of Wellington (IX. 1–13) and England (X. 66–8) for missing a great opportunity in liberal action. Byron had regarded his country, as did Pope, as potentially the world's exemplar and liberator. Now all monarchs are suspect. The Empress's delighted receipt of the news of 'thirty thousand slain' (IX. 59) needs little comment; and yet Byron does not like 'mobs' any better than 'tyrants' and is no facile 'demagogue' (IX. 25); what he does like his whole life-work is left to define. He is aiming to swing over certain powerful human instincts from a destructive to a creative direction.

Juan's move to England occasions a social satire following mainly Pope's, and most other satirists', aversions: hypocrisy (X. 34; XI. 86), supposed purity (XI. 10), respect for 'fashion' (XI. 33), literary critics (X. 14), the mentalization of passion (XI. 34), sexual coldness (XII. 63), gossip (XII. 43), pride (XIII. 19), politicians' 'double front' and tendency to lie without daring a 'bold' wickedness (XI. 36), the dangers of wealth and the growing power of capitalism over Europe (XII. 5–14), England's pretence to freedom (XI. 9). England is a race of 'haughty shopkeepers' (X. 65) which nevertheless 'might have been' the 'noblest nation' (X. 66). The satiric arrows are multi-directional and ironic: kings must nowadays at least 'talk of law before they butcher' (X. 74). Byron fights, like Pope, a swarming complex of insincerities, at one moment attacking sophisticated and cold women who 'hate all vice except its reputation' (XII. 25), at another those who fear discovery without being ashamed of deeds (XII. 80). Aristocratic sport gets a lash, with a kindly wink at poachers (XIII. 75); so does,

typically, the lack of sympathy with post-horses (XIII. 42).
The 'ennui' of aristocratic pleasures (XIV. 17) and the 'dreary
void' of 'high life' (XIV. 79) are well characterized. A miniature
drama is conjured up of a pretty country girl brought before a
justice for immorality (XVI. 63–5). Though the fluid technique
cannot be expected to maintain the compacted energy of
Pope, yet individual phrases or lines may have an equal sting,
as in the dynamic compression of 'ambrosial cash' (XIII. 100)
and 'the snake Society' (XIV. 96). Were we to strip off appearances and reveal the psychological fact, what new geography of
the social problem would be revealed:

> What icebergs in the hearts of mighty men,
> With self-love in the centre as their pole!
>
> (XIV. 102)

Byron matches Pope in epigrammatic pith, as also in so running
and swift a grammatical lucidity as 'Caesar himself would be
ashamed of fame' (XIV. 102).

There are many analyses of love. No writer has less shirked
its complexity. Its vanity and selfishness are admitted together
with an ironically humorous emphasis on the idealistic:

> The noblest kind of love is love Platonical
> To end or to begin with; the next grand
> Is that which may be christen'd love canonical,
> Because the clergy take the thing in hand . . .
>
> (IX. 76)

Both neglect those awkward realities, the 'senses'; and love
and lust are not easily distinguished (IX. 73–7). Marriage is
satirized: men are snared into it by an unfair social technique
(XII. 58–60). Why do we indulge romantically in poetic
phrases concerning love's supremacy which we next contradict
by pretending we regard all love outside marriage as sinful?
(XII. 13–16). Passion is admired in a lover but is considered
'uxorious' in a husband (III. 6.) The union of sensual and
sentimental has a dangerous aspect (XIV. 73). No sex really
understands the other and only a Tiresias can make love
properly (XIV. 73). We do not understand ourselves: 'She
knew not her own heart; then how should I?' (XIV. 91). The
marriage state may be either the best or worst of any (XIV. 95);

yet the essence of love is change (xiv. 94), and female friends have proved truer than lovers in trouble (xiv. 96). From this tangle emerges a simple faith in the romantic essence: in feelings which, since they are 'divine', are therefore 'real' (xvi. 107); in the revelatory quality of 'moments when we gather from a glance more joy' than from any of those causes for pride that may 'kindle manhood' but never 'entrance the heart' with its own, yet selfless, existence (xvi. 108). Since the poem is working through complexities to essences, the essence of love is given a theological dignity. Anacreon alone has properly honoured 'Eros' with 'unwithering myrtle', and Byron therefore, just before the long poem's climax, offers formal respect to 'Alma Venus Genetrix' (xvi. 109).

The opposition of the Byronic Eros to war and social insincerity is clear and, in so far as there is conflict, its victory easy. A sterner and subtler problem awaits our attention. Briefly, the poem's last movement which takes us to Norman Abbey (based on Newstead) offers the old 'dark eternity' of ancestry, ruins, death, and the Church.

Byron is no facile rationalist in his approach to final mysteries. All philosophical schemes, he suggests, are vain. We know only that we are born to die, and even that may be untrue (xiv. 3). Some 'Font of Eternity', some ever-springing source of immediate essence, may be attained where 'new' and 'old' (that is, time) lose meaning (xiv. 3). We fear death, yet what is sleep? (xiv. 3). The suicide often dies paradoxically through the very 'dread of death', as men desire to leap down a precipice (xiv. 4). Byron hints at that perversity of mind that makes man aim, like Macbeth, at what he fears most, since in all fear there is a fascination, just as there is in fascination a necessary fear: a paradox through which a new equation of love and death might be reached. The unknown draws us with a 'secret prepossession' (xiv. 6); a thought relevant to many passages in Wordsworth's *Prelude* and the normal human interest in horror-stories and ghosts. The poet claims to have once had an experience he prefers to suppress, and will not mock that 'source of the sublime and the mysterious', the supernatural (xv. 95). His comprehensive awareness sees man as inhabiting 'two worlds', as a star on the horizon between 'night and morn', a mighty mystery enclosing and awaiting our destiny: we know neither what we are nor what we may be (xv. 99). The Black Friar on whose ghostly legend so much depends is shown as not conquered:

> Amundeville is lord by day
> But the monk is lord by night.
>
> (xvi. 40–1)

This might serve as a motto for Byron's work, its balance of the two eternities, dark and light, the historic and the prophetic, death and love. His respect for the Church is one with his respect for what I call 'dark eternity' and both are integral to the conception of Norman Abbey.

The description occurs at xiii. 55–74, balancing a different architecture and sculpture against former examples. Once an old monastery, it lies in a valley where a 'Druid oak' stands 'like Caractacus'. The 'Gothic pile' rises with a 'grand arch' awaking thought of ruinous time. A Virgin image with God-born Child in her 'blessed arms' alone survives among the empty niches, making the poet feel the ground 'holy' in super-stitious reverence. There is a window once filled with stained glass through which the sun's 'deepen'd glories' used to pass, but now the gale 'sweeps through' the 'fretwork' and the owl sings his anthem. At full moon, if the wind be from a certain quarter, there 'moans a strange unearthly sound', soaring and sinking, which Byron says he has heard 'once too much'. The courtyard has a fountain with weird facial carvings; the mansion 'huge halls' and 'long galleries' joined by architectural styles out of period, in grand irregularity. The ancestral pictures are described, of ladies, churchmen, soldiers, and classic land-scapes. All is weighty with the past. In our latter cantos we again find plastic metaphors. The world of yesterday is gone like a shivered 'globe of glass' (xi. 76). Hypocritical society is, or pretends to be, a 'china without flaw' (xii. 78). The reserved dignity of an aristocratic dinner-table is

> polish'd, smooth, and cold,
> As Phidian forms cut out of marble Attic . . .
>
> (xiii. 110)

Here, though the intended tone is correct, the bright Hellenic reminder may slightly disturb the balance; for the poem itself

is to be now 'high and solemn' like 'an old temple dwindled to
a column' (XIII. 1). The tone is to be heavy, weighted with
the dark eternity of historic ruins.

From this setting grows Aurora, as important as Haidée.
Though she is a 'gem', that is, more spiritual, in comparison
with Haidée's natural 'flower' (XV. 58), she is also a rose 'with
all its sweetest leaves yet folded' (XV. 43); and, like Marina in
Shakespeare's *Pericles*, an 'orphan'. She dwells in eternity: her
eyes shine as a 'seraph's' wearing an 'aspect beyond time', at
once 'radiant' and 'grave'. She is seen pictorially as though
she were 'pitying man's decline', mourning sins not her own:

> She look'd as if she sat by Eden's door,
> And griev'd for those who could return no more.
>   (XV. 45)

She is a 'young star' above our world, 'too sweet an image' for
its 'glass' (XV. 43), and her spirit

> seem'd as seated on a throne
> Apart from the surrounding world, and strong
> In its own strength . . .   (XV. 47)

She resembles Shakespeare's 'Patience gazing on kings' graves
and smiling extremity out of act' in *Pericles* (V. i. 140). Byron
himself feels the kinship. She was 'more Shakespearian', since

> The worlds beyond this world's perplexing waste
> Had more of her existence . . .

Her 'depth of feeling' embraces thoughts infinite yet 'silent' as
space (XVI. 48). Both Haidée and Aurora have affinities with
the younger heroines of Shakespeare's last period. They
personify respectively the bright and dark eternities, Eros and
religion, though in each there is a blend of both, Haidée being
herself 'devout as well as fair' (II. 193) and expressly maternal,
and Aurora 'radiant' as well as 'grave'. Aurora is a Catholic,
loving that 'fallen worship' partly because of its fall (XV. 46).
She is Haidée fully conscious of Haidée's tragic fate.

Juan is alone (XVI. 15–19). He moves from his Gothic
chamber with its ornaments of 'chisell'd stone and painted
glass' to the gallery with its pictures of 'knights and dames'. All
is ghostly in the moonlight. At this hour 'voices from the urn'

of death are aroused in a world where all else 'should sleep'. He watches the 'pale smile of beauties in the grave', their 'buried locks' still waving on the starlit canvas. The portrait of even a living subject records an uncapturable past (xvi. 19): the mystery of stillness, of time, of eternal essence is transmitted, something akin to that shadowed in Keats's *Ode on a Grecian Urn*. When the ghost appears Juan is himself turned to stone, 'petrified', and stands as a 'statue' (xvi. 23). The next night (xvi. 113–23) he waits all but undressed, uneasy lest the ghost return. It does. There is the last vivid scene, Juan putting out his arm only to touch the moon-silver'd 'tracery' of the old walls, the monk's eyes not precisely those of 'stony death', Juan's hand pressing on a 'hard but glowing bust', which strangely 'beat as if there was a warm heart under', his seeing a 'dimpled chin' and 'neck of ivory' – how *sculptural* it all is – and, behold, the amorous Duchess of Fitz-Fulke!

All our solemn impressions of ancestral ruin and statued dignity, the whole poem's plastic symbolism, piles up to this climax. The Monk's ghost[1] symbolizes haunting mystery, Church tradition, death itself, the dark eternity in its most forbidding aspect. The merry Duchess, a flirtatious 'full-grown Hebe', the most trivial of our long gallery of ladies, with more prettiness than intelligence (xvi. 49), symbolizes, as would none of the others, that erotic *essence* with which Byron would challenge our culture. The staggering humour is one with a profound conflict: it is Byron's equivalent to Shakespeare's resurrection of Hermione in *The Winter's Tale*, and hence the at first sight unnecessary statue-impressions at the conclusion. It is the final, humorous, opposition of essences, of the bright and dark eternities in *extreme* forms; though their best human incarnations, Haidée and Aurora, include elements of both.

Byron's outlook in *Don Juan* is kindly, radiating from a spontaneous affection, especially for women, good or bad. His Julia, Haidée, Gulbeyaz, Leila, Catherine, Adeline, Aurora, and Fitz-Fulke make a striking company. His reverence for petticoats (xiv. 23–8) is central and from that heart no ultimate

---

[1] I take its first appearance to be that of a real ghost, otherwise there would be little point in Byron's introductory comments at xv. 95–9 and xvi. 4, 7. [1967]

bitterness can arise. He defends himself against charges of both
bitterness and irreligion, though only a blunted criticism could
accuse him of either: *The Vision of Judgement* (comp. 1821), at
least on the theological side, might serve as a test of healthy
reaction. He finds himself accused of scoffing at 'human power
and virtue' when all he says is covered by Solomon, Cervantes,
and Dante (VII. 3). His satire is light; his muse has no reproof
worse than a 'smile' (XI. 63), she is a butterfly that does not
'sting' and rarely even alights, though were she a hornet there
are vices that would feel it (XIII. 89). 'Bitters' are mixed
'slightly' with her 'sweets' (XVI. 3). It is true. Byron is not out
for 'poetic war' (IV. 98). While sharply attacking 'hatred', he
would 'rather check than punish crimes' (XIII. 6–8), and is
indeed 'the mildest, meekest of mankind' who has never been
cruel, whose sins were of the instinctive and warmer kind
only – why then is he charged with misanthropy? 'They hate
me,' he says, 'not I them' (IX. 21). As for religion, the world is
at the very worst a 'glorious blunder' (XI. 3) and he in half-
seriousness – and here that can mean a great deal – subscribes
explicitly to orthodoxy (XI. 6); an implicit reverence is continual. The poem is an attempt at elucidation of his relation to
the 'creed and morals of the land' (IV. 5). However, he discovers that 'a jest at Vice by Virtue's called a crime' (XIII. 1).
He lived in an age when poachers were caught in a steel trap,
and, wounded, awaited prison instead of hospital (XVI. 61).
We should understand many of his revulsions the better for a
century's advance. He compares himself humbly with other
'persecuted sages', Locke, Bacon, Socrates,

> and thou, Diviner still,
> Whose lot it is by man to be mistaken,
> And thy pure creed made sanction of all ill,
> Redeeming worlds to be by bigots shaken,
> How was thy toil rewarded?
>
> (XV. 18)

An old thought, but not a dead one. His own Muse is 'the most
sincere that ever dealt in fiction' (XVI. 2): though that is not
to deny its humour. He believes all poetry to be true con-
ditionally on the reader's proper understanding of its nature;
and that religion has the 'clue' to reality; perhaps all the varied

sects are right (xv. 89–90). It is time 'some new prophet should appear' or else some 'old' one indulge mankind with 'second sight' (xv. 90).[1] The prophets are there, waiting for us, and among them Byron's work stands high. Especially, perhaps, is his humour profound. He feels humour to be close to tragedy, and *Don Quixote* is to him the saddest of tales because it 'makes us smile' (xiii. 9). Again:

> And if I laugh at any mortal thing,
> 'Tis that I may not weep . . .
> (iv. 4)

The cosmic philosophy to which he strains is a monistic faith like Pope's, believing all things ultimately 'kind' (xiii. 41); and with a short notice of the kindly quality in Byron's humour I must close my summary account of his poetry.

A deep human sympathy enweaves with light irony, as in Shakespeare's last plays, where the simple and the romantic assert themselves against a play of critical intelligence. In *Don Juan*, manner and matter alike, this sympathy is basic.

When Haidée's pirate father is called 'the good old man' (ii. 130) we know that he is, in one very obvious sense, the precise opposite:

> A fisherman he had been in his youth,
> And still a sort of fisherman was he . . .
> (ii. 125)

Within the fun exists a wide comprehension, almost *sub specie aeternitatis*, wherein the distinction between suffering fishes and suffering men may not be so all-important as we think. He is next a 'fisher of men' like 'Peter the Apostle' and we balance piracy and proselytizing (ii. 126). The humour depends on recognition of a possible breakdown of our most cherished illusions, with nevertheless a *happy* result. When Haidée makes love 'whilst her piratical papa was cruising' (iii. 13), the word 'papa' enlists soft family emotions on the side of villainy. It is next suggested that were he a 'prime minister' his way of 'raising cash' would be 'nothing but taxation'; he just practises as a 'sea-attorney' (iii. 14). As so often in writers like Byron, the

---

[1] This is an important statement which should be considered in relation to Byron's various spiritualistic apprehensions studied in my *Byron and Shakespeare*. [1967]

obvious crime is thrown into sharp and significant relation to
the more subtly insidious dangers of respectability.

The pirate's ruthlessness is not watered down (III. 16), but
he remains 'the best of fathers' (III. 17), bringing back a
present for Haidée. A slight shift of perspective and we recognize a man no worse than ourselves, with a certain delight in
the recognition. Besides,

> He was the mildest manner'd man
> That ever scuttled ship or cut a throat . . .
>
> (III. 41)

He had been hardened in part by continual abuse of his mercy
(III. 54); the 'spirit of old Greece' was in him, with no honest
way open for expressing his force of personality (III. 55); and
he loves music and flowers (III. 56). He is a usual Byronic
figure. What first appeared a light humour gradually reveals
itself as a wide and deep recognition of common humanity
beneath the level of moral distinctions.

Whatever the variations played, and they are many, a
certain optimistic universal underlies the poem's humour.
Apparent cruelties are superficial. A slave-market is lightly,
and it may seem callously, described: yet, look deeper, and
are we not all slaves (v. 25)? 'By God's grace' (II. 132) many
wrecks throw up firewood on Haidée's island: yet what philosophy has yet penetrated God's certainly non-human categories?
Suffering and advantage are reciprocal throughout the fabric of
the universe: we recognize a sudden truth with an equally
sudden delight. Continually we are so directed to a pleasing
profundity:

> Let us have wine and women, mirth and laughter,
> Sermons and soda-water the day after . . .
>
> (II. 178)

The thought circles above the diurnal rhythms of psychic
variation too often supposed a unity. Attacks of ill-health, we
are told, have developed the poet's orthodoxy until the Trinity
is so uncontrovertibly established

> That I devoutly wish'd the three were four
> On purpose to believe so much the more.
>
> (XI. 6)

This is, in fact, true, since the whole poem dallies with the thought of a new sanctity, a new Eros-god, or 'Alma Venus'. Meanwhile the mockery hints at the provisional nature of man-made schemes. The humour is substantial, resolving conflicts of importance and never existing for itself alone. When the parched survivors from the wreck eat Juan's tutor, the manner of approach is its own solution, not allowing our emotions to get too seriously involved. Where the satiric attack is fierce, as in the war incidents, the humour fades out. Pope and Byron are alike in their inability to be at once humorous and cruel, the best *humour* of *The Dunciad* tending to blunt the edge of its attack. The light irony of *Don Juan* acts like Swift's, only with far less bitterness, to raise our own instinctive judgements. Social insincerities are neatly handled, but the deeper human substance which those insincerities obscure is never suspect or slighted. I cannot here analyse the many variations; and my remarks aim only to characterize at least the prevailing spirit and the main incidents. The approach might be defined as one of good-natured mockery through which certain human qualities, and in particular sexual desire, kindliness, and bravery, assert themselves pleasingly, while certain respectable vices, especially those concerned with social insincerity and war, appear to condemn themselves. The Pharisaic is forced to reveal itself. People are attacked, but no person, not even Catherine, is created in cruelty: as persons, they are either partly sympathetic or comically dignified, as is the Sultan (at v. 147–55).

A distinction of sympathetic from derisive humour may help. Smiles or any lighting up of eye or face may in child or savage reflect states more ultimate than any intellectual categories or humour as their derivative. They reflect simply joy, with in maturity close sexual affinities, the ripple of laughter being perhaps not unrelated to sexual rhythms. Whenever some intellectual mechanism releases such primal joy in terms of ideas troubling us, we have rich humour: a brittle surface, itself either akin to or poles apart from the happy substance, comparison or contrast being variously employed, is either merged in, or shattered to make way for, a larger recognition. That recognition involves a certain basic and golden human centre, and therefore basic human dignity, especially the often questionable dignity of sex-rhythm and joy, must on no account suffer degradation. The lilting and titillating rhymes that percolate through Byron's narrative mark an inclusive subjugation of *mock* dignities to a spontaneous merriment which itself accordingly gains prestige. You can see why humour decrying the basic instincts will be necessarily unhealthy. Two main elements are involved: (A) a basic humanity with its 'golden' centre and (B) a host of conventional value-judgements. When B is dissolved in A we have a pure unity-experience comparable to that of tragedy, suffused by forgiveness of all elements dissolved and joy in the golden centre revealed. But if certain values (e.g. ethical) of B are so inextricably entwined with any concept of the good that no dissolution occurs; still worse, if, as, to hazard a suggestion, in Ben Jonson's great comedies, A seems deliberately dissolved into B; we have what I call 'derisive' humour, hostile on the whole to basic instincts and cosmic penetration, cruel rather than loving. This sort will always seem at first sight the more moral and important, but the other humour, as with tragic insight, exerts a slower yet more lasting ethic. There is often point in satiric bitterness, but not perhaps humorous point. One should not know the joy of comedy in the act of knowing *Volpone* to be a true statement: bitter satire demands the manner of Pope on Sporus or Byron's Angiolina on Steno. Otherwise the golden centre is desecrated, than which we can have no worse blasphemy. That is my reason for not giving approval to the humour of Jonson in *Volpone* or Marlowe in the sadistic incidents of *Tamburlaine* and, more widely, in *The Jew of Malta*.

My use of the word 'golden' relates to Byron's strong feeling for the sun in relation to sexual instincts. It is itself the 'golden centre' of the macrocosm, exerts royalty over true humour, and must have place in any bright eternity:

It was upon a day, a summer's day –
  Summer's indeed a very dangerous season,
And so is spring about the end of May;
  The sun, no doubt, is the prevailing reason . . .
            (*Don Juan*, I. 102)

'That indecent sun' (I. 63) stimulates licence (V. 157), while Russian chastity is related to the cold north (VIII. 128; X. 33).

The moon in contrast is 'chaste' (x. 11). The Juan-Haidée romance with its 'feelings universal as the sun' (ii. 167) stands as a direct flowering of what is implicit in the humour of the whole. Juan is the erotic personified: hence bisexual, courtly, at once reserved and fascinating (xv. 12), loved by all the ladies in turn. Less a realized person than an essence vitalized by the poetic approach, he runs as a gold thread through the vast design. Incidents are contrived to reveal love-instincts shattering conventional surfaces, as when, on the occasion of Juan's first affair, Julia defends herself to her suspicious husband with a list of her would-be seducers:

> Is it for this that General Count O'Reilly
> Who took Algiers, declares I used him vilely?
>
> (i. 148)

The list includes two bishops. The humour marks an ability to break free from conventional values, if only for a moment, in service to what is however healthy and 'universal as the sun' (ii. 167). The qualification is necessary: Swift's use of ordure performs a vastly different function for a different, non-humorous, purpose. Much of Byron's enjoyment in paradox is distilled in the phrase 'that indecent sun' (i. 63). The spring-like and rebirth quality of the sheep-shearing scenes in *The Winter's Tale*, a play dominated by Apollo as the 'fire-robed' and 'golden' god (iv. iii. 29–30), naturally produces Autolycus, whose essence[1] is (i) melody, sunshine and flowery song, and (ii) shameless disrespect for social values. In Falstaff there is a similar antinomy of cosmic physical proportions against the refinements of conventional ideals. Our most deep-rooted, least questionable, and most dignified value is that of death, the dark eternity, religion: and see how towards the end of *1 Henry IV* the lumbering resurrection of Falstaff, whom we thought dead and for whom we were getting our best tragic emotions in order, shatters the dark eternity itself with the other eternity of a vast, but living, body. Falstaff serves as an introduction to that purest essence of humour in *Don Juan* when, after the long last movement has been studiously at pains to create a

---

[1] I refer to his *first* entry. The reservation is necessary: see *The Crown of Life*, 111–13. [1967]

nobly dark eternity, with all its legendary and ghostly fears, architectural ruins and ancestral portraits, the whole poem's meaning is crystallized in the unexpected revelation of a warm and amorous duchess beneath the ghostly cowl; of a 'warm heart', as the poem says, instead of 'stony death' (XVI. 121–2). Essence is pitted against essence, flesh against stone. The last conventional value, death, is melted by rays from the heart of life as surely as in the restoring of Hermione. Resurrection is in its essence comic, just as in true humour there is always a re-creation and rebirth from the golden centre, from Byron's 'bright eternity' (VIII. 115); which is nothing if not resurrection.[1]

A full treatment of Byron's poetry would give detailed notice to *The Deformed Transformed* (pub. 1824), which has an importance in conception perhaps not borne out in execution: involving realization of a power-dream, desecration by war of a church and a heroine, with a revival after apparent death recalling Shakespeare's *Pericles*, of the lady concerned. I should also like to have noticed the psychological tension of *The Two Foscari* (1821) and the dramatic excellences of *Werner* (1822) with its dark background of guilt and Oedipus-discovery.

Byron's poetic interests are, like Shakespeare's, subjective, personal, social, political, naturalistic, and cosmic. No writer has exposed a more agonized sense of sin and psychological conflict, yet none finally mastered a happier unity. His revolutionary thinking is grafted on to as keen an awareness of and feeling for tradition, social and religious, as any in our literature: no one but Milton and Blake has made such use of Biblical mythology. He is master equally of deepest pathos and richest comedy, showing in the latter a fine Chaucerian kinship. In

---

[1] 'Resurrection' naturally includes surprise, the particular attribute of Shaw's comic genius (*The Golden Labyrinth*, 352–3); and Shaw's humour is near the Byronic wavelength. Statues, or statue-equivalents, may be involved with the surprise, as in *The Winter's Tale*, the Resurrection Piece of Ibsen's *When We Dead Awaken* and Yeats's *The Resurrection*. Compare Yeats's 'The heart of the phantom is beating' (the word 'statue' also occurs) with 'beat as if there was a warm heart under' (*Don Juan*, XVI. 122) and Shakespeare's emphasis upon blood, warmth and breath, in his statue scene (*The Winter's Tale*, v. iii). Living sculptures occur in the final act of Shaw's *Back to Methuselah*. For a reference of such resurrection statue symbols to a possible origin in spiritualistic materializations, see my *Ibsen* (Writers and Critics Series; U.S.A. Evergreen Pilot Books), 102–3, 106, note 6. For Byron's more general interest in statues see p. 238, note. [1967]

Shakespeare alone do we find such stabs of human insight. His feminine sympathy approaches Shakespeare's and surpasses Pope's, with a fine and varied succession of heroines. In the eight hundred double-column pages of his stupendous poetic output – he died at the age of thirty-six – there is scarcely one weak line, and perhaps not a single obscure one. He is equally at home with the primary symbols of sea, mountains, and human architecture, and is our first poet of the sun. His sympathy with animals and ability to create either animal or human life in convincing action is matched by Shakespeare only.[1] No poet shows a more delicate sympathy for the lighter aspects of human love-intercourse, seen best in his many references to the dance culminating in the fine description of Juan's grace and skill (*Don Juan*, xiv. 38–40): a quality found also in Lyly, Shakespeare and Pope, but later diverging into the novel to leave poetry the worse. His progress reflects Shakespeare's with the main difference of a more challenging and less provisional humour and erotic faith at the close. He is from the start as ready as Shakespeare to use the conventionally established emotion or phrase for his own more complex purposes, but he is also happy with and uses the best 'romantic' insight of his day, while relating it, as others do not, to the further complexities of action. Master of two periods in English poetry, he is mastered by neither: he is as often above as within his own creation. No English poet has left a message more directly relevant to our own twentieth-century problems. His sympathies are equally European and Oriental: he is our only cosmopolitan poet. As a satirist, he stands second only to Pope, though his own field of inspection is the wider: his balance of religious orthodoxy with sexual sympathy recalls Pope's. Outside Shakespeare no one even distantly approaches him in range and variety: while that disturbing sexual complex in Spenser, Marlowe and Milton, not *directly* attacked in Shakespeare, is, within his humour, resolved. His blend of vitality and plastic or sculptural image to create a living eternity is matched by Keats alone. He is at once, to use his own phrase from *Manfred* (ii. ii.

---

[1] I was probably thinking of the animals in *Venus and Adonis*. Drama gave Shakespeare less opportunities for such sympathetic writing, and his references are there often otherwise motivated. Probably Byron and D. H. Lawrence are our two best animal specialists. [1967]

142), a 'Croesus in creation', and, to use Shelley's remarkably precise title in *Adonais* (xxx), 'the Pilgrim of Eternity': though we must remember that in Byron both eternities, the solemn and the radiant, get equal notice: his work shows a balancing of the one against the other similar to that dramatized in Nietzsche's *Thus Spake Zarathustra*; the similarity to Nietzsche's teaching being felt also in the development from Satanic power to rich generosity in his sequence of protagonists. He is deeply, because essentially, Christian. A human figure burns through his pages either thunder-scarred or touched with some new sovereignty from a height which civilization as we know it can only with difficulty conceive. He is the only English poet of the modern world making contact with the ideals of chivalry.

ADDITIONAL NOTE, 1967

As a supplement to this essay I would point to my article 'Byron as Poet', reviewing Mr W. W. Robson's Chatterton lecture *Byron as Poet* in *Essays in Criticism*, I. 9, January 1959, where I observed, and quoted from, Mr Roy Walker's notice of a production of *Marino Faliero* by the Hovenden Theatre Club in *The Times* (as below; and see p. 210 above, note).

On the dramas I have written elsewhere as follows: 'The Plays of Lord Byron', *The Times Literary Supplement*, 3 February 1950, wherein I made a plea, on general cultural and especially European grounds, for an annual Byron festival; 'Shakespeare and Byron's Plays', *Shakespeare-Jahrbuch*, 95, 1959; in *The Golden Labyrinth*, x; and throughout *Byron and Shakespeare*, wherein I record (9, note) a number of other contemporary studies.

There was also a letter of mine 'Byron's Dramatic Verse' in *The Times Literary Supplement* of 20 February 1959, which may be worth reprinting in this context:

> Contemporary criticism does not find the appreciation of Byron's dramatic verse easy; and yet, as we read in the report of a recent production headed 'Unexpected Merits of *Marino Faliero*' in *The Times* of 21 May 1958, his language can, if correctly spoken, be effective. Were it otherwise, these dramas could hardly have had so distinguished a stage record as was theirs during the

last century. As I pointed out in an article in your columns on 3 February 1950, Byron was deliberately aiming to part with tradition and 'break down' the 'poetry' into a style of translucent clarity. The rhythm is often non-poetic, and it is interesting to study the effect gained by writing certain passages in prose.

Here is one, from *Marino Faliero*. I have changed 'o'er' to 'over', and used my own punctuation:

> I will be what I should be, or be nothing. But never more – oh! never, never more – over the few days or hours which yet await the blighted old age of Faliero, shall sweet quiet shed her sunset. Never more those summer shadows rising from the past of a not ill-spent nor inglorious life, mellowing the last hours as the night approaches, shall soothe me to my moment of long rest. I had but little more to ask or hope, save the regards due to the blood and sweat and the soul's labour through which I had toiled to make my country honoured. As her servant – her servant, though her chief – I would have gone down to my fathers with a name serene and pure as theirs: but this has been denied me. Would I had died at Zara!   (II. i. 453)

The actor would do better by cutting out his own phrase-blocks, pauses and variations, from this version than by constricting his freedom by attention to line-units which can hardly be said to exist.

Sharp dialogue-interchanges can often be regarded with dramatic advantage as prose, as in this from *Cain*:

> *Lucifer:* You have forgotten the denunciation which drove your race from Eden: war with all things and death to all things and disease to most things: and pangs and bitterness. These were the fruits of the forbidden tree.
> *Cain:* But animals – did they too eat of it that they must die?
> *Lucifer:* Your Maker told ye, they were made for you, as you for him. You would not have their doom superior to your own? Had Adam not fallen all had stood.   (II. ii. 148)

This is fairly typical of the long dialogues between Cain and Lucifer. The points are made dramatically by a prose rather than a poetic intonation: and when so understood they gain in effect.

But the prose is a studied prose, on the borderline between colloquial speech and literary dignity and colour. Sometimes the uncertainty as to whether we are listening to prose or verse has its own appeal, as in this lyrical rhapsody from *Sardanapalus*. The hero is speaking of the stars:

> Oh, for that – I love them. I love to watch them in the deep blue vault and to compare them with my Myrrha's eyes. I love

to see their rays redoubled in the tremulous silver of Euphrates'
wave, as the light breeze of midnight crisps the broad and
rolling water, sighing through the sedges which fringe his banks.
But whether they may be gods as some say, or the abodes of
gods as others hold, or simply lamps of night; worlds or the
lights of worlds, I know nor care not. There's something sweet
in my uncertainty I would not change for your Chaldean lore.
Besides, I know of these all clay can know of aught above it
or below it: nothing. I see their brilliancy and feel their beauty.
When they shine on my grave I shall know neither.

(II. i. 252)

But here, too, despite the poetic rhythms, an actor studying the
speech would be well advised to make prose his basis. Often he
will be forced to do so, as in this sample of forensic argument from
The Two Foscari:

> But in all things I have observed the strictest reverence. Not for
> the laws alone, for those you have strained – I do not speak of
> *you* but as a single voice of the many – somewhat beyond what I
> could enforce for my authority were *I* disposed to brawl: but,
> as I said, I have observed with veneration like a priest's for
> the high altar – even unto the sacrifice of my own blood and
> quiet, safety, and all save honour – the decrees, the health, the
> pride and welfare of the state. And now, sir, to your business.

(II. i. 248)

That holds a high dramatic potentiality relying on vocal changes
and speed-variations that have nothing whatsoever to do with
verse.

There are clearly many occasions when urgency of thought or
sublimity of conception creates and demands poetic rhythm and
response. But the tone of these finely wrought dramas is often
nearer prose, though prose of a strange, at times rather Shavian,
perhaps more Jamesian (I am thinking of Henry James's plays),
variety. Shaw, who regarded Byron's as the 'best brain' in the
England of his day (*Everybody's Political What's What?* XXXVII),
wrote plays showing a similarly intellectualized approach to substances traditionally poetic; and that they were both led to adopt
a medium fighting shy of both colloquial idiom and rhetorical
exuberance was a natural result of the dramatic tasks to which
they devoted themselves.

For the verse form of the passage from *Sardanapalus*, see pp.
224–5 above. I should add that my reference to Henry James
is an afterthought that did not appear in the original letter.

VI

Byron's Dramatic Prose

Byron Foundation Lecture, The University of Nottingham, 1953, published at Nottingham, 1954. With two exceptions my reference numerals for Byron's prose apply to *The Works of Lord Byron, Letters and Journals*; ed. R. E. Prothero (Lord Ernle), 6 vols. For this edition I use the designation '*LJ*'.

I

There is much to say of Lord Byron. There can be few famous persons whom it is profitable to approach in so many ways; and some of them have scarcely as yet been attempted.

He died at the age of thirty-six. His poetry, extending to eight hundred double-columned pages, shows a quality, weight and substance, enough to constitute the life-work of any major poet. His prose, in historical and literary comment, oratory, letters and journals is in range, variety, and power, among the great achievements of English literature. In politics at home, Byron was an active force, his speeches in the Lords remaining for us as a verbal record of his challenge to the ruling classes. Abroad, he engaged in two movements of national liberation, Italian and Greek, leaving his mark, as a man of action, on European History and the story of human enlightenment. His reading was, according to Lady Blessington, probably more comprehensive than that of any man of his time. Throughout his life part of every day was regularly given over to physical exercise. There were also certain love-affairs. Some people regard these as a good thing, and some regard them as a bad thing; but on this, at least, we can agree – they take up time. And yet there has always been talk – he himself started it – of Byron's 'indolence'. If he won time for indolence, that was surely his crowning achievement.

Our business tonight is with his prose; especially his prose as drama. Of course, everything about Byron was dramatic. He had himself had dramatic experience. 'When I was a youth', he tells us in his *Detached Thoughts*, with words that recall Polonius, 'I was reckoned a good actor'; at Harrow he shone in dramatic declamation; and he acted in a number of plays, with considerable success, at Southwell (*Detached Thoughts*, 71 and 88; *LJ*, v. 445, 453; and see *LJ*, I. 118, note). He was later a member of the Drury Lane Committee, and devoted time and care to his duties; no art moved him so greatly as the art of acting. His whole life was, moreover, dramatic; so was his poetry; and his prose. But these elements were dramatic in different ways. Tonight we shall consider the drama, or dramas, so vigorously active in Byron's prose writings. His prose is, in fact, more obviously dramatic than his poetry.

My friend Francis Berry once remarked to me that Byron's poetry is poetry 'on the far side of decision'. We receive no 'processes' of thought, since 'the working out has all been done before'. This he contrasted with Hamlet's thinking; and also with *The Prelude* and *In Memoriam*, which he called 'evolving processes of thought', 'one long business of arriving at a thought'; and with other famous poems. With Byron, 'All that', he said, 'has been done before.'

This judgement, coming from a master, like Byron, of poetic narrative, challenges attention. Byron's poetry, as surely as Pope's, is the poetry not of searching but of statement; introducing us not to any shadow-land of dimly apprehended mystery but rather to a Mediterranean scene of clear definition and intellectual light. Now this, though it lends itself naturally to narrative, may well appear rather too conscious, too mental, too settled, for drama. Perhaps only Corneille – the French poet whom Byron, at least in youth, most admired – was completely successful in making such a style dramatic. It can, in various degrees, be made so elsewhere; in Dryden, and in Byron's own plays. But this is not easy.

Poetically, Byron stands above us, above even the rise and fall of empires, like a Colossus. Great though they be, Shakespeare's people, with the possible exception of Timon, seem much nearer to us. A Shakespearian speech normally represents not only something said, but also the striving of the spirit of man to say it; and we cannot help but identify ourselves with this striving, moment by moment, inserting ourselves into the process and so sharing the *katharsis*, or the re-creation, that such a process offers us. But with Byron we feel a little uneasy. He does not normally speak in terms of our confusions, unless indeed we be of Napoleonic stature; and even when writing of Napoleon, as in his *Ode to Napoleon* and *Childe Harold* (III. 36–45), he writes as though he has seen through it all, and is not himself confused. Despite the most baffling of conflicts, there is nothing confused in *Manfred*.

In *The Birth of Tragedy* Nietzsche defined drama, or life dramatically conceived, as the interplay of two principles which he called the 'Dionysian' and the 'Apollonian'. The first is the music behind, or beneath, the world we see; it is the creative origin, thrusting up, making, destroying, and remaking that world. The Apollonian is the created ideal, forms of visionary beauty that can be seen, sight rather than sound, intellectually clear to us. Creation, and drama as its supreme artistic expression, exists through the interplay of these two principles.

Creation comes from below; it is not a surface development; and drama exists not so much as a logical sequence of events and thoughts, the one causing the next, but rather through a more vertical action, a moment-by-moment thrusting up, from the unseen. That is why in Shakespeare, and still more in Webster, we find, and may have to forgive, the occasional hiatus, or gap, the shadowed gulf or chasm, in the logic of event or thought. Dramatically such gaps may often constitute an attraction. Attention is riveted by shock-tactics. The continual surprises and sudden inconsequences of Shaw's humour are in this way essentially dramatic. You can enjoy them without knowing, or liking, the story. Chesterton once said of Dickens' dramatic novels that you can open the book and start anywhere, adding, 'This is not chaos: it is eternity.'

Byron's poetry, though it certainly holds dramatic and oratorical qualities of a high order, is always aiming at the Apollonian perfection, the Augustan clarity; in language, and in event. It is very tidy. *Marino Faliero* and *Sardanapalus* are two of the most perfect works of art in our literature; and part of their perfection lies in their intellectual lucidity, their exact working out of a reasonable action on themes of greatest importance to man. In this very perfection lies, if not a risk, certainly a technical difficulty. As plays, they presuppose an audience of keen intellectual perception; it could not rest back, as we do when witnessing Shakespeare, to enjoy linguistic grandeurs and startling events in a semi-conscious state of dramatic coma; it would have to think, and think hard.

In Byron's prose however we find exactly those more obviously dramatic qualities which his poetry at least appears to have left behind. It is, of course, a question of emphasis. All great art is made, in Nietzsche's terms, of a fusion of Dionysian and Apollonian; but in Byron's poetry the balance is tilted one way, and in his greatest prose the other. I do not mean that his is an incantatory prose, nor that it is ever obscure, but in its general movement it is, or appears, uncontrolled, a torrential rush, like poetry as defined by the poet in Shakespeare's *Timon of Athens*:

> A thing slipp'd idly from me.
> Our poesy is as a gum, which oozes
> From whence 'tis nourish'd: the fire i' the flint
> Shows not till it be struck; our gentle flame
> Provokes itself, and, like the current, flies
> Each bound it chafes. (I. i. 20)

So, too, Byron's more informal prose has 'slipped' from him, as by instinct. It normally owes little to external pressure but rather 'provokes itself', rising as a natural, self-generated growth; and once started it moves torrentially with all the dramatic discontinuities and sharp deflections in mood and manner hinted by Shakespeare's lines.

True, Byron's poetry came fluently to his pen, too; but whether in the act of creation or in recopying his work, a critical faculty was in action such as you do not suspect in his prose. He did not, as he records on 6 December 1813 (*LJ*. II. 366), re-read his 1813–14 Journal. Even the famous *Memoirs* which were destroyed at his death were sent off, as he told Isaac D'Israeli on 10 June 1822, without re-reading (*LJ*. VI. 88). Of his poetry he says, writing to his publisher John Murray on 18 November 1820:

I am like the tyger (in poesy); if I m ss my first spring, I go

growling back to my jungle. There is no second. I can't correct.
I can't, and I won't.   (*LJ*. v. 120)

This was not always true of his poetry, but it was far more true
of his prose.

Bryon, when he wished, could write more formal prose.
There is the historical commentary of his early notes to *Childe
Harold*, written at Athens in the year 1811. These are marked
by maturity of judgement and dignity of phrase. Byron had
already in early manhood reached, in these matters at least,
what we should call an urbane 'maturity', and such a style was
always at his command. These notes witness the classic,
Augustan, basis of Byron's prose.

We have also the speeches in the House of Lords (*LJ*. ii.
App. ii. 424–45). The art of oratory is close to the art of drama.
In his *Detached Thoughts* Byron tells us how Dr Drury thought
well of his promise as an orator; and one of his meditations
surveys, with what might be called the acumen of a practitioner,
the abilities and limitations of the greatest exponents (*Detached
Thoughts*, 88 and 5; *LJ*. v. 453 and 411–13). Of Byron's political
challenge Professor Pinto has spoken in an earlier lecture
Byron and Liberty, Byron Foundation Lecture, 1944; and I have
discussed it in *Lord Byron: Christian Virtues*. The importance of
these three speeches is great: in them Byron joins the company
of Milton, Swift and Burke, as one of the great succession of
literary figures through whom literature has entered the arena
of political action.[1]

II

We pass now to the letters. Good letters are necessarily dramatic,
being a kind of natural speech, with the bloom of the moment
on them, showing us a close-up of the writer's mind in the act of
communication. We can, for example, say that Richardson's
Pamela is dramatic in contrast to the more epic structure of
Fielding's *Tom Jones*. Pamela's letters keep us in excitement with
a moment-by-moment suspense, continually reinforced: we are

[1] For Byron's political engagements see also David V. Erdman in *PMLA*, LVI. 4
and LVII. 1 Dec. 1941 and March 1942; in *Science and Society*, XI. 3, Summer 1947;
and in *Keats-Shelley Journal*, XI, Winter 1962.

far closer to her than to Fielding's hero. Such, exactly, is the
effect on us of Byron's letters to Lady Melbourne about his
flirtation with Lady Frances Wedderburn Webster (published
in *Lord Byron's Correspondence*, ed. John Murray, vol. I. 180–219).
They are as good as, or better than, Richardson or a Restoration comedy, and the more excellent for the critical judgement
active throughout, together with the moral feeling that paradoxically starts the adventure and finally determines Byron's
refusal of the lady's surrender. It has all the quality of a work
of art – with Byron as both composer and actor – wherein we
enjoy the immoral content of a whole which is not immoral. In
form it resembles an epistolary novel, where the big or little
adventures spring fresh from the page. On 30 October 1815
Byron concluded some remarks to Leigh Hunt with:

> I write in great haste, and, I doubt, *not* much to the purpose; but
> you have it hot and hot, just as it comes, and so let it go.
>
> (*LJ*. III. 241)

All good letters have something of this, but Byron's have it pre-
eminently.

There was never a more impulsive letter-writer. What wants
to come is allowed to come, whatever the sharp turns in subject-
matter or the reversals of mood. There is no critical tidying up:
the letters read as though they have gone into their envelopes
almost before the ink is dry. Byron's poetry, however fast some
of it may have come, is far more exactly devised, and his
greater single works, except for *Don Juan*, beautifully and carefully shaped. *Don Juan*, with its personal tone and easy variations, marks a blend of his two main literary tendencies.

The range of these letters is wide. Their most marked characteristic is, probably, friendliness. In reading them we are aware
of an easy communication between a man of culture and others
of similar mental equipment, the numerous literary, dramatic,
and historical allusions, lightly carried, signifying an order of
cultured intercourse strange to our own century. Humour
subtle, ironic, gay, broad, obscene, bitter, caustic, witty, is on
page after page. But there is no cruelty in it; often, perhaps
most often, it is just sheer fun, together with joy in a self-
expression which is also an assured communion with some

K

kindred mind. Friendliness was never more infectiously expressed.

But there is more: there are accounts of violent action and adventure, with a fine mixture of conscious *braggadocio*. There is pride, scorn, irascibility, and on rare occasions a dark fury. Single letters sometimes contain a rich assortment of contrasted elements, and the complete collection is of almost 'infinite variety'. But the results are never chaotic. The language is bold, lucid and definite, with a firm diction, a fine play of antithesis, and sentences of structural weight. The native pith and sap of English speech tingles in it, but it is also, the more so for its wealth of literary reference and allusion, a literary speech. It is colloquial on a sound basis of Augustan tradition and Augustan learning; the language of a man in whom a literary heritage has become a natural colloquialism. You hear the speaking voice, but the speaking voice speaks in literature. That is dramatic speech.

Let us turn to a letter illustrating some of these qualities. It starts chattily, works up irritably, and closes in an urbane yet conversational manner. Byron is writing to Thomas Moore from Venice on 1 June 1818 (*LJ*. IV. 236–40). He starts by admitting the probable validity of Moore's criticism of *Childe Harold IV*, but is glad that he likes *Beppo*. He then goes on to write of Leigh Hunt:

> Hunt's letter is probably the exact piece of vulgar coxcombry you might expect from his situation. He is a good man, with some poetical elements in his chaos; but spoilt by the Christ-Church Hospital and a Sunday newspaper – to say nothing of the Surrey gaol, which conceited him into a martyr. But he is a good man.

That is a typical judgement, perhaps most notable for the astute comment on the temptations of martyrdom. The largest issues are continually found rising from a context that appears mere friendly chat. The last phrase, 'a good man', is to be repeated later. We pass to some critical aspersions on Hunt's poetry:

> He believes his trash of vulgar phrases tortured into compound barbarisms to be *old* English; and we may say of it as Aimwell says of Captain Gibbet's regiment, when the Captain calls it an 'old corps' – 'the *oldest* in Europe, if I may judge by your uniform'.

He is referring to *The Beaux' Stratagem.* Some of his most fervent
emotions have been roused, and the letter warms up with:

> ... of all the ineffable Centaurs that were ever begotten by Self-
> love upon a Night-mare, I think 'this monstrous Sagittary' the
> most prodigious.

Byron may be recalling 'the dreadful Sagittary' of *Troilus and
Cressida* (v. v. 14). 'Self-love' and 'night-*mare*' are to be precisely related to, and indeed make, the 'centaurs'. Byron's
seemingly most haphazard gestures of speech can stand exact
analysis. But all is carried easily. I do not know where else we
shall find a crisp sentence so effortlessly defining the kind of
poetry which one happens not to like.

Having got into his stride, he leaves Hunt: bigger game is
viewed. Hunt has been praising Wordsworth. See how the
irritation grows, burns from the page, as we read:

> Did you read his skimble-skamble about Wordsworth being at the
> head of his own *profession*, in the *eyes* of *those* who followed it? I
> thought that poetry was an *art*, or an *attribute*, and not a *profession*;
> – but be it one, is that x x x x x at the head of *your* profession in
> *your* eyes? I'll be curst if he is of *mine*, or ever shall be. He is the only
> one of us (but of us he is not) whose coronation I would oppose.
> Let them take Scott, Campbell, Crabbe, or you, or me, or any
> of the living, and throne him; – but not this new Jacob Behman,
> this x x x x x whose pride might have kept him true, even had
> his principles turned as perverted as his *soi-disant* poetry.

'Skimble-skamble' is Hotspur's (*1 Henry IV*, III. i. 153). Much
of Byron's epistolary prose, especially where literary judgements are the concern, is on a Hotspur wavelength. Like
Hotspur, he warms up in irritation and temper, and the temper
is our entertainment. Let us not worry as to whether his political
principles have here perverted his judgement of *The Excursion.*
On a purely 'literary' assessment – if there be such a thing –
there are surely few passages in that poem of equal length which
we would not exchange for one of Byron's greater letters. Of
The Prelude, which had not been published, Byron knew nothing.

The surge of anger has risen and broken. Now he returns,
circles back, with a Shakespearian movement, to Hunt, harking
back to his earlier phrase:

> But Leigh Hunt is a good man, and a good father – see his Odes
> to all the Masters Hunt; – a good husband – see his Sonnet to

Mrs Hunt; – a good friend – see his Epistles to different people; – and a great coxcomb and a very vulgar person in every thing about him. But that's not his fault, but of circumstances.

We have, compactly, an attempt to do justice to a man genuinely admired and a tribute to the domestic virtues, balanced by an impression of the subject's triviality, vulgarity and self-satisfaction. There is a characteristic slighting of personal poetry, and a final, and sincere, exculpation. The little piece cannot be properly received without a free play of humour.

We pass to more congenial matters. Moore was to write a life of Sheridan, whom Byron admired. The style now assumes a more considered, more responsible, gravity of tone, but with no loss of intimacy:

> I do not know any good model for a life of Sheridan but that of *Savage*. Recollect, however, that the life of such a man may be made far more amusing than if he had been a Wilberforce; – and this without offending the living, or insulting the dead.

This might make a text for a biography of Byron, too. Simple virtue alone, the virtue of normal, easily placed goodness, lacks drama, and therefore interest: 'amusing' suggests cultured enjoyment. But the great man must not be maligned:

> Were his intrigues more notorious than those of all his contemporaries? and is his memory to be blasted, and theirs respected? Don't let yourself be led away by clamour, but compare him with the coalitioner Fox, and the pensioner Burke, as a man of principle, and with ten hundred thousand in personal views, and with none in talent, for he beat them all *out* and *out*.

Here Byron is, as a prose writer, or talker, in his natural vein. Never were classic style and intimacy of tone more happily wedded. This is fresh air to him after Hunt and Wordsworth. Men of action and affairs fascinated him, and he was never more effective than when saving genius, as when he defended Pope against Bowles, from detraction. Where Byron admires, his admiration is uncompromising: there was never a more magnificent praiser.

Sheridan's failings are nevertheless admitted, and seen in perspective:

> But alas, poor human nature! Good night, or rather morning. It is four, and the dawn gleams over the Grand Canal, and un-

shadows the Rialto. I must to bed; up all night – but, as George Philpot says, 'it's life, though, damme, it's life!'

Again, the reference is to a play, this time Arthur Murphy's *Citizen*. A postscript apologizes for possible errors: 'no time for revision'.

The letter is a miniature work of art: an essay could be written on the themes raised by nearly every sentence. Its structure is quite unconsidered; but the balance in point of political principle of Sheridan against Wordsworth, together with the difference in Byron's tone of approach, is deeply revealing. It is all firmly built, staged, in our minds: that dawn lives for us with the immediacy of an aroma, in simple words.[1]

Such simplicity is, perhaps, the finest of all literary gifts – the ability, I mean, to use the obvious word with no loss of immediate sense-perception, as when Chaucer writes effectively, as we could not, of 'the grene gras'. Byron's dawn has that quality. So has this, from the letter to Isaac D'Israeli on 10 June 1822:

> I write to you from the Villa Dupuy, near Leghorn, with the islands of Elba and Corsica visible from my balcony, and my old friend the Mediterranean rolling blue at my feet. (*LJ.* VI. 89)

I cannot say why, but that obvious word 'blue' appears to have all the freshness of Chaucer's 'grene'. It comes, I suppose, of saying exactly what you mean; no more and no less. This is far from easy, but it is throughout a characteristic of Byron's peculiar ease.

In his comments on Hunt and Wordsworth we were aware less of the writer's opinions than of his annoyance; a nervous energy, or quality, was being transmitted. Such prose is more than statement; it is momentarily at least infectious. Something was lost when English prose was tidied up in the age of Dryden. If you read Roger Ascham inveighing against the 'Englishman Italianate' in his *Scholemaster*, you hear the old gentleman getting angrier and angrier; his prose expresses, not just statement, but irascibility, and we are more strongly aware of the irascibility than of the statement. Often enough, Milton's prose

---

[1] The passage on Sheridan and the conclusion were singled out for especial attention by Ruskin when writing in praise of Byron's prose work in *Praeterita*: see Peter Quennell's *Byron: a Self-Portrait*, I, Intro. x–xi. [1967]

warms to a denunciation which is more than literary, his vocabulary and syntax being strained, whipped up, as his own violent feelings demand more and yet more of it. In those days there was no good basis for such heated adventures. Writers had all the resource of vocabulary and phrase that was needed, but the emotions, irritable to start with, are yet further irritated – or at least the reader is – by being hopelessly entangled in a Latinistic syntax that had never been assimilated into spoken English. The result was too often a wild tangle of almost inextricable meanings and feelings.

In Byron's Letters and Journals we have all the emotional intensity, variation and resource of that older style, with no loss of lucidity. A century of new, lucid prose, the familiar styles of Dryden and Addison, the ironic simplicities of Swift, the weightier formations of Johnson, Gibbon and Burke, have all gone into the melting pot, like one of Medea's victims, and something comes out, young, valiant, resilient – Byron's prose is like nothing so much as the spring of a horse's hoof from turf – which has at its command any or all of the qualities of those recent masters, yet may serve an intensity as fierce as the impassioned fire of Milton, be almost as thickly inlaid with scholarly allusions as Browne, or pass in review the meditative profundities of a Burton.

Byron had affinities with those older writers, but his affinities with Shakespeare are even more striking. I doubt if there is any writer in English who can compare with either in the ability to say a great deal in small space without labour or straining.[1] Surely never was so much transcendental and human philosophy so lightly announced as when, in a letter to Augusta Leigh from Venice on 18 December 1816 (published in Lord Lovelace's *Astarte*, enlarged edition, 279), Byron remarks: 'At present I am better – thank Heaven above – and woman beneath.' The idiom is purely Byronic, but the easy carriage, the accomplishment, of it, Shakespearian. In no major writer do we find so many Shakespearian reminiscences, direct or submerged, as in Byron. He generally quotes enough to make

[1] But what of Pope? His brevity tends towards the condensing of known profundities rather than the awakening of new ones. Shakespeare's extraordinary genius, by the way, is as successful in inflating the obvious as in condensing the mysteries. [1967]

recognition inevitable, but there may be single words or embedded phrases, such as Hotspur's 'skimble-skamble', that are easily missed; or as when in his letter to Isaac D'Israeli of 10 June 1822 he says that the exact status of a man's genius can never be known 'till the Posterity, whose decisions are merely dreams to ourselves, has sanctioned or denied it, while it can touch us no further' (*LJ*. vi. 88).

These Shakespearian quotations are never mere additions, never just stuck in; they are thoroughly organic. It is because Byron feels like Shakespeare's greater persons, and often finds himself in similar circumstances, that his thoughts and emotions clothe themselves so regularly in Shakespearian dress. When, on 6 April 1819, angered at certain of Murray's remarks as to what the English public would like from him, he refuses to flatter their 'sweet voices', he is remembering Coriolanus (ii. iii. 119). In the same letter, lashing himself into histrionic anger at recollection of what the English have done to him, he cites Shylock for his purpose:

> I know the precise worth of popular applause, for few Scribblers have had more of it; and if I chose to swerve into their paths, I could retain it, or resume it, or increase it. But I neither love ye, nor fear ye; and though I buy with ye and sell with ye, and talk with ye, I will neither eat with ye, drink with ye, nor pray with ye. They made me, without my search, a species of popular Idol; they, without reason or judgement, beyond the caprice of their good pleasure, threw down the Image from its pedestal; it was not broken with the fall, and they would, it seems, again replace it – but they shall not.   (*LJ*. iv. 285)

Shylock's words in *The Merchant of Venice* were:

> I will buy with you, sell with you, talk with you, walk with you, and so following; but I will not eat with you, drink with you, nor pray with you.   (i. iii. 36)

The regrafting is perfect. Shakespeare flowers naturally within the context of Byron's drama; indeed, nothing else could so assist our understanding of that drama. Byron feels himself, again and again, in the position of Shakespeare's protagonists, knowing in himself their good and their evil, their passions and their greatness. It may be the scorn of a Coriolanus, or the

outcast bitterness of a Shylock; but it may just as well be something from Falstaff, or even Nym. All Shakespeare was in Byron.
That is precisely why, in characteristic fashion, he called Shakespeare a 'barbarian'.[1]

Such borrowings are only one very obvious symptom of what
may be called the Shakespearian quality of Byron's informal
prose. What, we, today, most respect in Shakespeare's poetry,
and miss in Byron's poetic plays, is the rough, untrimmed, wild
growth of language, which gives us the sense of thought or
feeling at each instant shaping its own expression regardless of
any preconceived structure; the language of Falconbridge's
'Commodity' speech in *King John*, of Falstaff's prose, of Lear's
madness. There are, of course, numerous set-pieces of more
studied artistry: the choric patterns of *Richard III*, the operatic
solos of *Richard II*, Portia's 'quality of mercy', the modulated
soliloquies and lyric prose of Hamlet, the Othello music, the
farewells of Buckingham and Wolsey. Probably Shakespeare
rated these higher than the more hurried and unconsidered
style in which he often elsewhere indulged; but it is precisely
that more wild manner which, grafted on to the rhetorical
patterns, fuses with poetic custom to make the supreme speeches
of a Macbeth, a Lear, a Timon, a Leontes. This is what we
normally mean when we speak of Shakespeare's dramatic poetry.

In such poetry we are aware less of any surface than of a
turbulent power, a heave and swell, from deeps beyond verbal
definition; and, as the thing progresses, a gathering of power, a
ninth wave of passion, an increase in tempo and intensity.

These are qualities in Byron's greatest letters. They possess
what Sir Herbert Read would call 'organic form'. True, his
diction remains clean, firm and simple, the words speeding to
their mark like the well-trimmed arrows of Chaucer's Yeoman.
His prose units are the established forms of clause and sentence,
used with balance, precision and clarity. And yet Byron's use
of his Augustan material is also deeply Shakespearian: his prose
is fluent without loss of solidities. Syntax is certainly tossed like
a tennis-ball, but it is never tormented; without ceasing to be
correct, it enjoys its new freedom and takes, not only dashes –

---

[1] I have mislaid the reference. For Byron's views on Shakespeare and his contemporaries, see *LJ.* v. 217–18, 243, 323, 371–2.

of which there are many – but wings. The repertory of tricks is inexhaustible. In both Shakespeare and Byron we meet a vigour which we feel to be in essence non-literary, which yet finds perfect expression through words; a discipline which is in its very nature wayward and Dionysian, yet never chaotic; at an extreme, the negation of all rules of composition, yet even so a standard for future critics. Different as may be the traditions used, the rhetorical schools behind Shakespeare and the eighteenth-century prose idiom behind Byron – superficially the two styles have often little in common – yet these techniques are mastered and moulded in similar manner. I would hazard the suggestion that there is no more Shakespearian writing in English than the prose of Byron's Letters and Journals.

Before leaving the letters, I would notice two more, chosen as extremes of fun and fury.

The first is one purporting to be written by Fletcher, Byron's valet, to J. C. Hobhouse, recording Byron's supposed death. It is dated from Venice, June 1818 (*L.J.* IV. 234–5). It had been inspired by the reports current regarding Byron's dissipated life in that city. It starts:

> Sir – With great grief I inform you of the death of my late dear Master, my Lord, who died this morning at ten of the Clock of a rapid decline and slow fever, caused by anxiety, sea-bathing, women, and riding in the Sun against my advice.

It is worth once again observing that Byron's life at Venice was, whatever its rumoured dissipations, a time of keen and daily exercise, and an almost incredible literary activity.

The supposed Fletcher goes on to talk of his unpaid wages: 'You, Sir, who are his executioner won't see a poor Servant wronged of his little all.' Shakespeare, who, according to Richard Davies, 'died a Papist', comes inevitably into the picture:

> My dear Master had several phisicians and a Priest: he died a Papish . . .

Though dying 'a Papish', he is nevertheless, with perhaps another recollection of Shylock, to be buried 'in the Jewish burying ground'. He died well:

> He suffered his illness with great patience, except that when in

extremity he twice damned his friends and said they were selfish rascals – you, Sir, particularly and Mr Kinnaird, who had never answered his letters nor complied with his repeated requests. He also said he hoped that your new tragedy would be damned – God forgive him – I hope that my master won't be damned like the tragedy.

His nine whores are already provided for . . .

A humorously ambivalent report for those who want first-hand evidence as to Byron's Venetian life.

We pass now to another, and very different, letter. It is perhaps the most frightening letter in existence. I risk doing Byron an injustice in selecting it for attention from the great mass of his good-humoured and kindly correspondence. But it is, from a dramatic view, too interesting to pass over.

When you know, or think you know, the truth about anything, you write a sermon, or a political tract, propaganda of some kind. But drama grows from the simultaneous knowledge of incompatible, or at least contradictory, truths, and so we put them on the stage to fight it out. In all most vitally important and difficult matters some such technique is necessary: in Parliament and Courts of Law we regularly put our final trust in a dramatic conflict. Though drama itself need not express a synthesis in so many words, yet its very form may shadow, or symbolize, a dimly apprehended solution.

Byron, as Professor Heinrich Straumann has observed (in *Byron and Switzerland*, Byron Foundation Lecture, 1948–9), baffles us by his ability to hold in his mind contradictory thoughts, or emotions; and I have myself written at length of his balancing of opposites. Here we see the dramatic quality of his mental structure, and, in fact, of his life; he was by instinct and honesty forced beyond all premature, one-way solutions.

Our letter, as fascinating an example of 'organic form' as we shall find in English, is written to Murray from Bologna, dated 7 June 1819 (*LJ.* IV. 313–17). It starts:

Tell Mr Hobhouse that I wrote to him a few days ago from Ferrara. It will therefore be idle in him or you to wait for any further answers or returns of proofs from Venice, as I have directed that no English letters be sent after me. The publication can be proceeded in without, and I am already sick of your remarks, to which I think not the least attention ought to be paid.

I have been criticized for my high rating of Byron as a man; but it is difficult not to deny superlative status to an author who has the courage to write like that to his publisher.

Having dismissed literary business, he proceeds to describe the cemetery at Bologna, where he has discovered a custodian who reminded him of the grave-digger in *Hamlet*, showing him with pride a certain skull of a merry Capuchin who, 'wherever he went, he brought joy'. This custodian loved his work and, says Byron, 'had the greatest attachment', not only to the cypresses he had planted, but also 'to his dead people'. Byron next recalls certain monumental inscriptions at Ferrara, with 'Implora pace' or 'Implora eterna quiete' under the names. These phrases had moved him deeply:

> Those few words say all that can be said or sought . . . There is all the helplessness, and humble hope, and deathlike prayer, that can arise from the grave – '*implora pace*'.

His thoughts pass naturally to his own death. He would like to be buried at the Lido, with those simple words inscribed, for his bones 'would not rest in an English grave'. He compares himself to Mowbray in *Richard II*, who also died at Venice, recalling how Mowbray, after fighting

> Against black pagans, Turks, and Saracens,
> And toil'd with works of war, retir'd himself
> To Italy; and there, at *Venice*, gave
> His body to that *pleasant* country's earth,
> And his pure soul unto his Captain Christ,
> Under whose colours he had fought so long.

Every phrase of the quotation (*Richard II*, IV. i. 92–100) is to be applied to himself.

He speaks again of correspondence and proofs; of the Hoppners and their boy, and his own Allegra. His thoughts turn bitterly to his domestic tragedy:

> I never hear any thing of Ada, the little Electra of my Mycenae; the moral Clytemnestra is not very communicative of her tidings.

His own drama is momentarily equated with Aeschylus' *Oresteia*.

Now his bitterness increases. If our next passage is read

coolly, it is certainly unpleasant; but it must not be read coolly. To understand it – and this means to understand some of Byron's deepest and darkest emotions – we must read it dramatically. He is speaking of Sir Samuel Romilly who, after having held a retainer for Byron in his legal dispute with his wife, had later passed over to the opposing side, and had become to Byron a symbol of all that drove him from England. This Sir Samuel Romilly had recently committed suicide on the death of his wife. Our passage, a truly remarkable instance of passionate abandon burning through lucidity of phrase and serenity of syntax, runs:

> I have at least seen Romilly shivered who was one of the assassins. When that felon, or lunatic (take your choice, he must be one and might be both), was doing his worst to uproot my whole family tree, branch and blossoms; when, after taking my retainer, he went over to them; when he was bringing desolation on my hearth and destruction on my household Gods, did he think that, in less than three years, a natural event – a severe domestic – but an expected and common domestic calamity – would lay his carcase in a cross road, or stamp his name in a verdict of Lunacy? Did he (who in his drivelling sexagenary dotage had not the courage to survive his Nurse – for what else was a wife to him at his time of life?) reflect or consider what my feelings must have been, when wife, and child, and sister, and name, and fame, and country were to be my sacrifice on his legal altar – and this at a moment when my health was declining, my fortune embarrassed, and my mind had been shaken by many kinds of disappointment; while I was yet young and might have reformed what might be wrong in my conduct, and retrieved what was perplexing in my affairs. But the wretch is in his grave. I detested him living, and I will not affect to pity him dead; I still loathe him – as much as we can hate dust – but that is nothing.
> What a long letter I have scribbled!

You see how a dramatic reading does not merely make the passage more effective: it changes its meaning. What you took to be a cool statement of implacable hatred, becomes – to anyone with stage experience it will happen automatically – an agonized emotion at the experience of that hatred. Byron was deeply concerned with all matters of sin, retribution, hell, punishment, revenge – and forgiveness. He did, as I have elsewhere shown (*Lord Byron: Christian Virtues*, 262–71), in his own life, attain a remarkably high standard of Christian forgiveness. But this letter is no place for it. Letters, like dramatic speech, may, and often should, give us emotion in the raw. We do not want our Lears and Timons to withhold their curses; and theirs is the world to which this passage belongs.

True, it is rather terrible, with the terror of Aeschylus, of Dante's *Inferno*, of Hamlet's words over the praying Claudius. It is also true that the darker elements in great literature are merely parts within their greater artistic wholes, and that those wholes do not breathe an uncharitable spirit. But then, neither does Byron's whole letter: the anger is only part of it, and part only of Byron.

We started with business details, and moved on to the idyllic description of the graveyard and the inscription *'implora pace'*; and from that to the comparison of Mowbray's Christian warriorship and death with Byron's own life and death. We then passed, after a brief return to trivialities, to the Electra and Clytemnestra references, and thence to the dark passage on Romilly. This is a descent to Hell; for in this matter Byron is in Hell, and knows it. Lack of forgiveness, whatever the justification, was to him, as Teresa Guiccioli in her study of Byron makes clear to us, Hell; and that is why our reading underlined, as the actor of Timon should underline Timon's, his own agony in hatred. The very words, in all their melodramatic straining ('drivelling sexagenary dotage'), witness an ever-so-slight insincerity, like an overdone gesture: he is not wholly within the emotion. There is a momentary loss of balance. But poise is regained and all is, finally, controlled: the dark passage is known for what it is, and placed. For we have not finished. There is a postscript, which harks back, like the recapturing of a musical theme, to the start:

> Here, as in Greece, they strew flowers on the tombs. I saw a quantity of rose-leaves, and entire roses, scattered over the graves at Ferrara. It has the most pleasing effect you can imagine.

Most of us would claim, outwardly, to forgive our Romillys; Byron, with his keen sense of truth, cannot. But this is only one Byron; there is another, soft-hearted to the point of sentimentality, 'always loving', as Joseph Mazzini in his essay *Byron and*

Goethe so admirably put it, 'even when he seemed to curse'; and yet another, always cool, surveying from above his own passionate engagements. Those others, refusing to leave the letter as it stands, have, or hint, the last word.

At this period Byron was writing the third canto of *Don Juan*, which was completed in November 1819. Towards its close, we find, springing rather inconsequentially from some stanzas of delicate feeling, the line: 'Ah! surely nothing dies but something mourns' (III. 108). The thought is next expanded:

> When Nero perish'd by the justest doom
> > Which ever the destroyer yet destroy'd,
> Amidst the roar of liberated Rome,
> > Of nations freed, and the world overjoy'd,
> Some hands unseen strew'd flowers upon his tomb:
> > Perhaps the weakness of a heart not void
> Of feeling for some kindness done, when power
> Had left the wretch an uncorrupted hour. (III. 109)

So, too, 'some hands unseen' drop the roses of our postscript. No explicit relation is stated. Byron was very diffident, even afraid, of sentiment. Even in his poetry, its proper home as his prose is not, he follows this stanza on Nero with a comic disclaimer; and in his letter he deliberately concludes with an offhand and non-committal understatement: 'It has the most pleasing effect you can imagine.'

Keyserling once said that no great religious truth could be expressed except through some sharp, contrapuntal opposition. We may say the same of any great human truth. Byron's ability to live without loss of poise opposing thoughts and emotions marks his dramatic stature. It is significant that we cannot profitably discuss either his life or its reflection in his informal prose, to say nothing of his poetry, without continual reference to the mountain peaks of literature. This was the air, the air of Aeschylus, of Dante and of Shakespeare, which he, as a man, lived in, from day to day, in matters both personal and public.

III

If the Letters represent the dialogue of Byron's drama, the Journals are its soliloquies. These offer no revelation of intimacies such as you get from Pepys, Rousseau, or John Cowper

Powys. Byron's prose is in the main concerned mainly with external affairs: books, politics and people, including himself objectively viewed; the rest, especially the softer emotions, goes into his poetry. And yet it is precisely with such externals that many of his most personal and passionate feelings were regularly concerned.

What strikes us most in Byron's early 1813–14 Journal is his interest in people. He had the dramatist's or novelist's instinctive response to, and penetration of, the mysteries of personality, together with a Chaucerian ability of effortless characterization, though it may be couched in pithy, non-Chaucerian metaphor, as when, on 22 November 1813, thinking of revolutionary Holland, he notes that 'the bluff burghers, puffing freedom out of their short tobacco-pipes, might be worth seeing' (*LJ*. II. 329). Here is a pretty miniature, of the same date:

> Rogers is silent – and, it is said, severe. When he does talk, he talks well; and, on all subjects of taste, his delicacy of expression is pure as his poetry. If you enter his house – his drawing-room – his library – you of yourself say, this is not the dwelling of a common mind. There is not a gem, a coin, a book thrown aside on his chimney-piece, his sofa, his table, that does not bespeak an almost fastidious elegance in the possessor. But this very delicacy must be the misery of his existence. Oh the jarrings his disposition must have encountered through life! (*LJ*. II. 331)

Such little sketches are frequent.

The Journals hold the accents and impact of a living mind in a series of fascinatingly discontinuous pieces more impressive and true to actuality than any modern novelist's 'stream of consciousness' (which is too often, to use Nietzsche's valuable terms, merely a superficial Apollonianism aping the Dionysian activity). The Journals are personal, but in them we make contact with a man many of whose most personal emotions were inextricably entangled with world-affairs. Few people in history, and perhaps no man of letters, can have felt more passionately about the great issues of his day. Byron's interest in the fortunes of Great Britain and Europe, and the political destinies of man, almost took on the status of a mania. He and they become part of one drama, and the specifically dramatic impact of these soliloquies reaches, rather like the soliloquies of *Hamlet* in contrast with the dialogue, a greater intensity than anything in the Letters.

The 1813–14 Journal contains some remarkable pieces. There is that revelatory meditation of 23 November 1813, starting

> If I had any views in this country, they would probably be parliamentary. But I have no ambition; at least, if any, it would be *aut Caesae aut nihil*. (*LJ.* ii. 338)

The passage builds up to a fine meditation on republicanism, and ends by striking out his own epitaph as a potential leader: 'He might, perhaps, if he would' (*LJ.* ii. 340).

Even more impressive are two soliloquies at the Journal's conclusion. We have called Byron's use of language, with some important reservations, 'Shakespearian'; but it was there rather his use of language than the language itself to which we referred. Under sufficient dramatic pressure, however, his language itself becomes Shakespearian, as when, on 6 December 1813, cursing himself for inaction, he jots down that he has 'no more charity than a cruet of vinegar' (*LJ.* ii. 366), recalling Menenius on Coriolanus: 'There is no more mercy in him than milk in a male tiger' (*Coriolanus*, v. iv. 31).

Napoleon was Byron's symbol of human greatness, and his undignified survival of collapse left Byron without hope for man. Here is a bitter comment, dated Saturday, 9 April 1814, sprinkled with quotations from *Hamlet, Venice Preserved, Antony and Cleopatra, Hamlet* once again, and *Macbeth*:

> I mark this day!
> Napoleon Buonaparte has abdicated the throne of the world. 'Excellent well'. Methinks Sylla did better; for he revenged and resigned in the height of his sway, red with the slaughter of his foes – the finest instance of glorious contempt of the rascals upon record. Dioclesian did well too – Amurath not amiss, had he become aught except a dervise – Charles the Fifth but so so – but Napoleon, worst of all. What! wait till they were in his capital, and then talk of his readiness to give up what is already gone!! 'What whining monk art thou – what holy cheat?' 'Sdeath! – Dionysius at Corinth was yet a king to this. The 'Isle of Elba' to retire to! – Well – if it had been Caprea, I should have marvelled less. 'I see men's minds are but a parcel of their fortunes'. I am utterly bewildered and confounded.

I don't know – but I think I, even I (an insect compared with this creature), have set my life on casts not a millionth part of this man's. But, after all, a crown may be not worth dying for. Yet, to outlive *Lodi* for this!!! Oh that Juvenal or Johnson could rise from the dead! *Expende – quot libras in duce summo invenies?* I knew they were light in the balance of mortality; but I thought their living dust weighed more *carats*. Alas! this imperial diamond hath a flaw in it, and is now hardly fit to stick in a glazier's pencil: – the pen of the historian won't rate it worth a ducat.

Psha! 'Something too much of this.' But I won't give him up even now; though all his admirers have, 'like the thanes, fallen from him'. (*LJ.* ii. 409)

This must be read aloud, performed, to get its true quality. Shakespeare is present, not only in reference and modulation of language – how close it is to the self-torment of Ford's prose soliloquies in *The Merry Wives of Windsor* – but in vocabulary, turn of idiom, blazing metaphor, and dramatic detonation. It smells of the stage. But it is not the stage – it is life.

Shakespeare, when all is said, remains fiction. Here we have the Shakespearian power speaking direct through a pinnacle of human consciousness from out the heart of great events.

Our next entry, dated 10 April, records the composition of the bitter *Ode to Napoleon*. Napoleon to Byron meant primarily not his country's enemy but a challenge that took precedence over international wrangling: the possibility of man attaining a stature, both personal and political, beyond his present miserable inadequacies. Had Napoleon elected not to survive his fall, that greatness would have assumed tragic and eternal stature. Now Byron's hopes of man, and superman, had been falsified, and his values shattered. Our last entry is on 19 April 1814. Quotations from *Macbeth, Romeo and Juliet* and *King Lear* load a fragment of human significance and dramatic power like nothing else in our literature:

There is ice at both poles, north and south – all extremes are the same – misery belongs to the highest and the lowest only, to the emperor and the beggar, when unsixpenced and unthroned. There is, to be sure, a damned insipid medium – an equinoctial line – no one knows where, except upon maps and measurement.

'And all our *yesterdays* have lighted fools
The way to dusty death'.

I will keep no further journal of that same hesternal torchlight: and, to prevent me from returning, like a dog, to the vomit of memory, I tear out the remaining leaves of this volume, and write, in *Ipecacuanha* – 'that the Bourbons are restored!!!' – 'Hang up philosophy'. To be sure, I have long despised myself and man, but I never spat in the face of my species before – 'O fool! I shall go mad'.   (*LJ.* II. 411)

Byron is living the great moments of Shakespearian drama on the stage of Europe. In these terms his greater, dramatic personality is at home, and only there; and, when such are the issues, and he is writing merely for himself, his language blends the Byronic idiom of 'damned insipid medium' with the Shakespearian freedom of 'unsixpenced'. Observe the brilliant condensation of the lines from *Macbeth* (quoted here very exactly to underline the pointlessness of human existence without hopes of greatness) in 'that same hesternal torchlight'. The metaphoric opening demands our closest attention, the contrast of these twin, ice-cold extremes with mediocrity[1] sinking deep into the most ultimate problems of great drama and man's destiny on earth; and that is why the protagonist's fall, which is also, at this moment, Byron's, forces a conclusion on the pivot-instant of Lear's agony. In Byron Shakespearian drama has become actual and incarnate; in watching him we know what it – what all great drama – is *for*.

He wrote a short 'journal' for Augusta recording some of his experiences in Switzerland in 1816 (*LJ.* III. 349–65), and has left us a longer one done in Ravenna during January and February 1821 (*LJ.* V. 147–211). Of this last I have written elsewhere: in it he records his various daily activities, his visits to Teresa, poetic work, forest rides, acts of charity, historical and other reading, hearing of music, whilst awaiting the outbreak of hostilities in the cause of Italian liberation.

These passages show Byron's ability of varied and all but simultaneous activities; and also his strange way of rising, in the manner of Shaw's dramatic humour, above his own most deeply felt passions and purposes. He is not only an actor; he is also a dramatist composing and controlling his own play. Or we

---

[1] Observe the extraordinary psychological penetration of 'no one knows where, except upon maps and measurement': is what we call 'normality' an academic fiction? [1967]

might say that he enjoys the dualized consciousness of an actor who is inside his part and its emotions while remaining technically conscious and even cool. This fine edge, or tight-rope balance, of dramatic art, Byron lived, in actuality. That is why his bitterest emotions are, with no diminution of their intensity, nevertheless regularly related to their opposites, placed, seen in perspective, and surmounted. He is always riding his own storm.

After the liberation movement had failed, he wrote the short *My Dictionary* (*LJ.* v. 403–7) and the deeply important *Detached Thoughts* (*LJ.* v. 407–68). Action had failed, and Byron, with something of a stoic calm, was in a back-water mood. Among many dispassionate comments on himself and others, especially statesmen, thoughts which take pleasure in distancing his emotions, we have his most mature conclusions on death and immortality. It is his 'To be or not to be'.

He had already, in his 1813–1814 Journal, quoted both from *Hamlet* and *Henry VIII* in a similar meditation on 27 November 1813:

> All are inclined to believe what they covet, from a lottery-ticket up to a passport to Paradise – in which, from the description, I see nothing very tempting. My restlessness tells me I have something 'within that passeth show'. It is for Him, who made it, to prolong that spark of celestial fire which illuminates, yet burns, this frail tenement; but I see no such horror in a 'dreamless sleep', and I have no conception of any existence which duration would not render tiresome. How else 'fell the angels', even according to your creed? They were immortal, heavenly, and happy, as their *apostate* Abdiel is now by his treachery. Time must decide; and eternity won't be the less agreeable or more horrible because one did not expect it. In the mean time, I am grateful for some good, and tolerably patient under certain evils – *grace à Dieu et mon bon tempérament.* (*LJ.* II. 351)

'Frail tenement' appears to be a blend of Bolingbroke's 'this frail sepulchre of our flesh' in *Richard II* (I. iii. 196) and Dryden's 'tenement of clay' in *Absalom and Achitophel*.

On 'midnight' of 18 February 1814, Byron returned to the problem:

> Is there anything beyond? – *who* knows? *He* that can't tell. Who tells that there *is*? He who don't know. And when shall he know?

Perhaps, when he don't expect, and generally when he don't wish it. In this last respect, however, all are not alike: it depends a good deal upon education – something upon nerves and habits – but most upon digestion.   (*LJ.* II. 385)

His theological speculations are nothing if not realistic: there is as much of Falstaff in him as of Hamlet.

In his 1821 *Detached Thoughts* (96–8) he leaves us a more considered statement. There is nothing in it of obvious originality: in a man, as he told Murray on 2 April 1817 (*LJ.* IV. 93), who considered 'pure invention' but 'the talent of a liar', you do not look for theological surprises; he was normally averse from mysticism and metaphysics, but his conclusions, in this quiet entry, are conclusions based on a common-sense, a reading, and an experience of more than ordinary proportions. The grounding is solid, and what cannot be said in plain words will not be said at all. A mind of a calibre recalling variously Dante and Shakespeare – Mazzini was deeply aware of his affinities with Dante – speaks to us through the purified concepts of an Augustan and the common-sense, without the laboured abstractions, of a Johnson. Here is the passage (*Detached Thoughts, LJ.* v. 456–8; the italics are Byron's):

Of the Immortality of the Soul, it appears to me that there can be little doubt, if we attend for a moment to the action of Mind. It is in perpetual activity. I used to doubt of it, but reflection has taught me better. It acts also so very independent of body: in dreams for instance incoherently and madly, I grant you; but still it is *Mind*, and much more *Mind* than when we are awake. Now, that *this* should not act *separately*, as well as jointly, who can pronounce? The Stoics, Epictetus and Marcus Aurelius, call the present state 'a Soul which drags a Carcase': a heavy chain, to be sure; but all chains, being material, may be shaken off.

How far our future life will be individual, or, rather, how far it will at all resemble our *present* existence, is another question; but that the *Mind* is *eternal*, seems as probable as that the body is not so. Of course, I have ventured upon the question without recurring to Revelation, which, however, is at least as rational a solution of it as any other.

He proceeds to record his aversion from all doctrines of Hell and the corresponding brutality of penal codes among men. Then:

Matter is eternal, always changing, but reproduced, and, as far as we can comprehend Eternity, Eternal; and why not *Mind*? Why should not the *Mind* act with and upon the Universe? as portions of it act upon and with the congregated dust called *Mankind*? See, how one man acts upon himself and others, or upon multitudes? The same Agency, in a higher and purer degree, may act upon the Stars, etc., ad infinitum.

Materialism is discounted. If there must be a choice, he says, 'I own my partiality for Spirit'.

We have noticed certain salient characteristics of Byron's Letters and Journals. His poetry is very different; it subscribes regularly to the established disciplines of stanza and rhyme, and these themselves on occasion lift him, as such patterned disciplines will, into worlds untouched by his prose. Through such impersonal techniques a man may speak beyond his conscious thinking; and, though it may seem dangerous to set limits to a Byron's self-consciousness, he has left us some authority for it. Once, in a letter to Murray on 2 January 1817, after contrasting his poetry and his prose, he wrote:

> As for poesy, mine is the *dream* of my sleeping Passions; when they are awake, I cannot speak their language, only in their Somnambulism, and just now they are not dormant.   (*LJ*. IV. 43)

His most careless analogies are regularly both precise and profound: poetry, when too self-conscious, contradicts its own nature in the same way as somnambulism is an offence to sleep. He had said as much in his earlier journal (20 February 1814; *LJ*. II. 388). His poetry, he tells us, was written to get away from his burning self-consciousness, from his own personality, from the self dramatized in the Letters and Journals (Journal, 27 Nov. 1813; Miss Milbanke, 10 Nov. 1813; *LJ*. II. 351; III. 405).[1] Even so, Byron's was a peculiarly *conscious* poetry.

His best poetic dramas are among the great things in that kind. In conception, in dramatic incident, in human delineation under dramatic pressure, in symbolic overtone, they are comparable with Sophocles, with Shakespeare, with Corneille. And yet the language is, in contrast to his prose, less dramatic than we might expect, or wish. Why is this?

[1] The date '10 Nov.' should it seems be '29 Nov.' See Malcolm Elwin, *Lord Byron's Wife*, 496. [1967]

When I first saw the Comédie-Française do a play of Racine, I was struck by the violence of the emotions displayed, and it occurred to me that here I had glimpsed the reason for the stern concentration on classic canons in the literature of France: they dared not let themselves go. So was it with Byron. Throughout his life, though himself living Shakespearian drama on the stage of Europe, his poetic ideal was, not Shakespeare, but Pope;[1] just as, though a man of strong and wayward passions, his life's aim was true – I do not say conventional – righteousness. He searched, in both literature and in life, for control and order; but the world he would order was far greater than Dryden's or Pope's. It was the world, or soul, of Greek drama, of Dante, of Shakespeare, brought to bear on the complexities of nineteenth-century Europe. In his dramas he of set purpose forced his supreme dramatic genius into a semi-classic mould, confining himself within a stern economy of diction and a strict adherence to logic. His aim was to reject dramatic intoxicants for language like 'a clear spring bubbling in the sun' (Murray, 4 July 1821; *LJ*. v. 218; and see v. 323). This is no excuse for shirking the task of production, though it may be an excuse for choosing our producers and actors with care. Anyone can make a moderate success of Shakespeare; but with *Marino Faliero* or *Sardanapalus* there will be either a superb achievement, or disaster.

Our brief review has touched wide areas of literary art, and yet something has been left out. Byron's prose is robust, the prose of a 'man of the world'. His poetry is either rhetorical with the rounded diction of *Childe Harold* or forthright with the unadorned lucidities of the plays and *Don Juan*. It handles, as the prose does not, delicate sentiments of the sweetest, most intimate kind; and it is deeply aware of the eternal dimension. But what of verbal magic? Of phrases touched by what Wordsworth in his *Elegiac Stanzas suggested by a picture of Peel Castle* called 'the light that never was, on sea or land'? Of

> magic casements, opening on the foam
> Of perilous seas, in faery lands forlorn.

What of these? Such magic comes, after all, from a twilight awareness, from moving about, as Wordsworth in his *Immor-*

[1] For Byron's relation to Pope see 'The Book of Life' in *Laureate of Peace*, reissued as *The Poetry of Pope*; also *Byron and Shakespeare*, 9–11.

tality ode has it, 'in worlds not realised'. That Byron could not do, since in him those worlds *had* been realized. He already had them, or much of them, within himself; and that is why the concept 'eternity' sounds like a gong through his poetry; why he handles the supernatural throughout with the cold precision of a man speaking of it *on equal terms*; and why those who knew him have left us those extraordinary descriptions of personal magnetism. Such a man will not be content to adumbrate the mysteries. He must act, and live, them. What to others was a half-fearsome, numinous mystery was to Byron simple 'truth'. In his letter to D'Israeli of 10 June 1822 he wrote:

> Such is Truth! Men dare not look her in the face, except by degrees: they mistake her for a Gorgon, instead of knowing her to be a Minerva. (*LJ.* vi. 89)

Characteristically, he disclaims reference to himself: 'I have only to turn over a few pages of your volumes to find innumerable, and far more illustrious, instances.' But to us the phrase is a valid pointer. The Gorgon's head was placed on the Goddess's *shield*, and it is simply the hostility at first aroused by genius which next forces the defence which finally so terrifies society.

For us Byron may, if we so choose, be in himself Keats's 'magic casement'. True, there is nothing 'forlorn' about him: as we, in our directionless century, study his life and all that he stood, and died, for, it is we who are 'forlorn', not he; and though at times we may fear the 'perilous seas' to which he invites us, yet perhaps they are only so from the hither viewpoint. Byron was, despite everything, a happy man; his letters, like his *Don Juan*, are characterized above all by buoyancy. Perhaps, should we adventure with him, we shall find nothing more fearful, nor less beautiful, than 'my old friend the Mediterranean rolling blue at my feet'.

Index

Material in footnotes is indexed simply under the numeral of the page on which the note occurs, without further designation